RadioTimes Family Video Guide

Barry Norman and Emma Norman

Family Video Guide

The A-Z guide to over 1500 videos for all the family

Network Books

Acknowledgements

Our grateful thanks go to all those who have given us such invaluable help in making this book as free of errors as possible, in particular project editor Kate Lock and Susan Oates, head of the *Radio Times* film unit. We would also like to thank her team of helpers Jane Anderson, Gill Crawford, Diana McAdam, Paula Pfaff, Kim Jarvis, Narinder Flora, Nick Vaudrey and Caroline Bullough.

Every attempt has been made to ensure that the information given in this book is accurate. However, the authors and the publishers would be pleased to hear from readers who spot any errors so that they may be corrected in future editions of the book.

Published by Network Books,
an imprint of BBC Worldwide Publishing.
BBC Worldwide Publishing Limited, Woodlands,
80 Wood Lane, London W12 0TT

First published 1995
Reprinted 1995
© Barry Norman and Emma Norman 1995
The moral right of the authors has been asserted

ISBN 0 563 37183 8

Designed by Edward Moody Design Ltd
Cover photograph by Ruth Jenkinson

Set in Franklin Gothic and Adobe Garamond
Printed and bound in Great Britain by Butler & Tanner Ltd, Frome
Cover printed by Richard Clays Ltd, St Ives plc

Contents

Introduction

by Barry Norman

When Emma and her elder sister Samantha were growing up, deciding which films they might watch presented no real problem. In those prehistoric days twenty-odd years ago there were no such things as videos. If you wanted to see a movie you either went to the cinema or caught it on TV. An element of parental control was therefore easier to maintain.

Furthermore, at that time no film with what might today attract an 18, a 15 or even a PG certificate was likely to be shown unexpurgated on the box. Sex and violence were toned down, four-letter words smoothed away. Even so, a certain amount of vigilance was required. A child's natural curiosity urges it to reach for the forbidden fruit and the trick seemed to be for parents to make that fruit sound unappetising. So there'd be conversations like this:

'What about this film, Dad?'

'Nah, you wouldn't like that.'

'Why not?'

'Well, I dunno, it's about a couple of men who fancy the same woman and she leaves her husband, who is poor, to go off with the other bloke, who is rich, and the husband wants her back and there's very little action. Personally, I thought it was rather dull and very hard to believe.' And that would be something on the lines of *Indecent Proposal* neatly circumvented.

I was lucky, I suppose. Even before I was on TV I was writing about films, as of course I still do every week in *Radio Times*. So I was regarded as the household's mobile movie guide and the girls tended to listen to me, possibly on the assumption that if people were actually paying me to watch movies there was at least a chance that I knew what I was talking about.

As time went by, my wife Diana and I pointed them in the direction of the classic Disneys, *The Adventures of Robin Hood*, *Bringing Up Baby*, the great old musicals and later *Gone with the Wind*, *Casablanca*, *Citizen Kane* and the like. We didn't force such films upon them; we merely suggested, casually, that they might like them, so whether they watched or not was always their own choice.

If there was any policy behind all this I suppose it was simply a belief that, with films as with books, if you bring children up to appreciate good stuff they're less likely to develop a taste for cheap trash.

It's not so easy now, though. The proliferation of videos has meant that all kinds of movies are commonly available and it's harder for parents to keep an eye on things. Hence this book – the *Radio Times Family Video Guide*.

And what, you may ask, is that exactly? Well, quite simply it's a compendium of films on tape that can be brought home with equanimity by parents of children under 18. Nothing in this book has more than a 15 certificate. In the cinema, of course, 15s should be approached with caution by those worried about violence, sex and bad language. On video a 15 gives far less cause for concern. Quite often video 15s were PGs in the cinema and even if they were 15s to begin with they have usually been pruned – at times quite drastically – to avoid causing offence. This is not to say, however, that there will be positively no violence, no sex and no strong language on the tape you take home. There will, however, be much less of them and where they occur we give a warning. In other words, both of us as parents agreed that each film had to be considered in the context of family viewing.

Now this is neither the time nor the place to discuss the rights and wrongs of censorship. Suffice it to say that many people are worried and embarrassed by four-letter words, overt sexual displays and violence on screen and they tend to be even more worried and embarrassed if these things are on a screen in their own homes rather than in the local cinema.

Understandably so, because a video might easily be watched by someone much younger than the age for which the movie was originally intended.

The films in this book can be watched, with ease of mind, by both parents and their offspring – though not necessarily by all their offspring. This is a *family* video guide, not a *children's* video guide. Families include adults and teenagers who might well be looking for more serious or sophisticated stories than their younger children or siblings but still don't wish to be distracted or annoyed by gratuitous sex, violent mayhem or language to make a stoker blush. Thus the 15 category films in this book are for them.

The 1500 or so films we list here are, obviously, only a small percentage of those that are, nominally, to be found on video. But they are, or should be, those most easily available either for hire or purchase.

A word of warning is necessary here, however. Videos tend to have a comparatively short shelf life, sometimes, as in the case of Disney, because they are only released for limited periods (*Fantasia* is a good example), but mostly because the average dealer does not carry a large stock. Indeed, the smaller shops tend to concentrate heavily on the latest releases.

This does not mean that you have to be fobbed off with whatever appears to be on display in your local corner store. We repeat – all the films in this book are available on video and can therefore be obtained for you by a dealer. Admittedly he or she is more likely to do that if you wish to buy, rather than rent the film, but they *can* get it.

And if they say they can't, that it doesn't exist, ask them to look it up in the Videolog, a comprehensive catalogue, frequently updated, to which all dealers worth their salt should subscribe.

As a general rule, the more recent the release the easier it should be to rent. Older videos – classic films, for instance – are more likely to be available for sale.

But they are usually quite inexpensive – a lot cheaper than hardback books anyway – and a good many supermarkets and other chain stores now carry quite comprehensive stocks.

As to the quality of the films we list, you will notice that not all of them are strongly recommended, though none is entirely without merit.

Those that come with the faintest praise are there, for the most part, mainly because they are recent issues and therefore not only more easily come by but also perhaps of more immediate interest, or because they were well known in their time.

The choice, of course, is yours and so, even more, is the final verdict on the quality of the films. After which, all that remains is to wish you many happy hours of family viewing.

Postscript by Emma Norman

Choosing a video for oneself is hard enough, although I hope my weekly *Radio Times* reviews help with that. Selecting for the rest of the family is trickier still. My father and I both hope this book will shoulder some of that responsibility and steer you towards movies which might just please all the clan.

Although I don't intend to turn my eighteen-month-old son into the world's smallest couch potato, I am looking forward to showing him some of my childhood favourites: *The Wizard of Oz, The Railway Children, Chitty Chitty Bang Bang* and all the Disney classics such as *Pinocchio, Bambi, Snow White* and *The Jungle Book.*

Whether he'll approve of my selection or prefer *Teenage Mutant Ninja Turtles* and *Home Alone* remains to be seen, but I'll shove a copy of our book at him and trust to his inherent good taste.

Happy viewing.

How to use
Radio Times Family Video Guide

Information about each film is displayed as follows:

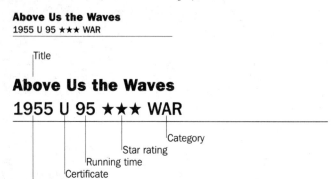

Above Us the Waves
1955 U 95 ★★★ WAR

Title

Above Us the Waves
1955 U 95 ★★★ WAR

Category
Star rating
Running time
Certificate
Release date

Title: films have been ordered strictly alphabetically, i.e. letter by letter, ignoring word breaks and punctuation. Articles of speech (A, An, The, Le, La, Les) have been placed at the end of titles to make this easier to follow. Abbreviations – e.g. Dr, Mr, Mrs, etc – are placed exactly as spelt, although films starting with numbers – *42nd Street*, for example – should be looked for as if they were spelt out.
Foreign language films are included under the title on the video box - usually the original foreign title.

Release date: this is the year the film was first shown to the public, not the date of the video release.

Certificate: this is the official classification given by the British Board of Film Classification (BBFC). Broadly speaking, certificates may be described as follows:

Uc universal films suitable for all, but especially suitable for very young children.

U means that a film is suitable for all and will contain nothing unsuitable for children.

PG indicates that on the whole the film is suitable for all, but younger children might be shocked or startled by the occasional scene and therefore a little parental guidance is advisable.

12 means that the film is unsuitable for anyone younger than twelve years of age. There may be stronger moments of violence and swearwords that aren't in a PG.

15 means that the film is unsuitable for anyone younger than fifteen. There may be a fairly adult theme or scenes of sex, violence or drugs. There may also be some sexual swearwords.

Uc, U and PG films can be legally supplied to people of all ages – including children. Supply of 12, 15 and 18s (films unsuitable for anyone younger than 18 – not included in this book) are restricted to people of the specified age and above. It is a criminal offence for a shopkeeper to supply a video with an age-restricted classification to someone below that age.

Running time: this refers to the running time of the video version, not the original cinema release. (Note: as this book went to press a handful of the very latest video releases were still awaiting final confirmation of their certificates and running times with BBFC.)

Star rating: to help in your initial selection we offer the following simple guidelines:

★★★★★ = excellent

★★★★ .. = very good

★★★ .... = good

★★ ...... = worth seeing

★ .... = yeah, well, OK, good in parts

Category: in addition we have described the films like this:

ACT/ADV . = action/adventure

COM ..... = comedy

DRA ..... = drama

FAM .... = films which can, without reservation, be watched
　　　　　　 by the entire family

FOR ...... = foreign language film

HOR ..... = horror

MUS ..... = musical

MYS/THR . = mystery/thriller

SCI/FAN .. = science-fiction or fantasy

WAR ..... = war

WES ..... = Western

B&W/Subtitles: if a film is only available in black and white, or has subtitles, this information is included in parentheses at the end of the review.

Above Us the Waves
1955 U 95 ★★★ WAR

One of those wartime dramas that Britain made so well and a nostalgic reminder of an older, more restrained school of film-making. A British submarine crew, among them John Mills, Donald Sinden and John Gregson, attacks a German warship in a Norwegian fjord. Realistic action and admirably stiff-upper-lipped heroism. (B&W)

Absence of Malice
1981 PG 111 ★★★ MYS/THR

A salutary warning of how newspapers can harm innocent bystanders. A Miami union leader disappears and local hack Sally Field is pressured by the FBI into accusing Paul Newman, blameless son of a mobster. Newman protests; Field claims press privilege. An excellent drama, as topical now as it was then.

Absolute Beginners
1986 15 103 ★ MUS

Julien Temple's attempt at a spectacular British musical was a pretty spectacular failure. This adaptation of Colin MacInnes's novel about youth and racism in 1950s London looks stylish, some of the musical numbers (especially David Bowie's title song) work well and there's a rousing climax. But the casting of Eddie O'Connell and Patsy Kensit as the romantic leads simply doesn't work because there is no sexual chemistry between them.

Abyss, The
1989 15 133 ★★ SCI/FAN

A poor man's *Alien* under water. Oil riggers, led by Ed Harris, attempt to rescue a nuclear submarine from teetering into an abyss. Complications ensue when Harris's estranged wife, Mary Elizabeth Mastrantonio, insists on taking part. The special effects, especially something strange and possibly extra-terrestrial floating in the depths, are good. The same, alas, cannot be said for the script.

Abyss, The: Special Edition
1993 15 163 ★★ SCI/FAN

The director, James Cameron, saw fit to add half an hour to an already overlong film. Main additions are to the special effects, which are technically brilliant. But the director's tinkering does little to improve the story.

Accident
1967 PG 101 ★★★ DRA

A formidable partnership of Dirk Bogarde, director Joseph Losey and writer Harold Pinter. An undergraduate dies in a car crash near Oxford and his female passenger is rescued by Bogarde, the philosophy don who taught them both. The film explores the complex relationships in a claustrophobic academic community. Fine performance by Michael York in his first important role.

Accidental Hero
1992 15 113 ★★ DRA

Surprisingly the problem here is Dustin Hoffman, whose performance seems ill-conceived and unsympathetic. He plays a ne'er-do-well who, by chance, rescues the survivors of an air crash in New York. But, through a combination of circumstances, down-and-out Vietnam war veteran Andy Garcia gets the credit, the reward and the romantic interest of TV reporter Geena Davis. Stephen Frears's film lacks focus.

Accidental Tourist, The
1988 PG 116 ★★★ DRA

William Hurt plays a travel writer whose wife, Kathleen Turner, has left him. The story focuses on his rite of passage from unhappiness to new-found love in the shape of zany dog trainer Geena Davis. This combination of the bleak, the romantic and the funny falls apart in the last half hour but generally director Lawrence Kasdan handles it with much skill.

Ace Ventura: Pet Detective
1994 12 82 ★★★ COM

The film that launched Jim Carrey, a comedian with the out-of-control approach of a more likeable Jerry Lewis, into the big league. You probably won't like him much at the start but he grows on you as a private eye who recovers lost or stolen pets. In a complex plot – about an American football team's kidnapped dolphin – the engaging Sean Young is not all she seems to be. It shouldn't work, but it does.

Adam's Rib
1949 U 97 ★★★★ COM

Spencer Tracy and Katharine Hepburn perfectly cast in a witty, sophisticated comedy about two squabbling lawyers, married to each other but on opposing sides of a murder trial. Ruth Gordon and Garson Kanin provided the script, George Cukor the seamless direction and Judy Holliday is outstanding as the bimbo on trial. (B&W)

Addams Family, The
1991 PG 95 ★★ COM

Inspired by the Charles Addams cartoons, the film looks a treat and the cast, headed by Raul Julia, Anjelica Huston and the grave, precociously talented Christina Ricci, could hardly be better. But the plot and dialogue would be more suited to a thirty-minute TV sitcom. The story has a crooked lawyer trying to pass off a fake Uncle Fester (Christopher Lloyd) to steal the family fortune.

Addams Family Values
1993 PG 90 ★★★ COM

For once the sequel is better than the original. The film's two plots have little to do with each other but run happily on parallel lines. In one, a scheming nanny (Joan Cusack) sets her cap at Fester and his money. In the other, Christina Ricci and brother Pugsley (Jimmy Workman) endure the horrors of an American summer camp. The latter storyline is more fun and young Ricci outshines the adult cast.

Adventures in Babysitting
1987 15 98 ★★ COM

Babysitter Elisabeth Shue's peaceful evening goes drastically wrong when she answers an SOS call from her friend, Penelope Ann Miller, who has run away from home. Shue packs her charges into a car, heads for downtown Chicago, blows a tyre and finds herself involved with a menacing ring of car thieves. Neat concept, nice performances.

Adventures of Baron Munchausen, The
1989 PG 126 ★★ COM

Terry Gilliam's uneven, sometimes dazzling tale of the eighteenth-century Prussian fantasist (a miscast, because rather too old, John Neville) is certainly ambitious and beautiful to look at but the parts are better than the whole. The baron's tall stories include, memorably, an encounter on the moon with a manic Robin Williams and another, at the centre of the Earth, with the outrageous Oliver Reed.

Adventures of Robin Hood, The
1938 U 102 ★★★★★ ACT/ADV

Quite simply the best example of its genre – swashbuckling historical action adventure – ever made and certainly far better than any other cinematic version of the legend. Everyone, from Errol Flynn as Robin, to Olivia de Havilland as Marian and Claude Rains and Basil Rathbone as the arch villains, is perfectly cast. The direction, by Michael Curtiz (mostly) and William Keighley, is first-rate and Flynn gives the most appealing performance of his career.

African Queen, The
1951 U 100 ★★★★★ ACT/ADV

Magnificent romantic adventure. Prissy missionary Katharine Hepburn and drunken riverboat captain Humphrey Bogart brave a perilous journey down the Congo, culminating in an attempt to destroy a German battleship during the First World War. John Huston's superb direction and the offbeat casting make for a movie classic. Bogart won an Oscar; Hepburn, sadly, had to be content with a nomination.

After Hours
1985 15 93 ★★★ COM

A dark, funny, disturbing comedy – an unusual venture for director Martin Scorsese – wherein Griffin Dunne's potentially romantic assignation becomes a nightmare as he finds himself penniless and victimized in downtown Manhattan. Rosanna Arquette is the seductive catalyst. One for the older members of the family.

Age of Innocence, The
1993 U 133 ★★★ DRA

Again a departure for Martin Scorsese as he invades cinematic territory more familiarly occupied by Merchant and Ivory. His adaptation of Edith Wharton's novel of nineteenth-century high society in New York is beautifully detailed. But the story of a man (Daniel Day-Lewis) caught between desire for the slightly scandalous Michelle Pfeiffer and duty towards his fiancée, Wynona Ryder, lacks drama.

Agnes of God
1985 15 94 ★★★ DRA

Norman Jewison's adaptation of a stage play about a young nun, Meg Tilly, accused of murdering her child to which, allegedly, she gave birth in the convent. Drama is provided by confrontations between Jane Fonda, as the psychiatrist appointed to discover what really happened, and Anne Bancroft as the streetwise Mother Superior.

Air America
1990 15 107 ★ ACT/ADV

Mel Gibson and Robert Downey Jr are pilots for an airline covertly run by the CIA as a drug-running operation to finance the Vietnam war. This fascinating can of worms, however, is never fully opened. The film goes for comedy and the odd thrill and shirks the more interesting option of exposing CIA corruption, leaving Gibson and Downey with little to work on.

Airplane!
1980 PG 84 ★★★★ COM

This irreverent romp has but one objective – to make the audience laugh. Many a film aims at a similar goal and hits the corner flag instead but *Airplane!* – a glorious satire on those doomy *Airport* movies – is on target more often than not. Every joke that doesn't work is swiftly followed by some that do and the cast (including Leslie Nielsen and Lloyd Bridges) is spot on.

Airplane II: The Sequel
1982 15 80 ★★★ COM

Much the same as *Airplane!* only not quite so good. The jokes are too often a reprise of those that worked best in the original. Robert Hays captains an ill-fated space shuttle carrying passengers to the moon. Hays, Julie Hagerty and Lloyd Bridges return from the first film and are joined, engagingly, by a self-mocking William Shatner in his Captain Kirk guise.

Air Up There, The
1994 PG 103 ★★★ COM

Kevin Bacon is an ambitious college basketball coach who needs to recruit a star player but all the talent has gone to other teams. So he heads for Africa to sign up a skyscraper of a Winabi warrior, Charles Gitonga Maina. But Maina isn't interested in the American way of life and in this delightful, amusing tale it's Bacon who has to make the concessions.

Aladdin
1992 U 87 ★★★★ FAM

Disney's thirty-first animated feature, based on the *Arabian Nights* folk tales, became the highest-grossing cartoon ever made. A doe-eyed heroine and an Aladdin who looks like a deeply tanned Tom Cruise had much to do with that. But it's the extraordinary virtuosity of Robin Williams as the voice of the genie that really grabs the attention of adults and children alike. The film won Oscars for the score and Tim Rice's song, *A Whole New World*.

Alamo, The
1960 PG 154 ★★ WES

At the battle of the Alamo in 1836, 185 Americans (including Davy Crockett and Jim Bowie) heroically but vainly resisted 7000 Mexican troops. John Wayne's screen tribute (he directed as well as playing Crockett) pays over-lengthy homage to the men who took part. Not a bad film but it would have been better without super-patriot Wayne's homilies on all-American virtues.

Alice
1990 15 101 ★★★ COM

Sometimes Woody Allen thinks he's Ingmar Bergman, sometimes Federico Fellini. Here he's in Fellini mode with a loose version of *Juliet of the Spirits* set in contemporary Manhattan. Mia Farrow is the rich, bored housewife whose visit to a Chinese herbalist leads her into mystical and sexual encounters. Directed by – but, alas, not featuring – Allen. Enjoyable but uneven.

Alice Doesn't Live Here Anymore
1974 15 107 ★★★ DRA

The widowed Alice (Ellen Burstyn in Oscar-winning form) doesn't live here any more because she, along with her twelve-year-old son, has set off in search of a new life. A discursive tale which becomes most engaging with the entrance of Kris Kristofferson as Burstyn's new suitor. Interesting study of ordinary people doing slightly extraordinary things.

Alive
1992 15 121 ★★★ ACT/ADV

A planeload of South American rugby players and supporters crashes in the Andes. When hopes for rescue are abandoned the survivors resort to eating those who died. A true story that would have been better developed if the film had addressed the moral problems more courageously. Good cast, headed by Ethan Hawke, and the crash sequence is terrifyingly realistic. The cannibalism, however, is handled with some discretion.

All about Eve
1950 U 133 ★★★★★ DRA

A perfect example of how a brilliant writer-director (Joseph L Mankiewicz) and a stunning cast can spin straw into gold. An essentially trite tale – great but fading actress (Bette Davis) threatened by sugary but ruthless ingénue (Anne Baxter) – is magicked into a classic by a witty, literate script and superb performances. The film won Oscars galore, including two for Mankiewicz. (B&W)

All Creatures Great and Small
1974 PG 87 ★★★ COM

This feature-length version is very different from the TV series, though equally as involving and charming. Simon Ward plays James Herriot, the young, inexperienced vet taking up his first post in an initially hostile Yorkshire community. Anthony Hopkins is his senior partner. A sequel, *It Shouldn't Happen to a Vet*, followed with John Alderton and Colin Blakely.

All Dogs Go to Heaven
1989 U 81 ★★ FAM

Disney-style animation made in Ireland but set in New Orleans. Burt Reynolds provides the voice of the canine hero, Charlie, who is killed by his old gambling partner, goes to heaven and seeks a second chance at life to rescue a cruelly

exploited little girl. Not as alarming for small children as it might sound, though rather more lightness would not have come amiss.

All I Want for Christmas
1991 U 88 ★ FAM

A cast that includes Leslie Nielsen as Santa Claus and Lauren Bacall as granny to a pair of quite appealing children promises something better than this relentlessly sentimental story. What the children want for Christmas is for their divorced parents to reunite. A cynical tear-jerker that could raise unrealistic hopes in young viewers whose parents are indeed divorced.

All of Me
1984 15 87 ★★★ COM

Like Woody Allen, Steve Martin aspires to be more than merely funny. This is sometimes regrettable because Martin is a brilliant comic. Here, fortunately, he is close to his manic best as a lawyer who finds that half his body has been occupied by the soul of the late, cranky Lily Tomlin. An opportunity for a welter of funny man/woman jokes and some inspired clowning by Martin.

All Quiet on the Western Front
1930 PG 103 ★★★★ WAR

The first classic film of the sound era. Based on the novel by Erich Maria Remarque, it follows the fortunes of a group of young Germans from the outset of the First World War to their respective fates in the trenches. The final shot of a doomed soldier reaching out to touch a butterfly is one of the most memorable scenes in the cinema. It looks dated now but the battle sequences are still remarkably effective. (B&W)

All That Jazz
1979 15 118 ★★★ MUS

An unusual and often compelling piece that stars Roy Scheider as a dance director working himself into the grave. It's said to be based on the life of its director, Bob Fosse. Much here that is self-indulgent and irritating but also much to admire, especially Scheider's storming performance – not necessarily likeable but powerful – and stirring musical numbers. Spicy and explicit in places.

All the President's Men
1976 I5 132 ★★★★ DRA

How two reporters on the *Washington Post*, Bob Woodward (Robert Redford) and Carl Bernstein (Dustin Hoffman), exposed the Watergate break-in and brought down President Nixon. William Goldman's script, Alan J Pakula's direction and the two star performances make a lengthy, convoluted story both exciting and absorbing. Winner of two Oscars.

Almost an Angel
1990 PG 91 ★ COM

Paul Hogan trying – and failing – to cash in on the popularity he won from the '*Crocodile' Dundee* films. A soppy, purportedly comic fable about a soft-hearted crook who is given a second chance at life. Hogan's OK, so is Linda Kozlowski, but the comedy and the determinedly feel-good nature of the film grow irksome.

Always
1989 PG 117 ★★★ DRA

Steven Spielberg's remake of the 1944 Spencer Tracy movie, *A Guy Named Joe*. In this contemporary version Richard Dreyfuss is a firefighter pilot who dies and returns as an unseen, unheard ghost to watch over his girlfriend, Holly Hunter. Overly sentimental but Dreyfuss and Hunter are appealing and there's neat support from John Goodman.

Amadeus
1984 PG 152 ★★★★ DRA

Once you accept the brashly American accents (especially Tom Hulce, as Mozart) this is a superb adaptation of Peter Shaffer's play. The music is magnificent and the story, concerning the possibly murderous jealousy of court composer Salieri (F Murray Abraham) for the divinely gifted but scatalogical Wolfgang Amadeus, is riveting. Oscars include Shaffer, director Milos Forman and Abraham, who has rarely been seen in a leading role since.

Amazing Stories
1985/6 ★★★ DRA

Made-for-TV movies on eight videos, ranging in length from 70 to 105 minutes and in certification from U to PG to 15. They were all made under the auspices of Steven Spielberg, who directed some of the stories. Other directors include Martin Scorsese, Robert Zemeckis and Joe Dante. Each video is an anthology, consisting of an assortment of short, fantastical stories, many inspired by such 1950s TV shows as *The Outer Limits*. The first compilation, directed by Spielberg, is also the best. The stories are variable in quality but the performers include the likes of Kevin Costner, Patrick Swayze, Danny DeVito, Kiefer Sutherland and Mary Stuart Masterson.

American Friends
1991 PG 91 ★★★ COM

Michael Palin's likeable account of how his great-grandfather found true love. Palin stars as his own Victorian ancestor, an Oxbridge don and confirmed bachelor, who falls for a young American woman (Trini Alvarado) he meets in Switzerland on a walking holiday. Romance blossoms when she visits him at his college. The humour is gentle and affectionate with sharp observation of university back-biting.

American Graffiti
1973 PG 107 ★★★★ COM

George Lucas's cult movie set in smalltown America in l962. The protagonists are a bunch of kids celebrating high school graduation on an action-packed, coming-of-age night out. It's funny, it rings true and there's a great rock 'n' roll soundtrack. An impressive cast includes such (then) unknowns as Harrison Ford, Richard Dreyfuss and Ron Howard, now himself a successful director.

American Heart
1993 15 109 ★★ DRA

The main attraction here is Jeff Bridges's first-rate performance as a recently parolled, penniless convict who discovers that his teenage son (Edward Furlong) wants to become a part of his life. The relationship between the two, as each seeks a better future, is sometimes bitter, sometimes loving. A thoughtful film that has disturbing things to say about America's dispossessed.

American in Paris, An
1951 U 108 ★★★ MUS

Gene Kelly is an ex-GI-turned-artist torn between the conflicting charms of his rich patroness, Nina Foch, and the waif-like Leslie Caron (in her screen debut). Kelly's dance routines are all you would expect and they, along with George and Ira Gershwin's smashing songs, turn a hackneyed story into a satisfyingly spectacular musical.

American Tail, An
1986 U 77 ★★★ FAM

Steven Spielberg's first venture (as a producer) into animation tells of a family of Russian mice emigrating to turn-of-the-century America, where they hope to find the streets paved with cheese. Young Fievel gets separated from the others and it's his adventures we follow as he searches for his family. Voices are provided by, among others, Christopher Plummer, Madeline Kahn and Dom DeLuise.

American Tail, An: Fievel Goes West
1991 U 72 ★★ FAM

All successful films are followed by a sequel and the sequel, except in the case of *Addams Family Values* and a few other notables, is usually weaker than the original. So it is here with the further escapades of the Mousekewitz family who, disillusioned with New York, head west to improve their fortunes. The plotting is thin and though the animation is fine there is more to a good cartoon than skilled draughtsmanship.

Anchors Aweigh
1945 U 133 ★★★ MUS

A highly enjoyable musical in which Gene Kelly and Frank Sinatra are sailors enjoying shore leave and the company of toothsome young women such as Kathryn Grayson. Dean Stockwell completes the male trio as an aspiring matelot. Not much plot but the songs (by Jule Styne and Sammy Cahn) are pleasing and there's a classic sequence in which Kelly dances with an animated mouse – Jerry, of *Tom and Jerry* fame, no less.

Anderson Tapes, The
1972 15 95 ★★★ MYS/THR

Sean Connery plays an ex-con in New York who plans to rob an entire apartment building and recruits a specialist team that includes gay art dealer Martin Balsam. Meanwhile, various law agencies are snooping on Connery's

activities without quite understanding what they hear. A tense, often funny thriller. Connery, as usual, plays an American role with an uncompromising Scottish accent.

... And Justice for All
1979 15 116 ★★★ DRA

Essentially a showcase for Al Pacino, Norman Jewison's film is an exposé of the inadequacies of the American legal system. Pacino, a Baltimore lawyer, has to defend a judge (John Forsythe) accused of raping a young girl. While the message of the film is strong, the approach is confused since it opts for an uneasy mixture of drama and comedy. The title, as you will swiftly gather, is ironic.

And Now for Something Completely Different
1971 PG 85 ★★★ COM

A treat for Monty Python fans – a collection of the best sketches from the well-loved TV series. Some are dated now but others, such as the Dead Parrot, Hell's Grannies, the Lumberjacks' Song and Upper-Class Twit of the Year remain perennially fresh. Besides, if things begin to pall you can always say, 'This is getting silly' and fast-forward.

Andre
1994 U 90 ★★ FAM

Sentimental, clichéd fare, but that always seems to go down well with the youngsters and, since this is based on a true story, all the family may care to take a peep. Andre's a cute orphaned seal cub adopted by the local harbourmaster and his family. Keith Carradine and Tina Majorino (*Waterworld*) are among the human actors but they don't get much of a look in beside the seal.

Angel
1982 15 88 ★★★ DRA

Neil Jordan's directorial debut is a riveting thriller. Stephen Rea stars as an Irish musician who witnesses the killing of a deaf-mute girl at a dancehall and sets out to seek retribution from the terrorists who murdered her. A tense, marvellously atmospheric piece which brought instant attention to both Jordan and Rea. One for the older members of the family.

Animal Crackers: see Marx Brothers

Anna Karenina
1935 U 90 ★★★ DRA

A fair – if shortish – adaptation of Tolstoy's novel featuring Greta Garbo as the tragic wife of Russian aristocrat Basil Rathbone. It's tragic because she falls in love with cavalry officer Fredric March and in nineteenth-century literature such affairs always ended with tears before bedtime. An ideal part for Garbo, who had already played it in a silent film. (B&W)

Anna Karenina
1948 PG 134 ★★ DRA

Same story as above only longer and not quite so well done. Vivien Leigh is less convincing than Garbo and Kieron Moore is no match for Fredric March. Ralph Richardson, though, is good in the Basil Rathbone role. (B&W)

Anna Karenina
1978 PG 365 ★★★ DRA

They just can't leave Tolstoy alone, although in this two-cassette BBC version you do get a heck of a lot more of the book. This is the kind of production that the Beeb mounts better than anyone else. It looks great and moves at just the right tense but leisurely pace. Nicola Pagett and Eric Porter are fine in the leading roles.

Anna Karenina
1985 PG 130 ★★ DRA

And yet again. Anyone studying Anna Karenina for A-levels and looking for a crib is positively spoilt for choice. Another honest and earnest endeavour this, with Jacqueline Bisset doing a fair job as Anna, Paul Scofield as the betrayed and understandably glum husband and Christopher Reeve as the dashing young officer.

Anne of Green Gables
1985 U 130 ★★★ FAM

Not at all a bad adaptation of the well-loved children's book by Lucy Maude Montgomery. Megan Follows plays the spirited orphan who pluckily and cheerfully suffers a series of unpleasant foster homes before finding happiness with an elderly couple. Richard Farnsworth and Colleen Dewhurst provide excellent support in an engaging, likeable film.

Anne of Green Gables: the Sequel
1988 U 164 ★★ FAM

Being the further adventures of Anne, who is now eighteen, teaching at the local school and still played by Megan Follows. Love enters her life and so does a problem: an attractive teaching post can be hers in another town and what she has to decide is whether or not to leave Green Gables and all her friends. Tough choice, as you can imagine. (Available as a boxed set with the previous film under the title of *Anne of Green Gables: the Complete Story*.)

Anne of the Thousand Days
1969 PG 140 ★★ DRA

Never mind the quality, feel the width. Charles Jarrott's film concentrates on style rather than substance – lavish costumes, handsome sets. But despite Richard Burton and Genevieve Bujold this story of the short, tragic life of Henry VIII's second wife, Anne Boleyn, never really comes to life, flipping too quickly through the pages of history and never giving its cast the time to develop the characters they portray.

Annie
1982 U 122 ★★★ MUS

John Huston directed this adaptation of the Broadway musical, itself based on Harold Gray's 1930s comic strip about Little Orphan Annie. Aileen Quinn plays Annie, rescued from an orphanage by billionaire Daddy Warbucks (Albert Finney). All vastly improbable but the songs are fine, there's some lively dancing and, so long as you don't think too deeply about it, the movie is quite a lot of fun.

Annie Hall
1977 15 90 ★★★★ COM

Many people regard this as Woody Allen's masterpiece. Whether it is or not this touching, believable, frequently hilarious love story won Oscars for Best Picture, Best Director (Allen), Best Screenplay (also Allen) and Best Actress (Diane Keaton). Allen is a neurotic New York Jewish comedian; Keaton, the kooky, disorganised young WASP whom he meets, falls

for and quarrels and breaks up with. It's
probably Keaton's finest hour and Allen's script
is a delight.

Another Country
1984 15 86 ★★★ DRA

A fine adaptation of Julian Mitchell's stage
play about a pair of young misfits at an
English public school. As the homosexual
Rupert Everett and the quasi-Communist
Colin Firth rebel against a system that will
inevitably thwart them both, what we are
watching is the British Establishment in
microcosm. The story is told in flashback by
Everett, who has grown up to be a kind of
Guy Burgess figure. No explicit
homosexuality but the 15 certificate should
be heeded.

Another Stakeout
1993 PG 104 ★ MYS/THR

Emilio Estevez and Richard Dreyfuss play
happy families with Assistant DA Rosie
O'Donnell as they search for a witness to a
murder before the Mob gets her. A witless
sequel to a much superior film (see *Stakeout*)
made six years earlier. How can it have taken so
long to come up with a load of codswallop like
this?

Another Time, Another Place
1983 15 102 ★★★ DRA

Phyllis Logan as a Scottish farmer's wife who
falls in love with an Italian POW (Giovanni
Mauriello) in the Second World War. Michael
Radford's film depicts beautifully the aridity of
the woman's home life and the way she
blossoms as her guilty affair develops. A tender,
moving portrait of two decent people who
should indeed have met at another time and in
another place.

Another You
1991 15 91 ★ COM

Fresh from the loony bin, Gene Wilder is put
in charge of con man Richard Pryor, who has
been ordered to do community service. Not a
bad start but a silly plot – the gullible Wilder
persuaded to impersonate a missing heir –
leaves us with a raucous, frantic comedy that's
weakly written and poorly directed.

Apartment, The
1960 PG 119 ★★★★ COM

The kind of film they don't make 'em like any
more, probably because there aren't any writer-
directors like Billy Wilder around any more.
Jack Lemmon is the office worker who lends his
flat to his bosses for illicit sex and falls for
elevator girl Shirley MacLaine – the lover of the
firm's personnel chief, Fred MacMurray. Which
will triumph – love, or Lemmon's desire for
promotion? Lovely sharp dialogue and a cynical
view of inter-office politics. Suggestive rather
than explicit. (B&W)

Apple Dumpling Gang, The
1975 U 96 ★★★ FAM

An amusing comedy Western from Disney
wherein three homeless children fall into the
care of a gambler, Bill Bixby. There's plenty of
knockabout fun as Bixby tries to rob a bank.
Don Knotts and Tim Conway are the inevitable
– and inevitably inept – bad guys. Slim Pickens
and Susan Clark also contribute to the good-
natured comic capers. The film was popular
enough to lead to a sequel (see below).

Apple Dumpling Gang Rides Again, The
1979 U 85 ★ FAM

This is best avoided by all except those addicted
to dumplings. Conway and Knotts now head
the cast in a slapstick yarn that tries, but fails, to
recapture the freshness and zest of the original.

Arachnophobia
1990 PG 104 ★★★ COM

A small American town is threatened when
killer spiders from South America breed with
the local arachnids and run amok. No, no,
don't worry – it's more comic than frightening
but those with a spider phobia might have to
peep through their fingers from time to time. A
slick comedy-thriller with Jeff Daniels as the
local doctor and John Goodman as the not-
always-infallible spider exterminator.

Aristocats, The
1970 U 75 ★★★ FAM

Very agreeable piece of Disney animation,
directed by Wolfgang Reitherman, concerning
the plight of a cat (voiced by Eva Gabor) and

her kittens, villainously cast out of their home by a wicked butler, who wants his employer to leave her fortune to him rather than them. Excellent animation and a better-than-average script which, mercifully, goes easy on the sentimentality, give the film considerable appeal. As do the actors who lend their voices to the characters, among them the incomparable Phil Harris, who memorably voiced Baloo the bear in Reitherman's *The Jungle Book*.

Army of Darkness: The Medieval Dead
1993 15 85 ★ HOR

The final part of director Sam Raimi's *Evil Dead* trilogy – a time-travel caper in which Bruce Campbell is transported back to medieval England and becomes involved in a local war. A touch gruesome in parts but also quite tongue-in-cheek. The result is neither one thing nor the other, neither funny nor horrific. A fair bit of violence, though.

Around the World in 80 Days
1956 U 135 ★★★ FAM

Producer Mike Todd's sprawling epic, based on the novel by Jules Verne, is noted for the forty-odd guest stars who turn up in walk-on parts. The main characters – Phileas Fogg and his manservant – are nicely played by David Niven and the Mexican comedian, Cantinflas. Shirley MacLaine is good, too, in a film that is somehow smaller than it looks but is most entertaining nevertheless.

Arsenic and Old Lace
1944 PG 113 ★★★★ COM

Frank Capra in more playful mood than usual. Cary Grant is at his effortless, boneless best as the nephew trying to stop his little old aunts, Josephine Hull and Jean Adair, bumping off lonely old men. They do it, of course, from the nicest possible motives. Raymond Massey and Peter Lorre are much meaner villains than the two old girls. A time-honoured classic in splendid bad taste. (B&W)

Arthur
1981 15 93 ★★★ COM

Some say *10* was the best film Dudley Moore has made in his uneven Hollywood career but *Arthur* is arguably better. Moore plays an alcoholic millionaire playboy who must choose between his inheritance plus an arranged marriage and penury with the girl he loves, Liza Minnelli. Moore makes an excellent drunk and Minnelli is engagingly kooky but it was John Gielgud, as the unflappable valet, who walked off with an Oscar.

Arthur 2: On the Rocks
1988 PG 108 ★ COM

The dreaded curse of the sequel strikes again. Goodness knows why, seven years later, Moore chose to make this awful little film in which Arthur, now married to Minnelli, loses his inheritance and strives to get it back. If he thought this might be the hit he needed at the time, he was wrong.

Asphalt Jungle, The
1950 PG 107 ★★★★ DRA

John Huston's excellent, much-copied thriller tells of a scam seen from the point of view of the criminals and is notable, among other things, for bringing Marilyn Monroe to prominence as the mistress of a smooth crook, Louis Calhern. Sam Jaffe is the old con who comes out of jail to pull off one last jewellery heist. Calhern and Sterling Hayden are among the helpers he recruits. (B&W)

Atlantic City
1980 15 105 ★★★★ DRA

If Burt Lancaster ever gave a better performance than he did here, would somebody please point it out to us. He is marvellous as an ageing petty crook who befriends harrassed waitress Susan Sarandon in Louis Malle's beautifully observed thriller set in one of America's gambling capitals. Malle's wickedly sharp view of transatlantic idiosyncracies is another huge plus in a film full of surprises.

At Play in the Fields of the Lord
1991 15 179 ★ DRA

A film of noble intentions overcome by its own ambition. Adapted from Peter Matthiessen's novel, it tells a politically correct tale warning against messing about with ecology and native culture. Tom Berenger, Aidan Quinn, Kathy Bates, John Lithgow and Daryl Hannah are among those involved. Worthy, yes, but worthy here is also rather dull.

Attack of the 50 Ft Woman
1993 12 85 ★★ SCI/FAN

It could happen to anyone: Daryl Hannah is looking for her wayward husband when she's zapped away by an alien spaceship. By the time she returns she is fifty feet tall. Would you believe that what this film is really about is Hannah's dodgy marriage and her father's attempts to take over her business? No, probably not. Still, Hannah is fun to watch.

Aunt Julia and the Scriptwriter
1990 15 102 ★★ DRA

Budding radio writer Keanu Reeves falls for his divorced aunt, Barbara Hershey, in 1950s New Orleans. Peter Falk, another writer on his way down, incorporates their love talk, along with fiercely anti-Albanian sentiments, in his radio soap. An entertaining, unconventional and hugely untidy film.

Au Revoir les Enfants
1987 PG 100 ★★★★ FOR

A marvellously moving slice of autobiography by director Louis Malle. In an exclusive boarding school in occupied France in 1944 three Jewish boys are hidden from the Nazis by the masters. The main story – of the friendship between a Jewish and a Catholic boy (based on the young Malle himself) – builds through detail and incident to a heart-rending climax. Neither sentimental nor manipulative but keep a handkerchief close by. (Subtitled)

Avalon
1990 U 122 ★★ DRA

Despite its strong cast, Barry Levinson's vaguely autobiographical story of Russian Jewish immigrants in America fails to grip. A sprawling, overlong saga spanning fifty years of family tribulations, tensions and change, although nothing very dramatic seems to happen. Aidan Quinn and Elizabeth Perkins are personable but the eye-catching performances come from Joan Plowright and Armin Mueller-Stahl.

Awakenings
1990 15 115 ★★★★ DRA

The remarkable and, broadly speaking, true story of how in 1969 a New York doctor (Robin Williams) awakened a group of encephalitic patients – some of whom had been in a trance-like state for thirty years – with the aid of the drug L-DOPA. But the apparently miracle cure did not have quite the hoped-for happy ending. Williams is outstanding as the doctor and Robert De Niro is highly sympathetic as the chief guinea pig.

Babette's Feast
1987 U 103 ★★★★ FOR

Stéphane Audran is the French refugee who
decides to thank the two Danish sisters who
have helped and befriended her by preparing
the most sumptuous meal in the world. Based
on the book by Isak Dinesen (who also wrote
Out of Africa), this is not recommended to
weak-willed dieters since a gastronomic feast to
end all feasts is presented. Gentle and uplifting,
it won a richly deserved Oscar for Best Foreign
Film that year. (Subtitled)

Baby Boom
1987 PG 106 ★★ COM

Diane Keaton's the self-absorbed yuppie who
(reluctantly) inherits a baby, loses her job and
boyfriend, uproots to life in a backwater and
finds it a small price to pay for fulfilment. It's a
charming story and the best of the baby movies
that flooded the screen around that time.
Keaton's good performance is well supported by
Harold Ramis, James Spader, Sam Shepard and
Sam Wanamaker. Possibly responsible for a
mini population explosion, since even the
hardest heart turns broody.

Baby's Day Out
1994 PG 94 ★★ COM

Fans of *Home Alone* will like this since it's made
by John Hughes to a similar formula – namely,
the little guy wins out over the big guys. A
pampered toddler is taken hostage by
incompetent kidnappers, wanders away and
embarks on a danger-filled journey through the
big city. Typically with Hughes, sentimentality
takes prominence over humour and the
slapstick comedy verges on the violent. Joe
Mantegna provides more class than the film
deserves.

Baby... Secret of the Lost Legend
1985 PG 89 ★★ DRA

Dinosaurs are alive and well and living in the
African jungle as a group of palaeontologists
discover when they happen upon a whole
family of them. It's cute, if a little cutesy,
though Sean Young brings a bit of bite with
her. The dinosaurs are most appealing and
technically impressive, but it's not up to the
standard set later by *Jurassic Park*. Nothing less
than you'd expect from a Disney movie. Note

the certificate, especially if very young children
are about.

Backbeat
1994 15 96 ★★★ DRA

The story of the fifth Beatle, Stuart Sutcliffe
(Stephen Dorff), and set during the band's early
days in Germany when Sutcliffe was still part of
it. The fab five worked hard at the Kaiser Club
and played even harder. In between gigs and
rows, Sutcliffe fell in love with German
photographer Astrid Kirchherr (Sheryl Lee)
and, while the rest of the boys went home to
Liverpool and legend, Sutcliffe preferred Astrid,
Germany and art college. Solid performances
and an interesting slant on the Beatles.

Backdraft
1991 15 131 ★★ ACT/ADV

Kurt Russell and William Baldwin are firemen
brothers, more competent at fighting each other
than fires. When faced with a mad arsonist
Russell stays with the force (where he's a big
hero) while Baldwin helps fire investigator
Robert De Niro. Despite a glittering cast
(including Scott Glenn and Donald Sutherland)
it's the fire sequences, photographed to
stunning, almost loving effect, that captivate.

Back in the USSR
1991 15 85 ★★ DRA

A brave attempt at a post-Cold War thriller
with a younger protagonist than usual – Frank
Whaley, an American teenager looking for
action on his last night in Moscow. He certainly
finds it after falling in with Natalya Negoda, a
beautiful local girl, who leads him into a rather
flat, rather disappointing story involving Brian
Blessed as a black marketeer and Roman
Polanski as a Russian gangster.

Back to the Future
1985 PG 111 ★★★★ COM

A terrific movie that led to two sequels.
Michael J Fox is Marty McFly, a college kid
sent back to the past thanks to his eccentric
friend Dr Emmett Brown (Christopher Lloyd),
who has devised a time-travel machine in the
shape of a De Lorean car. Back in the 1950s,
Marty has to ensure that his future mother gets
together with his gawky father-to-be (Crispin

Glover) and not with nasty bully Biff. Lovely stuff.

Back to the Future II
1989 PG 103 ★★ COM

A shade disappointing, since it's harsher, crueller and more violent than the original, but still quite appealing. This time, Biff is now a mega-rich swine married to Marty's mother. Something's got to be done. Fox and Lloyd nip to and fro through time as if there's no tomorrow and poor old Elisabeth Shue (as Marty's girlfriend) spends practically the entire film unconscious – nice work if you can get it.

Back to the Future III
1990 PG 113 ★★★ COM

Now this is much better. Everyone shows a welcome return to the gentler form of the first film as Doc goes back to the Wild West and Marty follows to get him out of trouble. In the bad old days of shoot-outs at high noon, the Doc finds romance with Mary Steenburgen. Marty, of course, once again has problems with Biff. Better than *II*, not quite as good as the original and a nice point at which to end the series.

Bad Day at Black Rock
1955 PG 78 ★★★★ DRA

A one-armed man (Spencer Tracy) arrives in a small Western town to present a dead Japanese-American soldier's medal to his father and encounters a hostile, tight-knit community with a guilty secret to hide. Terrific atmosphere and tension and great support from Robert Ryan and Ernest Borgnine. Under John Sturges's direction Tracy gives one of his finest performances.

Ballad of Little Jo, The
1993 15 116 ★★★ DRA

The true story of a woman in the old West who, after being ostracized for having an illegitimate child, found the only way to survive was as a man, which is just what she did, living in a log cabin outside a mining community. When she saves a Chinese man from hanging, the pair set up home, ostensibly as man and man but secretly as man and wife. Suzy Amis gives a most effective performance as Jo.

Bamba, La
1987 15 105 ★★★ MUS

At seventeen Ritchie Valens was an international pop star. At seventeen he was also dead – killed in the plane crash that also carried off Buddy Holly. 'La Bamba' the song was Valens's biggest hit; *La Bamba* the movie does a likeable job of telling his (brief) life story, from Mexican fruit-picker to pop legend. As Valens, Lou Diamond Phillips turns in a well-judged performance.

Bambi
1942 U 67 ★★★★ FAM

One of the best of the early Disneys – both joyful and a notorious tear-jerker. Remember the death of Bambi's mother, a scene that has caused generations of kids to weep buckets? Bambi, the fawn growing up in the forest, Thumper the rabbit and other woodland residents have also delighted those same generations. A classic of animation.

Bananas
1971 15 78 ★★★ COM

Woody Allen as his customary neurotic New Yorker, this time embroiled in a South American revolution. Due to his fascination for and with political activist Nancy (Louise Lasser – Allen's wife at the time) he becomes the rebel leader. There are some splendid Allen gags, though not perhaps as many as in some of his other comedies. But then this was only his second film as a director.

Band Wagon, The
1953 U 108 ★★★ MUS

The attractions of Fred Astaire, Cyd Charisse, Jack Buchanan, Ava Gardner and the song 'That's Entertainment' (among many others) in an enjoyable, sophisticated musical. Astaire plays a Hollywood dancer on the skids who is attempting a comeback in a Broadway musical. But the show's director (Buchanan) leaves much to be desired and Astaire's co-star (Charisse) is less than enamoured of him. Predictable but fun.

Barefoot in the Park
1967 PG 101 ★★★ COM

Neil Simon is quite profligate with his sparkling one-liners in this story of a couple of newlyweds (Robert Redford and Jane Fonda) who make their home in a fifth-floor flat, with no elevator, in Manhattan. Problems abound for Redford's mother-in-law (Mildred Natwick) and everyone else who has to climb the stairs. The interference of Bohemian neighbour Charles Boyer does little to help. Every performance is a gem.

Barkleys of Broadway, The
1949 U 104 ★★★ MUS

A lush, warm, nostalgic emotional bath for fans of Fred Astaire and Ginger Rogers. This was the last time they appeared together – after a break of ten years. And, appropriately, they play a showbiz couple who reunite after having split up. There never was a team like Fred and Ginger and, though they may not be at their very best here, there is enough to make us regret that we would never see them in harness again.

Barry Lyndon
1975 PG 177 ★★★ DRA

Stanley Kubrick's bold, not entirely successful attempt to film Thackeray's novel. Ryan O'Neal plays the roguish eighteenth-century Irishman Barry who is enamoured of his cousin (Gay Hamilton). Via a duel, plus encounters with a highwayman, a Prussian and a spy, he emerges as a self-centred social climber. What distinguishes the film is John Alcott's cinematography, which has never been bettered.

Barton Fink
1991 15 111 ★★★ COM

The jury at the Cannes Film Festival awarded this oddball comedy from the Coen brothers its major prize that year. The eponymous hero (John Turturro) is an earnest young playwright lured to Hollywood under the delusion that he can write what he wants. Wrong. Once there, he suffers from writer's block, pushy producers and a serial killer. Wild and uneven but nicely played, especially by John Goodman as a travelling salesman.

Basil, the Great Mouse Detective, The
1986 U 80 ★★★ FAM

Modelled on Mr Rathbone, Basil is Walt Disney's rodent Sherlock Holmes and an endearing little know-all. This animated cartoon is a jolly caper which sees Basil investigating the disappearance of a toymaker and coming head-to-head with his arch enemy, Professor Rattigan.

Batman
1989 15 121 ★★★ ACT/ADV

It's not that Michael Keaton's laid-back representation of the hero is bad, it's just that Jack Nicholson is so outrageous and hammy as the Joker that Batman himself is overshadowed. Kim Basinger provides some love interest for the Caped Crusader in a dark, menacing Gotham City. Indeed it's the impressive Gothic sets – plus Tim Burton's moody direction – that dominate the film.

Batman Returns
1992 15 121 ★★★ ACT/ADV

More romance and action for Michael Keaton as he dons the Batman cape for a second outing. This time he takes on the Penguin (Danny DeVito, who looks so cute with webbed feet), Catwoman (Michelle Pfeiffer, who took over the role when Annette Bening became too pregnant to wear the skintight suit) and evil entrepreneur Christopher Walken. The sets are still impressive but more attention has been paid to plot and character development and it's none the worse for that.

*batteries not included
1987 PG 102 ★ SCI/FAN

The residents of a block of crumbling Manhattan flats are being pushed into moving out of their homes so that a sleek, modern office can be built in its place. But no-one has reckoned with stubborn couple Hume Cronyn and Jessica Tandy, nor, for that matter, the aliens who help the poverty-stricken oldies' battle to stay put. The comedy's a little on the thin side but the story is wholesome and the aliens are appealing.

Battleship Potemkin
1925 PG 65 ★★★★★ FOR

Eisenstein's silent epic is widely recognised as one of the greatest – and certainly most influential – films of all time. It tells of the mutiny of the crew of the battleship *Potemkin* during the 1905 Russian Revolution. The massacre on the steps at Odessa is one of the most memorable scenes in the cinema and has been frequently imitated. It's a film that everyone interested in the movies really ought to see. (B&W)

Beaches
1988 15 118 ★ DRA

Bette Midler and Barbara Hershey as a mismatched pair of childhood friends. Midler, a working-class Bronx kid, is from the wrong side of the tracks. Hershey is the refined, wealthy child from San Francisco. As they grow up, men, careers, family and fate play an ever-increasing role in their friendship. The emotion is too calculated to make much of an impression, but it doesn't mean you won't be brushing away the odd tear.

Beanstalk
1994 U 78 ★★ FAM

A modernized version of *Jack and the Beanstalk*. Here, though, Jack's a streetwise American boy who, trying to provide for his impoverished single mother, acquires some eggplant seeds. These soon sprout into an enormous tree at the bottom of their garden with a whacking great giant residing at the top. It's a touch silly, but the kids should like it.

Bear, The
1989 PG 89 ★★ DRA

This is either a touching, very well-made study of a bear cub's struggle to survive or an excruciatingly anthropomorphic tale of ursine folks. Actually, it's both. Filmed in British Columbia, the story follows a young bear whose life is shattered when its mother is killed. Hunters pursuing an adult male bear are the villains of the piece. Essentially not unlike *Bambi* but with real, highly trained animals instead of Disney sketches.

Beauty and the Beast
1991 U 81 ★★★★ FAM

Belle, the beauty, scorned by the townsfolk for being brainy, is courted by the macho local stud. The Beast, who kidnaps her father, lives in a gloomy castle along with singing teapots and the like. Angela Lansbury is one of many stars

who lend their voices to an excellent fairy tale, which was the first animated film ever to be Oscar-nominated as Best Picture. Quite right, too, for Disney proves it can still make this kind of thing better than anyone else.

Bedknobs and Broomsticks
1971 U 112 ★★ FAM

Here Disney mixes live action with animation, ultimately to disjointed effect. The year is 1940 and three children are evacuated to the country where a witch provides them with a magic bedstead which will take them wherever they wish to go. Angela Lansbury and David Tomlinson star. The special effects won an Academy Award. It looks a little dated now but at the time the editing and camera trickery were considered impressive.

Bedroom Window, The
1986 15 108 ★★ MYS/THR

Steve Guttenberg plays an affable young man who is having an affair with his boss's wife. One passion-filled night she witnesses a young girl (Elizabeth McGovern) being assaulted in the street outside. Later that night a similar assault results in rape and murder and the police need witnesses, so Guttenberg steps forward, pretending it was he who witnessed the assault. Neat idea, a touch over-plotted. Isabelle Huppert is the boss's naughty wife. Contains sex and violence.

Beethoven
1992 U 83 ★★★ FAM

A thirteen-stone St Bernard dog takes over and creates bedlam in the house of dog-hating Charles Grodin. The rest of the family, of course, love the mutt and so Grodin must perforce spring to the rescue when Beethoven is kidnapped by Dean Jones and company. Beethoven may be the star of the film but the dry, sharp, unsentimental Grodin provides the fun for adults. Any film benefits from his presence in the cast.

Beethoven's 2nd
1993 U 85 ★★ FAM

Even Charles Grodin has his work cut out to make much of a story in which Beethoven finds himself a girlfriend. She, however, is caught in the middle of a custody battle between her master and his soon-to-be ex-wife. Grodin's kids take control when the St Bernardette produces a litter of pups. In a repeat of the original joke, Grodin is not at all pleased at having his house wrecked by Beethoven's brood.

Beetle Juice
1988 15 88 ★★★ COM

Husband and wife Alec Baldwin and Geena Davis die in a car crash and their ghosts return to haunt their much-loved house. When it's sold to a yuppie family, the spectral couple's efforts to evict them as quickly as possible fail to work, so they call on the expert help of wacky Betelgeuse, Michael Keaton, who specialises in exorcizing the living. Tim Burton (he of *Batman*) directed this – very well, too.

Being Human
1993 15 116 ★ DRA

Hard to imagine that Bill Forsyth, the writer/director of such whimsical delights as *Gregory's Girl* and *Local Hero*, could come up with something so comparatively poor, but then this was a big-budget Hollywood venture and Forsyth's original ideas were, allegedly, messed about with. The film is a series of tales spanning the centuries from Roman times to the present day and the only thing they have in common is Robin Williams as the central character. Most are very sentimental and few are as dramatic as they might be.

Being There
1979 15 124 ★★★★ DRA

Arguably Peter Sellers's finest performance as an idiot savant who, after chance encounters with influential people, is taken out of his familiar environment and heralded as the great mind of the century. Despite the undercurrent of black humour it's a sombre piece, performed to perfection by the entire cast (Melvyn Douglas won an Oscar) and proves Sellers's considerable ability as a straight actor.

Belle Epoque
1993 15 105 ★★★ FOR

A saucy, amusing Spanish offering, which won the 1994 Oscar for Best Foreign Film. In a bittersweet way it portrays life, love (and a touch of sex) against the background of the Spanish Civil War. Fernando, a young army deserter, finds sanctuary on the country estate of an elderly, liberal painter, where he is seduced by his host's four beautiful daughters with results that include pleasure, joy, sadness and pain. This is to be the best time of his life. Well, it would be, wouldn't it? (Subtitled)

Belles of St Trinian's, The
1954 U 87 ★★★ FAM

The first and best of the series which introduced the schoolgirls from hell. The school is not only anarchic but on the verge of bankruptcy as the girls, instead of studying, concentrate their efforts on betting on horses. Alastair Sim and Joyce Grenfell are on sparkling form as the adults outwitted by the girls, as is George Cole as Flash Harry, who helps the pupils sell the moonshine they make in the science lab. Often sold in a double bill with *Blue Murder at St Trinian's*. (B&W)

Bellman and True
1987 15 117 ★★ MYS/THR

A British thriller that has Bernard Hill as a computer programmer forced by thieves, who kidnap his son, into knocking out a bank's security system. Gradually, he is drawn deeper and deeper into a plot that involves death as well as theft. Realistic and with plenty of suspense, plus a fine performance by Bernard Hill. Violent in places.

Belly of an Architect, The
1987 15 113 ★★★ DRA

Peter Greenaway is one of the most artistic of British directors and this is a very beautiful film. Beautiful, but rather cold, as it tells of a dying American architect, Brian Dennehy, in Rome. Although there to celebrate an eighteenth-century French architect, Dennehy becomes obsessed with the idea that his abdominal pains are caused by his young wife (Chloe Webb) trying to poison him. Dennehy lends human warmth to an otherwise cerebral and adult story.

Ben-Hur
1959 PG 203 ★★★ ACT/ADV

The American comedian Mort Sahl said: 'Loved Ben, hated Hur'. Not fair. There's much to enjoy in William Wyler's epic wherein Charlton Heston's revenge-seeking galley slave takes on the Roman masters – especially in a terrific chariot race. A touch ponderous elsewhere and one hates to think of the damage caused to the horses. But the film did win a record eleven Oscars.

Benji
1974 Uc 86 ★★★ FAM

Almost, though not quite, a modern-day *Lassie*. Lovable mongrel Benji may not have the famous collie's pedigree but he does save a pair of kidnapped children in heroic style. His adventures here spawned a couple of sequels. Neither of them matched the calibre of this, much of which is recorded from the canine's point of view. It'll have you crying, laughing and crying again.

Benny and Joon
1993 15 95 ★★★ DRA

Aidan Quinn has neglected his own life to take care of his lovably daffy sister, Mary Stuart Masterson, who has learning difficulties. However, when Johnny Depp moves in things change. Depp is a Buster Keaton-type clown who is also one sandwich short of a picnic and he and Masterson fall in love. An original, unusual little drama with nice performances and a great deal of charm.

Best Years of Our Lives, The
1946 U 159 ★★★★ FAM

William Wyler's poignant examination of the difficulties faced by American servicemen returning from the Second World War and reverting to civilian life. The story follows three veterans – Fredric March, Dana Andrews and Harold Russell – as their homecoming is plagued by memories of the war and fears for the future. The performances are all top-class and the script is warm and emotional without being over-sentimental. (B&W)

Betsy's Wedding
1990 15 90 ★★ COM

Alan Alda wrote this marital story after one of his own daughters got married – it must have been a traumatic occasion. Molly Ringwald plays the bride, Madeline Kahn her mother.

Alda himself plays the father, who is determined to do the best for his child even though he can't afford it. Rather a bittersweet story, if not a terribly original one.

Beverly Hillbillies, The
1993 PG 90 ★★ COM

The country bumpkin Clampett family strike oil on their farmland and rush to the big city to spend their millions – the first few of which go on a pink palace in Beverly Hills. Scheming yuppies make a bid for the rest. The humour, such as it is, is about naive hicks adapting to cosmopolitan life. Erika Eleniak (of TV's *Baywatch* fame), Jim Varney and Lily Tomlin star in this unnecessary cinema version of a long-running television series.

Beverly Hills Cop
1984 15 99 ★★★ ACT/ADV

The best friend of Detroit cop Eddie Murphy is murdered by LA thugs, so Murphy goes to Beverly Hills to investigate. The plot doesn't matter too much, since the film's appeal depends upon watching Murphy at his very best. Judge Reinhold is also most appealing as an easy-going LA detective. Enjoyable, fast, amusing entertainment and one of the last really good things Murphy has done. The language may be salty, except in the specially edited-for-TV version.

Beverly Hills Cop II
1987 15 99 ★★ ACT/ADV

Tony (*Top Gun*) Scott directed this flaccid, self-congratulatory, disappointing sequel. Loads of action (or movement, anyway) and violence but little in the way of characterization and plot. Murphy merely drifts through the story; the wooden Brigitte Nielsen, as a villainness, can't even manage that. Reinhold and his partner (John Ashton) also go through the motions. Dean Stockwell lends a touch of distinction as the main heavy. The same warnings apply about swearing as above.

Beverly Hills Cop III
1994 15 100 ★★ ACT/ADV

A slight improvement on *II* but still falling short of the original. This time Murphy – you may be surprised to learn – has gone back to

LA on the trail of an evil gang who've murdered his police chief. Why he doesn't just relocate to California is a mystery. Anyway, old pal Reinhold returns for his third outing but instead of Ashton, Hector Elizondo is his new partner. Again, beware of possible strong language.

Bhaji on the Beach
1993 15 96 ★★ DRA

A funny, touching portrayal of a bunch of Asian women on a day trip to Blackpool to see the lights. What begins as a break from normal routine becomes a day of re-evaluation and reappraisal as the women confront the realities of their lives. The predominantly Indian cast does a fine job of exploring and exposing the difficulties faced by Asian women in modern Britain.

Big
1988 PG 105 ★★★ COM

In which Tom Hanks plays a twelve-year-old boy who suddenly finds himself in the body of a thirtysomething man. A marvellous opportunity this, splendidly taken, to explore the absurdities that dominate the lives of ambitious adults. A fine performance by Hanks – suddenly becoming an executive in a toy company – in a role that, too conveniently perhaps, extols the virtues of childhood innocence.

Big Blue, The
1988 15 114 ★ ACT/ADV

Luc Besson's somewhat baffling film has developed a cult following, though goodness knows why. It tells of an insurance investigator, Rosanna Arquette, who follows her boyfriend (Jean-Marc Barr) from place to place as he takes part in deep-sea diving competitions. The underwater scenes are fine but they tend to submerge any vestige of human interest.

Big Chill, The
1983 15 101 ★★★★ DRA

Much imitated since, this is the story of a bunch of old college friends who are reunited at the funeral of one of their number and compare notes on their progress to date. Marvellously evocative sixties soundtrack and a superb cast of then unknowns (Tom Berenger, Glenn Close,

Jeff Goldblum, Kevin Kline, JoBeth Williams and William Hurt), with a keenly intelligent script by writer-director Lawrence Kasdan. (Kevin Costner was originally in it too, but his entire role ended up on the cutting-room floor.)

Big Country, The
1958 PG 160 ★★★★ WES

What it all boils down to is a heated feud about water rights, such things being vital in the old West. But it begins with a sailor, Gregory Peck, coming ashore to settle on land and being taught a few things – not all of them pleasant – by Jean Simmons, Charlton Heston and Burl Ives. Apt title, since the vistas are expansive and the scenery threatens to dwarf the story. William Wyler directed.

Big Easy, The
1986 15 98 ★★★ MYS/THR

A most enjoyable romantic thriller in which a free-and-easy New Orleans cop, Dennis Quaid, becomes professionally – and sexually – involved with the beautiful assistant DA (Ellen Barkin) who is looking into police corruption. Quaid, of course, is a suspect, but that's just a red herring. Cajun music and the New Orleans background add greatly to a nicely plotted mystery. Some sex and violence.

Bigfoot and the Hendersons
1987 PG 107 ★★ COM

Known in the USA as *Harry and the Hendersons*, this mild comedy is directed by William Dear. John Lithgow accidentally runs into a sort of Yeti and finds his family's life considerably overturned when the amiable Bigfoot moves in. Hunters are on the trail of hairy Harry, so the question is: can Lithgow return him to his own environment in time?

Big Picture, The
1988 15 96 ★★★ DRA

A sharp and amusing satire on Hollywood and its ethics. Kevin Bacon is the promising young film-maker embraced by the studio system, who finds that artistic integrity is all very well but it doesn't actually pay the bills. Well, not if your bills include running a Porsche and a home in Beverly Hills. A sly little sideswipe at the corrupting effects of success.

Big Sleep, The
1946 PG 110 ★★★★★ MYS/THR

Not just a marvellously twisting and complex murder mystery but also the best attempt yet to bring Raymond Chandler's Philip Marlowe to the screen. Humphrey Bogart makes a terrific Marlowe, Lauren Bacall is a slinky *femme fatale* and Howard Hawks directs the whole thing with tremendous verve and pace. The plot, still somewhat baffling at the end, simply doesn't lend itself to a brief summary but in fact that hardly matters. (B&W)

Big Store, The: see Marx Brothers

Bill and Ted's Bogus Journey
1991 PG 89 ★★ COM

Being the sequel to the film below. Here the two dudes (Keanu Reeves and Alex Winter) must visit both heaven and hell in order to save the world – to say nothing of themselves. Pretty good jokes, amiable performances, neat special effects and a splendid turn by Bill Sadler as the Grim Reaper, inevitably outwitted by our heroes' cunning naivety.

Bill and Ted's Excellent Adventure
1989 PG 85 ★★★ COM

Introducing Reeves and Winter as the high-school dudes for whom life will be unpleasant if they fail their history test. Fortunately, George Carlin, a dude from the future, helps them out by means of a phone box which takes them back to the past and enables them to collect famous dudes such as Socrates, Napoleon, Billy the Kid and Joan of Arc. The delight of the film is the boys' casual treatment of these luminaries. As Bill and Ted would say: excellent!

Billy Bathgate
1991 15 102 ★★ DRA

Given the cast (Dustin Hoffman as the notorious Dutch Schultz, Bruce Willis and Nicole Kidman) and the writer (Tom Stoppard, adapting E L Doctorow's novel), this tale of gangland life in the 1930s should have been a great deal better. Basically, it tells how young Billy (Loren Dean) becomes Schultz's trusted assistant just as the law moves in on him. The main problem is that Hoffman is simply not menacing enough.

Billy Liar
1963 PG 94 ★★★ DRA

John Schlesinger's fine screen version of Keith Waterhouse and Willis Hall's gritty, funny urban comedy. Tom Courtenay is the North Country lad whose daydreams of escape into a more glamorous life spill over and complicate intensely the life he is actually living. Julie Christie, Wilfred Pickles and Rodney Bewes complete an excellent cast. (B&W)

Biloxi Blues
1988 15 102 ★★★ COM

The second of Neil Simon's autobiographical plays (the first was *Brighton Beach Memoirs*) deals with raw, rueful, funny memories of life as an army recruit in Mississippi during the Second World War. Matthew Broderick is the innocent-at-arms, facing the hazards of sex, bigotry and Christopher Walken's psychotic drill sergeant. As ever with Simon, the humour is in the dialogue and the observations, which hit the mark every time.

Bingo
1991 PG 86 ★★ COM

Robert J Steinmiller wants to get a dog but his parents say no. But when a dog gets him, that's different. Bingo is a runaway circus dog who has landed in Steinmiller's lap and must be hidden from the parents. All goes along nicely until the Steinmiller family have to move away and Bingo must be left behind. Or must he? Only the dog is worth writing home about.

Bird
1988 15 154 ★★★ MUS

Director Clint Eastwood's Cannes prize-winner about the life of saxophonist Charlie 'Bird' Parker, one of the seminal figures of jazz – an alcoholic, a womanizer, a drug addict and, also, a genius. Forest Whitaker is marvellously sympathetic in the title role. Parker died at thirty-four and the film, which is cool, fond and compassionate, consists of a collage of scenes from his life.

Bird on a Wire
1990 15 106 ★★ ACT/ADV

Mel Gibson is the man in the Witness Relocation Programme, Goldie Hawn the ex-girlfriend he accidentally re-encounters. Together they go on the run when the man on whom Gibson grassed (David Carradine) gets out of jail and seeks vengeance. So begins a high-speed romantic chase with a novel setting for the finale. The stars are better than the plot which, in turn, is better than the script.

Birds, The
1963 15 114 ★★★ HOR

Not one of Alfred Hitchcock's very best but it could certainly put you off feeding the dickies. Tippi Hedren (mother of Melanie Griffith, for what that's worth) is the young woman picked on for no very clear reason by a most menacing flock of birds. It's all very allegorical, tense and actually quite scary.

Birdy
1984 15 115 ★★★ DRA

Although the original book – by William Wharton – is set during the Second World War, the film successfully updates the story to the post-Vietnam era when a war-traumatized Matthew Modine believes he can fly. As a result, he's committed to a military mental hospital but his best friend, Nicolas Cage – physically wounded in the war – determines to bring him back to reality. Smashing performances and great direction by Alan Parker make this a thoughtful study of the human aftermath of war.

Bishop's Wife, The
1947 U 106 ★★★★ COM

Second-best movie to watch during the Christmas hols – *It's a Wonderful Life* being the first. David Niven is a bishop who is so fixed on raising money for a new cathedral that he neglects his wife (Loretta Young) and child. Cary Grant is the all-too-attractive angel sent down to help them. It's set during the festive season and if it doesn't soften your heart then you must be a Scrooge indeed. (B&W)

Blackbeard's Ghost
1968 U 103 ★★ FAM

They run this kind of film off the conveyor belt at the Disney studio. It's pleasing enough, but formulaic and predictable. Here Dean Jones with the help of friendly ghost Peter Ustinov fights off sharks wanting to get their teeth into

his family home. Knockabout fun and lots of 'ahh' moments.

Black Beauty
1971 PG 101 ★★★ DRA

There have been several screen versions of Anna Sewell's children's classic and this is probably as good as any of them. It doesn't capture the full horror of Beauty's descent from pampered colt to often ill-treated hack pulling a hansom cab and a great big cart, but this is probably deliberate. An unexpurgated visual form of Sewell's book would be far too heart-rending for small children. But the happy ending is there, so that's all right. Mark Lester and Walter Slezak lead the human cast but it's the horses that catch the eye.

Black Beauty
1995 U 85 ★★ FAM

If you overlook the young Beauty's temporary but astonishing change of colour, this, too, is an acceptable version. Quite faithful to the book but again delicately toning down such tear-jerking moments as Beauty's sad reunion with his filly friend Ginger. Again the horses are splendid and Caroline Thompson's film is very handsome to look at. A fine British cast includes David Thewlis, Sean Bean, Peter Davison, Eleanor Bron and the late Peter Cook as a most snooty aristocrat.

Black Narcissus
1946 U 96 ★★★★ DRA

A Himalayan convent proves a great setting for a terrifying drama about the emotional and underlying sexual problems facing a group of nuns. Deborah Kerr and Jean Simmons are particularly effective as, respectively, the young ambitious sister and a seductive native girl in Powell and Pressburger's haunting story. The film deservedly won Oscars for colour cinematography and art direction.

Black Stallion, The
1979 U 110 ★★★ FAM

A young boy (Kelly Reno) and a horse battle valiantly through a number of adventures but win out in the end. Great cinematography, and Mickey Rooney is smashing as the racehorse trainer.

Black Stallion Returns, The
1983 U 99 ★ FAM

An unsuccessful attempt to match the charm of
the original. This time young Reno, now a
teenager, has lost his stallion to Arab thieves so
he stows away on a plane to the Middle East
and scours the Sahara Desert to get the animal
back. The thriller aspect of the tale means that
what had been so charming in the original –
the boy-horse relationship – is pretty well
neglected.

Black Widow
1987 15 97 ★★ MYS/THR

Debra Winger plays an enthusiastic Justice
Department agent who notices that a beautiful
woman, Theresa Russell, is waxing rich after the
untimely death of three husbands. Winger sets
out to snare the presumably murderous widow
and prove to her that crime doesn't pay – but
then finds her judgement impaired by her
attraction to the woman. A strong, steamy
psychological thriller.

Blade Runner: The Director's Cut
1992 15 112 ★★★★ SCI/FAN

This is Ridley Scott's director's cut and a big
improvement on the film as first released in
1982. The unnecessary voiceovers have gone
and the story is much clearer and cleaner as
blade runner (i.e. cop) Harrison Ford tracks
down a group of murderous replicants (i.e.
androids), among them Rutger Hauer and
Daryl Hannah, who have illegally returned to a
futuristic Earth. A cult classic and
understandably so.

Blame It on the Bellboy
1992 15 75 ★ COM

Dudley Moore has had little luck with his
movies since *Arthur* and this one doesn't help
him much. It's a pretty feeble comedy of errors
involving a hit man, an estate agent and a man
on a blind date, all with similar names, who
check into the same Venetian hotel. Bryan
Brown, Richard Griffiths, Bronson Pinchot (as
the bellboy) and Patsy Kensit are also in the
cast but Alison Steadman emerges best.

Blank Cheque
1994 PG 89 ★★ COM

When eleven-year-old Brian Bonsall is knocked
off his bike, he demands compensation from
the car driver. The driver, a thief who doesn't
want involvement with the police, writes a
cheque – forgetting to specify an amount. The
greedy kid fills it in for one million dollars and
he starts to live the high life – lavish house,
chauffeur, the lot. But the FBI is after the thief,
and the thief and his thugs are after the boy
and the money…

Blazing Saddles
1974 15 89 ★★★★ COM

One of Mel Brooks's most glorious comedies –
an outrageous Western spoof with Gene Wilder
as a former gunfighter and Cleavon Little as a
black sheriff. It's all in magnificent, politically
incorrect bad taste – especially the farting
sequence that follows the cowboys' traditional
bean supper. There's also a wicked take-off of
Marlene Dietrich by Madeline Kahn.

Blind Date
1987 15 91 ★ COM

A bunch of none-too-funny jokes loosely held
together by a semblance of a story. Bruce Willis,
in need of a partner for his company's 'do',
reluctantly agrees to take his sister-in-law's
cousin, Kim Basinger. But after a drink or two
it soon becomes clear why such a knockout is
unattached. The woman is unhinged and can't
hold her booze. There follow mayhem and
madcap chases that are more desperately farcical
than funny.

Blithe Spirit
1945 U 92 ★★★★ COM

A comic gem based on a stage play by Noël
Coward. Rex Harrison is a remarried widower,
Constance Cummings being wife number two.
However, the ghost of wife number one, Kay
Hammond, is accidentally conjured up during a
seance by scatty medium Madame Arcati (a
quite perfect performance by Margaret
Rutherford) and proceeds to menace the happy
couple. Harrison then asks her, in turn, to
exorcise the haunting spouse. Or maybe not…

Bloodhounds of Broadway
1989 PG 88 ★★ COM

Madonna does keep trying to establish herself as a movie star but this adaptation of four Damon Runyon stories set on Broadway on New Year's Eve, 1928, doesn't do it for her. Matt Dillon co-stars in an inconsequential but quite amusing farce about gangsters. The trouble is, the film is never sure whether to go all out for the comic or concentrate on style. Most unbelievable concept: Madonna wanting to abandon stardom and raise chickens instead.

Blue Ice
1992 15 101 ★ MYS/THR

Michael Caine as a retired secret service agent somehow co-opted to help a glamorous young woman (Sean Young) out of a nasty jam. What happens afterwards lands them both in even nastier jams, as well as a romantic pairing that is a million miles from convincing. Let us say that Young is simply too young – for Caine anyway. Still, the film does at least view London from a more realistic angle than the usual Hollywood image of Big Ben and chirpy cockneys.

Blue Murder at St Trinian's
1958 U 83 ★★★ FAM

The little fiends, originally created in Ronald Searle's cartoons, run amok while their school is without a headmistress and the army has to be deployed to control the girls. Diamond robberies, trips to Rome and princes provide the merest outline of a plot. Joyce Grenfell, Terry-Thomas, George Cole and Lionel Jeffries as the older members of the cast contribute much to the fun. (B&W)

Blues Brothers, The
1980 15 127 ★★ MUS

A John Landis comedy, starring John Belushi and Dan Aykroyd, which has developed a strong cult following. The plot is a feeble thing about two musicians trying to save an orphanage and, in the process, creating all manner of havoc in Chicago. There's a great score, plus appearances by the likes of Aretha Franklin and James Brown. But why it has such a devoted following only those who belong to the cult can explain.

Blue Thunder
1983 15 105 ★★★ ACT/ADV

A John Badham movie with Roy Scheider as the pilot of a state-of-the-art police helicopter. His surveillance duties include anti-terrorist activities – and more. It's mostly an excuse for thrilling aerobatics and special effects but Scheider, Warren Oates and Malcolm McDowell put some meat on the bones of a thinnish yarn.

Bob Roberts
1992 15 99 ★★★ DRA

A most impressive debut by Tim Robbins as a cinematic one-man band – writer, director, singer, star. The result is a sharply satirical look at right-wing American politics, Robbins himself playing the hypocritical candidate. With the aid of Alan Rickman and Susan Sarandon he provides a freshly observant slant on a fairly familiar theme.

Bodies, Rest and Motion
1993 15 90 ★★★ DRA

The chief attraction here is the cast, since it consists of four talented and attractive young actors: Bridget Fonda, Tim Roth, Eric Stoltz and Phoebe Cates. In a small American town, the relationships between them shift and change as all, in their different ways, look for some kind of fulfilment in life. Fonda catches the eye particularly as the one who is actually prepared to do something constructive. It was billed as a comedy but it's more dramatic than funny.

Bodyguard, The
1992 15 124 ★★★ MYS/THR

Interesting pairing of Kevin Costner and, in her first acting role, Whitney Houston. He's the bodyguard she employs after receiving death threats; she is an enormously successful pop singer (typecasting?). The plot is fairly conventional but cops out of full-scale romantic entanglement between the stars. Enjoyable nevertheless, though many grew to loathe it for keeping the title song, 'I Will Always Love You', top of the charts for months. Houston sings beautifully, of course, and also gives a very commendable acting performance. Contains a certain amount of violence.

Body Snatchers
1994 15 83 ★★ HOR

The *Invasion of the Body Snatchers* reprised yet again, this time by director Abel Ferrara. In this modern version the aliens take over the bodies and souls of an entire US army camp. Gabrielle Anwar is the officer's daughter who suspects something fishy is going on. Not badly done but with the Cold War over there seems little point in the story nowadays. After all, in the first two films for 'aliens' we were expected to read 'Russians'.

Boiling Point
1993 15 88 ★★ MYS/THR

Not too much in the way of mystery and thrills but watchable performances by Wesley Snipes, Dennis Hopper and Viggo Mortensen. Snipes is a treasury agent bent on revenge against the counterfeiters who killed his partner; Hopper has a more nefarious agenda to follow. Lolita Davidovich provides the female interest.

Boomerang
1992 15 112 ★★ COM

Eddie Murphy forsakes his normal action-man mode to play a ladies' man. He has Halle Berry but he wants perfection in his mate so he makes a play for his beautiful new boss, Robin Givens. But in the game of loving them and leaving them she is at the very least his equal. All terribly corny but the women are good and sassy and Murphy projects a nice swaggering charm.

Born Free
1966 U 91 ★★★★ FAM

Maybe the best-loved animal movie of them all. It's based on the true story of how Joy Adamson (Virginia McKenna) and her husband (Bill Travers) raised Elsa, an orphaned lion cub, in Kenya. The humans are good but the real stars are Elsa and the African countryside. A three-hanky movie at least, since the Adamsons have to face the agonising decision whether to force Elsa back to the wild or send her to a zoo.

Born Yesterday
1993 PG 96 ★ COM

Don Johnson and Melanie Griffith helped, in this *Pygmalion*-style comedy, by the presence of John Goodman. But it's not a patch on the 1950 original with Judy Holliday. Griffith is a bimbo (and she only has to speak in that juvenile voice to convince us of that) whose wealthy lover, Goodman, enlists the help of Johnson to educate her. Predictable consequences in a quite unnecessary remake.

Bounty, The
1984 15 128 ★★★ DRA

If you want to understand the probable reason why the mutiny on the *Bounty* happened, this is the film for you. Mel Gibson's portrayal of a charming but spoilt and headstrong Fletcher Christian makes the showdown with Anthony Hopkins's stern martinet of a Captain Bligh not merely understandable but inevitable. If the film is less exciting than the Gable/Laughton *Mutiny on the Bounty* it's certainly better than the Brando/Trevor Howard version and Robert Bolt's script gives the impression of having been much more carefully researched than either of the other two films.

Boyz N The Hood
1991 15 107 ★★★ DRA

An impressive debut by twenty-three-year-old director John Singleton – a study of under-privileged young blacks trying to cope and survive in the violent, crime-and-drug-ridden ambience of South Central Los Angeles. Although bleak, it does leave room for hope and, by concentrating on characterization, makes you care about the people. Cuba Gooding Jr and Larry Fishburne head the cast. Ice Cube co-stars and provides the soundtrack. Contains sex and violence and, particularly, profanity and strong language.

Brannigan
1975 15 107 ★★★ MYS/THR

A fish-out-of-water movie – John Wayne as the Chicago cop sent to London to claim an American fugitive. Richard Attenborough, as a Scotland Yard commander and Judy Geeson, the policewoman assigned to escort the big guy round town, provide the British counterparts whom Wayne, of course, dazzles with his American get-up-and-go. Utterly daft but quite fun with nice characterization and relationships.

Brazil
1985 15 137 ★★ SCI/FAN

Another cult movie, dazzlingly directed by
Terry Gilliam. Jonathan Pryce leads as a diligent
civil servant forced to confront a system he'd
never previously questioned. Excellent cameo
appearances by Robert De Niro, Bob Hoskins
and Michael Palin, among others. The trouble
is that as futuristic social satire it's too much
like Orwell's *1984* to gain many marks for
originality, except in the way it is filmed. To be
fair, though, Gilliam did originally want to call
it *1984 1/2*.

Breakfast at Tiffany's
1961 PG 109 ★★★ DRA

Did any woman ever look as perfect as Audrey
Hepburn does here? She plays Holly Golightly,
a free-spirited young woman who intrigues her
neighbour, George Peppard. Actually, she's a call
girl but Hollywood didn't mention such things
in 1961. Set against a glossy Manhattan social
scene, what transpires is a touching love story
with a good score, dominated by Henry
Mancini's 'Moon River'.

Breakfast Club, The
1985 15 93 ★★★ DRA

John Hughes directed this OK teen flick before
moving down a generation and embarking on
the *Home Alone*-types. It's set in a school
detention class, consisting of brat-packers
Emilio Estevez, Molly Ringwald, Ally Sheedy,
Anthony Michael Hall and Judd Nelson, who
fixes the doors so they remain closed. Locked
in, the famous five indulge in navel
contemplation which raises teenage issues but
lacks the conviction to follow them through.

Brewster's Millions
1985 PG 97 ★★ COM

The mixture of comedians Richard Pryor and
John Candy and action director Walter Hill
makes for uncomfortable bedfellows but Pryor
is endearing and the pace is fast. Brewster
(Pryor) is given a month to squander thirty
million dollars in order to inherit ten times that
amount. Best friend Candy helps, with frenetic
results. The seventh version of the story, but as
good as any.

Brideshead Revisited
1981 15 664 ★★★★ DRA

Award-winning ITV series based on Evelyn
Waugh's story of a young student and a fateful
encounter he makes while at university.
Everything is beautiful, from the Oxford colleges
to the Venice canals, from Castle Howard –
which doubles for Brideshead itself – to Anthony
Andrews as the doomed Sebastian Flyte. Available
on three videos (664 minutes is the total running
time) and a must for any household.

Bridge on the River Kwai, The
1957 PG 155 ★★★★ WAR

British soldiers in a Japanese POW camp
during the Second World War are ordered by
their captors to build a bridge. For reasons of
morale, their obsessed colonel – Alec Guinness,
in one of his most masterly performances –
determines it should be the best bridge possible.
But the Americans (William Holden, assisted
by Jack Hawkins) plan to blow it up. A classic
war story, superbly played and magnificently
directed by David Lean.

Bridge Too Far, A
1977 15 169 ★★★ WAR

Another fine war film, this time directed by
Richard Attenborough and telling of the
doomed Allied assault on Arnhem in 1944. The
plan was to drop 35 000 troops into Holland to
secure six bridges leading into Germany. The
film tells how – and why – it didn't work. The
starry cast reads like a *Who's Who* of the movies
– Anthony Hopkins, Ryan O'Neal, Dirk
Bogarde, Michael Caine, Sean Connery, James
Caan, Robert Redford, Laurence Olivier and
many more.

Brief Encounter
1945 PG 82 ★★★ DRA

A famous love story, based on a play by Noël
Coward and directed by David Lean. In
wartime England Trevor Howard, a doctor, and
Celia Johnson, a housewife, happen to be
travelling on the same train to London one
Thursday. On the fateful day he is called upon
to remove a piece of smut from her eye and
they embark on a doomed, albeit innocent, love
affair. It's dated now but the performances are
cherishable and the clock at Waterloo will never
look the same to you after this.

B

Brigadoon
1954 U 103 ★★ MUS

A musical fantasy of some charm, set in a mythical, disappearing Scottish village. Gene Kelly and Van Johnson are the Americans who stumble upon the place when it makes its regular, once-in-every-100-years appearance; Cyd Charisse is one of the villagers who entrance them. Unusually for a Hollywood musical, the sets are very disappointing. But Lerner and Loewe's score and the dancing by Kelly and Charisse make up for much.

Brighton Beach Memoirs
1986 15 105 ★★★ COM

The first part of Neil Simon's autobiographical trilogy is set in Brooklyn in a house occupied by the families of a pair of Jewish sisters. Young Jonathan Silverman discovers the joys of baseball and the perplexing attraction of sex while his elders worry about the impending Second World War. Richly enjoyable.

Brighton Rock
1947 PG 88 ★★★ DRA

The film that made Richard Attenborough a star. He plays Pinkie, an amoral, psychopathic young gang leader who commits a murder and, having used a waitress to provide an alibi, plans to drive her to suicide. Adapted from Graham Greene's psychological thriller, its violence and examination of the criminal mind caused a considerable stir in its day. (B&W)

Bringing Up Baby
1938 U 98 ★★★★★ COM

One of the great, timeless comedies of the cinema. The pairing of palaeontologist Cary Grant and scatterbrained heiress Katharine Hepburn – to say nothing of Baby, the leopard – is positively inspired. Director Howard Hawks handles this crazy, delightful story with impeccable lightness and speed. It's nearly sixty years old but still funnier and more polished than any comedy made today. (B&W)

Broadcast News
1987 15 127 ★★★ COM

A sharp, affectionate but critical look at the television news industry in America. It revolves around the relationships between the personable but none-too-bright newscaster (William Hurt), the energetic producer who fancies him (Holly Hunter) and the star reporter (Albert Brooks), who fancies Hurt's job and would have got it if he didn't sweat so much under the TV lights. An amusing, observant and witty script and a knockout cameo from Jack Nicholson.

Broadway Bound
1991 PG 90 ★★★ COM

The final part of Neil Simon's autobiographical trilogy. Here Jonathan Silverman (as the grown-up Simon) embarks on a scriptwriting career with his older brother. It doesn't go well… Family warmth and squabbles and the same amusing appeal as in the other two episodes – *Brighton Beach Memoirs* and *Biloxi Blues.*

Broadway Danny Rose
1984 PG 81 ★★★★ COM

Woody Allen in fine comic form as actor, writer and director. He plays the eponymous Danny, a struggling theatrical agent, most of whose clients would be flattered to be called third-rate. But his life takes a sharp new turn when he becomes involved with Mia Farrow, a Mafia moll. Lovely comic moments and a whole host of deliciously eccentric characters. (B&W)

Browning Version, The
1951 U 90 ★★★★ DRA

Michael Redgrave gives a superb performance as a school teacher who, upon retirement, has to face his failings as a master and the remnants of his marriage. It's a touching story, originally a play by Terence Rattigan, that won't leave a dry eye in the house. Jean Kent plays Redgrave's unfaithful wife; Nigel Patrick the fellow teacher who cuckolds him. (B&W)

Browning Version, The
1994 15 112 ★★★ DRA

A lesser version, though the central performance, this time given by Albert Finney, is very impressive. The trouble here is that it's been updated and the story does not work so well in modern times. Greta Scacchi is good as the wife, Matthew Modine (in the Nigel Patrick role), Julian Sands and Michael Gambon lend fine support as fellow teachers. Still a moving tale but less effective than the original.

Buddy Holly Story, The
1978 PG 108 ★★ MUS

Gary Busey as the now legendary pop star in a very decent biopic that traces his life from the early days in Texas, through the rise to fame and on to his final, ill-fated plane ride. Busey's pretty good; what's more, he does his own singing along with co-stars Don Stroud (as Jesse) and Charles Martin Smith (Ray Bob). The film won an Oscar for its adapted score.

Buffy the Vampire Slayer
1992 15 82 ★★ COM

There's something quite appealing about this comic high-school horror in which the rather daffy Valley girl, Kirsty Swanson, and the handsome loner, Luke Perry, clean up their neighbourhood and school, which have become overrun by vampires. Rutger Hauer lends weight as the chief latter-day Dracula.

Bugsy Malone
1976 U 90 ★★★ FAM

Alan Parker's first big success – an ingenious musical yarn in which children play 1920s gangsters and bootleggers. Instead of bombs and bullets the warring hoods spray jelly, cream and custard pies around. It shouldn't work but it does. The cast is led by Scott Baio (of *Happy Days* fame) and a twelve-year-old called Jodie Foster. Wonder what happened to her?

Bullitt
1968 15 108 ★★★★ MYS/THR

Hectic car chases are ten-a-penny in the movies these days but the one shown here, through the streets of San Francisco, created the precedent. It has still rarely been bettered. Otherwise, this is a good exciting thriller with Steve McQueen at his best as a cop protecting a witness and coping with all manner of skulduggery. Robert Vaughn, Jacqueline Bisset and even Robert Duvall co-star but it was for McQueen – and that chase – that everyone flocked to see it.

Burden of Proof, The
1992 15 175 ★★ MYS/THR

In a way a sequel to *Presumed Innocent* in that the defence lawyer from that film (Hector Elizondo) here finds himself under suspicion after the mysterious death – was it suicide? – of

his wife. It's far too long but there's a strong cast (Brian Dennehy and Stefanie Powers among them) and the story unravels intelligently and with a fair degree of suspense.

Bus Stop
1956 U 90 ★★★ DRA

The film that provided Marilyn Monroe with her first dramatic role. A rodeo star, Don Murray, comes to the big city for the first time, meets sexy showgirl Monroe, kisses her and then more or less kidnaps her when she rejects his marriage proposal. Murray's good but the film is most notable for revealing that Monroe was a lot more than just a pretty face.

Buster
1988 15 98 ★★★ DRA

Part-comedy, part-biography that spawned the hit record by its star, 'Groovy Kind of Love'. Phil Collins more than adequately portrays Buster Edwards, the Great Train Robber who, after trying the high life in Acapulco, returns to Blighty, does his time in jail and ends up selling flowers outside London's Waterloo Station. Good though Collins is, it is Julie Walters who really shines as Buster's wife.

Butch Cassidy and the Sundance Kid
1969 PG 106 ★★★★★ WES

A superb Western from the 'them days is over' era when our heroes had to flee to South America to pursue their trade as bandits. Funny, exciting and romantic, with a great script from William Goldman and the unbeatable pairing of Paul Newman and Robert Redford. Not to mention the song, 'Raindrops Keep Falling on My Head'. Butch's line 'I can't help you, Sundance' has become an all-purpose catchphrase in our household.

Butcher's Wife, The
1991 15 100 ★★ DRA

If ever a film loses its way, this one does. It starts off as an intriguing, humorous tale of a clairvoyant, Demi Moore, who, misreading her own future, marries a butcher and leaves her remote seaside home for his town. Her gift soon changes the neighbourhood but the film disintegrates as it concentrates more on romance than mysticism and laughs.

C

Cabaret
1972 15 119 ★★★★ MUS

Liza Minnelli on Oscar-winning form as Sally
Bowles in Bob Fosse's dazzling musical
adaptation of Christopher Isherwood's
collection of short stories. The setting is 1930s
Berlin with the rise of Nazism – true decadence
– contrasting with the more obvious decadence
of the cabaret. Michael York is fine as
Minnelli's bisexual lover and Joel Grey
outstanding as the MC of the Kit Kat club
where Minnelli works.

Cactus Flower
1969 PG 99 ★★★ COM

Goldie Hawn's first starring role in a comedy of
errors involving a bachelor dentist, Walter
Matthau, his young mistress (Hawn) and his
receptionist, Ingrid Bergman, who blooms –
not unlike the cactus flower of the title – when
she realises she's in love with him. It flatters to
deceive a little and Bergman is miscast but it's
still an amusing piece.

Cadillac Man
1990 15 93 ★ COM

Robin Williams is a fast-talking Cadillac
salesman in danger of losing his job and
girlfriend unless he gets his act together. So far
pretty funny. But melodrama takes over when a
distraught husband (Tim Robbins) breaks into
the showroom and holds Williams hostage.
After that everything goes to pieces though
Williams has his good moments.

Caesar and Cleopatra
1945 U 122 ★★ DRA

Given Shaw's witty play, splendid spectacle and
a cast headed by Claude Rains and Vivien
Leigh we are entitled to expect more than
Gabriel Pascal's film delivers. It cost six million
dollars, a massive amount for the time, and
certainly looks it – indeed, that's one of the
problems. The protagonists and the story itself
are dwarfed by the lavish scenery, costumes and
settings.

Cage aux Folles, La
1978 15 87 ★★★ FOR

A French comedy, which is both funny and
risqué, about a gay couple, Ugo Tognazzi and

Michel Serrault, who pretend to be straight
when Tognazzi's son wants to get married. The
moral, of course, is: whoever you are, be
yourself. Lovely performances. The film
spawned two sequels of which the first is also
very funny. The second is dreary. (Subtitled)

Caine Mutiny, The
1954 U 119 ★★★ DRA

Humphrey Bogart leads an excellent cast,
including Jose Ferrer and Van Johnson, in
Edward Dmytryk's classy version of Herman
Wouk's novel. Bogart is the naval captain,
verging on a nervous breakdown, who has
control of his destroyer seized from him by his
junior officers. The best scenes are of the court
martial when Bogart begins to crack under
cross-examination.

Cal
1984 15 99 ★★★ DRA

Exceptional performance by John Lynch as a
Northern Irish teenager trying to sever his ties
with the IRA. Guilt about his part in the
murder of a policeman drives him to seek out
the man's widow, Helen Mirren, with whom he
falls in love. Mirren is in excellent form but the
haunted, touching Lynch is equally
memorable.

Calamity Jane
1953 U 97 ★★★ MUS

Doris Day as the gun-totin' female resorting to
feminine wiles to win Wild Bill Hickok,
Howard Keel. Day, the freckled, wholesome,
perennial virgin of the movies, is out of
fashion in this more licentious age but she and
Keel make a lusty, attractive team. OK, so the
plot's corny but the music and lyrics are
terrific.

California Man
1992 PG 85 ★ COM

Well, see this if you must but don't say you
weren't warned. Sean Astin digs up and defrosts
a Cro-Magnon man (Brendan Fraser) in his
back yard and causes a 'comic' stir when he
takes him to school. Hopelessly moronic stuff
which proves that cavemen had an IQ several
notches higher than that of the average
Californian teenager.

California Suite
1978 15 98 ★★★ COM

Four separate but intertwined stories set in the Beverly Hills Hotel at Academy Awards time. Neil Simon's sharp, funny script gives the best scenes to Maggie Smith – who, uniquely, won an Oscar for playing an Oscar-nominated actress – and her gay husband, Michael Caine. But Walter Matthau has delicious moments. The other stories, involving the likes of Jane Fonda and Alan Alda, are not quite so enjoyable.

Camelot
1967 U 175 ★★★ MUS

The notion of using straight actors – Richard Harris and Vanessa Redgrave – in an otherwise familiar, lavish musical actually works very well. They play King Arthur and Guinevere and though their singing isn't up to much they bring unusual drama and passion to the central story around which the musical numbers revolve.

Can-Can
1960 U 125 ★★★ MUS

Frank Sinatra, Shirley MacLaine, Maurice Chevalier – not a bad basis for a musical. But, in truth, the cast and the musical numbers – including 'Let's Do It' and 'You Do Something to Me' – are the only big attractions for the convoluted plot is a bit of a no-no. Well, you can't have everything…

Candidate, The
1972 PG 106 ★★★ DRA

A sharply cynical look at American politics, which won an Oscar for the writer, Jeremy Larner. Robert Redford plays a glamorous young candidate for the US Senate who, because he is sure he is going to lose, actually brings ideals and integrity to his campaign, something almost unheard of in politics anywhere. The plot twists and turns nicely and Redford gives one of his best performances.

Cannonball Run, The
1981 PG 91 ★★ ACT/ADV

When Burt Reynolds and Dom DeLuise take part in an illegal cross-country car race the accent is mostly on slapstick comedy. The film's main purpose is to allow a fairly starry cast – Roger Moore racing in an Aston Martin, Farrah Fawcett as the toothsome heroine, Dean Martin and Sammy Davis Jr – to ham around. It can become tiresome after a bit.

Canterbury Tale, A
1944 U 119 ★★★★ DRA

Very loosely, this is Chaucer transposed to wartime Britain. British soldier Dennis Price and a GI, John Sweet, plus land girl Sheila Sim make a pilgrimage to Canterbury and unmask an over-patriotic nutter who is narked by local girls who go out with Americans. The beauty of the film lies in its simplicity and the marvellous quality of mystery and near-magic that imbues it. (B&W)

Canterville Ghost, The
1944 U 100 ★★★ COM

Charles Laughton on great form as a 300-year-old ghost terrifying American GIs billeted in the house he haunts. Drama, too, in this adaptation of an Oscar Wilde short story. Laughton, a coward in battle in his own lifetime, must witness an act of bravery by one of his descendants before he can rest in peace. The latest descendant is Margaret O'Brien, who nearly steals the picture. (B&W)

Captain Blood
1935 PG 94 ★★★ ACT/ADV

Errol Flynn's first starring role. He plays a country doctor, wrongfully sold into slavery in the West Indies, who re-emerges as a dashing pirate. Flynn was always at his best in this sort of yarn. There's plenty of action, excitement and tension, plus one of the screen's finest villains (Basil Rathbone) and Olivia de Havilland to provide the romantic interest. (B&W)

Captive Heart, The
1946 PG 95 ★★★ DRA

Intriguing wartime drama with Michael Redgrave as a Czech POW who, to escape the Gestapo, takes on the identity of a dead British officer and begins writing to the man's wife. What happens when, finally, he reveals the truth to her is only one of many aspects which give the film its strength. A fine cast who expertly portray the grim reality of prison camp life.

Care Bears Movie, The
1985 U 75 ★★ FAM

The very young will probably love this animated tale of cuddly bears befriending two small children who have fallen foul of a nasty spirit. Older viewers might consider the story slack and over-sentimental and the animation a touch amateurish, especially when compared with Disney. In chronological order this was followed by...

Care Bears Movie II: A New Generation
1986 U 73 ★ FAM

Wherein a little girl is tricked by the wicked Dark Heart into trapping the bears, later of course to repent of her actions. The story in this one is even soppier than in the first and you begin to suspect that the merchandising of the Care Bears products is actually more important than the films.

Care Bears Adventure in Wonderland!, The
1987 U 72 ★ FAM

This time the bears follow Alice through the looking glass and into Wonderland. Lewis Carroll might have been a touch bemused by the story of how the bears rescue the Princess (and future Queen) of Wonderland who has been captured by an evil wizard. The Princess of Wonderland – who she?

Carousel
1956 U 123 ★★★ MUS

Gordon MacRae is the shiftless fairground barker who marries and mistreats pretty Shirley Jones. The story of their lives and his redemption is told in flashback with MacRae already dead but preparing for a one-day return to life to make amends. Sounds pretty glum but it's actually a charming film with a great score by Rodgers and Hammerstein.

Carry On Abroad
1972 PG 85 ★★ COM

Well-loved regulars Sid James and Peter Butterworth plus the rest of the *Carry On* team

in a disastrous holiday on the Spanish island of Elsbels. (The *Carry On* series, listed here alphabetically, has become as much a British institution as fish and chips and wet bank holidays. It began with *Carry On Sergeant*, although it was *Carry On Nurse* that established the style that we have come to love – or, depending on taste, loathe.)

Carry On Again, Doctor
1969 PG 85 ★★ COM

The familiar cast (which now included Barbara Windsor) in another hospital story.

Carry On at Your Convenience
1971 PG 86 ★★ COM

This one has the absolutely perfect setting for a *Carry On* movie – a lavatory factory. We leave you to imagine what the team makes of that.

Carry On Behind
1975 PG 87 ★★★ COM

Elke Sommer guest stars in the absence of some of the regulars. Most of them are still around though in a story that plunges archaeologists into a busy camp site. With Sommers showing a nice comic touch and Kenneth Williams in excellent form, this is actually among the funniest of the series.

Carry On Cabby
1963 PG 88 PG ★★ COM

No Williams or Sims in this tale of husband-and-wife team James and Jacques running rival taxi firms. (B&W)

Carry On Camping
1969 PG 85 ★★ COM

The title is self-explanatory – high (or rather low) jinks in what Sid James et al hope is a nudist camp.

Carry On Cleo
1964 PG 88 ★★★★ COM

Incomparably the best of the entire series. Set in ancient Rome, Williams is Julius Caesar, James is Mark Antony and Amanda Barrie makes a delightful, scatterbrained Cleopatra. A glorious send-up of the dull Elizabeth Taylor epic. Talbot Rothwell's script is not just very funny, it's also very witty – Caesar, for example, declaiming, 'Infamy, infamy – they've all got it in for me'.

Carry On Columbus
1992 PG 88 ★ COM

The latest – to say nothing of very possibly the worst – in the long-running series. A decent cast (Jim Dale, Peter Richardson, Bernard Cribbins, Alexei Sayle and the like) are defeated by an appalling script about – what else? – Columbus's discovery of the Americas. It's best avoided.

Carry On Constable
1960 U 83 ★★ COM

The fourth in the series. Eric Barker, Leslie Phillips and Shirley Eaton join the rep company in sending up the cops.

Carry On Cowboy
1965 PG 90 ★★★ COM

Sid James is the notorious Rumpo Kid and Jim Dale is the sanitary engineer mistakenly appointed to rid a Wild West town of its more rowdy outlaw elements. This is *Carry On* in a broad – and often very funny – send-up of classic Westerns. The town is called Stodge City, so you can guess the kind of Western it targets.

Carry On Cruising
1962 U 85 ★★ COM

Sid James is the captain of a cruise ship on board which, inevitably, everything goes wrong. Amiable enough, though much of it is predictable. Sea-sickness, for instance, plays a strong part in the comic capers – now there's a surprise for a *Carry On* at sea…

Carry On Dick
1974 PG 86 ★★ COM

Even lewder than usual as the title might suggest, though in fact it refers to Dick Turpin (Sid James). For him, as for Hattie Jacques, it was the last *Carry On*. Coincidentally or not, the series grew progressively coarser after this.

Carry On Doctor
1968 PG 90 ★★ COM

More patients-versus-staff capers; more well-tried jokes revisited.

Carry On Don't Lose Your Head
1966 PG 89 ★★ COM

The saga of the Scarlet Pimpernel – except that here we have the Black Fingernail (Sid James) plus Citizen Camembert, Citizen Bidet and the rest.

Carry On Emmannuelle
1978 15 84 ★ COM

A deeply misguided attempt to – so it would seem – inject more 'adult' humour into the series. This is an attempt to parody the soft-core porn *Emmanuelle* movies but, despite the presence of the delicious Suzanne Danielle, the result is simply crude.

Carry On England
1976 PG 84 ★ COM

Even before *Carry On Emmannuelle* the writing was on the wall with this listless farce about a wartime anti-aircraft battery. Too many unsuitable newcomers in the cast; far too few jokes.

Carry On Follow That Camel
1966 PG 91 ★★ COM

The veteran Phil Silvers, presumably replacing Sid James, makes a guest appearance in this tale of the French Foreign Legion.

Carry On Girls
1973 PG 84 ★★ COM

Sid James organizes a beauty contest in the seaside town of Fircombe and enrages the local feminists.

Carry On Henry
1971 PG 87 ★★ COM

Another send-up (this time of *Anne of the Thousand Days*) with Sid James as Henry VIII.

Carry On Jack
1964 PG 87 ★★ COM

Usual bawdy humour but, for the first time, a costume 'epic' as the team takes on the Armada.

Carry On Loving
1970 PG 86 ★★ COM

Wherein Sid James and Hattie Jacques run a marriage bureau.

Carry On Matron
1972 PG 85 ★★ COM

And, yes, we're all back in hospital again, together with comic crooks and a lot of expectant mums.

Carry On Nurse
1959 PG 83 ★★★ COM

Williams and Hawtrey, now joined by other regulars such as Kenneth Connor, Joan Sims and Hattie Jacques in the second *Carry On* film – a hospital-based romp wherein the patients attempt to outwit the staff. Like all the others it was directed by Gerald Thomas and produced by Peter Rogers and set the pattern for its successors, being a compendium of bawdy, often lavatorial jokes apparently inspired by seaside postcards. (B&W)

Carry On Regardless
1960 PG 87 ★★ COM

With Sid James as the employer of the world's most bungling bunch of odd-job men. (B&W)

Carry On Screaming
1966 PG 92 ★★★ COM

A spoof on horror movies, this time with Kenneth Williams among the undead and Fenella Fielding as a vampire.

Carry On Sergeant
1958 U 80 ★★ COM

Although this is the first *Carry On* film, it turned out to be atypical. Apart from Kenneth Williams and Charles Hawtrey, few of what was to become the regular repertory company were included. Bob Monkhouse and William Hartnell are the leads in a so-so farce about a platoon of army recruits trying to win the best squad award. (B&W)

Carry On Spying
1964 U 84 ★★★ COM

Television's *The Man from UNCLE* gets the *Carry On* treatment here. Williams is the incompetent spy-catcher; the villainous STENCH (Society for the Total Extinction of Non-Conforming Humans) provides the opposition. (B&W)

Carry On Teacher
1959 U 83 ★★ COM

More of a story – pupils versus headmaster Ted Ray – in this, the third in the series. The films became less well-structured and more anarchic later, with a few notable exceptions. (B&W)

Carry On Up the Jungle
1970 PG 87 ★ COM

Pretty dismal stuff, also pretty crude, as ornithologist Frankie Howerd seeks a rare bird in the Pinewood jungle.

Carry On Up the Khyber
1968 PG 85 ★★★ COM

Back we go to the days of the British Raj. The Scottish Foot and Mouth regiment versus the revolting Burpas, to say nothing of the Khasi of Kalabar. The familiar team in one of their best efforts.

Carve Her Name with Pride
1958 PG 114 ★★★ DRA

The true and very moving story of Violette Szabo, the British widow of a French soldier, who twice parachuted into Occupied France as a spy during the Second World War. Director Lewis Gilbert handles this ultimately tragic story with commendable restraint and sincerity. As Szabo, Virginia McKenna gives a nicely understated performance and receives excellent support from Paul Scofield as an intelligence officer. (B&W)

Casablanca
1942 U 99 ★★★★★ DRA

Quite simply one of the best movie romances ever made. A great script, which includes some of the most cherishable lines in the cinema, a dazzling cast and crackling chemistry produced by the unlikely pairing of Humphrey Bogart and the young Ingrid Bergman. It's a compendium of delights, not least among them Claude Rains as the utterly amoral police chief. A special fiftieth anniversary edition of the film is also available; it includes a thirty-minute documentary and runs for a total of 132 minutes. (B&W)

Casanova's Big Night
1954 U 82 ★★ COM

Bob Hope was well-suited to this kind of costume caper. He plays a tailor's apprentice and cowardly braggart who pretends to be Casanova to help the genuine article (Vincent Price) through a cash-flow crisis. The jokes don't quite justify the high budget but there's a splendid supporting cast including Basil Rathbone, Joan Fontaine and Lon Chaney Jr.

Casino Royale
1967 PG 126 ★★ COM

Notable mainly for being the film in which David Niven played James Bond. Based very loosely indeed on Ian Fleming's first 007 novel and played strictly – though not often successfully – for laughs. Five directors (including John Huston) lent a hand, as did a multitude of stars – Peter Sellers, Woody Allen, Orson Welles, George Raft, etc. A severe case of over-egging the pudding. Even with all that talent the movie never really gets off the ground.

Cat Ballou
1965 PG 92 ★★★ WES

Well, yes, this is a Western in that it's set in the old West but it's much more of a comedy, memorable for Lee Marvin's Oscar-winning double performance as a deadly gunfighter and his drunken twin brother. Jane Fonda hires the drunk to protect her father and, when this fails, she herself picks up a gun and goes after revenge. An uneven mixture of action and laughs but it has some splendid moments.

Catch-22
1970 15 116 ★★★ DRA

Joseph Heller's savagely effective and painfully funny anti-war novel becomes a somewhat disappointing film despite Alan Arkin's fine performance as Yossarian. Indeed, the entire cast (Richard Benjamin, Art Garfunkel, Orson Welles et al) is very good and Mike Nichols directs it pretty well. But, as so often, too much of what is cherishable in the book fails to make the transition to the screen.

Champions
1983 PG 109 ★★ DRA

John Hurt plays Bob Champion, the jockey who overcame cancer to ride to victory in the Grand National, but not on any old horse. The steed in question was Aldiniti, who himself came back from the brink of death to run the race of his life. Despite the story being true it's played too sentimentally for a lot of tastes.

Champions
1992 PG 99 ★★ COM

In America this was called *The Mighty Ducks* and took its title from the name of a hopeless team of young ice-hockey players which Emilio Estevez is sentenced to coach as a form of community service. The rest – concerning people, not least Estevez, learning lessons all round – is as predictable as rain in winter.

Chaplin
1992 15 138 ★★★ DRA

Richard Attenborough's solid biopic of the comic genius is greatly enhanced by the title performance from Robert Downey Jr. A very honourable and commendable movie though it does, perhaps fatally, gloss over Chaplin's predilection for young girls, which caused much of the turbulence in his life. Anthony Hopkins, James Woods, Dan Aykroyd and Kevin Kline lend excellent support to the remarkable Downey.

Charade
1963 PG 108 ★★★ MYS/THR

The 1960s spawned a spate of caper movies with bags of style and very little substance. This one, featuring Cary Grant and Audrey Hepburn charging around Paris pursued by crooks and sniffing after red herrings as they look for a lost fortune, was one of the best of them. It owes a lot to Grant, Hepburn and Walter Matthau but Stanley Donen's direction is good, too.

Chariots of Fire
1981 U 118 ★★★★ DRA

David Puttnam's excellent Oscar-winner about the rivalry between two British sprinters, the Scots missionary Eric Liddell and the Jewish undergraduate Harold Abrahams, who won

gold medals in the 1924 Olympic Games. Ian
Charleson and Ben Cross are first rate and
Colin Welland's script (also an Oscar-winner)
combines drama and tension with a thoughtful,
probing examination of the period.

Charlotte's Web
1973 U 94 ★★★ FAM

Hanna and Barbera's animated version – the
animation not quite up to Disney standards –
of E B White's children's story about a pig, a
spider, magic and friendship. Pleasant songs
and the voices of Debbie Reynolds, Agnes
Moorehead and Henry Gibson, among others.

Château de Ma Mère, Le
1990 U 95 ★★★ FOR

The concluding part of Marcel Pagnol's
poignant look at his childhood in rural France.
The young Pagnol is older now and learns some
of life's harsher lessons. Not as charming as the
earlier film, La Gloire de Mon Père, but again
it's beautifully shot and performed. You don't
need to have seen the first part, though it helps
if you have. (Subtitled)

Children of a Lesser God
1986 15 115 ★★★ DRA

The touching story of a love affair between a
teacher, William Hurt, and his deaf student,
Marlee Matlin. The film is particularly good at
showing how Matlin blossoms, how her
repressed hopes and aspirations re-emerge as the
relationship develops. Hurt is very appealing
and Matlin, who is indeed deaf, won the Oscar
for her remarkable performance.

Chitty Chitty Bang Bang
1968 U 135 ★★★★ FAM

Four stars for this kiddies' musical, since it has
more sentimental value than an old teddy bear.
Memories of childhood Christmases are evoked
as soon as hero Dick Van Dyke appears.
Chitty's the magical car which carries the Potts
family and friend, Truly Scrumptious, to a land
where children are banned. Brilliant for the
children, though the child-catcher can be
terrifying.

Chorus Line, A
1985 PG 112 ★★ MUS

Richard Attenborough's movie version of the
highly successful stage play is surprisingly
uninvolving, despite the nice numbers, the
lavish production and the cast. Michael
Douglas leads as the director holding auditions
for a Broadway musical, but despite the navel-
contemplation of the hopefuls, the characters
remain one-dimensional. Not even granny
would be able to sit still through this one.

Chorus of Disapproval, A
1988 PG 95 ★★ COM

Alan Ayckbourn's shrewd, funny play about a
widower (Jeremy Irons) who joins a seaside
dramatic society fairly zipped along. Michael
Winner's film version simply plods. The cast,
including Anthony Hopkins and Prunella
Scales, is fine but comedy has never been
Winner's strong point. And here he proves it
conclusively.

Christmas Carol, A
1938 U 69 ★★★ FAM

A made-in-America MGM version of Charles
Dickens's classic tale, originally designed as a
starring vehicle for Lionel Barrymore. He,
however, dropped out and was replaced as
Ebenezer Scrooge by the British character actor
Reginald Owen, who is very good in a perfectly
decent production with a largely American
supporting cast. (B&W)

Christmas Carol, A
1984 U 100 ★★★ FAM

The perennial Yuletide favourite, prettily staged
by director Clive Donner in a version produced
for television but also released in the cinema.
The roles are reversed from the earlier American
production in that a splendid cast of British
actors here lends support to an American
Scrooge, George C Scott. He's good though –
OK, fatter than the average Scrooge perhaps –
but always worth watching.

Christopher Columbus: The Discovery
1991 PG 116 ★ ACT/ADV

Of the three movies celebrating the 400th
anniversary of Columbus's historic voyage this

rivals *Carry On Columbus* as the worst. Just about everything is wrong with it – it's slow, old-fashioned and, at times, downright laughable. George Corraface isn't bad as Columbus but Tom Selleck is unintentionally hilarious as the King of Spain and Marlon Brando does a mumbling moody as Torquemada.

Cinderella
1950 U 71 ★★★★ FAM

Delightful Walt Disney version of the classic fable with some inspired touches, including the dear little mice, Gus and Jaq, without whom Cinders would be bereft, and some catchy songs. Perfect for the whole family.

Cinema Paradiso
1988 PG 118 ★★★ FOR

A Franco-Italian gem about a young Sicilian boy's love of the cinema. A flawed gem, though, because the final act is so truncated as to amount to anti-climax. The first section, however, is sheer delight as Salvatore Cascio, a marvellous imp with a rasping voice, befriends the local cinema projectionist, Philippe Noiret. The charm and nostalgia fade as the boy grows up but there's a lot to like here. (Subtitled)

Citizen Kane
1941 U 114 ★★★★★ DRA

A good many critics insist that this – the twenty-five-year-old Orson Welles's first movie – is the finest film ever made. They could even be right. Welles co-wrote, directed and starred in the life story of a newspaper tycoon (clearly inspired by William Randolph Hearst) that is told in flashback after Kane's death. Miraculously, it remains as fresh now as it was in 1941. A film that everyone, not just serious students of the cinema, should see. (B&W)

City Lights
1931 U 87 ★★★ COM

Chaplin's silent movie in which the Little Fellow falls in love with a blind flower seller (Virginia Cherrill) and pays to have her sight restored plays more for pathos than laughs. Sweet and touching, certainly, but also grossly sentimental. For those who adore Chaplin it's a must; for those who admire his genius but are irked by his calculated attempts at pathos it can be a little too much. (B&W)

City of Hope
1991 15 124 ★★★★ DRA

John Sayles's study of an eastern American city and the corruption therein. A splendidly rich tapestry of interwoven stories that paint a vivid, not altogether hopeful, picture of modern urban life. The pivotal characters are Vincent Spano, a boy in trouble with the cops, and Tony Lo Bianco, as his father, forced into a criminal act to save him. The dialogue and the unusual camera shots produce a grippingly naturalistic effect.

City of Joy
1992 15 130 ★★ DRA

Roland Joffe's film (based on a bestselling book) is always honourable but never really sparks into life. Patrick Swayze is the disillusioned American doctor trying to find himself in India; Pauline Collins the lay Mother Teresa figure who gets him involved in the slum clinic she runs. Unfortunately, Swayze's moral dilemma, set against the reality of Calcutta's poverty, seems hardly worth bothering about.

City Slickers
1991 15 110 ★★★★ COM

Notable for the fact that, thirty-eight years after his previous nomination for *Shane*, Jack Palance finally won an Oscar (as Best Supporting Actor). He's the biggest attraction in this witty, amusing story of three urban types – Billy Crystal, Bruno Kirby and Daniel Stern – working out their mid-life crises by joining a modern cattle drive.

City Slickers II: The Legend of Curly's Gold
1994 12 111 ★ COM

Crystal, Stern and Jon Lovitz (replacing Bruno Kirby, who was smart enough to drop out) are back in the West, now looking for Curly's hidden gold. Curly died in the first film but, never fear, this one brings Palance back as his own twin brother. Sadly, it also brings back most of the original jokes and they taste no better than anything else that's been regurgitated.

Cliffhanger
1993 15 106 ★★★ ACT/ADV

The film that resurrected Sylvester Stallone's career after such flops as *Rocky V* and *Oscar*. A story of breathtaking banality is redeemed by equally breathtaking stunts as ace mountain rescuer Stallone chases psychotic villain John Lithgow across high and treacherous terrain. One or two nasty, violent bits but otherwise the action is non-stop and thrilling. Lithgow, incidentally, plays an Englishman. Is it the accent that makes Hollywood think all Englishmen are villains?

Clockwise
1986 PG 92 ★★★ COM

A madcap vehicle for John Cleese, desperately trying to get to Norwich and take his place as chairman of the lofty headmasters' conference. Cleese's frantic antics stem from his obsession with punctuality and the way a malignant fate keeps holding him back. The comedy flags occasionally but, happily, not too often.

Close Encounters of the Third Kind
1977 PG 127 ★★★★ SCI/FAN

Steven Spielberg's sci-fi epic about non-threatening aliens landing in America and communicating through music. François Truffaut is the scientist who makes the communication breakthrough with the extra-terrestrials. Richard Dreyfuss is the ordinary Joe led by irresistible influences to the spacecraft's landing site. Great special effects and a lovely tale with a message of tolerance and understanding.

Cocktail
1988 15 99 ★★ DRA

Tom Cruise tends bar, services women and juggles a good cocktail in a pretty pointless romantic drama. Bryan Brown comes across better as Cruise's fellow barman, advocating an easy, love-'em-and-leave-'em kind of life. Cruise begins to query this when he meets Elisabeth Shue and true love ups and bites him. A satire perhaps on 1980s materialism but really too mild to register.

Cocoon
1985 PG 112 ★★★ SCI/FAN

Mysterious pods from outer space fetch up in a Florida swimming pool and rejuvenate local wrinklies such as Don Ameche (who won a Best Supporting Actor Oscar), Hume Cronyn, Jessica Tandy and Wilford Brimley. A rather charming fantasy for senior citizens and indeed anyone who is young at heart and would rather be young in body again, too.

Cocoon: The Return
1988 PG 110 ★★ SCI/FAN

Always a mistake to go back as not only the wrinklies but also the audience discover in this rather sorry sequel. Brimley, Ameche and Cronyn return to earth from the distant planet to which they had emigrated in the first film to visit aged Jack Gilford, who had stayed behind. The formula, fresh the first time round, looks pretty tired here.

Coeur en Hiver, Un
1992 15 100 ★★★★ FOR

The kind of film only the French seem able to make with any real conviction. A sophisticated, believable love triangle involving a concert violinist (Emmanuelle Béart), Daniel Auteuil and André Dussollier, friends and partners in a violin-making business. The hub of the story is Auteuil, who is unable or unwilling to show his love for Béart. Beautifully played and splendidly directed by Claude Sautet. (Subtitled)

Colditz Story, The
1954 U 93 ★★★ WAR

The ever-popular wartime escape saga, which inspired a BBC series in 1972. John Mills plays the officer, who with fellow British POWs plans to prove that Colditz, the 'escape-proof' German castle, is anything but. They do it, too. Nicely understated in that stiffish-upper-lip way and the blend of tension, melodrama and comedy works well. (B&W)

Color Purple, The
1985 15 148 ★★ DRA

Spielberg's first real attempt at a 'grown-up' movie. Doesn't quite work, though. Despite a fine performance from Whoopi Goldberg (making her film debut, as does Oprah

Winfrey) this study of life for black people in the Deep South starting around 1910 and covering a decade or two looks simply too glamorous to be convincing. Besides, Spielberg seems uncomfortable with blacks, poverty and lesbianism.

Come See the Paradise
1990 15 127 ★★ DRA

Alan Parker's worthy exposé of the persecution of Japanese Americans in the USA during the Second World War. Dennis Quaid is the husband whose Japanese wife and daughter are taken from him and interned. There's no doubting Parker's indignation at the treatment of the internees but it's a slight story carrying too much historical and moral weight.

Comfort and Joy
1984 PG 100 ★★ COM

A quirky story by writer-director Bill Forsyth about the strife between rival ice-cream vendors in Glasgow. Bill Paterson is splendid as a disc jockey who inadvertently becomes involved but the story is pretty thin and there's not enough of the humour we might expect from the director of *Gregory's Girl* and *Local Hero*.

Commitments, The
1991 15 113 ★★★★ COM

This is a great delight – foul-mouthed, certainly, but fast, lively and very funny indeed. Alan Parker directed this joyous adaptation of Roddy Doyle's novel about the rise and fall of a Dublin soul band. A previously unknown cast performs marvellously in what amounts to a warm and warming paean to the optimism of the human spirit.

Compromising Positions
1985 15 94 ★★★ MYS/THR

Housewife Susan Sarandon gets involved in a lively, amusing murder investigation, led by detective Raul Julia, when her dentist is killed because of his habit of photographing his female patients in compromising positions. The setting is well-to-do suburbia, the sex is not explicit and the appeal of the film lies in the cleverly drawn characters and witty dialogue.

Conan the Barbarian
1982 15 121 ★★★ ACT/ADV

The film that made Arnold Schwarzenegger an international star. He plays a barbarian from the Dark Ages seeking revenge on the tribal leader who killed his parents. Violent, lusty stuff with Arnie doing what he does best – he looks strong and tough but you couldn't really say he acts. Mind you, he still hasn't quite got the hang of that even now.

Conan the Destroyer
1984 15 96 ★★ ACT/ADV

Much like the first film only a bit shorter. Arnie's on a quest this time in another mystical adventure. The production is less grand, maybe less grandiose, than the original and the performances are perhaps a little more tongue in cheek. Grace Jones provides a typically curious portrayal of a camp villainess.

Concierge, The
1993 PG 91 ★★★ COM

Michael J Fox as the Mr Fix It concierge of a Manhattan hotel who can solve everyone's problems but his own. He can get you anything you want, even a girl, and saves his money to build the hotel of his dreams. Then he falls in love, only to discover that his girlfriend is the mistress of his wealthy potential partner. A nice showcase for Fox, who makes the script appear better than it is.

Conversation, The
1974 15 109 ★★★ MYS/THR

Francis Ford Coppola's deeply plotted thriller in which surveillance operator Gene Hackman begins to worry about the use being made of a tape he recorded in a bugging investigation. His concern leads to involvement in a murder case. This is a darker, much more thoughtful film than most thrillers. Intense and with a climax well worth waiting for.

Convoy
1978 15 115 ★★ ACT/ADV

Sam Peckinpah's rather daft but romping yarn about a trucker, Kris Kristofferson, leading his mates in a fight for freedom on the freeways in a trek across the south-west of America. Danger is provided by a nasty cop, Ernest Borgnine, romance by Ali MacGraw. There's a fair bit of violence but what else would you expect from Peckinpah?

Cool Hand Luke
1967 15 121 ★★★★ DRA

Paul Newman gives probably the performance of his life as a convict on a chain gang in the Deep South who refuses to let the system and the sadistic guards break him. A tough tale much enlivened by humour, and the supporting cast, in particular George Kennedy, are knock-out. The film is similar in theme (and compares favourably) to *One Flew Over the Cuckoo's Nest*.

Cool Runnings
1993 PG 95 ★★★ COM

Notable mostly for being based on a remarkable true story – Jamaica entering a bobsleigh team in the Olympic Games. But as American coach John Candy, a disgraced former bobsleigh medallist, assembles his squad, we wave goodbye to reality and welcome fiction. An uneven picture but funny enough, often enough to entertain.

Cop and a Half
1993 PG 89 ★★ COM

Cop and kid is an amusing twist on the familiar buddy movie. The cop is Burt Reynolds; the kid a small black youngster, Norman D Golden II, who bribes Reynolds into taking him on as his partner in return for eye-witness evidence that will solve a killing. A nice idea but it could and should have been worked out better.

Cop au Vin
1984 15 105 ★★★ FOR

The kind of deeply engaging *policier* that Claude Chabrol makes so well. Nasty murders take place in a provincial town where the young postboy is investigating a local cartel's nefarious affairs. Jean Poiret is splendid as the cop brought in to solve the crimes. Chabrol turns his mocking eye on the bourgeoisie to delightful effect. Stéphane Audran plays the postboy's crippled mother. (Subtitled)

Cops and Robbersons
1994 PG 89 ★★ COM

Chevy Chase is the hapless householder who is forced to play host to hardbitten detective Jack Palance on a stakeout. The family's life, not to mention its house, is turned upside down by the policeman's presence. Palance is good but Chase is better, with Dianne Wiest practically unrecognisable as the mother.

Corrina, Corrina
1993 U 111 ★★ DRA

When his wife dies suddenly and his young daughter stops talking, advertising executive Ray Liotta employs a nanny. The most suitable candidate, Whoopi Goldberg, is a black woman, a significant point in the race-conscious America of the 1950s. Matters become even more complex when Liotta and Goldberg find more than platonic comfort in each other's company. It's a gentle piece, a bit gooey in places, but there's nothing to offend and a lot to coo over.

Corsican Brothers, The
1941 U 96 ★★ ACT/ADV

Alexandre Dumas's story of Siamese twins, separated at birth but not at heart, makes good swashbuckling stuff. Douglas Fairbanks Jr plays the twins – one a smart Parisian, the other raised in Corsica by a former family servant. Akim Tamiroff is the arch enemy as the reunited twins seek to avenge the murder of their forebears. (B&W)

Cotton Club, The
1984 15 123 ★★★ DRA

Francis Coppola's flawed but vivid tribute to Harlem's famous Cotton Club, home in the late 1920s to great jazz and dancing, not to mention bootleggers and gangsters. It takes the form of several loosely connected stories involving the likes of Richard Gere, Gregory Hines and so on. Outstanding performances by Bob Hoskins and Fred Gwynne as the club owners. Overall, though, it lacks the coherence of Coppola's earlier gangster movies.

Coupe de Ville
1990 15 93 ★★ DRA

A bittersweet comedy-drama about three brothers – Patrick Dempsey, Arye Gross and Daniel Stern – driving their father's 1954 Cadillac across country to Florida. The journey helps them come to terms with themselves, each other and dad, Alan Arkin, who is quite the best thing in it. There's some heavy-duty sentimentality in all this but a good few laughs as well.

Court Jester, The
1956 U 97 ★★★ FAM

Danny Kaye as the medieval clown who joins up with a gang of outlaws, not entirely unlike Robin Hood and his merry men. A lovely opportunity for Kaye to strut his stuff with the aid of Glynis Johns, Basil Rathbone and Cecil Parker among others.

Cousins
1989 15 108 ★★ DRA

An American remake of the French film *Cousin Cousine*. The French do these things better. Ted Danson and Isabella Rossellini are cousins and married to other people – Sean Young and William Petersen – who are having an affair. Danson and Rossellini seek revenge by pretending to have an affair of their own and… well, you can probably guess the rest. Amusing, but lacks the sophistication of the original.

Cover Girl
1944 U 102 ★★★ FAM

One of those pleasingly moral tales that Hollywood used to make. Rita Hayworth is the dancer who becomes a cover girl and jilts her sweetheart in search of fame and fortune. Ah, but are these assets better than true love? Gene Kelly is the boyfriend, Phil Silvers provides much of the humour.

Cowboys, The
1972 PG 121 ★★ WES

John Wayne is the cattleman unwillingly leading youngsters on a cattle drive. Bruce Dern is the rustler who actually shoots Wayne dead, something that didn't happen often in old Duke's movies. Rites of passage stuff, really, the boys growing up as they plan revenge for Wayne's murder. A gently paced film with far less violence than the average Western.

Crazy People
1990 15 88 ★★ COM

Dudley Moore is the advertising executive who flips and ends up in a mental institution – no bad place to be because he finds not only Daryl Hannah and sanity but a bunch of other inmates, who write advertising slogans which tell the truth and – most improbably – impress Madison Avenue. All very silly but not disagreeable.

Crimes and Misdemeanors
1989 15 100 ★★★★ COM

One of Woody Allen's best – a blending of two separate stories involving comedy, murder and adultery. In one, Allen is unhappily married, in love with another woman (Mia Farrow) and patronised by his insufferable brother-in-law (Alan Alda). In the other, Martin Landau is a doctor whose mistress (Anjelica Huston) threatens blackmail and must be dealt with. Funny, warm, thoughtful and beautifully done.

Criminal Justice
1990 15 87 ★★ MYS/THR

A courtroom drama notable for Forest Whitaker's performance as a black ex-convict accused by an assistant DA (Jennifer Grey) of attacking a prostitute. A high-quality supporting cast includes Rosie Perez. This is harder hitting and rather better written and directed (by Andy Wolk) than most made-for-TV dramas. Some violence and 'fresh' language.

'Crocodile' Dundee
1986 15 93 ★★★★ COM

Woodsman, hunter and tall-story teller Paul Hogan beguiles smart New York reporter Linda Kozlowski in the Australian outback, then wins both her and the admiration of Manhattan when she takes him home with her. The laconic, laid-back Hogan, unfazed by the big city and still less by muggers, makes a refreshingly different and delightful hero.

'Crocodile' Dundee II
1988 PG 107 ★★★ COM

By no means a bad sequel but with more violence and fewer jokes. This one starts in Manhattan with Hogan and Kozlowski falling foul of drug dealers, then – reversing the structure of the earlier film – luring the villains to Australia so that Hogan can confront them in his own back yard. Familiarity breeds not contempt but, well, familiarity.

Crossing Delancey
1988 PG 93 ★★★ COM

A warm, wistful tale about romance and arranged marriage in New York's Jewish community. Amy Irving is the thirtysomething bachelor girl whose grandmother tries, through a matchmaker, to fix her up with Peter Riegert, a pickle seller. Jeroen Krabbe is the sophisticated writer who nearly ruins everything. A bit schmaltzy but nicely romantic all the same.

Cruel Sea, The
1953 PG 126 ★★★★ WAR

This adaptation of Nicholas Monsarrat's novel is an outstanding British war film. Jack Hawkins plays the corvette skipper who has to weld his crew of conscripts and part-time sailors into a fighting unit able to take on U-boats and the sea itself. Eric Ambler's script, Charles Frend's direction and the performances of a top-notch cast – including, in his debut, Donald Sinden – are splendidly convincing. (B&W)

Cry Freedom
1987 PG 151 ★★★ DRA

Richard Attenborough's fiercely anti-apartheid drama about the friendship between South African journalist Donald Woods and the black activist Steve Biko. The first half of the story – the events leading up to Biko's death in jail – is by far the more gripping. Kevin Kline and Denzel Washington are excellent in a film that should be seen even now as a reminder of the way things were.

Cry in the Dark, A
1988 15 116 ★★★ DRA

Meryl Streep is exceptional as the Australian mother wrongly accused of infanticide when her baby vanishes on a camping trip. Though Streep is adamant that a dingo snatched the child, public hostility is so great that she and her husband (Sam Neill) are convicted of murder until a chance discovery casts serious doubt on the legal verdict. Based, of course, on a true story.

Curly Sue
1991 PG 98 ★ COM

Pure slush all the way through, even by the manipulative standards of its director, John (*Home Alone*) Hughes. A precocious eight-year-old orphan (Alisan Porter) pals up with a con artist (James Belushi) and together they melt the heart of divorce lawyer Kelly Lynch. But since it's very difficult indeed to like the child it's also very difficult to care.

Cutting Edge, The
1992 PG 97 ★★ DRA

A dumb, sentimental tale of an American ice-hockey star-turned-figure skater (D B Sweeney), teamed by coach Roy Dotrice with rich, haughty champ Moira Kelly. Naturally, they hate each other but they're in the Olympics so they have to try to get along and, well, you know… Still, let's not be too harsh – viewers have been spotted smiling happily through their tears.

Cyrano de Bergerac
1950 U 112 ★★★ DRA

Earlier American version with the Oscar-winning Jose Ferrer as Cyrano and Mala Powers as Roxanne. A very decent production, actually, but it lacks the gusto of the French film (see below) and, besides, Gérard Depardieu's Cyrano is better. (B&W)

Cyrano de Bergerac
1990 U 132 ★★★★ FOR

This outstanding adaptation of Rostand's play owes almost as much to Anthony Burgess's poetic subtitles as to Gérard Depardieu's moving, flamboyant portrayal of the poet-soldier with the huge, inhibiting nose. A fine cast (Anne Brochet and Vincent Pérez) and director Jean-Paul Rappeneau's lavish production give this edge over the 1950 version. (Subtitled)

Da
1988 PG 98 ★★★ DRA

An autobiographical tale that yanks at the heartstrings. Irish-American playwright Martin Sheen returns home – a humble Irish cottage – for his father's (Barnard Hughes) funeral. There he is visited by his father's ghost and together they examine their relationship. It's not all sad; there's a lot of humour and warmth and a good performance by Sheen, who laboured for years to bring Hugh Leonard's play to the screen.

Dad
1989 PG 112 ★ DRA

This film stands out for providing one of the worst performances of modern cinema and by Jack Lemmon, no less. He's doused with make-up and bent double to play the ailing father of Ted Danson, a Wall Street hot-shot summoned to look after his aged parents (Olympia Dukakis plays his mother) and reconcile family differences. Dead slushy and unforgivable for woeful miscasting.

Daddy Long Legs
1955 U 120 ★★ MUS

Fred Astaire makes an unlikely playboy in this good-natured, *Pygmalion*-type romp. Leslie Caron's gorgeous as the waif whose improvement he finances and with whom he falls in love. Nice numbers and great choreography.

Dam Busters, The
1954 U 120 ★★★ WAR

The story of Barnes Wallis (Michael Redgrave) who invented the bouncing bomb. This splendid film follows the blood, sweat and tears that went into the invention and the daring raid, led by Guy Gibson (Richard Todd), to blow up the Ruhr dams. Brilliant music helps to distinguish one of the most exciting, intelligent and moving Second World War tales. (B&W)

Dance with a Stranger
1985 15 98 ★★★ DRA

The story of Ruth Ellis, the last woman to be hanged in Britain. The excellent Miranda Richardson plays Ellis; Rupert Everett is David Blakely, the shiftless lover for whose murder she was executed. It's a sympathetic examination of both her crime and the events that gave rise to it and the trial. Richardson's performance is quite stunning.

Dances with Wolves
1990 15 173 ★★★★ WES

Twelve nominations and seven wins at the Oscars gave this film more prestige than perhaps it warrants. Beautifully shot, politically correct (holding out for the Indians against the white man) and dramatic, its length does work against it. Producer-director Kevin Costner also stars as a post-Civil War soldier who, appointed to an outpost on the border of Indian country, becomes converted to the Sioux way of life. Intelligent and well worth seeing, but make sure you're sitting comfortably.

Dancin' thru the Dark
1989 15 91 ★★★ COM

Written by Willy Russell, who also gave us the rather better *Shirley Valentine*. Still, this one – also set in working-class Liverpool – is also quite funny and, at times, bitingly observant. The original play was called *Stags and Hens*, possibly because a group of friends, out on a separate hen night and stag night, converge on the same disco with disastrous results.

Dangerous Liaisons
1988 15 115 ★★★★ DRA

Glenn Close and John Malkovich as debauched eighteenth-century French aristocrats who, bored with their own sexual shenanigans, turn their corrupting attentions to the loyal and pure Michelle Pfeiffer. Malkovich's intentions are dishonourable, Close's downright evil as she plots Pfeiffer's downfall. Uma Thurman also stars in Stephen Frears's very well made film.

Danton
1982 PG 130 ★★★★ FOR

Gérard Depardieu plays the eponymous Danton during the Reign of Terror which followed the French Revolution in eighteenth-century Paris. In Andrzej Wajda's absorbing film, Danton, the incorruptible humanist, returns to Paris after a spell of retirement in the country to challenge former colleague Robespierre (Wojciech Pszoniak), whose Committee of Public Safety has become as oppressive as the monarch they helped overthrow. (Subtitled)

Dark Crystal, The
1983 PG 87 ★★★ SCI/FAN

Frank Oz's and Jim Henson's tale of good versus evil is surprisingly dark considering it's by the man who brought us the Muppets. In a world mainly inhabited by the evil Skeksis only a few good and wise creatures have been able to survive. But all is not necessarily lost if a little boy and girl can replace a missing shard in the Dark Crystal and ward off Doomsday. Splendid animation.

Dark Star
1974 PG 83 ★★★ SCI/FAN

A low-budget sci-fi send-up of, among other things, *2001*. A bunch of layabout astronauts, charged with destroying obsolete planets, amble through space. They pass the time making videos, having sunbeds, playing ball with a rotund alien and generally shooting the breeze until their talking computer malfunctions and their rocket breaks down. This was John Carpenter's first feature and cost only $60,000, which makes the special effects even more impressive.

Dark Victory
1939 PG 100 ★★★ DRA

Boxes of chocolates were designed with this type of film in mind – so were paper tissues. Keep both handy and enjoy a classic Bette Davis melodrama in which she plays a spoilt little rich girl who discovers she is dying from a brain tumour and marries the doctor (George Brent) who is treating her. Watch for Ronald Reagan and a woefully miscast Humphrey Bogart. (B&W)

Darling
1965 15 122 ★★★ DRA

The kind of film that epitomized the 1960s. It's about very smart, amoral people – especially a young fashion model (Julie Christie) and the men (Dirk Bogarde, Laurence Harvey) she exploits in her ruthless pursuit of success. Both Christie and Frederic Raphael's screenplay won Oscars, while the movie itself and director John Schlesinger won nominations. (B&W)

Daughters of the Dust
1993 PG 107 ★ DRA

A not uninteresting but also not very gripping study of the African-American Gullah people, who in the early 1900s settled on an island off the Georgia coast. The main concern is with one particular family, headed by an aged matriarch, who in various ways are celebrating their last evening on the island before starting a new life on the mainland.

Dave
1993 15 105 ★★★ COM

A pleasing romp in which philanthropic employment agency boss Kevin Kline is forced to impersonate his look-alike, the president of the USA, when the latter has a stroke. The question is not so much whether Kline can deceive the nation but whether he can fool the philandering president's bitter wife, Sigourney Weaver. Very funny and with a fair sprinkling of satirical points to make about American politics.

David Copperfield
1935 U 124 ★★★★ FAM

MGM's painstaking and affectionate version of Dickens's masterpiece looks like an Oscar roll call of cinema's early years. Freddie Bartholomew, Lionel Barrymore, Maureen O'Sullivan, Edna May Oliver, and of course W C Fields, who's nothing short of hilarious as a juggling Mr Micawber. A *juggling* Mr Micawber? Hey, come on – this is Hollywood, what do you expect! (B&W)

Day at the Races, A: see Marx Brothers

Day of the Jackal, The
1973 15 136 ★★★ DRA

Edward Fox as a top-notch hit man employed to assassinate President Charles de Gaulle. We all know he didn't succeed, but even so there's plenty of suspense in Fred Zinnemann's thriller. The gendarmerie is wise to the plot and sets out to hunt the Jackal down. Two stories run parallel as one man makes his preparation to kill while the police work against time to find and stop him. Everything builds to a thrilling climax.

Days of Heaven
1978 PG 89 ★★★★ DRA

An engrossing American film that tells of a
ménàge-a-trois in Texas in 1916. Richard Gere
and Brooke Adams are migrant workers who,
posing as brother and sister, find work on Sam
Shepard's farm. Shepard and Adams marry and
that's when the emotional turmoil begins. A
powerful, dramatic story, brilliantly written
and directed by Terrence Malick, which has
developed considerable cult status.

Days of Thunder
1990 15 102 ★★ ACT/ADV

Tom Cruise and Nicole Kidman met and fell in
love while making this movie but the only
sparks in evidence are those from the stock cars'
pistons. This is formulaic stuff – a *Top Gun* on
the racing-car circuit. Looks good but not
much of a story and a surprising lack of
chemistry between the leads. Robert Duvall
brings it some welcome clout but it's essentially
a leaden offering from director Tony Scott.

D-Day the Sixth of June
1956 PG 106 ★★★ WAR

Detailed saga centred on the 1944 Normandy
landings and concentrating on the personal and
professional relationship between an American
(Robert Taylor) and an English officer (Richard
Todd). Some spectacular action sequences
interspersed with romance involving Dana
Wynter as the woman in Taylor's life.

Dead, The
1987 U 79 ★★★★ DRA

In 1904, two spinster sisters throw their
traditional Epiphany party for family and
friends. But this year two guests (Anjelica
Huston and Donal McCann) discover things
about each other that they had never suspected
before. That's the basis of John Huston's
memorable last film, a faithful recreation of
James Joyce's moving, funny, short story, and
beautifully played by a splendid and, other than
Anjelica Huston, all-Irish cast.

Dead Again
1991 15 103 ★★★ MYS/THR

A double helping here of Emma Thompson and
Kenneth Branagh, who play both an amnesiac

and a private eye, and a murdered wife and her
composer husband. The plot, as gripping as it is
convoluted, revolves round whether the
composer did his wife in. A hypnotist, Derek
Jacobi, helps private eye Branagh investigate.
Andy Garcia and Robin Williams crop up in
scene-stealing cameos.

Dead Calm
1989 15 92 ★★★ MYS/THR

A happily married couple (Nicole Kidman and
Sam Neill) are hijacked aboard their yacht. The
calm of the Pacific contrasts strongly with the
raging fury of killer Billy Zane who boards the
couple's boat on the pretence that something
dreadful has happened on his own and proceeds
to terrorize them. Good, tense action with Zane
easily taking the acting honours. (Colour and
B&W)

Deadly Affair, The
1967 15 103 ★★★ MYS/THR

Based on *Call for the Dead*, an early John Le
Carré novel about murder and espionage. James
Mason, as intelligence officer George Smiley,
looks into the apparent suicide of a colleague.
As a subplot, Mason is married to a
nymphomaniac whose affairs threaten his
career. Mason finds secure support from
Simone Signoret, Maximilian Schell and Lynn
Redgrave.

Deadly Pursuit
1988 15 105 ★★ MYS/THR

A thrilling first scene makes a terrific opening
for this murder mystery but things go downhill
from there. After a violent diamond robbery,
the killer hides out on a mountain expedition
led by Kirstie Alley. She's ignorant of the danger
but detective Sidney Poitier and Alley's
boyfriend, Tom Berenger, are on their trail. The
film marked Poitier's return to the screen after
an all-too-lengthy absence.

Dead Men Don't Wear Plaid
1982 PG 84 ★★★ COM

Appropriately shot in black and white because
this is an affectionate send-up of *film noir*.
With the aid of some smart editing, private eye
Steve Martin meets such late movie greats as
Humphrey Bogart, Joan Crawford and Ingrid

Bergman. Martin calls for help from Philip Marlowe (Bogart) in the case he's investigating. Rachel Ward provides the romance. All very light and enjoyable. (B&W)

Dead Poets Society
1989 PG 123 ★★★★ DRA

Robin Williams is inspired in the serious role of an English teacher at a disciplinarian prep school. He has no respect for tradition and rips up the text books as he seeks to imbue in his charges the spirit of poetry. But his unorthodox methods have varying effects on a handful of pupils, principle among them Robert Sean Leonard and Ethan Hawke. Directed by Peter Weir.

Death Becomes Her
1992 PG 99 ★ COM

First you marvel at the special effects. Then you marvel even more at what a distinguished cast (Meryl Streep, Goldie Hawn, Bruce Willis) and director (Robert Zemeckis) thought they were doing with anything quite as fatuous as this half-baked story about wealthy women seeking rejuvenation and immortality. Nobody – except the FX department – comes out of it with any credit at all.

Death in Venice
1971 15 125 ★★★ DRA

Dirk Bogarde proving, in his post pin-up boy era, what a fine actor he is. The story, based on Thomas Mann's novel, is set before the First World War when an elderly artist, taking an Italian holiday, confronts his obsession with a young boy (Bjorn Andresen). A very good-looking film which, under Luchino Visconti's direction, takes its time – perhaps too much time – but Bogarde's performance is remarkable.

Deceived
1991 15 104 ★★★ MYS/THR

Goldie Hawn thinks she was happily married – until she learns that her late husband, John Heard, had been deceiving her. What's more, she herself is now in danger. A complicated plot, nicely handled, especially by Hawn who, not before time, abandons the kooky, cute roles of her youth and proves herself an

accomplished, serious actress. Heard, as always, is good in support.

Defence of the Realm
1985 PG 92 ★★★ MYS/THR

When a tough investigative journalist (Gabriel Byrne) follows up the near-crash of a nuclear bomber on an American air force base in England, events lead to the resignation of a radical politician. Then unfolds a fast-paced thriller about government cover-ups, political conspiracies and murder. Byrne is fine, Greta Scacchi looks good in the romantic role and Denholm Elliott shines as the older journalist caught between a rock and a hard place.

Delicatessen
1991 15 95 ★★★ FOR

This is a really black French farce centred on an apartment block whose landlord is a butcher. So? So the time is post-apocalypse and, meat being scarce, the butcher tends to feed his tenants to his customers. Unfortunately, some of his tenants are his customers. Very dark, very funny, bleakly stylish. (Subtitled)

Demolition Man
1993 15 110 ★★ ACT/ADV

In the twenty-first century a cop, Sylvester Stallone, and a villain, Wesley Snipes, both long deep-frozen for their misdemeanours, are defrosted to chase each other all over again. What's more, they are in a post-modern Los Angeles where crime is unknown. If you can believe that, you can believe anything – even this preposterous yarn, the satirical aspects of which are quickly tossed aside lest they get in the way of the action and violence, which is liberally distributed throughout.

Dennis
1993 PG 92 ★★ COM

A John Hughes movie in which long-suffering Walter Matthau and his wife Joan Plowright agree to look after the little boy next door (Mason Gamble) when his parents go away. Matthau grows fond of the obnoxious kid though it's hard to see why. Not Gamble's fault; just that John Hughes's idea of what constitutes 'cute' in a child is not everybody's.

Desert Fox, The
1951 PG 85 ★★★ WAR

The Desert Fox was, of course, Field Marshal Erwin Rommel (James Mason) who, after the battle of El Alamein, was recalled to Germany to explain the 'disgrace' of his defeat. Too late, Rommel realises that Hitler is quite mad and must be stopped. Impressive action footage in a tale well told and immaculately acted by Mason. Jessica Tandy is good, too, as Frau Rommel. (B&W)

Desert Rats, The
1953 U 84 ★★★ WAR

Rommel (James Mason again) and the war in North Africa once more, though this time the protagonist is a British captain (Richard Burton) leading a group of Australians at the battle of Tobruk. He and Mason meet only briefly in a nicely played scene. Otherwise there's plenty of action as the Brit and the Aussies gradually develop respect for each other. (B&W)

Desperate Hours
1990 15 100 ★★ MYS/THR

Mickey Rourke as a psycho who busts out of jail with the aid of his lawyer, no less, played by Kelly Lynch. To aid his escape he bursts into the home of Anthony Hopkins and Mimi Rogers, who are on the brink of divorce, and holds them hostage. The story was done much better in William Wyler's 1955 version with Humphrey Bogart and Fredric March. Michael Cimino's remake is violent but rather dull.

Desperately Seeking Susan
1985 15 99 ★★★★ COM

This was Madonna's first significant role and, in truth, she has never been as good since. As the Susan whom everyone – boyfriend, bad guys and bored housewife Rosanna Arquette – is desperately seeking, she's tough, raunchy, funny and appealing. Even so, Arquette is even better and Aidan Quinn, too, contributes heftily to an unusual and delightful comedy.

Dial M for Murder
1954 PG 100 ★★★ MYS/THR

Ray Milland as the murderous husband, Grace Kelly as the wealthy wife whose death he plans.

Not, of course, that the plans necessarily work out. Not one of Hitchcock's best, though the old master's familiar touches are there. The studio insisted it be made in 3D, which didn't help anybody much. Still, no Hitchcock film is entirely without merit and this certainly has its moments.

Diamonds Are Forever
1971 PG 115 ★★★ ACT/ADV

After a break that saw George Lazenby take over as Bond, Sean Connery was lured back for his sixth and penultimate outing as 007, this time in Las Vegas. The script's more tongue-in-cheek than most, but much of the rest is pretty familiar really. Scantily clad women, the future of the planet threatened, state-of-the-art gadgets, Jill St John for romantic relief and Shirley Bassey singing the title song.

Dick Tracy
1990 PG 100 ★★★ ACT/ADV

Warren Beatty directed and played the title role in this beautifully designed – all vivid primary colours – re-creation of the comic-strip character. Lots of action and (not too offensive) violence. But the fun comes in spotting the guest stars – Dustin Hoffman, Dick Van Dyke, James Caan and, especially, Al Pacino – all hidden under excellent make-up. Madonna is not bad as the *femme fatale* and Glenne Headly is Tracy's loyal girlfriend.

Die Hard 2: Die Harder
1990 15 118 ★★★ ACT/ADV

The original warranted an 18 certificate so, as second best, make do with the sequel. Well, it's almost a reprise really and not much less violent than the first. Here Bruce Willis, the wise-cracking cop, is waiting at Dulles Airport to pick up his wife for Christmas when terrorists seize the place. Willis goes to the rescue, of course. Non-stop action (and a hefty amount of violence) and quite good fun, but the original was a lot better. (Be warned: there is also an 18-certificate version available in widescreen.)

Diner
1982 15 106 ★★★ DRA

Barry Levinson's debut as writer-director introduces a group of young players, all of whom were to find fame later. The setting is a café in Baltimore in the 1950s where a bunch of early twentysomethings hang out and prepare to face adulthood. Among them are Mickey Rourke, Ellen Barkin, Steve Guttenberg, Kevin Bacon and Daniel Stern. It doesn't amount to much, but it's funny and thoughtful and very well written.

Dirty Dancing
1987 15 99 ★★★ DRA

Patrick Swayze wins Jennifer Grey's heart in this musical set in the 1960s. She's the bored daughter of a doctor who during a vacation wanders into the staff-only area of the hotel. There – Basil Fawlty would have a field day – the employees are hot-hoofing it in time to music, inspired by the resident twinkletoes Swayze. Rites of passage stuff ensues. A pleasing tale with good song and dance.

Dirty Dozen, The
1967 15 147 ★★★ ACT/ADV

Lee Marvin is the major who assembles a squad of felons for an apparent suicide mission – to infiltrate and destroy a high-powered Nazi conference. The twelve hardened convicts he recruits include Charles Bronson, Ernest Borgnine, John Cassavetes and George Kennedy. Best part of the film is at the training camp but the mission itself is exciting stuff.

Dirty Rotten Scoundrels
1988 PG 106 ★★★ COM

Steve Martin and Michael Caine as two con men who team up to rip off the rich on the French Riviera. The main object of their scam is Glenne Headly, though she may not be the easy mark they expect. The setting is lovely and the stars give lively performances but the plot is a touch sloppy and it's not always quite as funny as you had hoped.

Distant Voices, Still Lives
1988 15 80 ★★★ DRA

The first, strongly autobiographical film by Terence Davies about working-class life in post-war Liverpool. It's divided into two parts: the *Distant Voices* section centres on a wedding and a funeral; *Still Lives*, filmed with the same actors but different crew two years later (not

that you'd notice), culminates in another wedding. Deceptively simple and quietly riveting.

Distinguished Gentleman, The
1992 15 107 ★★ COM

After a few box office flops, Eddie Murphy returns to a form not seen since *Beverly Hills Cop* as a con man who runs for Congress. It's the only way he can see of earning loads of money without doing anything for it. A funny and romantic satire of American politics which, being neither deep nor original, would not hold half the charm if it weren't for Murphy.

Diva
1981 15 112 ★★★ FOR

Stylish high-tech melodrama by Jean-Jacques Beineix about a French music lover unwittingly involved with the underworld after illicitly taping a diva's concert. Said singer has never made a recording so he's already in hot water, which becomes scalding when his tape is confused with one involving the activities of a bunch of gangsters. Good-looking, violent and a little over-ambitious. (Subtitled)

D.O.A.
1988 15 93 ★★ MYS/THR

Remake of an earlier and better film. Dennis Quaid is an English professor who discovers he's been poisoned and has only a day or so to live. So with the help of a student, Meg Ryan, he devotes his last hours to finding his killer. A good performance by Quaid.

Doc Hollywood
1991 15 99 ★★★ COM

An old-fashioned feel-good movie. Dr Michael J Fox, en route to a lucrative career as a Hollywood plastic surgeon, is stranded in a small town full of people with hearts of gold and falls for both it and unmarried mother Julie Warner. Fox and the corny plot exude a great deal of charm.

Doctor Dolittle
1967 U 138 ★★★ FAM

Pleasing enough – though it should have been better – musical version of Hugh Lofting's popular children's stories. Rex Harrison is the doctor who can talk to the animals, among them the Great Pink Sea Snail and the Pushme-Pullyou. Leslie Bricusse's decent songs include the Oscar-winning 'Talk to the Animals'.

Doctor in the House
1954 U 88 ★★★ COM

The first and the best of the series inspired by Richard Gordon's novels. Dirk Bogarde is Simon Sparrow, the medical student torn between his studies and the nurses. James Robertson Justice gives marvellous support as the terrifying consultant. (The five sequels are all PG and not bad, though not as funny as the original.)

Doctor Zhivago
1965 PG 200 ★★★★ DRA

Boris Pasternak's Russian Revolution love story splendidly adapted by writer Robert Bolt and director David Lean. Julie Christie and Omar Sharif are the star-crossed lovers. A big, rich, lush movie, which earned more money than any of Lean's other films. Excellent cast includes Alec Guinness, Tom Courtenay, Rod Steiger and Geraldine Chaplin. Bolt won an Oscar.

Dog Day Afternoon
1975 15 120 ★★★★ DRA

You might not believe this but Sidney Lumet's film – about a man (Al Pacino) robbing a bank to fund his male lover's sex-change operation – is based on a true story. The bank raid goes hopelessly wrong but the film goes splendidly right, being in equal measure exciting, funny and very touching. Pacino in particular is on peak form.

Don Bluth's Thumbelina: see
Thumbelina

Don't Tell Mom the Babysitter's Dead
1991 15 100 ★★ COM

Situation comedy about a family of horrible children whose mother shoves off on holiday leaving them in the care of a babysitter. But the sitter drops dead, so the kids (led by Christina Applegate) keep the news from mom and settle back to enjoy themselves. What follows is wild,

coarse and ultimately sentimental. Applegate's appealing, though.

Down and Out in Beverly Hills
1986 15 99 ★★ COM

Richard Dreyfuss and Bette Midler are a wealthy but unhappy Beverly Hills couple whose life is changed when a tramp, Nick Nolte, tries to drown himself in their pool. They adopt the tramp and he teaches them and their children lessons in living. A neat idea, not fully developed, but it has its share of comic and poignant moments.

Downhill Racer
1969 PG 102 ★★ ACT/ADV

The most striking aspect of this Alpine-based drama is the beautiful scenery, not least of which is a young Robert Redford. He takes an anti-hero role as an ambitious but ruthless skier seeking a place in the US Olympic team. Trouble is, Redford is so good that it's hard to like the character. Gene Hackman is quite sympathetic, though, as the coach and the skiing is spectacular.

Dracula
1979 15 104 ★★★ HOR

Interesting and not too bloodthirsty or horrific slant on the Dracula tale. This version explores the seductive side of the count (Frank Langella) as he comes to England and meets tasty Kate Nelligan. Laurence Olivier overacts as Van Helsing; Langella makes a more than usually sexy bloodsucker. Lush, lavish and steamy.

Dragnet
1987 PG 101 ★★★ COM

Tom Hanks and Dan Aykroyd as a pair of naff cops who run into trouble with a mad evangelist, Christopher Plummer, and their own police commissioner, Elizabeth Ashley. The film never really gets anywhere and doesn't live up to its initial promise but it's an amusing, affectionate send-up of the old TV series and some of the gags are great.

Dragon: The Bruce Lee Story
1993 15 114 ★★★ ACT/ADV

Biopic about the cinematic king of kung fu, Bruce Lee (very well played by the unrelated Jason Scott Lee). It follows the young Bruce from Hong Kong to California, to stardom and to death. Action, romance and – for devoted Bruce Lee fans – plenty of tears as he meets his untimely end. (Further tragedy befell his widow Linda when their twenty-seven-year-old son, Brandon, was killed in a film stunt that went wrong while he was making *The Crow*.)

Dream Team, The
1989 15 108 ★★★ COM

The eponymous team consists of four mental patients – Michael Keaton, Christopher Lloyd, Peter Boyle and Stephen Furst – who find themselves accidentally on the loose in downtown New York and become involved in a murder. Such an idea is a gift to these actors and they make the very most of it. Keaton shines particularly in a well worked-out and frequently hilarious film.

Dresser, The
1983 PG 113 ★★★ DRA

Albert Finney, as a cantankerous grand old man of the British stage, and Tom Courtenay, as his often exasperated but faithful dresser, were both nominated for Oscars and deservedly so. Finney's obsession with his art makes life hard for those around him. Only his dresser understands him. Ronald Harwood, the writer, apparently based Finney's character on actor-manager Donald Wolfit.

Driver, The
1978 15 87 ★★★ ACT/ADV

Walter Hill (who went on to do *48 HRS*) made his directorial debut with this tense, fast-moving story of the conflict between a professional getaway driver (Ryan O'Neal) and a cop (Bruce Dern). The story's a little confusing but Dern gives a fine performance and Hill directs the action with his now familiar skill.

Driving Miss Daisy
1989 U 95 ★★★ FAM

Over-rewarded with its Oscar for Best Picture. It's an extremely engaging film, beautifully played by Jessica Tandy (who deserved her Oscar as the elderly Southern matriarch) and Morgan Freeman, as her black chauffeur and unlikely friend. But it always reveals its origins as a stage play, nicely but not spectacularly opened out by director Bruce Beresford. Dan Aykroyd provides lighter moments as Tandy's son, concerned by his mother's increasing fragility.

Dr No
1962 PG 105 ★★★★ ACT/ADV

The first of the Bond films and the one that set the pace for the others. Sean Connery, as 007, shot to international stardom. Most people think he is still the best Bond of them all. Thrills, excitement, chases, a mad Chinese scientist (Joseph Wiseman) and Ursula Andress coming out of the sea with little more than a couple of conch shells on her.

Dr Strangelove
1963 PG 91 ★★★★ COM

Stanley Kubrick's magnificent, satirical anti-war comedy is still hilarious even now thanks to Peter Sellers, who excels in three different roles. Russo-American Cold War brinkmanship gone mad. Lovely performances by, among others, George C Scott and Sterling Hayden, but best remembered as perhaps Sellers's finest hour.

Duel
1971 PG 86 ★★★★ MYS/THR

One of the most terrifying monsters of the big screen was created by none other than Steven Spielberg as first-time director. The monster? A truck that pursues inoffensive motorist Dennis Weaver with murderous intent. You never see the truck driver's face and that only adds to the menace. Overall, so atmospheric and chilling as to be a lesson in film-making.

D2: The Mighty Ducks
1994 U 102 ★ FAM

The first *Mighty Ducks* or *Champions* as it was otherwise known was good fun but this is not up to that standard. Emilio Estevez is lured back, again, to coach a national team of ice-hockey players for the junior Olympic Games. A fresh idea might have helped it along a little. Only for the most faithful fans of the first.

Duck Soup: see Marx Brothers

Duel in the Sun
1946 PG 125 ★★★ WES

A Western of epic length, directed by King Vidor, which tells of two brothers, Gregory Peck and Joseph Cotten, in love with the same half-breed girl, Jennifer Jones. Pretty sexy for its time – critics dubbed it 'Lust in the Dust'. The casting is of interest since Peck plays the love-'em-and-leave-'em rotter while Cotten is the dependable heroic type.

Dumbo
1941 U 61 ★★★★ FAM

One of the Disney classics, the ever-enchanting story of the baby elephant whose ears are so big he can fly. As ever, marvellous animation and masses of cute animal characters. But, a word of warning: the scene where Dumbo is forced to part from his mother is a perennial tearjerker among the smaller fry. At just under one million dollars, this was the shortest and cheapest of the Disney studio's feature films.

Dune
1984 15 131 ★★ SCI/FAN

Or, as the American cast called it, 'Doon'. David Lynch's futuristic tale (based on Frank Herbert's novel) of a warrior leading the inhabitants of the planet Dune in their conflict with a wicked emperor looks good but always remains uninvolving. Still, the special effects are fine and the cast – including Kyle MacLachlan, Francesca Annis, Max von Sydow and Sting – struggle through manfully.

Dunkirk
1958 PG 130 ★★★★ WAR

Directed by Leslie Norman, father/grandfather of the authors (and all bias aside), this is the terrific tale of the mass beach evacuation seen through the eyes of three men: John Mills, a cockney soldier; Bernard Lee, a sceptical journalist and Richard Attenborough, a civilian who has avoided military service. The style is semi-documentary and underplayed, allowing the dramatic events to speak volubly for themselves. (B&W)

Eagle Has Landed, The
1976 15 118 ★★ WAR

A Second World War adventure adapted from Jack Higgins's novel and dealing with a dastardly Nazi plot to assassinate Churchill. What it provides mostly is a decent star vehicle for the likes of Michael Caine, as a disgraced German officer, Donald Sutherland, as an IRA man, and such others as Robert Duvall. Trouble is, there's precious little tension or credibility around.

Earth Girls Are Easy
1988 PG 100 ★ COM

A feeble comedy about three licentious, hairy aliens – Jeff Goldblum, Damon Wayans and Jim Carrey – invading the home of Geena Davis. She shaves them, finds out they're kind of sexy and romance ensues. The gags are predictable and rarely funny. The best line is in the publicity material: 'He's from Outer Space. She's from Los Angeles. At least they have something in common'.

Earthquake
1974 PG 116 ★★★ ACT/ADV

One of the better disaster movies of the 1970s, thanks mainly to Oscar-winning special effects. Poor old construction engineer Charlton Heston has to save shattered buildings, their occupants and his marriage – all on the same day. Ava Gardner, George Kennedy and Genevieve Bujold are among those who lend a hand or get in the way.

Easter Parade
1948 U 99 ★★★★ MUS

Irving Berlin, Fred Astaire, Judy Garland – what more could you ask? It's the familiar, well-loved showbiz story: Astaire, deserted by his partner (Ann Miller), decides to show her he can make anyone a star. So he plucks a girl – Garland, who else? – from the chorus. All right, so it's a corny plot but who cares? The music, the lyrics, the dancing and the stars are all marvellous.

East of Eden
1955 PG 110 ★★★ DRA

The film, based on John Steinbeck's novel, that made James Dean a star. Two films later (*Rebel without a Cause* and *Giant*) he was dead and became an instant legend. Here he gives a brooding performance as the bad son vying with his brother for the love of their father. In the context, Dean's mumbling Brandoesque delivery was just right. Elia Kazan directed.

Eat the Peach
1986 PG 91 ★★ COM

Engaging account of unemployed Irish friends, Stephen Brennan and Eamon Morrissey, who decide to build a wall of death after seeing Elvis's biker movie *Roustabout*. They've got the site – what they haven't got is the money. That comes from a spot of bootlegging across the border. But will the crowds come, too? Likeable, light-hearted and nicely put together.

Educating Rita
1983 15 106 ★★★ DRA

Both the stars – Michael Caine and Julie Walters – were Oscar-nominated. And both are fine in Willy Russell's story about a Liverpudlian hairdresser who decides to better herself by taking an Open University degree under the tutorship of alcoholic Michael Caine. Warm, funny and skilfully directed by Lewis Gilbert.

Edward Scissorhands
1990 PG 100 ★★★★ COM

Vincent Price sets out to create a boy with a loving heart (Johnny Depp) but dies before he can finish the job. Depp, left with scissors for hands, tries to make his way in 1950s American suburbia. He, Dianne Wiest and Winona Ryder shine in a warm, gentle fantasy whose moral is that we should set out to understand, rather than fear, the unusual. The ending seems a little harsh but, sadly, it's probably what would happen.

18 Again!
1988 PG 96 ★★ COM

Aged George Burns and his grandson, Charlie Schlatter, swap bodies with the result – pretty feeble, too – that Burns goes to college while Schlatter takes granddad's place. There were many such movies around in the late 80s and this was about par for the course. Burns, incidentally, was ninety-two when the film was shot but did a good job of playing a man eleven years younger than himself.

Eight Men Out
1988 15 114 ★★★ DRA

John Sayles directed this fascinating film about the 1919 Chicago White Sox, eight of whom took money to throw the baseball World Series. A fine cast includes Charlie Sheen, John Cusack, Christopher Lloyd and D B Sweeney. The scandal rocked America but the gloomy moral is that only the players lost. They were all banned for life.

84 Charing Cross Road
1986 U 95 ★★★ DRA

The deceptively simple and charming story of the transatlantic correspondence between American writer Helene Hanff (Anne Bancroft) and an English bookseller (Anthony Hopkins), which lasted two decades. The couple never met but the affection that builds between them is palpable. A film full of quiet pleasures, beautifully played.

El Cid
1961 U 172 ★★★ ACT/ADV

Charlton Heston plays the legendary Spanish hero who divides his time between attempting to rid his country of the invading Moors and wooing Sophia Loren. A very good-looking film, directed by Anthony Mann, with plenty of rousing action and battle scenes. Loren is beguiling; Heston as stolid as ever.

Electric Horseman, The
1979 PG 120 ★★★ DRA

A satire on big business, commercialism and also commercials, as has-been rodeo star, Robert Redford, makes his final protest by stealing a valuable horse and heading off into the Nevada desert. Jane Fonda is the journalist who gets an exclusive on the story. A charming if improbable and overpadded yarn, attractively played. Lovely horse, too.

Elenya
1992 PG 78 ★★ DRA

The tale, told in flashback by an elderly woman, of her lonely girlhood in wartime Wales and of the injured German airman she befriended. Muted colours lend visual splendour to an equally muted story. Often slow, never very exciting but nicely done. The film's composition makes it pleasantly suited to a quiet evening in front of the telly.

Elephant Man, The
1980 PG 118 ★★★ DRA

The dignity of John Hurt's portrayal of the grossly deformed John Merrick is somewhat marred by director David Lynch's oversentimental approach. Hurt is superb as the apparent freak who simply wants acceptance as a man and Lynch does at least paint a convincing portrait of Victorian society. Fine support from Anthony Hopkins and Anne Bancroft. (B&W)

Emerald Forest, The
1985 15 109 ★★★ DRA

John Boorman's film provides both a gripping human narrative and a strong ecological message. Based on a true story, it tells of a man (Powers Boothe) who spent ten years trying to recover his son (Charley Boorman, son of the director) from the tribe that had kidnapped him in the Amazon rain forest. A jungle adventure which, unlike *Tarzan*, leaves us with something to think about.

Emily Brontë's Wuthering Heights
1992 PG 102 ★ DRA

'Withering Lows' would be a more accurate title for this woefully bad adaptation. The casting was the first mistake: Ralph Fiennes as Heathcliff and Juliette Binoche as Cathy have as much sex appeal as a pair of snails. The script was the second mistake, messing with the dialogue of Emily Brontë's novel. Making the film was the third. Read the book, it's superb.

Empire of the Sun
1987 PG 146 ★★★ DRA

Steven Spielberg's scrupulous but over-pretty adaptation of J G Ballard's novel about a boy (Christian Bale) who is separated from his parents and learns the art of survival in a Japanese POW camp during the Second World War. John Malkovich is the American prisoner who both helps and uses him. Bale is very good but somehow the film lacks tension and any real sense of danger.

Empire Strikes Back, The
1980 U 120 ★★★★ SCI/FAN

Mark Hamill, Harrison Ford, Carrie Fisher, R2-D2 et al are back again for episode two of the struggle against Darth Vader and the evil Empire. Rousing stuff this, packed with action, derring-do and more than a modicum of laughs. The special effects – which won an Oscar – are maybe even better than they were in *Star Wars*.

Enchanted April
1991 U 89 ★★★ DRA

The kind of British period piece which the Americans love. Four middle-to-upper-class Edwardian women – Miranda Richardson, Joan Plowright, Josie Lawrence and Polly Walker – spend a month in an Italian castle and come to terms with their lives and each other. A very nice little film, beautifully acted and sensitively directed by Mike Newell, who went on to make *Four Weddings and a Funeral.*

End of the Golden Weather, The
1992 PG 99 ★★ DRA

A film whose reach exceeds its grasp. Nostalgic, yes, but not as moving and poignant as it wants to be. In the last idyllic summer before the Second World War a twelve-year-old New Zealand boy, who believes in miracles, befriends a backward neighbour and finds that miracles do happen – though not perhaps as he had expected.

Enemy of the People, An
1977 U 102 ★★ DRA

A curiosity for Steve McQueen fans. His portrayal of Ibsen's scientist, who seeks to expose the dangerous pollution of a town's water supply, was McQueen's one attempt at a classic role. He's a lot better than you might expect, too, as indeed is the film itself. It wasn't popular, though, and he swiftly returned to more familiar screen heroics.

Enemy Within, The
1994 12 86 ★★ MYS/THR

A political thriller in which an American army colonel comes to the conclusion that his own commanding officer is part of a group which plans to overthrow the President. The President is a bit of a pacifist, an attitude that's never popular with the military. Excellent cast includes Forest Whitaker, Sam Waterston and Jason Robards.

Enfants du Paradis, Les
1945 PG 181 ★★★★ FOR

One of the most admired of all French films. Marcel Carné's theatrical extravaganza set in 1840s Paris was made during the German occupation of France in the Second World War. A sumptuous, poetic evocation of an age and of an actress (Arletty) and the four men who love her. Arletty gives us one of the great romantic heroines of the cinema. (Subtitled; B&W)

Englishman Abroad, An
1985 PG 61 ★★★★ DRA

If you missed this on the box, get it now and give yourself a treat. It's Alan Bennett's witty, poignant account of how the actress Coral Browne (here playing herself) met the traitor Guy Burgess (Alan Bates) in Moscow and found herself doing his shopping in London. It's a perfect miniature, superb in every department, with not a second wasted.

Erik the Viking
1989 15 89 ★★ COM

It's the supporting cast (Eartha Kitt, John Cleese and Mickey Rooney among others) that catches the eye and this tells you all you need to know about Terry Jones's vaguely Pythonesque story of a Viking (Tim Robbins) who sets out to find the home of the gods. Funny in parts, very flat in others and at times seems a great deal longer than it is.

Escape from Alcatraz
1979 15 107 ★★★ ACT/ADV

A not-at-all-bad Clint Eastwood thriller, directed by Don Siegel and based on fact, about the only man who ever escaped from the notorious prison and was never seen again. Patrick McGoohan scores as the warden and

Danny Glover makes his screen debut, but it's Eastwood who holds everything together. Pretty violent in places.

ET The Extra-Terrestrial
1982 U 110 ★★★★★ FAM

Until *Jurassic Park* came along this was the biggest-grossing film in cinema history – deservedly so. Steven Spielberg's tale of an ugly little extra-terrestrial, stranded on Earth and befriended by a small boy (Henry Thomas), provides the yardstick against which every other fantasy movie must be measured. Warm, moving, never overly sentimental, and see how menace is depicted not by guns but by keys.

Eversmile, New Jersey
1989 PG 87 ★★ COM

A Daniel Day-Lewis movie which kind of crept out on video, never a good augury. He plays an Irish dentist motor-cycling across Patagonia and fixing people's teeth, free, on the way. Complications, trouble – and romance – ensue when he meets a feisty runaway, Mirjana Jokovic.

Everybody's Fine
1990 PG 121 ★★ FOR

An elderly Sicilian, Marcello Mastroianni, travels to the mainland to see his five children and becomes caught up in their respective problems. The darker side of nostalgia as Mastroianni's dreams for his offspring are dashed by reality. Made by Giuseppe Tornatore, who also directed *Cinema Paradiso*, but without the flair of the earlier film. (Subtitled)

Everybody Wins
1990 15 93 ★★ MYS/THR

No they don't, not really. Arthur Miller's first screenplay for nearly thirty years – a story of corruption and intrigue in a small New England town – tries hard to be significant and ends up being simply confusing, slightly pretentious and a touch dull. Nick Nolte stars

as the private eye called in to investigate by an enigmatic prostitute, Debra Winger.

Every Which Way but Loose
1978 15 110 ★★ COM

Lots of brawling, chases and knockabout fun – some, but not enough, laughs, too – as a dumb prizefighter, Clint Eastwood, wins an orangutan and takes it with him as he seeks, and tries to win, Country and Western singer Sondra Locke. For Eastwood a deliberate, but not necessarily wise, change of pace. The ape is good, though.

Evil under the Sun
1982 PG 111 ★★ MYS/THR

Peter Ustinov as Hercule Poirot again, here investigating murder at an Adriatic hotel run by Maggie Smith. Diana Rigg is the bitchy, irritating actress whom all the guests want to kill. Agatha Christie's quiet, English seaside story becomes gaudy and over-flamboyant in this version but it passes the time agreeably enough.

Excalibur
1981 15 135 ★★★ ACT/ADV

John Boorman's lavish, surprising, rather eccentric version of the Arthurian legend. It looks terrific and has some splendid moments. Sexually aware and sometimes pretty sexy, too, especially in the scenes between Cherie Lunghi, as Guinevere, and Nicholas Clay, as Lancelot. A very good cast also features Nicol Williamson as an offbeat but impressive Merlin.

Eye of the Needle
1981 15 108 ★★★ ACT/ADV

Donald Sutherland as a Nazi agent washed ashore on a remote island and desperate to get vital information back to his masters in Germany. Kate Nelligan is the local housewife who dallies briefly with him. An appreciable amount of suspense and menace in a crisp tale, nicely directed by Richard Marquand.

Fabulous Baker Boys, The
1989 15 109 ★★★ DRA

Overly plotted drama about a cabaret act incorporating two brothers – played by real-life brothers Beau and Jeff Bridges – who take on a female singer (Michelle Pfeiffer) and find their lives are turned around. The relationships are examined in depth and Pfeiffer's rendition of 'Makin' Whoopee' while wearing a dress so tight it must have been sprayed on is memorable.

Falcon and the Snowman, The
1985 15 126 ★★★ DRA

John Schlesinger creates taut atmosphere in this astounding account of a true story. In the late 1970s a couple of wealthy Americans boys (Sean Penn and Timothy Hutton) were convicted of selling state secrets to the Russians. With the help of two fine performances – Penn's in particular – the movie examines why.

Fallen Angels
1993 15 108 (x2) ★★ DRA

These are made-for-TV movies in which faces better known for appearing in front of the camera – Toms Cruise and Hanks among them – walk round the back to try their hand at directing, with various degrees of success. There are three short films on each of the two tapes, stories of crime and redemption for the most part, but they're a mixed bag of offerings.

Fall of the Roman Empire, The
1964 U 172 ★★★ DRA

Magnificent account of the declining days of the Roman Empire, examined from a number of perspectives including those of Alec Guinness as Marcus Aurelius and James Mason as a freed slave. A little earnest in parts, but seriously made and with a cast that ranges from Sophia Loren to Stephen Boyd and Omar Sharif. The set pieces are exquisite; only the script is occasionally found wanting. Good history lesson for the young.

Fame
1980 15 128 ★★★ MUS

Energetic musical with a great score that follows the hopes, aspirations and varying fortunes of a group of wannabes at the New York High School for the Performing Arts. Alan Parker keeps a tight grip on the enthusiastic and talented young cast headed by virtual unknowns Irene Cara, Laura Dean, Lee Curreri and Paul McCrane. The long-running TV series followed but don't let its sentimentality put you off this movie which, thanks to Parker's touch, has bite.

Family Business
1989 15 110 ★★ MYS/THR

This story about three generations of men – two immoral, one as straight as a die – who plan one last big criminal heist is dream casting for any red-blooded female. Sean Connery is the granddaddy who has consistently led a life of crime, Dustin Hoffman the daddy, as honest as the day is long, and Matthew Broderick the young catalyst who's attracted by his grandfather's lifestyle. It would have been very good if as much care had gone into the script as into the casting.

Family Way, The
1966 15 110 ★★★ COM

A tidy British tale of newlyweds, Hayley Mills and Hywel Bennett, whose marriage has yet to be consummated, mainly due to the fact that they're still living with his parents (John Mills and Marjorie Rhodes). The Boulting brothers produced and directed; and Paul McCartney provided the score. Enjoyable and light; sex was handled much more discreetly in those days.

Fanny and Alexander
1982 15 163/138 ★★★ FOR

Ingmar Bergman's last film as a director ranks alongside some of his best. It's a lavish (often autobiographical) family saga which follows the fate and fortunes of two children in Sweden during the early part of the century. It deservedly won the Oscar for Best Foreign Film when it was cut to 188 minutes. That version is not available in Britain yet. What we are offered is the original TV series in two parts. (Subtitled)

Fantasia
1940 U 114 ★★★★ FAM

Owing to the Disney Studio's policy of releasing their most popular films on video only for a certain length of time this is not that easy to get hold of, but, if you can, do. Children, adults and oldies adore it, which, considering it's a superb sequence of animated films set to popular pieces of classical music, isn't surprising. Vibrant colours, amusing choreography and a smashing score make this nothing short of a masterpiece.

Fantastic Voyage
1966 U 96 ★★★ SCI/FAN

A lot of fun is to be had in this scientific romp which involves a medical team, including Raquel Welch, being reduced to microscopic size and injected into the bloodstream of a sick doctor in order to save his life. (Does memory play tricks or did Welch, navigating a main artery, really say, 'I never thought it would be like this'?) In its day the special effects were state of the art; now they're pretty standard but the action and story remain impressive. Fine family fare.

Far and Away
1992 15 134 ★★ DRA

Far and away the worst film Tom Cruise has yet made. He's a poor 'Oirish' lad who, accompanied by the local squire's stuck-up daughter, Nicole Kidman, heads for the promise of a better life in America. The story begins with the Ascendancy in nineteenth-century Ireland and ends with the Oklahoma land rush, but very little of it is convincing. Most curiously, there's precious little romantic chemistry between Mr and Mrs Cruise.

Farewell, My Concubine
1993 15 151 ★★★★ FOR

Melodramatic but powerful account of two male Peking opera stars (one who played the emperor, the other his concubine) and their dramatically varying fortunes between 1920 and the 1970s as China goes through the Japanese invasion, the Long March, Communist domination, the Cultural Revolution and so on. Chen Kaige's film is absorbing, moving and spectacular to look upon. What's more, as a lesson in Oriental history, it beats the stuffing out of a classroom. Contains some violence. (Subtitled)

Far from Home: The Adventures of Yellow Dog
1995 U 77 ★★ FAM

When a young lad (Jesse Bradford) and his faithful dog are washed overboard during a stormy boat trip, all the boy's powers of survival are called in to play as he faces the hostile wastes of the North Pacific in an attempt to get home. Mimi Rogers and Bruce Davison are the parents desperate for news of their missing son. There have been better one-boy-and-his-dog tales, but this is generally pleasing and offers some useful tips for the stranded.

Far from the Madding Crowd
1967 U 156 ★★★ DRA

Julie Christie is the heroine of Thomas Hardy's story – a beautiful country girl who wreaks havoc with the lives of three men (Alan Bates, a shepherd, Terence Stamp, a soldier, and Peter Finch, the local squire). Nicolas Roeg's breathtaking photography complements John Schlesinger's artful direction. It's a leisurely, painstaking film in which Finch's performance is outstanding.

Fatal Instinct
1993 15 86 ★★ COM

Armand Assante, that smouldering Latino, heads the cast of a hit-and-miss spoof. Carl Reiner attempts to do to *Basic Instinct* and *Fatal Attraction* what *Airplane!* did to the *Airport* movies. It's certainly not of that calibre but there are funny moments, most of them involving Kate Nelligan and Sherilyn Fenn.

Fatal Vision
1984 15 177 ★★ MYS/THR

Made-for-TV movie which exploits true life tragedy by somehow glamorizing it. This is a straightforward account of an American army doctor, to all intents and purposes a well-rounded guy, who is accused of murdering his wife and young daughters. As the father-in-law seeking justice against the man, Karl Malden is excellent. The film packs a disturbing punch so don't let the nippers near it.

Father Goose
1964 U 112 ★★★ COM

Cary Grant plays the boozy guardian of a South Sea island during the Second World War – a plane-spotter for the Australian navy – whose tropical idyll is ruined by the arrival of a troupe of shipwrecked schoolgirls under the supervision of Leslie Caron, and the impending arrival of the Japanese. Grant is at his most charming in this, his penultimate film. An engaging piece of entertainment, ideal for a slurpy Sunday.

Father of the Bride
1950 U 89 ★★★★ COM

Spencer Tracy experiences every father's nightmare as his cherished little girl, Elizabeth Taylor, turns into a woman and plans to marry. A small wedding turns into a huge affair and the entire family begins to buckle under the strain. All the characters are likeable and believable and you sympathize with every one of them, though most of all with the splendid Tracy. (B&W)

Father of the Bride
1991 PG 104 ★★ COM

The dictum 'If it ain't broke, don't fix it' applies to this unnecessary remake, which tends more towards the slapstick than the romantically comic and is much broader than the earlier movie. Steve Martin plays the father, Diane Keaton his wife, Kimberly Williams the bride and a new character is introduced – the wedding caterer, played by Martin Short. Short is very funny but there's not enough of him and the rest of the film lacks charm. Try to get the original version.

Fearless
1993 15 117 ★★★★ DRA

A haunting story about the survivors of an aeroplane crash who help each other through the trauma of returning to everyday life. Jeff Bridges is superb as a man who, now believing himself virtually immortal, finds he can no longer identify with his wife (Isabella Rossellini) and his child. Rosie Perez is very good, too, as the mother whose only child died in the crash and threatens to crack up under the grief and guilt. The relationship between the two survivors is sensitively developed under Peter Weir's thoughtful direction.

FernGully, the Last Rainforest
1992 U 73 ★★★ FAM

Delightful animated tale (not Disney) which is as green as they come, condemning the destruction of the rain forest. Robin Williams, Christian Slater and Samantha Mathis are among the voices of the wood-dwelling folk who must fight for their lives against the lumberjacks. Great ecology lesson for the little 'uns since the message is strongly leavened by humour. Williams is hilarious as a crazy bat.

Few Good Men, A
1992 15 132 ★★★★ DRA

Also known as 'A Few Big Names' since it stars Tom Cruise, Jack Nicholson, Demi Moore (though her role would have been better edited out) and Kevin Bacon. A cocky naval lawyer (Cruise) finds he's fighting the case of his life when he is brought in to defend two marines accused of murder. In the opposing corner are the prosecutor (Bacon) and – as the chief witness – the marine colonel (Nicholson). Scintillating stuff. Moore, by the way, provides little more than an ample bosom and a tight shirt.

Fiddler on the Roof
1971 U 171 ★★ MUS

'If I Were a Rich Man' is just one of the smashing numbers featured in this musical story about an eastern European Jew (Topol) trying to maintain his family, friends and traditions despite the changes taking place around him. Young children may get bored since its length could be off-putting to the fidgety.

Field, The
1990 15 106 ★★ DRA

A curate's egg of a film. In parts, the drama works very well: it's moving, evocative and touching; in others it goes hurtling off the rails into melodrama as director Jim Sheridan loses control of the tale of an Irish peasant's obsession with a piece of land. Richard Harris plays the peasant like an Irish King Lear (King O'Leary?) Tom Berenger provides a cameo as an American who wants Harris's field. Interesting but bleak and somewhat violent towards the end.

Field of Dreams
1989 PG 101 ★★★★★ DRA

If you're feeling down, pick up this film because it's guaranteed to make you believe that all's right with the world again. Kevin Costner is delightful as an Iowa farmer who turns a field into a baseball diamond after a mysterious voice tells him: 'If you build it, he will come'. But who will come? The ghosts of late, great baseball players, yes, but also others, far more significant. Ideal for everyone who believes you should be true to your dreams.

Fille de l'Air, La
1993 15 102 ★★★ FOR

The astonishing, and true, story of a French woman (Beatrice Dalle) who risked losing her children to bust the man she loved (an armed robber played by Thierry Fortineau) from prison. To pull off the jailbreak she even took flying lessons. Maroun Bagdadi's film tells the whole story. There is some violence here – a lot of it caused by the French police when they burst into Fortineau's home. (Subtitled)

Filofax
1990 15 103 ★★ COM

The pairing of James Belushi and Charles Grodin is a good one but, as so often happens, the script doesn't match up to the cast. Grodin is a businessman whose life simply collapses when he loses his Filofax. Belushi is the escaped convict who finds it and begins to live. When the two men get together it is, of course, Belushi who gives lessons in living to the uptight executive. Funny at times but not often enough.

Final Analysis
1992 15 119 ★★★ MYS/THR

Tissues out again, this time to wipe the sweat off your brow, for this psychological thriller has more twists than a corkscrew. The casting's good too, with Richard Gere as a psychoanalyst treating Uma Thurman but getting romantically involved with her big sister (Kim Basinger). Politically incorrect since the overall message seems to be: never trust a woman. So yes, it was obviously written by a man (Wesley Strick).

Firefox
1982 15 119 ★★ ACT/ADV

Stick to the Westerns and the thrillers, Clint. Eastwood directs and stars in this utterly implausible Cold War yarn as an all-action US pilot despatched behind Moscow lines to steal the latest in Russian war planes. The plotting is too dull and laborious for the action sequences to provide adequate compensation. Some violence (inevitable with Eastwood) but not too much.

Fire in the Sky
1993 15 104 ★★ SCI/FAN

If you believe in UFOs then this is the stuff for you; otherwise it might strike you as mind-bogglingly daft. It recounts the supposedly true abduction by aliens of an American lumberjack (played by D B Sweeney), who is wafted to their spaceship and studied and experimented upon. James Garner provides welcome relief as a sceptical marshal. Only those who regularly see Elvis in the local supermarket will love it.

Firm, The
1993 15 148 ★★★ MYS/THR

Have your wits about you for this clever but complicated thriller adapted from a novel by John Grisham. Newly qualified lawyer Tom Cruise lands what seems to be the ideal job in the ideal firm of attorneys, only to face a moral and life-threatening dilemma when he uncovers his employers' dark secret. Gene Hackman is great as a fellow lawyer and there's strong support from Holly Hunter and Gary Busey. Too long and a touch self-indulgent but intriguing nevertheless.

First Great Train Robbery, The
1978 15 106 ★★★ ACT/ADV

Jurassic Park author Michael Crichton wrote and directed this fast-moving tale about a planned robbery from a moving train. What gives it added interest is that it's set in England in the 1850s (so don't expect to find Buster Edwards cropping up). Dramatic weight is added to the tale by the casting of Sean Connery and Donald Sutherland as the leading train robbers. Lesley-Anne Down provides the love interest.

First of the Few, The
1942 U 114 ★★★ WAR

A stirring biopic about R J Mitchell, the man and his life and how he invented the Spitfire, the plane that won the Battle of Britain. Leslie Howard directs and stars with David Niven as his friend and test pilot. Rosamund John plays Mitchell's wife. It's fascinating material, nicely played and offering nostalgic glimpses of wartime Britain. (B&W)

Fish Called Wanda, A
1988 15 103 ★★★★ COM

Dog lovers be warned. Certain parts of this film contain some wince-making material; for everyone else it's hilarious. John Cleese wrote and also stars as a stuffy British lawyer seduced by an American thief, Jamie Lee Curtis, to help her find the key to the booty. Michael Palin, as the stuttering, fish-loving, accidental dog-killer and Kevin Kline, who won an Oscar as Curtis's homicidal ignoramus lover, run off with the best gags, though all the cast are brilliant. A little sexy in places.

Fisher King, The
1991 15 132 ★★★ DRA

There's something for everybody in this offbeat, part-drama, part-comedy with a bit of magic and fantasy thrown in. A New York tramp (Robin Williams) rescues a once-successful DJ (Jeff Bridges) from despair following a personal tragedy. Mercedes Ruehl and Amanda Plummer are superb in supporting roles as the two men help each other to salvation. Lavishly shot and splendidly directed by Terry Gilliam.

Fistful of Dollars, A
1964 15 96 ★★★ WES

This was the first of the 'spaghetti' Westerns and remains one of the best. Clint Eastwood rides into town as the gunfighter with no name and finds himself in the middle of a feud. Sergio Leone's direction keeps the action flowing and the suspense taut. This movie (adapted from Kurosawa's *Yojimbo*) made Eastwood an international star. A lot of gunfights and violence, though.

Fitzcarraldo
1982 PG 150 ★★★ FOR

Obsession marks this intriguing Werner Herzog film in which a deeply eccentric Irishman (Klaus Kinski) drags his boat across a hill in the Peruvian jungle to the Amazon in order to bring opera to the native inhabitants. It's grippingly watchable and is based on fact. The man who actually did this mad deed was called Fitzgerald; Fitzcarraldo was the Peruvian corruption of his name. (Subtitled)

Flash, The
1990 PG 90 ★★★ SCI/FAN

If you like your heros in luminous Lycra, with more daring and dash than James Bond, you'll love this comic book he-man who never obtained the legendary status of Superman nor Batman nor, come to that, Spiderman. But he's just as brave and his adventures just as predictable. Wholesome stuff, starring John Wesley Shipp and Amanda Pays and followed by *The Flash 2: Revenge of the Trickster* and *The Flash 3: Deadly Nightshade* (both PG), being two more occasions for Flash to save Central City from the villains. Family entertainment, yes, but with that PG proviso indicating that things might get a little too rough and ready for the younger element.

Flashdance
1983 15 90 ★★ MUS

This thin story about a female welder (Jennifer Beals) who longs to make it as a dancer is stretched to breaking point. But then the hoofing and the soundtrack (including 'What a Feeling') are the real stars of the show. If you are a *Dirty Dancing* fan this is right up your street.

Flash Gordon
1980 PG 106 ★★ SCI/FAN

Another comic-book hero whose tailor has a thing for Lycra. This time the real stars are the special effects and the supporting cast: Brian Blessed, Max Von Sydow, Timothy Dalton and a suitably camp score by Queen. Children will love it, adults may not. Ornella Muti makes a fine villainess and Flash himself is played by Sam J Jones, of whom little has been heard since.

Flatliners
1990 15 109 ★★ HOR

An imaginative tale about the afterlife never delivers what it promises since the characters, though interesting, spend too much time soul-searching and not enough experimenting. Five medical students experience life after death by scientifically 'killing' and, as it were, resurrecting one another. Julia Roberts, Kiefer Sutherland, Kevin Bacon, William Baldwin and Oliver Platt star. Dark stuff, not to be watched when at a low ebb.

Flight of the Navigator
1986 U 85 ★★ FAM

Appealing and imaginative sci-fi adventure in which a twelve-year-old boy (Joey Cramer) is captured by aliens sent to study earth and is returned, to the general astonishment of those at home, several years later but not a day older. How he fits in to a world that has moved on provides the basis for the subsequent action and indeed for the kind of fun that twelve-year-olds and younger will particularly enjoy. Smart special effects are complemented by cute characters, including a robot voiced by Pee-Wee Herman.

Flintstones, The
1994 U 87 ★★ FAM

An expensive attempt to re-create those Stone Age cartoon characters in the flesh for the big screen. The casting is superb – John Goodman was born to play Fred Flintstone, as was Rick Moranis to be Barney Rubble – but the script, cobbled together by over thirty writers, is abysmal. 'Gravel' would be nearer the mark. The film earns its two stars only for its look, design and costume.

Flipper
1963 U 86 ★★★ FAM

Everybody born in the sixties grew up thinking all dolphins were Flipper and wishing they had a friend like him. The story, which later became a TV series, is about a young American lad who befriends and tames a dolphin. Typical family fare which the kids are bound to love. You may need to be on hand to do some comforting in the more anxious moments.

Flirting
1989 15 95 ★★ DRA

Should keep the teenagers quiet for a while since it's all about pubescent angst, emotions and acne. Marks an early appearance by young Nicole Kidman, too. Two Aussie single-sex schools stand close to one another – anyone could have told the authorities this was asking for trouble. The pupils meet regularly (sometimes surreptitiously) for school dances. The story takes a long time to say little.

Fog, The
1980 15 86 ★★ HOR

A horror story from John Carpenter which is more creepy than scary. Ghosts drift in on the sea mists to terrorize a small fishing village in California. Among those frightened witless are Jamie Lee Curtis and her real-life mummy, Janet Leigh (best known for being murdered while taking a shower at Norman Bates's motel).

Folks!
1992 15 104 ★ COM

What's so funny about senility? You may well ask and this film won't tell you, since there are few laughs to be had as Tom Selleck returns to the family fold to care for his father, Don Ameche, who is suffering from Alzheimer's disease. The joke's supposed to be that, thanks to a chapter of accidents, Selleck is the one who spends most time in hospital, but it's a pretty thin joke. The film's heart is actually in the right place but, in its attempts to be sympathetic, it just ends up being patronising.

Footloose
1984 15 100 ★★ MUS

Kevin Bacon's the best thing in what amounts to a very slight story. He plays a dancer from the big city who finds himself in a community where the local preacher has banned rock 'n' roll (some may think this not such a bad thing) and even dancing. Bacon wants to show the locals what they're missing but his plans are complicated by his attraction to the preacher's daughter. Ably co-starring are John Lithgow, Dianne Wiest, Lori Singer and Chris Penn.

For a Few Dollars More
1966 15 127 ★★★ WES

Pasta anyone? This is Sergio Leone's 'spaghetti' Western sequel to *A Fistful of Dollars*. Clint's back as the man with no name on the trail of Mexican bandits. Lee Van Cleef plays a fellow bounty hunter and Klaus Kinski makes an exceptional baddy. A very good film of its kind. Inevitably there's plenty of gun play and associated violence.

Forbidden Planet
1956 U 94 ★★★ SCI/FAN

Family entertainment, really. This is a very intelligent piece of science-fiction in which an astronaut lands on the planet Altair-4 in the twenty-third century and encounters the sole survivors of an earlier space voyage – a scientist, his daughter and their robot. And they don't welcome the newcomer's intrusion. Very soon you realise that this is an ingenious version of Shakespeare's *The Tempest*. Excellent performances by Walter Pidgeon, Anne Francis and Leslie Nielsen among others.

Forever Young
1992 PG 97 ★★★ DRA

A fine opportunity for a wallow in old-fashioned romance. Mel Gibson plays a pilot who, in 1939, volunteers for cryogenics (freezing) when his fiancée is seriously injured in an accident. Some fifty years later he is defrosted and finds himself being looked after by Jamie Lee Curtis and her son, Elijah Wood. He's a fish out of water until the unexpected happens and… well, it's a lot of nonsense really but it gets the happy tears flowing.

For Queen and Country
1988 15 101 ★★ DRA

Thatcher's Britain is the target of this moving tale of a black paratrooper's struggle for survival in a thankless country after his demobilization from the British army. Denzel Washington does a superb job (give or take a curious London accent) as the soldier who finds the country he defended doesn't want him and virtually drives him to crime. Pretty grim and tough in places.

Forrest Gump
1994 12 136 ★★★★ DRA

This story of a simpleton, Tom Hanks, who somehow manages to be brilliant at everything, from football and ping-pong to war heroism and money-making, yet remain unaffected by it all, touched a special chord in the heart of America. Delightful acting from all concerned, including Gary Sinise as Gump's great friend and Robin Wright as the object of his affections. The special effects, in particular, are amazing, from the – as it seems literally – legless Sinise to scenes in which Forrest meets presidents Kennedy, Johnson and Nixon. The film won six Oscars but you would have to be an American to believe it deserved quite so many.

Fort Apache
1948 U 122 ★★★ WES

An interesting piece of casting has Henry Fonda as a stubborn US cavalry colonel at loggerheads with his subordinate, John Wayne, over the best way to tackle the menace of the warring Apaches. It all builds up to some stirring action. In this, the first of director John Ford's 'cavalry trilogy' (the others were *She Wore a Yellow Ribbon* and *The Horse Soldiers)*, Shirley Temple makes a rare grown-up appearance in a romantic role. (B&W)

For the Boys
1991 15 139 ★★ DRA

'Melodrama with the odd song thrown in' best describes this overlong story of the fate, fortune, friendship and love of Bette Midler and James Caan as they sing and dance their way through three major wars to entertain American troops. The sentiment is laid on with a trowel, as is the make-up which, as time goes by, gives the impression that the duo didn't so much age as get caught in the fall-out of an explosion at a talcum powder mine.

Fortress
1993 15 92 ★★ DRA

Futuristic prison dramas by their very nature tend to be bleak affairs but this is almost boring. Christopher Lambert fails to master the acting bit as he plays a convict planning to break out from an escape-proof jail. The only problem is that he wants to take his wife with him and she's in the same prison. Some interesting ideas, though few are fully explored.

Fortune Cookie, The
1966 U 121 ★★★ COM

This was the first time director Billy Wilder brought together Jack Lemmon and Walter Matthau. The result was an Oscar for Matthau as a devious lawyer who persuades Lemmon, a TV cameraman injured at a football game, to sue for a fortune. A perfectly amoral tale with a witty, spiky script from Wilder and I A L Diamond and lovely performances from the two stars. (B&W)

42nd Street
1933 U 86 ★★★★ MUS

The archetypal backstage musical, the one that showed the way for all its successors. Bebe Daniels is the leading lady who can't go on because of injury, Ruby Keeler the understudy who replaces her with instructions to 'come back a star.' Warner Baxter co-stars and there's even an early appearance by Ginger Rogers thrown in. Toes just can't help tapping along to the title tune or 'Shuffle Off to Buffalo'. And for good measure the choreography was provided by the peerless Busby Berkeley. (B&W)

For Your Eyes Only
1981 PG 122 ★★★ ACT/ADV

Roger Moore fans reckon this to be among the best of the Bond movies. A lot of the technical gimmicks are gone, to be replaced by good old-fashioned adventure and action. James and the KGB are both after an anti-nuclear device. Guess who gets it first. Carole Bouquet makes a spicy Bond girl, Topol has a strong supporting role and Charles Dance plays a gunman, but you'll have to keep your eyes peeled to spot him.

Foul Play
1978 PG 111 ★★ COM

Cute – a little too much so – romp in which Goldie Hawn unwittingly finds herself privy to a plot to kill the Pope and nobody will believe her except investigating detective Chevy Chase. But since he has fallen in love with her, nobody's much inclined to believe him either. Dudley Moore and Burgess Meredith lend a

comic hand. It was funny enough to spawn a short-lived TV series.

Four Feathers, The
1939 U 109 ★★★★ ACT/ADV

Upper lips are so stiff they might have been starched in Zoltan Korda's lavish adaptation of A E W Mason's adventure yarn. John Clements plays the soldier who determines to prove himself after being unfairly branded a coward by his friends and colleagues, Ralph Richardson and Clements's fiancée, June Duprez, among them. Cracking, understated, heroic stuff which everyone should enjoy.

Four Feathers, The
1977 U 100 ★★★ ACT/ADV

It took five remakes before they came up with one that could nearly match the original. This is an enjoyable romp, faithful to the book, which casts Beau Bridges as the soldier receiving feathers from colleagues Robert Powell and Simon Ward and girlfriend Jane Seymour. If you can't find the original film this is a pretty good substitute.

Four Seasons, The
1981 15 103 ★★★ DRA

Alan Alda wrote, directed and stars in a clever and moving tale about friendship. It concentrates on the changing relationships between three couples who holiday together over the four seasons. A great deal of warm humour in the script is enhanced by the casting, particularly of Carol Burnett and Rita Moreno. A TV series followed.

1492: Conquest of Paradise
1992 15 149 ★★ DRA

Looks aren't everything, which is perhaps something director Ridley Scott should have borne in mind while making this mammoth biopic about Christopher Columbus (Gérard Depardieu) before and after he discovered the Americas. It's lovely to look at and has a great cast (Sigourney Weaver as the Spanish Queen is splendid as, of course, is Depardieu), but it's far too long and self-indulgent.

Four Weddings and a Funeral
1994 15 113 ★★★★ COM

The most successful British film ever sees Hugh Grant as a bachelor whose entire summer is spent attending weddings where he meets attractive American Andie MacDowell and immediately falls in love. Trouble is, each time they meet either he's attached or she is. A great script by Richard Curtis and fine support from the likes of Simon Callow, Rowan Atkinson and especially Kristin Scott Thomas make this a delightful romantic confection.

Frances
1982 15 134 ★★★ DRA

Not to be confused with *Francis* – a movie about a talking mule – this is a harrowing account of the tragic life of 1930s movie star Frances Farmer (impeccably played by Jessica Lange). She was a girl who appeared to have everything but who cracked and ended up in a mental asylum. This, therefore, is not a jolly film, so anyone who likes happy endings should steer well clear. Worth watching for the power of Lange's performance, though.

Frankie and Johnny
1991 15 113 ★★ DRA

A café in downtown New York is a tidy microcosm of the world. Here lonely spinster waitress Michelle Pfeiffer is courted by the outgoing short-order cook, Al Pacino. Funnily enough this was not as good as it should have been, given the cast. Pacino and Pfeiffer are far too attractive to be lonely and the better performances are by the supporting cast – Hector Elizondo, Nathan Lane and Kate Nelligan. Some very nice moments, though.

Frantic
1988 15 115 ★★★ MYS/THR

An exciting Paris-based thriller with frantic Harrison Ford scouring the streets after his wife (Betty Buckley) mysteriously vanishes. Help takes the shapely form of Emmanuelle Seigner, director Roman Polanski's then real-life girlfriend. Gripping action and not a bad thriller, though the unchivalrous might wonder why Ford keeps looking for Buckley when the dazzling Seigner is so keen on him.

Frauds
1992 15 90 ★ COM

A rather thin comedy, set in Australia, about insurance fraud and blackmail is notable for starring Phil Collins. The singer does a good job, but the film – which deals with extortion and vengeance, attack and counter-attack – doesn't really do him justice and the humour is too broad and frenetic. (The director, Stephan Elliott, went on to make *The Adventures of Priscilla, Queen of the Desert*, which is much better.)

Freddie As FRO7
1992 U 87 ★★ FAM

A novel animated idea about a frog investigator – not any old frog investigator either because this one was once a prince. Famous bits of Britain's heritage have gone missing and Freddie has to find out how and why. Good animation with voices provided by Equity's best: Nigel Hawthorne, Jenny Agutter, Ben Kingsley, Brian Blessed, Michael Hordern, Prunella Scales, Billie Whitelaw, John Sessions and Jonathan Pryce.

Free Willy
1993 U 107 ★ FAM

Sick bags would be advisable since the sentiment is heaped on in truckloads and the story – of a potentially delinquent boy who finds redemption when he is ordered to help look after a killer whale in a marina – is pretty ludicrous. But the film did incredibly well at the box office. Children in particular seem to love it, especially the climax when the boy (Jason James Richter) hatches a plan to return Willy to the sea.

French Lieutenant's Woman, The
1981 15 119 ★★★ DRA

Double roles for Jeremy Irons and Meryl Streep as contemporary actors playing a nineteenth-century gentleman and his mistress. John Fowles's stirring novel about the love of a Victorian governess for a French officer is beautifully visualized by director Karel Reisz and the performances do justice to a Harold Pinter script which finds parallels between the experiences of the nineteenth and the twentieth century couples.

Freshman, The
1990 PG 98 ★★★★ COM

Quirky, often very funny variation on the
Godfather theme. Matthew Broderick is the
student of the title who gets involved with what
he believes to be a Mafia family, headed by the
mysterious Marlon Brando, and a plot
involving the smuggling of endangered species.
Good support from Maximilian Schell, Bruno
Kirby and Penelope Ann Miller but best of all is
Brando's superb, tongue-(and cotton wool)-in-
cheek reprisal of his Don Corleone role.

Fried Green Tomatoes at the Whistle Stop Café
1991 PG 125 ★★★★ DRA

Put your feet up and sit back for a real treat
with this humorous film about women. Two
stories run parallel – that of the plump,
browbeaten Kathy Bates, who is trying to find
self-esteem, and that which is told to her by
Jessica Tandy. Tandy's tale is of two sparky
young women, who ran the Whistle Stop Café
fifty years ago. Nice to see a film that offers
strong roles to women over 100lb in weight and
thirty years of age.

From Here to Eternity
1953 PG 113 ★★★★ DRA

A fascinating depiction of American army life
in Hawaii just before Pearl Harbor. It won eight
Oscars, including one for Frank Sinatra, though
the unrewarded Burt Lancaster rarely acted
better. A story of personal conflict, retribution,
redemption and love. Deborah Kerr, Ernest
Borgnine and Montgomery Clift are splendid.
The famous Lancaster/Kerr love scene on the
beach is fairly innocuous now but was regarded
as ultra-steamy in its day. (B&W)

From Russia with Love
1963 PG 110 ★★★ ACT/ADV

You can't beat these early Bond films. This was
the second and Sean Connery is the debonair
secret agent who comes up against one of the
all-time great baddies: a blond, psychotic
Robert Shaw (to say nothing of the equally
ruthless Lotte Lenya). Action in abundance and
lots of leggy lovelies to keep James happy.

Front, The
1976 15 91 ★★★ DRA

A rare appearance by Woody Allen in a fairly
straight role in a film written and directed by
other people. In the era of America's
McCarthy-inspired Communist witch-hunt,
Allen plays the man who lends his blameless
name to scripts written by blacklisted writers.
There is comedy and tragedy here, plus fine
performances by Allen and Zero Mostel. (In
fact Mostel, like the director Martin Ritt and
the writer Walter Bernstein, was indeed
blacklisted during that appalling period of
American history.)

Fugitive, The
1993 15 125 ★★★★ ACT/ADV

This action-thriller moves so fast you barely
have time to draw breath between incidents.
Harrison Ford is a bearded doctor who returns
home one night to find his wife has been
murdered. Charged with her homicide he
manages to escape from police custody and is
thenceforth pursued by relentless sheriff
Tommy Lee Jones. Watch it closely from the
very start since the train crash near the
beginning is one of the cinema's great stunts.

Funeral in Berlin
1967 PG 97 ★★ DRA

A sequel to *The Ipcress File* and although the
sixties spy story is a little dated, just to see
Michael Caine back as Harry Palmer is
enjoyable enough. Caine is sent to Berlin to
arrange the defection of a KGB colonel (Oscar
Homolka). A competent, well-plotted thriller
with nicely laconic stuff from Caine and a
richly hammy performance by Homolka. (This
was followed in turn by another sequel, *Billion
Dollar Brain*.)

Funny Face
1957 U 103 ★★★ MUS

A *Pygmalion*-type (and very tuneful) tale about a
fashion photographer (Fred Astaire) who turns a
young bookseller (Audrey Hepburn) into a top
model and socialite. Romance and romantic
complications inevitably follow. The score by
George Gershwin includes "S Wonderful' and
'How Long Has This Been Going On' and
provides Astaire with ample opportunity to do
his stuff as only he ever could.

Funny Girl
1968 U 141 ★★★ MUS

Barbra Streisand made her film debut here (and won an Oscar) as Fanny Brice, the Jewish girl who rose from the chorus to become the star of the Ziegfeld Follies but whose private life was far from funny. William Wyler directed, Omar Sharif provides the romantic interest – the husband Brice won and lost – but it is Streisand and the score by Jule Styne (including 'Don't Rain on My Parade') that linger in the memory.

Funny Lady
1975 PG 132 ★★ MUS

A competent sequel to *Funny Girl* sees Fanny (Streisand again) risen to stardom and falling for and marrying the legendary Broadway showman Billy Rose (James Caan). Romantic and amusing and with some good songs well served by Streisand but the original film had the best of the story.

Funny Thing Happened on the Way to the Forum, A
1966 PG 93 ★★★ COM

This was the film (based on a Broadway musical) that inspired the hugely successful TV series *Up Pompeii!* Here, however, the cunning, conniving slave looking to earn his freedom and a fair bit of loot is played not by Frankie Howerd but by Zero Mostel. It's broad and bawdy and fairly predictable. But it has songs and music by Stephen Sondheim and a supporting cast that includes Phil Silvers, Michael Hordern and the great Buster Keaton.

F/X: Murder by Illusion
1986 15 104 ★★★ ACT/ADV

An imaginative vehicle for lots of special effects (known as FX in the trade) as movie FX man Bryan Brown is hired to fake a Mafia killing, only to discover he's been set up. It's then that the excitement starts as Brown has to use all his ingenuity and specialised skills to save himself. The action moves along at breakneck speed and the thrills spill out like dry ice. Brian Dennehy is fine as the sympathetic cop. Contains some violence, as does the sequel.

F/X 2: The Deadly Art of Illusion
1991 15 104 ★★ ACT/ADV

Not much has changed since the first film. Bryan Brown is again employed to use his FX skills to help the police and again finds himself in no end of trouble. You'd have thought he'd have learned by now but no, he agrees to help catch a particularly nasty killer. Fortunately, Dennehy is back as good as ever to help him out, but the story's pretty thin.

Gallipoli
1981 PG 107 ★★★ WAR

If you want a good idea of how it must have felt to be a front-line soldier during the First World War, watch this marvellous drama by Peter Weir which follows two young Australian recruits, Mel Gibson and Mark Lee, whose youthful optimism is soon banished when they're sent to fight the Turks. The detail is minute and the atmosphere terrifying. Army recruitment figures must plummet every time this film is shown.

Gandhi
1982 PG 180 ★★★★ DRA

Overlong but thorough biopic of the life of the Indian leader, from his humble beginnings as a lawyer through his rise and to his fall. It's a meticulous piece of film-making by director Richard Attenborough and a splendid portrayal of the peace-bringer by Ben Kingsley, but it was – in our opinion – unfairly awarded the Oscars that year, when rightfully they belonged to *ET*, a more ingenious work of art.

Gaslight
1944 PG 110 ★★★ MYS/THR

Typical ironing film this, since it's passed its sell-by date. Charles Boyer plays a creepy man intent on driving his poor wife, Ingrid Bergman, into madness. Joseph Cotten's splendid as the saviour detective as is – pre-*Murder She Wrote* – Angela Lansbury. Ably directed by George Cukor, it's still very watchable but not shocking as it once would have been. (B&W)

Gay Divorcee, The
1934 U 100 ★★ MUS

No, not 'gay' in that sense – please, what are you thinking of? This is Fred Astaire for heaven's sake and Ginger Rogers, too. Nothing gay about them. The plot may be a little off-centre, perhaps, but they fall in love in the end. The Cole Porter score and the dance numbers are the film's main appeal. (B&W)

General, The
1927 U 73 ★★★★ COM

This is one of the all-time classic silent films, by one of the genre's very best: Buster Keaton. He's caught up in the American Civil War, where spies and stolen trains cause all kinds of trouble. Loads of stunts, lashings of slapstick and, if this humour's on your wavelength, you'll have a field day. (B&W; Silent)

Genevieve
1953 U 83 ★★★★ FAM

So often played on TV this meets with as familiar and welcome a viewing as an old family friend. John Gregson and Kenneth More are classic car enthusiasts and every year enter the London to Brighton race. Trouble brews with the women they have on board (Dinah Sheridan and Kay Kendall respectively) since the rivalry spills over beyond the race. Lovely image of how England might once have been.

Gentleman Jim
1942 U 101 ★★★ DRA

The 'Jim' of the title is boxer Jim Corbett (Errol Flynn) – the first world heavyweight champion of the post-bareknuckle era – whose fights, loves and life are depicted here. It's a competent biopic, though despite a good performance it's hard to believe in Flynn as a boxer, since his nose is so beautifully shaped. (B&W)

Gentlemen Prefer Blondes
1953 U 89 ★★★ MUS

And who can blame them when the blonde of the title is Marilyn Monroe? Mind you, the sequel to this light Howard Hawks charmer was entitled *Gentlemen Marry Brunettes*, so you can put down the bleach bottle. Monroe plays the man-eating fortune hunter and Jane Russell her best friend. The women are delightful and so are the songs, especially 'Diamonds Are a Girl's Best Friend'.

Germinal
1993 15 151 ★★ FOR

Remove all sharp objects before watching this since it's a heavy melodrama which could sink the morose into terminal gloom. On the plus side, it's an involving story (adapted from the novel by Emile Zola) about the hardship and exploitation suffered by a nineteenth-century French mining community and stars Gerard Depardieu. It's a well-made film, just a very bleak one. (Subtitled)

Getting Even with Dad
1994 PG 104 ★★ COM

Macaulay Culkin is the estranged son of jewel thief Ted Danson and is dumped on his father's doorstep on the very day his old man has pulled off the robbery of his life. Culkin, to grab his dad's attention, hides the booty, promising to tell where it is once Danson's spent a week doing everything Culkin wants. Not terribly funny since it's far too sentimental but the personable actors keep it ticking along.

Gettysburg
1994 PG 136/107 ★★★ WAR

Overlong but nonetheless absorbing account of the events leading up to and including the bloodiest – and probably most decisive – battle of the American Civil War. Good performances from the likes of Martin Sheen as Robert E Lee and Tom Berenger as the fellow Southern general whose advice Lee refuses to take, with tragic consequences. The beards look as if they were bought from a joke shop. (Available as two tapes.)

Ghost
1990 15 121 ★★★★ COM

Hankies at the ready because only the most sceptical fail to be touched by this corny story about a much-loved boyfriend (Patrick Swayze) who, after he has been murdered, returns to tell his lover (Demi Moore) that she too is in danger. Since she can't see or hear him it takes a medium (Whoopi Goldberg) to translate, and very funny she is too. Don't think too long or hard about it, just enjoy it for what it is – lovely gooey stuff.

Ghost and Mrs Muir, The
1947 U 100 ★★★★ FAM

Perfect piece of whimsy for a lazy afternoon as the widowed Gene Tierney takes herself and daughter to live on the coast in a house haunted by a salty old sea dog (Rex Harrison). Charming cast, fulfilling story and just the sort of film to put your feet up to. (B&W)

Ghostbusters
1984 PG 101 ★★★★ COM

Everyone has their favourite ghost from this movie; we particularly like the green slimer in the library, but he gets his comeuppance fairly early on. A bunch of scientists band together to form their own exorcising empire and great fun they have too as the hilarious Bill Murray leads Dan Aykroyd, Harold Ramis and Ernie Hudson to haunted places and manages to romance client Sigourney Weaver on the way.

Ghostbusters II
1989 PG 108 ★★★ COM

The story's not so good this time round, but then it never was the main appeal of the first. Murray and co are all back on great form, though, this time trying to prevent a city load of evil spirits (and they don't mean rancid whisky) creating havoc on New Year's Eve.

Ghost Goes West, The
1935 U 79 ★★★ COM

When a wealthy American buys a Scottish castle and takes it home with him brick by brick, he also takes along its resident ghost, Robert Donat. If you've got to be haunted, who nicer to do it than this dashing Scot. At least, that's how the daughter of the household feels. Curiosity value is added by the fact that it was made by the great French director René Clair. (B&W)

Giant
1956 PG 193 ★★ DRA

Giant in more ways than one (just look at the length of it). This melodrama is better for its cast than its substance. James Dean, Elizabeth Taylor and even Rock Hudson are outstanding in their portrayal of two generations of a Texas oil dynasty (no JR in sight). Old money versus new with passion, love and rivalry thrown in. The movie has a certain historical interest too, since Dean was killed in a road accident only days after the filming wrapped.

Gigi
1958 PG 111 ★★★ MUS

Lerner and Loewe's musical, set in turn-of-the-century Paris, which features such classic numbers as 'Thank Heaven for Little Girls' and 'The Night They Invented Champagne'. The story takes a back seat to the pretty people and pleasing sounds – a young beauty (Leslie Caron), who is being trained to become a courtesan, shows more interest in marrying the dashing Louis Jourdan. Maurice Chevalier and Hermione Gingold co-star in Vincente Minnelli's delightful film.

Gilda
1946 PG 105 ★★★ DRA

'Put the Blame on Mame' sings Rita Hayworth as the singer and wife of casino owner George Macready. She became as famous for the song as for her slinky (but subtle) sexuality in a plot that plunges her into a dangerous *ménage-à-trois* involving her husband and his right-hand man, Glenn Ford, who is also her former lover. There's a strong sexual frisson between Hayworth and Ford but such matters were handled with more delicacy in those days. (B&W)

Girl Can't Help It, The
1956 U 97 ★★ COM

Jayne Mansfield was billed as the rival to Marilyn Monroe. She was never that good but she's still not at all bad in this gentle, amusing spoof in which her modest ambition to be a simple housewife is confounded by her gangster boyfriend, Edmond O'Brien, who thinks she should be a rock 'n' roll star. Tom Ewell is the seedy agent O'Brien hires to promote her. Anyone who has seen *Born Yesterday* can guess what happens next and who falls in love with whom.

Girls, Les
1957 U 109 ★★★ MUS

A most pleasing musical, set in London, Paris and Spain, wherein Kay Kendall, former member of a song and dance team, writes an autobiography that leads to a libel action. The story of the group – Kendall, Gene Kelly, Mitzi Gaynor and Taina Elg – is told in flashback. Lots of zip, zest and laughs and great songs by Cole Porter.

Gleaming the Cube
1988 PG 99 ★★ MYS/THR

As a gimmicky thriller, this is as daft as they come. A troublesome teenager (Christian Slater) solves a murder – and finds his true self – with the aid of his trusty skateboard and a few friends. If it weren't for some nifty stunts and

the presence of Slater, who's always worth watching, this would not be much recommended. The title, incidentally, refers to a daring stunt done on skateboards.

Glengarry Glen Ross
1992 15 97 ★★★ DRA

When a group of estate agents learns that at least one of them is to lose his job at the end of the week, some of them begin to crack under the pressure. David Mamet's superbly written play has a dark and claustrophobic feel with a depth of character that is done full justice by a great cast. Al Pacino is outstanding but Jack Lemmon, Alan Arkin and Ed Harris are on top form, too, and there's a brilliant cameo by Alec Baldwin.

Glenn Miller Story, The
1954 U 108 ★★★ MUS

James Stewart does a smashing job portraying the band leader who met a tragic and mysterious death over the Channel in the Second World War. June Allyson is very likeable as his wife in a pleasingly affectionate story. The music – twenty or so great Miller numbers – rounds it all off nicely. Perhaps not to be watched if anyone in the family's about to take a plane trip, though.

Gloire de Mon Père, La
1990 U 106 ★★★★ FOR

One half of Marcel Pagnol's early autobiography which is completed in the film *Le Château de Ma Mère*. His childhood in southern France at the turn of the century would seem to have been idyllic. Beautifully shot and charmingly told, this is the better of the two films though they both have much to commend them. (Subtitled)

Gloria
1980 15 116 ★★★ DRA

John Cassavetes directs his wife, Gena Rowlands, in the title role as a former gangster's moll who protects a young Puerto Rican boy (John Adames) from the Mob. The pair go on the run as she plays and beats the Mafia at its own game. Rowlands gives a very assured performance in this, one of the most mainstream and generally accessible of

Cassavetes's films. Some violence, though not too much.

Glory
1989 15 117 ★★★ WAR

This is a much underrated account of the bravery shown by America's first black regiment formed during the country's Civil War. Matthew Broderick and Cary Elwes play the white officers; Denzel Washington and Morgan Freeman are two of the soldiers they recruit. The characterization and performances are every bit as impressive as the grand battle scenes. It loses some of its impact on the small screen but still packs a punch and the climactic battle is chillingly realistic.

Go-Between, The
1971 PG 111 ★★★★ DRA

A marvellously touching evocation of the Edwardian age, of British class distinction and of the impossible difficulties of love between people from different social strata. Harold Pinter wrote and Joseph Losey directed this adaptation of L P Hartley's novel. Dominic Guard is the young boy who secretly carries messages between the aristocratic Julie Christie and Alan Bates, the farmer who loves her. An emotional, intelligent film, beautifully performed by an impeccable cast.

Godfather Part III, The
1990 15 163 ★★★ ACT/ADV

The only one of the trio with less than an 18 certificate but also, alas, the weakest. It's still a very good gangster movie for all that. Al Pacino stars impressively as the elderly Michael Corleone trying, vainly, to break his family's ties with organised crime. Diane Keaton returns as his wife and Andy Garcia gives a standout performance as Pacino's nephew and new right-hand man. But be warned – there's plenty of violence, especially in the grand shoot-out on the steps of an Italian opera house.

Golden Child, The
1986 PG 89 ★ COM

If you're desperate for something to amuse the older children and they like Eddie Murphy, this may just keep them quiet but we're not promising. It's a pretty feeble story about a 'perfect' child with magical powers who is hailed as the Chosen One. Evil Charles Dance kidnaps him for nefarious reasons of his own and only Murphy can save the boy. Dance brings a touch of class but Murphy merely swaggers lazily through his role.

Golden Voyage of Sinbad, The
1974 U 100 ★★★ FAM

As a child's introduction to the *Arabian Nights* this is not at all bad, though reading the stories would be better. Sinbad (John Phillip Law) embarks on a dangerous voyage with the aid of a mysterious map. The journey leads him into peril from evil magicians and strange monsters, the creations of the splendid Ray Harryhausen. Excellent special effects and good support from Tom Baker and Caroline Munro.

Goldfinger
1964 PG 105 ★★★ ACT/ADV

In this, the third Bond film, Sean Connery finds himself doing battle with the evil Oddjob and his boss Goldfinger (Gert Frobe). At stake: the entire American gold reserve in Fort Knox. Luckily 007 has an abundance of clever gadgetry to hand. Watch out for the awful fate that befalls Shirley Eaton and for Honor Blackman who, as Pussy Galore, makes an unusually sassy and noteworthy Bond girl.

Gold Rush, The
1925 U 72 ★★★★★ COM

Maybe the best-loved of all Charlie Chaplin's feature films. This is the one in which he plays the starving gold prospector who, in the torments of hunger, mistakes his boot for a turkey dinner and their laces for spaghetti. It's full of marvellous sight gags – the dance of the bread rolls and the cabin teetering on the edge of a precipice, for example. If you wonder why people call Chaplin a comic genius, this is the film that provides the answer. (B&W; silent)

Gone with the Wind
1939 PG 224 ★★★★★ DRA

Quite simply one of the classics of American cinema – the story of Scarlett O'Hara (Vivien Leigh), her survival during the horrors of the American Civil War and, of course, her passionate relationship with Rhett Butler (Clark

Gable). Almost every young actress from Bette Davis to Lucille Ball wanted the role of Scarlett and now and then a special box set is on sale which includes their screen tests and a film about the making of *Gone with the Wind*. It's worth getting hold of a copy.

Goodbye Girl, The
1977 PG 106 ★★★ COM

A delightful romance about a single mother (Marsha Mason) and the dramatic changes that occur in her life when she and a struggling young actor (Richard Dreyfuss) are obliged to share the same small flat. The humour is gentle and warm with playwright Neil Simon's stamp all over it. It is, if you like, an intelligent feel-good movie, which won an Oscar for Dreyfuss.

Goodbye Mr Chips
1939 U 109 ★★★ DRA

An outstanding portrayal by Robert Donat of a shy, introverted schoolmaster who, having dedicated his life to his pupils, starts to live for himself on meeting Greer Garson. It's a tender, sentimental tale which takes Mr Chips from young manhood to old age and brought Donat an Oscar. Garson, too, won a nomination and overnight success on her screen debut. Gather the family – and a box of tissues – for this one. (B&W)

Good Morning Vietnam
1987 15 116 ★★★ COM

This film should go on a diet. In parts, it's lean, sharp and bitingly funny – but that's at the beginning when Robin Williams gives a virtuoso display as an achingly funny, fast-talking DJ entertaining American troops in Vietnam. After that, however, as the story begins to take the war seriously and, alas, sentimentally, it becomes heavy and plodding. Ideal to watch on video, though, since you can fast forward through the spare tyres and concentrate on Williams's irreverent jokes.

Goonies, The
1985 PG 109 ★★ COM

Vaguely disappointing given that the story was by Steven Spielberg, but that's probably because he didn't direct. Richard Donner (of *Lethal Weapon* fame) did and though he does a competent job, there's little that stands out in this movie about a bunch of teenagers and a gang of crooks in search of the same buried and long-lost treasure. Sean Astin leads a cast that otherwise was unknown then and pretty well remains so now.

Gorillas in the Mist
1988 15 124 ★★★ DRA

The heartbreaking tale of Dian Fossey, who gave her life to save the mountain gorillas of central Africa. It's gloriously shot and well directed by Michael Apted and the portrayal by Sigourney Weaver of a remarkable – though not always likeable – woman whose interest turns into obsession is immaculate. The ending could very well have you in tears, though.

Gorky Park
1983 15 123 ★★★ MYS/THR

Don't be deterred by the rather old-fashioned Cold War/spy thriller subject matter, for this is a gripping mystery. A Russian police detective (William Hurt) is assigned to investigate when three murdered bodies are found in Gorky Park. Keep your wits about you because the numerous twists and turns of the plot call for full attention. Helsinki does a good job doubling for Moscow and Lee Marvin adds to the mystery as an American businessman with remarkable Soviet connections.

Go West: see Marx Brothers

Graduate, The
1967 15 105 ★★★★ DRA

The film that brought stardom to Dustin Hoffman as the college graduate who falls in love with Katharine Ross, having been seduced by her mother, Anne Bancroft. First-class story and first-class acting (with honours) by Hoffman and Bancroft. It's a classic rites of passage saga with humour and warmth, a delightful score by Simon and Garfunkel and, of course, the famous 'Mrs Robinson' song.

Grand Canyon
1991 15 129 ★★★ DRA

Director Lawrence Kasdan here takes a disenchanted look at the horrors and dangers of life in modern Los Angeles. Through accident and mishap various disparate characters – a lawyer, Kevin Kline, a tow-truck driver, Danny Glover, and a movie producer, Steve Martin – are thrown together and help each other cope with the violence, loneliness and social problems of the big city. It's a thought-provoking piece with enough lighter moments to alleviate the seriousness of the subject.

Grand Hotel
1932 U 108 ★★★★ DRA

Perhaps the classic compendium movie, an Oscar-winner which revolves around a Berlin hotel and the heady mixture of guests therein – a ballerina and her lover (Greta Garbo and John Barrymore), a sick man (Lionel Barrymore) and a stenographer (Joan Crawford) among them. The formula has since been copied many times but few imitators have ever matched it for wit, pace and cast. (B&W)

Grapes of Wrath, The
1940 PG 128 ★★★★★ DRA

John Steinbeck's powerful story of the Depression years in America is brought movingly to the screen by John Ford. Henry Fonda stars as Tom Joad, son of a family whose Oklahoma farm has been turned into a dustbowl and who head for California in a desperate search for a better life. Superb photography by Gregg Toland emphasises the poverty and near-despair of the migrants. A great film with a timeless and universal message. (B&W)

Grass Is Greener, The
1960 U 100 ★★ COM

The cast is the best recommendation for this drawing-room farce in which the wealthy and aristocratic Cary Grant and his wife, Deborah Kerr, find their marriage is in trouble with the arrival of American millionaire Robert Mitchum and his old girlfriend, Jean Simmons. Mitchum, you see, sets his cap at Kerr. It's an amusing tale, worth watching if only for the polished cast.

Grease
1978 PG 105 ★★★ MUS

Never mind the story, listen to the songs. Rock 'n' roll classics belt out from every teenage pore

as high-school kids John Travolta and Olivia Newton-John skip their way along the rocky road to romance. 'You're the One That I Want', 'Grease' and 'Summer Nights' are just a few of the toe-tapping ditties that make it such a refreshing delight.

Grease 2
1982 PG 109 ★★ MUS

Sequel to the above in which Maxwell Caulfield replaced John Travolta, though not very successfully. Although it featured a young Michelle Pfeiffer it didn't amount to much.

Great Balls of Fire!
1989 15 102 ★ DRA

The 1950s rocker Jerry Lewis led quite a life! Shame it's not better told here, though Dennis Quaid, thumping out the numbers on the old joanna, does his best. So too does Winona Ryder as the young – very young – object of Lewis's affections, his thirteen-year-old cousin whom he married. Even the star's most ardent fans drew the line at that. A very good rock score doesn't compensate for the film's poor script and weak direction.

Great Escape, The
1963 PG 173 ★★★★★ WAR

Simply one of the best of all Second World War movies, based on the true story of how seventy-six Allied prisoners escaped from a maximum-security German POW camp. Everyone who has seen it remembers Steve McQueen's dash for freedom on a motorbike but there are plenty of other performances to cherish, among them those of James Garner, Richard Attenborough, Charles Bronson and James Coburn.

Greatest Story Ever Told, The
1965 U 191 ★★★ DRA

Originally one of the longest stories ever told when it was first shown at 260 minutes but even the most padded bottom would find this hard going so it was cut. The finished result is the story of Christ, over-solemnly told by director George Stevens and marred by distracting cameos. John Wayne, Telly Savalas, Angela Lansbury, Claude Rains, Sidney Poitier and Charlton Heston all crop up. Max Von Sydow plays Christ.

Great Expectations
1946 PG 113 ★★★★★ DRA

Despite a number of remakes, this remains the best adaptation of Dickens's novel. The direction is safe in the hands of David Lean, while the roles of young Pip and young Herbert Pocket are impeccably handled by John Mills and Alec Guinness, with splendid support from Bernard Miles, Valerie Hobson and Jean Simmons. Only the scary graveyard scene when Pip first encounters Magwitch and the harrowing fire that destroys Miss Havisham can have deprived the film of a U certificate. (B&W)

Great Outdoors, The
1988 PG 86 ★★ COM

A made-to-measure role for the late John Candy who takes his family on a country vacation only to find it ruined by the arrival of his in-laws, Dan Aykroyd and family. The story, by John Hughes, loses its way after a while but Aykroyd and Candy cope well with the farce.

Great St Trinian's Train Robbery, The
1966 U 90 ★★★ COM

The absence of Alastair Sim is deeply regrettable though Frankie Howerd, Dora Bryan and Reg Varney do their best in this, the fourth in the series directed by Frank Launder and Sidney Gilliat. The plot concerns an ingenious gang of train robbers hiding their loot on the new site for the infamous girls' school.

Greedy
1994 12 109 ★ COM

Greedy is what Michael J Fox and Kirk Douglas must have been to take part in a comedy that barely raises a titter but is worth watching for the cast. Long lost nephew Fox is recalled by his family to sweeten wealthy old uncle Douglas and ensure he doesn't leave his fortune to his new young girlfriend, Olivia d'Abo.

Green Card
1990 15 102 ★★★ COM

After a quick marriage of convenience to gain meat-eating, fag-smoking Frenchman Gérard Depardieu the green card which will enable him to work in the USA, he and fastidious vegetarian American Andie MacDowell scuttle off in opposite directions. Problems arise when the suspicious immigration authorities start sniffing around and the couple have to move in together. The blossoming romance between them is delightful and the direction by Peter Weir gives the unlikely tale a certain credibility.

Green Man, The
1957 PG 76 ★★★ COM

One of those cracking English comedies with such old favourites as Alastair Sim, Terry-Thomas and George Cole. The story revolves around a shy clockmaker (Sim) who moonlights as a professional hit man. Complications ensue when he accidentally assassinates a politician. Much blackish comedy as the action revolves in and around the pub of the title. (B&W)

Gremlins
1984 15 102 ★★★ COM

Packed with in-jokes, this is a charmer for the older members of the family. When a cute little furry creature called Gizmo is given to Zach Galligan, he fails to listen to the instructions that come with it: don't let him get wet and on no account feed him after midnight. Galligan does both these things and soon the town is overrun by rampaging, angry little critters. Only Gizmo can save the day. A little too much nastiness and sexual innuendo for younger people.

Gremlins 2: The New Batch
1990 15 102 ★★ COM

As is so often the case with a sequel, the special effects are as good as, if not better than the original but the plot's not up to much. Same cast – Galligan, Phoebe Cates and Gizmo – same story – Gizmo gets wet and nasty Gremlins go on the rampage. A case of been there, done that, but again it should keep the older teenagers amused. Same warning applies as with the original.

Greystoke: The Legend of Tarzan, Lord of the Apes
1984 PG 129 ★★ ACT/ADV

Forget Johnny Weissmuller swinging through the trees in his loin cloth. This is the apeman's story as written by Edgar Rice Burroughs, from Tarzan's abandonment in the jungle to his rescue and return to civilization as Lord Greystoke. Back in the baronial hall he is looked after by elderly relative Ralph Richardson. Andie MacDowell is the romantic interest but the jungle still calls. Christopher Lambert looks fine as the man who grew up in the wilds and the photography is exquisite. Hugh Hudson directed.

Groundhog Day
1993 PG 97 ★★★★ COM

Selfish, egotistical TV weatherman Bill Murray has to live the same day over and over again. Eventually he must get it right and become a better person. Well, that's the objective but can he manage it, especially after the worst side of his personality has had its moments. He gorges himself on junk food, contemplates suicide and robs a security van. Murray's at his best and is ably supported by Andie MacDowell.

Grumpy Old Men
1993 12 99 ★★ COM

A contrived vehicle for Walter Matthau and Jack Lemmon as a couple of warring old neighbours who fall out big time over pretty widow, Ann-Margret. 'Randy Old Men' would be a more accurate title.

Guess Who's Coming to Dinner
1967 PG 103 ★★★★ COM

Scintillating and progressive movie about parental reaction when the daughter (Katharine Houghton) of supposedly liberal Katharine Hepburn and Spencer Tracy brings her black boyfriend (Sidney Poitier) home. He's so educated, intelligent and likeable that they could only object to him on racial grounds. Poignant, since it was to be Tracy's last film. Hepburn won an Oscar; Tracy was nominated.

Guilty as Sin
1993 15 103 ★★ MYS/THR

A good performance by Rebecca De Mornay as a brilliant defence lawyer raises this thriller above the mediocre. Having done her best to defend the charming Don Johnson on a charge of wife murder, she begins to have her doubts as to his innocence, but by then it's too late.

Johnson's OK, the script could be better but the climax might have your palms sweating.

Guilty by Suspicion
1991 15 101 ★★ DRA

Over-wordy look at the Communist witch-hunts that took place in Hollywood during the 1950s. Movie-maker Robert De Niro, returned from Europe, finds himself guilty by association when he refuses to co-operate with the House Un-American Activities Committee. The film casts a chilling sidelight on the infamous McCarthy era in America.

Gunfight at the OK Corral
1957 PG 118 ★★★ WES

Burt Lancaster as Wyatt Earp, Kirk Douglas as Doc Holliday in a very good Western that climaxes, inevitably, with the famous gunfight against the Clanton gang in downtown Tombstone. Both the stars are in top form and director John Sturges handles the material with easy confidence.

Gunga Din
1939 U 112 ★★★ ACT/ADV

Based on a Rudyard Kipling poem but there's little of the original story here. Still, it's a cracking adventure anyway with a first-rate cast to boot. Cary Grant, Douglas Fairbanks Jr and Victor McLaglen play three roguish British soldiers based on India's North-West Frontier during a nineteenth-century native uprising. Sam Jaffe plays the heroic Indian Gunga Din. Lots of humour and dashing blades, great for a lazy afternoon. (B&W)

Guns of Navarone, The
1961 PG 149 ★★★ WAR

Action-packed adventure from start to finish as a crack squad of Hollywood's – and Britain's – finest are sent on a dangerous mission during the Second World War to destroy a German gun battery on a Greek island. First-rate *Boy's Own* adventure stuff featuring the likes of Gregory Peck, David Niven, Stanley Baker, Anthony Quinn and Richard Harris.

Guys and Dolls
1955 U 143 ★★★★ MUS

A delightful Frank Loesser musical featuring
Marlon Brando and Frank Sinatra as slick New
York gamblers. Jean Simmons is the Salvation
Army do-gooder who aims to reform them –
especially Brando. Packed with old favourites
such as 'Luck Be a Lady', 'Sit Down, You're
Rocking the Boat' and 'If I Were a Bell'.
Brando's at his most breathtakingly beautiful.
Oddly enough, he's also given most of the songs
while Sinatra has only a couple to deliver.

Hair
1979 15 116 ★★★ MUS

Nothing much wrong with the film but the timing was out – it was made too late to be topical, too early to have historical curiosity. Based on the stage musical hit of the 1960s about a soldier on his way to Vietnam who stops off to get involved with the flower people, it's well directed by Milos Forman and nicely played by a cast that includes John Savage, Treat Williams and Beverly D'Angelo. The passing of time has now lent it a nostalgic appeal. A warning to those who find the human body offensive – there is a certain amount of nudity.

Hairdresser's Husband, The
1990 15 78 ★★★ FOR

The story of a middle-aged Frenchman, Jean Rochefort, who, since childhood, has been obsessed by hairdressers (female) and Arab music. On impulse he marries a shy *coiffeuse*, Anna Galiena, and moves into her salon, there to lead a married life almost untouched by the world outside. Gently erotic; also both eccentric and charming. (Subtitled)

Hamlet
1948 U 147 ★★★★ DRA

Britain's first great success at the postwar Oscars with awards for Best Film and Best Actor (Laurence Olivier). Olivier's is a marvellous, brooding performance set in an impressive, though stagey, Elsinore. An excellent supporting cast includes the young Jean Simmons as an impressive Ophelia, plus the likes of Stanley Holloway and Peter Cushing. (B&W)

Hamlet
1990 PG 129 ★★★ DRA

If the Olivier version has the edge as far as speaking the verse is concerned – and it does – director Franco Zeffirelli, with the aid of Mel Gibson as an unexpectedly impressive Hamlet, gives a clearer reading of the text. You don't have to know the play to understand this film. Fine support, too, from Paul Scofield, Alan Bates, Glenn Close and Helena Bonham Carter as Ophelia.

Handful of Dust, A
1988 PG 113 ★★★ DRA

An emotional horror story, based on Evelyn Waugh's novel, of an aristocratic couple – James Wilby and Kristin Scott Thomas – whose life is disrupted by grasping, amoral Rupert Graves. Offensive, no; harrowing, certainly. Chilling appearance towards the end by Alec Guinness, but Scott Thomas makes the greatest impact. Directed by Charles Sturridge, who made *Brideshead Revisited*.

Hand That Rocks the Cradle, The
1992 15 106 ★★★★ MYS/THR

Rebecca De Mornay plays the nanny from hell, bent on destroying – for vengeful reasons of her own – the happy family life of Annabella Sciorra and Matt McCoy. Creepy rather than horrific, though the climax does go over the top. But that's usually the way with thrillers these days. Gripping and packed with suspense and De Mornay is chillingly believable.

Hangin' with the Homeboys
1991 15 85 ★ DRA

An ethnic, rites-of-passage tale about two blacks and two Hispanics who leave the Bronx for a bizarre night out in Manhattan. A low-budget picture with a largely unknown cast, it has a tendency to plunge towards the sentimental but the script is often funny and spiky and writer-director Joseph B Vasquez handles the material with confidence.

Hannah and Her Sisters
1986 15 102 ★★★★ COM

One of Woody Allen's very best, which is saying a lot. The story of three sisters – Mia Farrow, Barbara Hershey and Dianne Wiest – and the men, or lack of them, in their lives. For once Allen manages, triumphantly, to meld his desire to be a transatlantic Ingmar Bergman with rich comedy. He himself is hilarious as a hypochondriac TV producer and Michael Caine picked up the Oscar for Best Supporting Actor.

Hanover Street
1979 PG 104 ★★ DRA

Harrison Ford's first film after *Star Wars*. Bit of a mistake, really, though we expect he did it because his role was so different from Han Solo. He plays a bomber pilot stationed in London in the Second World War who, between missions, falls in love with the married Lesley-Anne Down. Pretty soppy stuff, written and directed by Peter Hyams. Christopher Plummer plays Down's husband.

Hans Christian Andersen
1952 U 108 ★★★ FAM

Danny Kaye as the village cobbler who goes out into the wide world and, in between making red shoes for a ballerina, becomes a wondrous spinner of tales for the younger set. The film is gentler than many of Andersen's stories. Kaye is on excellent form and Frank Loesser provided songs – 'The Ugly Duckling', for instance – that have become children's classics.

Happiest Days of Your Life, The
1950 U 78 ★★★★ COM

A ministerial error sends a girls' school to share premises already occupied by a boys' school. Result: chaos, farce and sheer comic delight. Margaret Rutherford and Alastair Sim are the respective head teachers; Joyce Grenfell and Richard Wattis are among their assistants. Beautifully played and directed with great zest by Frank Launder.

Hard Day's Night, A
1964 U 89 ★★★ MUS

This is really *the* Beatles film because nothing else they did was so vivid or original. Well, they weren't really actors – more like phenomena – and this documentary-style musical fantasy provided the ideal showcase for them. Great soundtrack, good comic support from Victor Spinetti, sharp script by Alun Owen and impressive visual flair in Richard Lester's direction. (B&W)

Hard Times
1994 U 102 ★★★★ DRA

Outstanding made-for-TV production of the Dickens classic, with Alan Bates, Richard E Grant and Bob Peck. Young literature students could do a lot worse than watch this; it's bound to whet their appetite for reading more of the great man's works.

Hard Way, The
1991 15 106 ★★★ MYS/THR

Michael J Fox as a grossly spoilt movie star who sets out to research his next role by pulling strings and getting himself an attachment as partner to a tough and hostile cop, James Woods. What happens, as they stumble into deep criminal waters, is hardly unpredictable but is nevertheless fun to watch. Fox is as agreeable as ever and Woods is one of the best screen actors around.

Harem Holiday
1965 U 81 ★★ MUS

Let's face it – Elvis Presley may, in other respects, have been the King but he really wasn't much of an actor. Still, he's adequate enough in this rather silly yarn about a movie star who is kidnapped and somehow finds himself involved in a dastardly plot to assassinate a real king. Elvis fans will probably love it – especially the soundtrack which includes 'Hey, Little Girl'. (The original US title was *Harum Scarum*.)

Harvey
1950 U 107 ★★★★ COM

Even people who have never seen the film have heard of Harvey, the invisible 6 ft rabbit which drunken James Stewart takes everywhere as his best friend. A comedy about alcoholism is, no doubt, politically incorrect these days but Stewart's performance is a gem – though Josephine Hull, as his sister, is equally good – and Mary Chase's play adapts delightfully to the screen.

Hawk, The
1993 15 83 ★★ MYS/THR

The premise here is interesting – how does a wife react when she begins to suspect that her husband is the local neighbourhood serial killer? The execution, however, is too superficial, although Helen Mirren, as the wife, is exempt from that criticism. Otherwise, there is very little tension and even less insight.

Hear My Song
1992 15 101 ★★★★ COM

Peter Chelsom's utterly charming Anglo-Irish sleeper of 1992 – the story of a nightclub manager (Adrian Dunbar) who seeks to redeem himself in the eyes of his girlfriend (Tara Fitzgerald) by tempting the noted tax-dodging Irish tenor Josef Locke to give a concert in Liverpool. Ned Beatty, as Locke, Dunbar himself and David McCallum head a smashing cast.

Heartbreak Kid, The
1972 PG 101 ★★★ COM

We have said before (*Beethoven*), and have no hesitation in saying again, that Charles Grodin is one of the best comedy actors in films. Elaine May's smashing, sharp comedy (written by Neil Simon), which gave him his first starring role, also gives full rein to his refreshingly unsentimental approach. He plays a newly married man who, on honeymoon, falls in love with another woman, Cybill Shepherd. The results, inevitably, are catastrophic.

Heartbreak Ridge
1986 15 125 ★★ ACT/ADV

Clint Eastwood is the tough old marine sergeant knocking a bunch of raw recruits into shape before America embarks on the perilous invasion of… Grenada! Bit hard to take any of it seriously in the circumstances. Lots of salty military language; obligatory love interest provided by Marsha Mason. It's Clint, though, who gives the film such class as it has.

Heartburn
1986 15 105 ★★★ COM

Meryl Streep and Jack Nicholson knock a few sparks off each other in this adaptation of Nora Ephron's autobiographical novel about her marriage to Watergate journalist Carl Bernstein. You know the marriage won't last when he starts having an affair just as she's having a baby. Serious, rather than sidesplitting comedy, entertaining nevertheless, though the combination of the megastars plus director Mike Nichols leads you to expect more than the film delivers.

Heart Condition
1990 15 96 ★★ COM

A buddy movie with a difference, but once you've said that you've pretty well said it all. Bob Hoskins plays a racist cop who, after a severe heart attack, is given the heart of a dead

black lawyer, Denzel Washington. Washington's ghost then returns to persuade Hoskins to investigate his (Washington's) murder and, naturally, to cure the cop of his intolerant beliefs. Well-meaning but unconvincing.

Heart in Winter, A: see Coeur en Hiver, Un

Heat and Dust
1982 15 124 ★★★ DRA

The story of two generations of Englishwomen (first Greta Scacchi, then, in modern times, Julie Christie) coming to terms with the exoticism of India. A subtle, absorbing story, adapted by Ruth Prawer Jhabvala from her own novel and made with the painstaking production values we have come to expect from the Merchant-Ivory team.

Heavens Above!
1963 PG 113 ★★★ COM

Engaging Boulting brothers comedy featuring Peter Sellers as a prison padre accidentally transferred to a posh parish where, somehow, he becomes involved in Britain's contribution to the space race. Nice satirical touches. It was this kind of film, far more than his later American efforts, that earned Sellers his reputation as a fine screen comedian.

Hello, Dolly!
1969 U 139 ★★ MUS

This was the film which 20th Century-Fox hoped would revive its flagging fortunes. It didn't. It's not bad – it's just not particularly good, despite Barbra Streisand's best efforts as a Jewish matchmaker. Good score and good support from Walter Matthau, Louis Armstrong and young Michael Crawford; solid, old-fashioned direction by Gene Kelly.

Henry V
1944 U 131 ★★★★ DRA

Laurence Olivier's film was made when the Allies were anticipating victory. Hence it is colourful, triumphant, jingoistic and mightily stirring. Nobody (except perhaps Gielgud) spoke Shakespeare's verse better than Olivier and his example rubs off on a splendid supporting cast.

The story begins in Shakespeare's Globe Theatre, then opens out superbly…

Henry V
1989 PG 131 ★★★ DRA

… whereas Kenneth Branagh's tougher, grittier version opens out from a sound stage in a film studio. Thus we know at once that this is a *Henry V* for contemporary times. Olivier's troops were the Household Cavalry; Branagh's are the SAS. Olivier celebrated victory; Branagh emphasises the grim brutality of war. Both readings are valid; both films are marvellous to watch.

Her Alibi
1989 PG 90 ★★★ MYS/THR

A comedy-thriller, actually. Author Tom Selleck becomes involved in what could be the plot of one of his own mystery stories when he ingenuously provides an alibi for a mysterious Romanian circus performer, Paulina Porizkova. You can't believe a word of it but both Selleck and the story are engaging.

Hidden Agenda
1990 15 104 ★★★★ DRA

Ken Loach's suspicion of the British Establishment is admirably paranoid. Here, with the aid of the excellent Brian Cox and Frances McDormand, he investigates allegations of a shoot-to-kill policy in Northern Ireland and finds it proven to his own satisfaction. A nail-biting thriller which, whether you agree with its politics or not, will get the adrenalin flowing.

High Anxiety
1977 15 94 ★★ COM

Sometimes Mel Brooks can be desperately funny; at other times – as here – he is just desperate. In what is intended as an affectionate pastiche of Alfred Hitchcock – films like *Psycho*, *Spellbound* and *Vertigo*, for instance – he misses the target as often as he hits it. A good comic cast includes Madeline Kahn and Cloris Leachman, plus Brooks himself.

High Hopes
1988 15 107 ★★★ COM

Mike Leigh is one of the cherishably few movie-makers who believe that film should reflect life. In this sharp-toothed satire on Britain under Margaret Thatcher he aims his fire most memorably at yuppies and greed. On the whole the characters he introduces to us are awful, but you can't help getting involved. Mind you, a fine – though mostly unknown – cast helps a lot.

Highlander
1986 15 111 ★★★ SCI/FAN

If you can accept Christopher Lambert (who not only is but sounds French) as a sixteenth-century Scot learning the arts of swordplay and survival from Sean Connery, then, having become immortal, being transposed to modern America to fight evil, the rest of this fantastical hokum is perfectly agreeable. It doesn't always make sense but it's good fun.

Highlander II: The Quickening
1990 15 86 ★ SCI/FAN

Alas, the same cannot be said of this sequel. Visually it's fine and the effects are good but the story is even more opaque and muddled than before. Lambert and Virginia Madsen do their best but it's hard to know why Connery bothered to be in it, unless his contract said he had to be.

High Noon
1952 U 81 ★★★★★ WES

The classic Western story, classically told. Gary Cooper is the marshal who must face the desperados getting off the noon train to kill him. A man's gotta do what a man's gotta do – but if Cooper goes ahead he risks losing his lovely Quaker bride, Grace Kelly. There are very few Westerns better than this. (B&W)

High Society
1956 U 103 ★★★★ MUS

The purists will tell you that this musical version (songs by Cole Porter) of *The Philadelphia Story* is not a patch on the original. Nonsense. It's glorious stuff, gloriously performed and sung by a cast that includes Grace Kelly, Frank Sinatra, Bing Crosby and Louis Armstrong. And the Porter songs are terrific.

His Girl Friday
1940 U 93 ★★★★ COM

Quite the best screen version of *The Front Page*, largely because here crime reporter Hildy Johnson is a woman (Rosalind Russell). Consequently the conflicts between her and her tetchy editor and former husband (Cary Grant) are given an added, though never explicit, sexual sparkle. The great Howard Hawks directed and both Russell and Grant are at their very best. (B&W)

Hobson's Choice
1954 U 102 ★★★★ FAM

The centrepiece of David Lean's lovely version of Harold Brighouse's play is a bravura performance by Charles Laughton as the tyrannical master bootmaker. But Brenda de Banzie, as his rebellious daughter, and John Mills, as the simple-minded assistant she chooses as her mate, run him very close. A warm, funny story with the 1890s setting beautifully evoked. (B&W)

Hocus Pocus
1993 PG 92 ★★ COM

A nice idea – pity it didn't work out too well. In a New England town three witches – Bette Midler, Sarah Jessica Parker and Kathy Najimy – are accidentally brought back to life after 300 years. The deal is that they can become immortal if they dispose of all the town's children before dawn. But it's Halloween and nobody takes witches very seriously. Note the PG certificate. Not for the very young, despite the Disney label.

Hoffa
1992 15 134 ★★ DRA

Jack Nicholson plays Jimmy Hoffa, the American union boss whose Mafia connections probably led to his mysterious disappearance. Danny DeVito (who also directs) plays Hoffa's fictional best friend in a film that, despite excellent performances, is far less than it should be. It ought to work but, in the end, it doesn't. A touch violent in places.

Holiday Inn
1942 U 100 ★★★ MUS

This wartime musical was notable not only for the pairing of Fred Astaire and Bing Crosby – a pretty formidable duo – but also for the introduction of such numbers as 'White Christmas' and 'Easter Parade'. Nuff said. Add to all that a pleasing, if thinnish, romantic triangle and you've got the kind of movie that slides down easily with a box of good chocolates. (B&W)

Home Alone
1990 PG 98 ★★★ COM

Good, if grossly sentimental, entertainment but there's something dubious about this John Hughes-produced tale of eight-year-old Macaulay Culkin accidentally left alone at home for Christmas by his exceedingly careless family. The bad taste is left by the violence with which the kid fights off two inept burglars, Joe Pesci and Daniel Stern, who decide to rob his apparently deserted house.

Home Alone 2: Lost in New York
1992 PG 115 ★★ COM

The bad taste recurs in the sequel in which – would you believe it? – Culkin is abandoned yet again and has to spend Christmas by himself in New York. In essence, it's the same story reprised, but the Culkin *vs.* crooks violence is even more explicit this time. Never mind the controversy over *Reservoir Dogs, Natural Born Killers,* etc. Surely a film that shows a little boy deriving intense joy from inflicting truly grievous bodily harm on adults (who, despite their awful wounds, apparently suffer no lasting damage) is even more dangerous?

Homeward Bound: The Incredible Journey
1993 U 81 ★ FAM

The sort of film that makes you despair of Hollywood. The Disney original about two dogs and a cat undergoing a perilous journey to rejoin their human owners was enchanting. This mindless remake with the animals crudely voiced by Don Ameche, Sally Field and Michael J Fox, who somehow manages to sound like Bruce Willis at his most unpleasant, is simply crass.

Honey, I Blew Up the Kid
1992 U 92 ★ FAM

A depressingly dim sequel to the film below. Here Rick Moranis, carrying on with his strange inventions, turns his new baby son into the 100 ft nappy-wearing monster that nearly eats Las Vegas. A pretty lousy sequel, even by sequel standards.

Honey, I Shrunk the Kids
1989 U 89 ★★★ FAM

Let us charitably excuse the appalling grammar ('shrunk'?). Nerdish scientist Rick Moranis develops a machine to shrink things and accidentally shrinks his, and his neighbours', children. The diminutive kids' fight for survival in a suburban garden, now become a jungle full of giant ants, makes for excellent family fun.

Honeymoon in Vegas
1993 15 92 ★★★ COM

Reluctant prospective bridegroom Nicolas Cage only realises how much he loves his fiancée, Sarah Jessica Parker, when he loses her in a poker game in Las Vegas to rich and sinister James Caan. There's a lot of plot and subplot involved, including a funny, ongoing gag about Elvis Presley impersonators, before all is resolved. Not perhaps one for the younger members of the family. Contains some sex and juicy language.

Hook
1991 U 135 ★★ FAM

Here is a lovely opportunity lost. Steven Spielberg could have made the definitive movie of *Peter Pan*. Instead, he projected the story into the future with a grown-up Peter (Robin Williams) trying to rescue his own children from Captain Hook (Dustin Hoffman) in Neverland. It just doesn't work. Maggie Smith, as an elderly Wendy, is fine; Julia Roberts as a Southern Tinkerbell is pretty awful. Good moments, certainly, but overall a grave disappointment.

Hope and Glory
1987 15 108 ★★★★ DRA

A wonderfully nostalgic trip down memory lane as director John Boorman revisits his childhood memories of the Second World War. This is a time of Britain under fire and at its best, of eccentric relatives and happy evacuation to the riverside. A fine cast includes Sarah Miles, Ian Bannen and the young Sebastian Rice-Edwards. War was like this only if you were a child.

Hot Shots!
1991 PG 81 ★★ COM

Director Jim Abrahams (part of the *Airplane!* team) turns his hand to a send-up of *Top Gun* and the like. With Charlie Sheen and Lloyd Bridges in the leading roles it works quite well, though not terribly well. Sometimes the jokes come off; just as often they don't. Indeed the sequel – see below – was for once rather better.

Hot Shots! Part Deux
1993 PG 83 ★★★ COM

The object of the spoof here is *Rambo* – though plenty of other films get the broad satirical treatment as well. Pretty good family fun, although – as with all such send-ups – the extent of your enjoyment depends heavily on the mood you're in when you sit down to watch. Charlie Sheen and Lloyd Bridges are again on good form.

House of Games
1987 15 98 ★★★ MYS/THR

Playwright David Mamet's first film as a director, splendidly ingenious apart from a dénouement which seems too obvious and unsubtle. It's the story of a psychiatrist (Lindsay Crouse) inadvertently involved in a convoluted scam. Joe Mantegna is the dextrous con man behind it all. An adult tale that demands that you keep your wits about you.

House of the Spirits, The
1993 15 132 ★★ DRA

Isabelle Allende's famous novel, recounting the adventures of the Latin-American Trueba family from the 1920s to the 1970s, loses much in its translation to the screen. All the ingredients are there in Bille August's film – ambition, mysticism, rape, murder and revolution – along with a strong cast that includes Jeremy Irons, Meryl Streep, Glenn Close and Winona Ryder. But somehow it's very hard to get involved.

Housesitter
1992 PG 97 ★★ COM

Goldie Hawn has a one-night stand with architect Steve Martin, occupies his new house in New England, claims to be his wife and indeed takes over his entire life. Hawn is at her kookiest, Martin at his most bemused and unselfish, giving too much of the funny stuff to her. Pity because he's a much better comedian than she is. The kind of romantic comedy that Hollywood made better in the 1930s.

Howards End
1992 PG 136 ★★★★ DRA

One of those beautifully made Merchant-Ivory costume dramas that critics tend to sneer at simply because they are beautifully made costume dramas. Ignore the denigrators. Anthony Hopkins and the Oscar-winning Emma Thompson are both splendid in this intelligent, sensitive adaptation of E M Forster's novel. A cool examination of the morals of Edwardian society which centres on the love which springs up between the young, liberated Thompson and the wealthy, autocratic and middle-aged Hopkins. Excellent support from Helena Bonham Carter.

How the West Was Won
1962 PG 157 ★★★ WES

Action-packed and often spectacular epic covering fifty turbulent years of American history and the fate of three generations of Western pioneers. The four directors include John Ford and Henry Hathaway, the star-studded cast features such names as Spencer Tracy, Henry Fonda, John Wayne, James Stewart and Gregory Peck. They must all, surely, have worked for the minimum wage otherwise nobody could have afforded them.

How to Get Ahead in Advertising
1989 15 90 ★★ COM

A surprisingly cold comedy in which Richard E Grant plays an unsympathetic advertising man who discovers that the boil on his neck is becoming his alter ego. Not a bad idea, written and directed by Bruce Robinson, who made *Withnail and I*, but it begins better than it goes on and tends to be too harsh to be really funny.

How to Marry a Millionaire
1953 U 92 ★★★ COM

A splendid opportunity to see three of the glamour icons of the 1950s – Monroe, Grable and Bacall – in the same film. They play a trio of young women who, desperate to marry money, rent a luxury flat and set out to trap

their men. Things don't work out quite as they planned. A funny, frothy entertainment in which Monroe is particularly delightful.

Hue and Cry
1947 U 78 ★★★ COM

The first postwar Ealing comedy, directed by Charles Crichton (who, 43 years later, made *A Fish Called Wanda*). A bunch of cockney kids discover that crooks are using a comic to pass messages to each other and, with the aid of Alastair Sim and Jack Warner, set out to hunt them down. Charming, lively and full of nostalgic glimpses of bomb-scarred London. (B&W)

Hunchback of Notre Dame, The
1939 PG 111 ★★★★ DRA

A very decent adaptation of Victor Hugo's novel, given particular distinction by Charles Laughton's remarkable, moving performance as Quasimodo, the bell-ringing hunchback. Laughton's work is rather neglected these days but, as he proves here, he was a very considerable screen actor. A fine supporting cast and excellent sets of Paris. (B&W)

Hunt for Red October, The
1990 PG 129 ★★★ ACT/ADV

Sean Connery (as the only Russian naval officer with a broad Scottish accent) steals his late-model nuclear submarine to help him defect to the Americans. Can the Yanks get to him before the Russians do? Exciting stuff – possibly the last Cold War thriller – which marks the first screen appearance of author Tom Clancy's CIA operative, Jack Ryan (here played by Alec Baldwin and not, as in *Patriot Games* and *Clear and Present Danger*, by Harrison Ford). *Boy's Own* adventure but pretty good of its kind.

Husbands and Wives
1992 15 103 ★★★ COM

A domestic comedy-drama, featuring Sydney Pollack and Judy Davis as one couple suffering marital traumas and Woody Allen and Mia Farrow as another. Sharp, spiky, beautifully observed and – bearing in mind the Allen-Farrow 'scandals' to come – a possible example of art predicting life, especially as, in the film, Allen goes off with a much younger woman (Juliette Lewis).

Ice Cold in Alex
1958 PG 124 ★★★ WAR

Wartime suspense and quite a bit of action as British captain John Mills, upper lip superbly stiff, leads an ambulance and its motley crew – Sylvia Syms and a sinister Anthony Quayle among them – through the Libyan desert to the safety of Alexandria. Based on a real-life incident and nicely understated, so that the sense of danger is stronger than if everyone was shouting and ranting as in some American war films. (B&W)

Icicle Thief, The
1989 PG 82 ★★★ FOR

Much visual humour in this often very funny confection by Italian writer/director/comedian Maurizio Nichetti, which is both a tribute to *Bicycle Thieves* and an anarchic swipe at the horrors of television. Nichetti plays a director invited on to TV to discuss his homage to De Sica, only to discover, to his increasing fury, that his own movie is constantly interrupted by commercials. (Subtitled)

If...
1968 15 107 ★★★ DRA

Lindsay Anderson's satire on the British Establishment, using a public school as a metaphor, was a landmark movie of the 1960s. Time, however, has not been too kind to it and it cannot be seen now as the classic people once thought it was. Nevertheless, the rebellion of Malcolm McDowell and his allies against the smugly corrupt power wielded by headmaster Peter Jeffrey is still remarkable in its constant switching from comedy to drama, to fantasy and ultimately to destructive violence. It ends in a massacre, so be warned.

I Know Where I'm Going
1945 U 91 ★★★★★ DRA

Drama, yes, but comedy, too. Wendy Hiller goes to Scotland to marry a rich old man but an almost supernatural combination of circumstances and strange climatic conditions leaves her stranded and throws her together with an attractive soldier, Roger Livesey. One of the most enchanting of Powell and Pressburger's films. Witty, tender and beautifully acted throughout. (B&W)

I Love You to Death
1990 15 93 ★★ COM

A blackish comedy inspired by a true, but still pretty unbelievable, story of a wife, Tracey Ullman, who seeks revenge on her philandering husband (Kevin Kline) by trying to kill him. And failing. Not once, but several times. River Phoenix and William Hurt are a pair of hopeless hit men; Joan Plowright is Ullman's mum. Enjoyable, though the sum is not as good as the parts.

I'm All Right Jack
1959 U 100 ★★★★ COM

On the whole Peter Sellers was at his best in the pre-Hollywood period and here, with his caricature of a British trade union official, he gives one of his finest performances. Ian Carmichael as the innocent abroad and Terry-Thomas also shine in a sharply funny satire on British industry, capitalism and the work ethic (or lack of it). Possibly the Boulting brothers's most successful comedy. (B&W)

I'm Gonna Git You Sucka
1988 15 85 ★★★★ COM

Keenen Ivory Wayans wrote, directed and starred in this hip, witty skit on those Blaxploitation movies that were so ubiquitous in the 1970s. Not unlike *Airplane!* in the way it hurls jokes at all manner of targets and is not too bothered if some of them miss. Wayans plays Jack Spade, out to avenge his brother, whose death was caused – please don't ask how; find out for yourselves – because of his passion for gold chains. (Blaxploitation? Exploitation of black people. OK?)

Importance of Being Earnest, The
1952 U 91 ★★★ COM

Even people who have never seen this film are known to imitate Edith Evans's immortal delivery of the line 'A haaandbag?' But Anthony Asquith's adaptation of Oscar Wilde's romantic comedy has many other delights to offer, not least a talented British cast (Michael Redgrave, Margaret Rutherford, Joan Greenwood) which handles this kind of elegant stuff with polished ease.

Indecent Proposal
1993 15 112 ★★ DRA

Wherein billionaire Robert Redford proves that money *can* buy anything by successfully offering Woody Harrelson one million dollars for a night with his wife, Demi Moore. Some sexual romping ensues but not much else does. The way the story works out, it's only the original concept and the spin-off question – for whom would you pay how much? – that are really interesting. Contains nudity and adult scenes.

Indiana Jones and the Last Crusade
1989 PG 121 ★★★★ ACT/ADV

In the third of the series Harrison Ford embarks on a double search: for his missing father, Sean Connery, and for the Holy Grail. As in the first film, *Raiders of the Lost Ark,* the Nazis are also after the religious icon to aid their quest for world domination. Connery's presence adds immeasurably to what is anyway a rattling good yarn and the best of the trilogy.

Indiana Jones and the Temple of Doom
1984 PG 113 ★★★ ACT/ADV

By contrast, this is the weakest of the Indiana Jones sagas. Again, the object of the search is a religious artefact – a sacred stone. Kate Capshaw is the girl trying to keep up with Jones. Spielberg rather overdid it this time, though. Plenty of derring-do, thrills, shocks and creepy-crawly horrors – too much, in fact, for there is never a pause for character development. Could be a touch terrifying for the very young.

Indiscreet
1958 PG 96 ★★★ COM

A frothy and beguiling romantic comedy set in London. Ingrid Bergman is the starry actress looking for love and marriage; Cary Grant the gadabout diplomat who wants romance but not commitment and weaves a web of lies and subterfuge to protect his freedom. Very light, very inconsequential and beautifully played, not least by Cecil Parker and Phyllis Calvert.

Indochine
1992 15 151 ★★ FOR

Romantic melodrama set in French Indochina from the early 1930s onwards. Great role for Catherine Deneuve, who plays the plantation matriarch vying for the favours of a French officer (Vincent Perez) with her adopted daughter. Half-way through, revolution takes precedence over love and divides the trio. An oddly rambling and somehow inconsequential tale but Deneuve makes the most of it. (Subtitled)

Inherit the Wind
1960 U 123 ★★★ DRA

A tense, intelligent courtroom drama based on the Tennessee Monkey Trial of 1925 when a young teacher was accused of preaching Darwinian theory instead of the Old Testament. Spencer Tracy as the defence attorney and Fredric March as the prosecutor deliver rousing histrionic goods in the court scenes. Gene Kelly is the journalist who stirs up the trouble. (B&W)

Innerspace
1987 PG 114 ★★★ SCI/FAN

Dennis Quaid is the hotshot pilot who, in the interests of science, is prepared to be miniaturized and injected into the bloodstream of a rabbit. But the bad guys are after the revolutionary formula and somehow the tiny Quaid is squirted into the buttock of hypochondriac Martin Short, to great comic effect. Meg Ryan is the girl both men want. (In real life Quaid won because he and Ryan were later married.)

Innocent Blood
1992 15 110 ★★ COM

Comedy, yes, and much camp horror, too. A John Landis film in which Anne Parillaud is a vampire who bites a Mafia boss, Robert Loggia, and sets him off on the rampage as well. Good, though often gross, special effects combine with a fair bit of humour, saucy sensuality and cinematic in-jokes. Fine if you're not too sensitive. Contains nudity.

Inn of the Sixth Happiness, The
1958 PG 151 ★★★★ DRA

Not quite a classic but nevertheless a perennial family favourite. Ingrid Bergman stars as Gladys Aylwood, the real-life English missionary who took Christianity to China in the 1930s and stayed to lead a bunch of refugee children through the war-torn countryside. Bergman is outstanding but Robert Donat and Curt Jurgens are very good, too.

Inspector Calls, An
1954 PG 76 ★★★ MYS/THR

A young girl has been found dead in a well-to-do Yorkshire household and a mysterious Scotland Yard inspector (Alastair Sim) turns up to investigate. Based on the play by J B Priestley and looks its age, but well worth a viewing, partly for the twists and turns in the plot but just as much for the typically bravura performance by Sim. (B&W)

In the Heat of the Night
1967 15 106 ★★★★ MYS/THR

Norman Jewison's excellent thriller not only provides a first-class murder mystery but also a sharp examination of racial prejudice in the Deep South. Rod Steiger is splendid as the initially bigoted local sheriff, Sidney Poitier equally so as the big-city black cop who, stranded in a small Southern town, reluctantly helps solve a murder. (This, incidentally, is far superior to the two sequels *They Call Me Mister Tibbs* and *The Organisation*.)

In the Line of Fire
1993 15 123 ★★★ ACT/ADV

Clint Eastwood as the veteran FBI agent who failed to save JFK and, thirty years later, is determined to do better now the current president is being stalked by psycho assassin John Malkovich. A well-above-average thriller with the interplay between Eastwood and Malkovich building tension solidly towards the inevitable showdown. Touches of violence, naturally, and some amusing sex between Eastwood and Rene Russo.

In the Name of the Father
1993 15 127 ★★★★ DRA

Director Jim Sheridan cuts a few corners and leans heavily on artistic licence in this story of the wrongful conviction of Gerry Conlon and the rest of the Guildford Four. A salutary – as well as tense, passionate and sometimes wickedly funny – reminder of how badly wrong British 'justice' can sometimes be. As Conlon,

Daniel Day-Lewis gives a marvellously powerful performance. Emma Thompson is effective in a supporting role as Conlon's solicitor.

Into the West
1992 PG 96 ★★★ ACT/ADV

An engaging Irish tale, much overhung with symbolism, of two small boys, sons of gypsy Gabriel Byrne, who find a mystical white stallion and go on the run, pursued by the police, to save it from a grasping capitalist. Fairly modest roles for Byrne and his then wife Ellen Barkin but the kids, the horse and the countryside are delightful.

Invasion of the Body Snatchers
1956 PG 77 ★★★★ SCI/FAN

The first, and by a long way the best version of this story of implacable aliens who invade a small town and take over the bodies of its inhabitants. Don Siegel's clever direction turns a good old B-picture into something much better, despite – or maybe because of – the thinly veiled right-wing political message that for aliens we should read Communists. It was made, after all, at a time when McCarthyism still had a strong influence. (B&W)

Invasion of the Body Snatchers
1978 15 111 ★★★ SCI/FAN

Not at all a bad remake, directed by Philip Kaufman, now set in San Francisco and starring Donald Sutherland. The story has been updated to reflect a more sophisticated and cynical age but oddly enough you miss the old anti-Communist message because it's not entirely clear what these new aliens are after. Good imagery, though, and, as a tribute, Don Siegel has a cameo appearance as a taxi driver.

In Which We Serve
1942 U 109 ★★★★ WAR

A classic British war film notable, among other things, for the acting debut of Richard Attenborough and the joint directing debuts of Noël Coward and David Lean. It's the story, based on the fate of HMS *Kelly*, of the survivors of a torpedoed destroyer. Coward himself wrote and starred and was strongly backed up by an excellent cast of stalwarts, John Mills among them. (B&W)

Ipcress File, The
1965 PG 103 ★★★ MYS/THR

Len Deighton's working-class secret agent, played by a bespectacled Michael Caine, is the very antithesis of his smooth contemporary, James Bond. No Beluga caviar and martinis – more like a glass of beer and scrambled eggs. The plot, similarly, is less escapist, more downbeat and very convoluted. But there's plenty of action and menace and none of the gratuitous violence that crept into thrillers later.

IQ
1994 U 92 ★★★ COM

You may not be aware of this – in fact, we're absolutely sure you're not aware of this – but Albert Einstein was just a loveable old hirsute Cupid. And you thought all he was good for was proving that $E = MC^2$? Well, listen up – according to this film he has this cute but ever-so-brainy mathematician niece, Meg Ryan, who is engaged to a nerdy psychiatrist (Stephen Fry). Einstein – Walther Matthau, no less – doesn't like Fry but does like Tim Robbins, the young garage mechanic who falls for Ryan. And guess who, with the aid of a complicated scientific scam, irons out the bumps on the path of true love? Yup, you've got it – good old Albert. Quite fun, really, though best taken with a large pinch of salt.

Ishtar
1987 PG 103 ★ COM

Probably one of the top ten flops of all time, a salutary reminder that even a mass of talent – writer-director Elaine May, Warren Beatty, Dustin Hoffman, Isabelle Adjani, Charles Grodin – can get things hopelessly wrong. Beatty and Hoffman are a pair of songsters mixed up in frenetic goings-on in the Middle East. Deeply, embarrassingly unfunny and it almost ruined Columbia Pictures.

Italian Job, The
1969 PG 95 ★★★ ACT/ADV

One of the best caper movies of the 1960s since it depends more than most on a decent plot. Noël Coward is the criminal mastermind who, from his English prison cell, plans a bank heist in Turin. Michael Caine leads those who carry it out. The getaway involves creating a humungous traffic jam that brings the city to a halt. Good rousing fun with a neatly suspenseful ending.

It Happened One Night
1934 U 101 ★★★★★ COM

The first and, for 40 years, only film to scoop all the major Oscars – Best Picture, Direction, Script, Actor and Actress. A delightful romance, directed by Frank Capra, about a runaway heiress (Claudette Colbert) and a hard-nosed reporter (Clark Gable). Particular delights, indeed classic and fondly remembered moments, include Colbert hoisting her skirt an inch or two above the knee (far more erotic than any modern bedroom romp) to show Gable how to hitch a lift and the scene in which he divides their shared bedroom by stringing up a blanket – the famous 'Walls of Jericho'. As enchanting a film as any of the principals ever made. (B&W)

It's a Mad Mad Mad Mad World
1963 U 147 ★★★ COM

Despite a spectacular cast – Spencer Tracy, Sid Caesar, Ethel Merman, Phil Silvers, Terry-Thomas – and a galaxy of guest stars, this comedy about a bunch of crooks on the trail of hidden booty, never quite matches its promise.

It's a Wonderful Life
1946 U 125 ★★★★ FAM

Frank Capra again, this time directing James Stewart as the potentially suicidal small-town banker and Henry Travers as the guardian angel who, to earn his wings, shows Stewart how much worse the town and life itself would be without him. Sentimental? Yes, but in its unequivocal celebration of human decency, also joyous and life-enhancing. (B&W)

It Shouldn't Happen to a Vet
1976 U 89 ★★★ COM

A sequel to *All Creatures Great and Small* but with a different cast. Once again the plot is based on James Herriot's tales of a Yorkshire veterinary practice and it's all quite gentle, amusing, nostalgic and enjoyable. John Alderton plays the Herriot character; Colin Blakely is his senior partner, Siegfried. Much bucolic humour and lovely scenery.

Jabberwocky
1977 PG 100 ★★ COM

The inspiration is Lewis Carroll; the settings are medieval and as imaginative as you would expect from Terry Gilliam. The rest, involving gormless Michael Palin's quest to kill a bothersome dragon, is a mishmash of jokes that work and jokes that don't. Palin's fine, so is Max Wall, as is the general ambience, but it needed a better script than the one provided.

Jacknife
1989 15 98 ★★ DRA

Adapted from a stage play and showing its origins. But the acting and the thoughtful approach to the theme make it worthwhile. A bearded Robert De Niro visits his old Vietnam buddy, Ed Harris, and forces him to confront his wartime nightmares, traumas and neuroses. Harris's sister, Kathy Baker, falls for De Niro, which only adds to the emotional problems.

Jack the Bear
1993 15 95 ★★ DRA

A film that can't make up its mind what it wants to be. Is it a family sitcom – widowed Danny DeVito bringing up two young sons in a bizarre San Francisco suburb? Or a satirical comedy – DeVito as host of a crazy late-night TV show? Or a melodrama – Gary Sinise as a neo-Nazi who kidnaps the younger son? In the end it's all of these things but also none of them, not in any satisfying sense at least.

Jane Eyre
1944 PG 96 ★★★ DRA

A nicely Gothic production of Charlotte Brontë's classic with Joan Fontaine toothsome and appealing as the heroine taken on as governess in a grim Victorian mansion. But it's Orson Welles as the mysterious, romantic Mr Rochester who romps off with the acting honours, though the early part of the film – detailing Jane's childhood – is as good as anything that comes later. Look out for eleven-year-old Elizabeth Taylor as young Jane's best friend.

Jason and the Argonauts
1963 U 99 ★★★ SCI/FAN

Wherein Jason (decently played by the now largely forgotten Todd Armstrong) and his loyal band set out in search of the Golden Fleece and encounter all manner of perils from the likes of Titans, sea monsters and skeletal warriors. Ray Harryhausen's special effects are very impressive even today – the best thing in the film, actually. Good, rousing adventure for all the family.

Jaws
1975 PG 119 ★★★★★ ACT/ADV

A New England seaside resort faces catastrophe when a great white shark starts eating the tourists. Pure hokum but brilliantly handled by Steven Spielberg. Not only is it superbly paced but Spielberg also finds time to establish the characters of the three disparate shark hunters – Roy Scheider, Richard Dreyfuss and Robert Shaw. The first shark attack is still a shock no matter how many times you've seen it.

Jaws 2
1978 PG 111 ★★ ACT/ADV

The sequel still has Roy Scheider and a shark but, alas, it doesn't have Spielberg. Instead it has the journeyman director Jeannot Szwarc and a juvenile story about kids being terrorized rather than adults being devoured. Less a sequel than an alternative version of the original – and a distinctly inferior one at that.

Jaws III
1983 15 94 ★ ACT/ADV

In the cinema this was Jaws 3-D, not that the added dimension did much to enhance a dreadfully feeble story which dispensed with everyone connected with the first two films and shifted the locale to a Florida Sea World complex menaced by a shark. Not even the young Dennis Quaid and steady old Louis Gossett Jr can breathe much life into it. (As the 15 certificate indicates here, and in the final film, Jaws: The Revenge below, the violence is cruder and more explicit – to make up perhaps for a shortfall in imagination.)

Jaws: The Revenge
1987 15 86 ★ ACT/ADV

And here we go again. This time Lorraine Gary takes the lead as the widow of Police Chief Brody (Roy Scheider's character) and mother of two sons who harbours dark suspicions that a shark is conducting a vendetta against her family. Michael Caine crops up as Gary's love interest in this weary old rehash. Heed the warning given for *Jaws III*.

Jean de Florette
1986 PG 122 ★★★★ FOR

A lush and satisfying epic of rustic greed and cunning (the story continues in *Manon des Sources*) in a Provence unknown to expatriate authors who might have spent a year there. Tax collector-turned-farmer Gerard Dépardieu, newly moved with wife and daughter to the countryside, is cruelly duped by Yves Montand and his nephew, Daniel Auteuil, with tragic consequences. Director Claude Berri concocts a marvellously rich brew that comes across like a superior, exotic soap opera. (Subtitled)

Jennifer Eight
1992 15 120 ★★ MYS/THR

A tense thriller which starts better than it finishes. Andy Garcia is a cop hunting a serial killer with a grudge against young blind women. Uma Thurman is a young blind woman and therefore appears destined to be the next victim. One or two gruesome moments – a severed hand and the discovery of a body on a city dump. The story rather loses its way but the performances are good. Contains some violent scenes.

Jeremiah Johnson
1972 PG 106 ★★★ WES

Robert Redford is pretty close to his best in this sometimes rambling but visually striking story, set in Utah in the 1830s, of a young trapper who, as he struggles to survive, becomes a hardened mountain man of almost mythical fame. Sydney Pollack's film sags a little in the middle but ends stirringly with Johnson hunted by the Indians whom, for one reason or another, he has offended.

Jerk, The
1979 15 90 ★★★★ COM

In his first starring role, Steve Martin plays a white foundling brought up by a poor black family who has a dreadful shock when he discovers that he's not black, too. He isn't very bright, you see. The subsequent adventures – joining a circus, making and losing a fortune –

give Martin plenty of scope for his wild, zany humour. Not all the jokes work but, at its best, the film is extremely funny.

Jesse James
1939 U 105 ★★★ WES

Jesse James and his brother Frank were outlaws, crooks, train robbers and killers. They're all those things here, too, but somehow they're also presented to us in Henry King's film as heroes. Well, with Tyrone Power playing Jesse and Henry Fonda as Frank they could hardly be anything else. If you can accept the dubious morality there's plenty of action and nicely charismatic performances.

Jesus Christ Superstar
1973 PG 102 ★★★ MUS

Director Norman Jewison overcame the problem of opening out the successful Andrew Lloyd Webber-Tim Rice stage musical by filming it on location in Israel. With Douglas Slocombe's cinematography and zippy performances, the story of American hippies acting out the last few days of Christ's life looks and sounds great.

Jewel of the Nile, The
1985 PG 101 ★★ ACT/ADV

Kathleen Turner, Michael Douglas and Danny DeVito reprise the roles they played in *Romancing the Stone* – this time in the Middle East – but not with the same success. Plenty of rollicking action but the enthusiasm of the original has been lost and there's something mechanical about it all.

JFK
1991 15 182 ★★★★ DRA

Oliver Stone's conspiracy theory concerning the assassination of John Kennedy is at least passionate and makes you doubt whether Lee Harvey Oswald (Gary Oldman) did it all by himself. Kevin Costner plays district attorney Jim Garrison, who sought to lump the CIA, the Mafia and even the White House together in the plot. Tommy Lee Jones is excellent as the only man ever brought to trial for the killing. A long, complex film but the interest rarely flags. (A widescreen director's cut version rated 15 is also available.)

Joe versus the Volcano
1990 PG 98 ★★★ COM

An underrated comedy in which Tom Hanks, told he has only a short time to live, is persuaded to sacrifice himself to appease the gods on a tropical island. Not, of course, that things turn out quite that way. The engaging Hanks, Lloyd Bridges, Robert Stack and Meg Ryan, looking cute in three different roles, make it an enjoyable fantasy.

Johnny Handsome
1989 15 89 ★★ MYS/THR

Walter Hill directed this crime story, so a certain amount of violence – well, actually, a great deal – is to be expected. A disfigured crook, Mickey Rourke, gets a handsome new face in jail and, on release, plots to avenge himself on those who set him up (principally Ellen Barkin). Tough and fast but hardly convincing.

Johnny Suede
1992 15 93 ★★★ DRA

A gently ironic and affectionate fantasy about a young dreamer (Brad Pitt) who sets out to become a pop star like his idol Ricky Nelson after a pair of blue suede shoes fall from the sky onto his head. (Surely *Blue Suede Shoes* was Elvis's song?) The setting is working-class big-city America in the 1950s. Romance is provided by Alison Moir and Catherine Keener.

Jolson Sings Again
1949 U 91 ★★ MUS

Only, this being a sequel, to rather less effect than he did the first time around (see below). Larry Parks again mimes and performs well in the story of the second and less interesting half of Jolson's life – the war years, illness, remarriage (to a nurse, played by Barbara Hale), and more. Lots of good songs – all the Jolson standards that weren't in the original – energetically performed.

Jolson Story, The
1946 U 124 ★★★ MUS

Larry Parks plays Jolson but fortunately, as in the sequel, Jolson himself does the singing. That's a big plus in an enjoyable, if perhaps over-respectful, screen biography of the cantor's son who became America's favourite entertainer and starred in the first sound feature, *The Jazz Singer*. Evelyn Keyes, as a thinly disguised Ruby Keeler, is the romantic interest. Loads of famous Jolson songs.

Joy Luck Club, The
1993 15 133 ★★ DRA

Overlong account of the lives of four women who were all born in China but are now living in America. Each story is fascinating, centring on the subsequent relationships this quartet now have with their Westernized daughters, but four of them are too much to sit through in one go and concentration is likely to wander.

Julia
1977 PG 112 ★★★ DRA

The title role is played by Vanessa Redgrave but Fred Zinnemann's fine, sensitive film is really about the writer Lillian Hellman (Jane Fonda) and her relationship with Dashiell Hammett (Jason Robards), as well as with Julia, the rich friend who involves her in the anti-Nazi movement in 1930s Germany. Alvin Sargent's script, tying together love, friendship and politics, won an Oscar. So, too, for their supporting roles, did Redgrave and Robards.

Julius Caesar
1953 U 116 ★★★★ DRA

A poignant reminder of what a marvellous screen actor Marlon Brando was before he turned away from it all in disgust. His Mark Antony, the focal point of Joseph L Mankiewicz's excellent production, gives the lie to the cynics who said he could never speak the verse and dominates the film. And since the cast includes John Gielgud (as Cassius) and James Mason (as Brutus) that's saying a lot. (B&W)

Jumpin' Jack Flash
1986 15 101 ★★★ MYS/THR

Comedy, thrills and a ration of violence in a caper that was given short shrift in the cinema. It plays enjoyably on the small screen, though. Whoopi Goldberg stars as a computer operator who receives messages on her machine from a British spy in peril in Eastern Europe and who, as a result, is caught up in intrigue and espionage. A bit muddled but fast and lively.

Jungle Book, The
1942 U 105 ★★★ FAM

Live action in this early version directed by
Zoltan Korda. Sabu plays Mowgli in a
spectacular production, which is certainly truer
to the original than Disney's effort (below). The
story is approached far more seriously, too,
though Korda sometimes seems unsure how
best to blend the lush backgrounds, the
wildlife, the fantasy and the drama.

Jungle Book, The
1967 U 75 ★★★★ FAM

Heaven only knows what Rudyard Kipling
would have made of this cartoon version of his
story but it's a perennial favourite with movie-
lovers. Splendid animation, terrific songs, a lot
of humour and the voices of George Sanders (as
the smoothly evil Shere Khan), Phil Harris
(Baloo the bear) and Louis Prima (King Louie
the ape) add up to sparkling entertainment.

Junior
1994 PG 105 ★★★ COM

When the funding's withdrawn from a
biological research project, scientist Arnold
Schwarzenegger continues experimenting at
home with the help of fellow boffin Danny
DeVito. Arnie implants an egg (stolen from
female egg-head Emma Thompson) into his
own stomach and the results are spectacular.
His belly swells, he craves strange food
combinations and he cries a lot. Arnie is
pregnant. Larks abound more than laughs and
it's heavier on slapstick than it is on subtlety,
but it's old-fashioned veg-out entertainment.

Jurassic Park
1993 PG 121 ★★★★ SCI/FAN

It wins its four stars for the special effects,
which are breathtaking, and Steven Spielberg's
superbly paced direction. The story – billionaire
Richard Attenborough running a theme park

packed with regenerated dinosaurs – is at best
perfunctory. But the dinosaurs are so realistic
you can almost smell them and when they start
running amok the excitement is marvellously
sustained. Pretty scary, too, in places.

Just Ask for Diamond
1988 U 89 ★★ COM

Two boy detectives (Dursley McLinden and
Colin Dale) are plunged into a Chandleresque
– well, sort of – mystery that involves the
obligatory *femmes fatales* (Susannah York and
Patricia Hodge), a real policeman (Bill
Paterson) and, of course, a sinister fat man (Roy
Kinnear). Quite a nice little spoof which
children will probably enjoy more than adults.

Just Cause
1994 15 98 ★★ MYS/THR

Two points to heed: first, that some of the
scenes are quite gratuitously violent; second,
half-way through the film the plot becomes so
obvious you might have written it yourself.
Sean Connery's a law professor who agrees to
investigate the dubious conviction of Blair
Underwood for the murder of an eleven-year-
old girl. Set in the red-neck South, it skips the
racism issue neatly by having the brutal police
officer (Laurence Fishburne) as black as the
accused. Connery and Fishburne are impressive,
but do be careful who gets to see it, as it could
offend.

Just Dennis: The Movie
1987 U 92 ★ FAM

This one went straight to video, so it's not that
good. Young Dennis (Victor Di Mattia) digs up
a dinosaur bone in his back garden and is
inundated by the media and people who want
to turn the entire area into a dead dinosaur
theme park. If they succeed, bang goes the
neighbourhood. Not to be confused in any way
with *Jurassic Park*.

Kagemusha
1980 PG 153 ★★★★ FOR

Akira Kurosawa is one of the masters of the cinema and here he gives us an absorbing, visually splendid recreation of medieval Japan. The story is of a thief who is spared execution to impersonate a warlord, so that neither his supporters nor enemies will know the warrior has died in battle. An epic film that has an almost Shakespearian sweep to it. Rousing and realistic battle scenes. (Subtitled)

Karate Kid, The
1984 15 122 ★★★ ACT/ADV

A sort of *Rocky* for kids – the story of a teenager, Ralph Macchio, who gives the local bullies a seeing to after Pat Morita, the janitor in his apartment building, teaches him karate. Thus the six-stone weakling gains revenge on those who kicked sand in his face. A small film, made with low expectations, which has become a favourite with teenagers, though it's not for the very young.

Karate Kid, Part II, The
1986 PG 108 ★★ ACT/ADV

This takes up where the first film stopped – Macchio beating the bullies etc. But then it heads off to Japan where Morita finds himself involved in an old feud. Something to do with the girl he had loved and (honourably) left. Macchio, of course, gets drawn into it, too.

Karate Kid, Part III, The
1989 PG 108 ★ ACT/ADV

Another example of the pitcher going too often to the well. The story and situation were slender enough in part II – here they're positively emaciated. The plot sees the return of Martin Kove, soundly beaten by Morita at the beginning of the second film, now seeking revenge. Macchio, though pushing thirty, still passes for seventeen pretty well.

Key Largo
1948 PG 97 ★★★ MYS/THR

As an adaptation of Maxwell Anderson's play, John Huston's *film noir* betrays its theatrical origins. It's wordy and static but the atmosphere and tension are excellent as Humphrey Bogart comes to grips with mobster Edward G Robinson in a Key Largo hotel. Lauren Bacall, Claire Trevor (who won an Oscar) and Lionel Barrymore lend fine support in an agreeably cynical and world-weary thriller. (B&W)

Khartoum
1966 PG 122 ★★★ DRA

Charlton Heston plays the doomed General Gordon but Laurence Olivier steals the show as the Mahdi. A sensible, often exciting account of the siege of Khartoum and of the conflict between two determined and very different men. Spectacular battle scenes, too.

Kidnapped
1971 U 102 ★★★ FAM

Robert Louis Stevenson's stirring adventure yarn has been filmed at least four times and this version, which also takes in part of another Stevenson novel, *Catriona*, is as enjoyable as any. In an eighteenth-century Scotland at war with England, young Lawrence Douglas seeks his rightful inheritance with the aid of swashbuckling cavalier Michael Caine.

Killing Fields, The
1984 15 136 ★★★★ DRA

Based on the true story of the friendship between American journalist Sydney Schanberg (Sam Waterston) and his guide/interpreter Dith Pran (newcomer Haing S Ngor, who won an Oscar for Best Supporting Actor), Roland Joffe's film gives a fiercely passionate portrayal of the war in Cambodia. The depiction of murder and cruelty by the Khmer Rouge is not for the over-sensitive but this is a moving, intelligent picture.

Kindergarten Cop
1990 15 107 ★★ ACT/ADV

Probably intended as a family film but too violent for that category. Arnold Schwarzenegger plays a tough cop posing as a kindergarten teacher to catch a killer. Arnie faced by unruly infants is quite funny, but Arnie licking them into shape like a Gestapo officer is a bit worrying. Good performances from Pamela Reed and from Carroll Baker as the bad guy's mum.

Kind Hearts and Coronets
1949 U 102 ★★★★★ COM

One of the true Ealing comedy classics, directed by Robert Hamer and full of wit, humour and superb performances. Dennis Price is the ruthless upstart who determines to murder the eight people, men and women, who stand between him and a dukedom. Alec Guinness plays all the unfortunate eight. A marvellously satisfying film that is not to be missed. (B&W)

King and I, The
1956 U 128 ★★★★ MUS

Yul Brynner's finest hour (and only Oscar-winning performance) as the King of Siam who employs English governess Deborah Kerr to take care of his multitudinous children. A stage production (songs and music by Rodgers and Hammerstein) simply and charmingly transferred to the screen. Splendid set pieces and pleasing performances throughout.

King David
1985 PG 109 ★★ DRA

A worthy but failed attempt to tell the story of David and Bathsheba. Richard Gere, miscast as King David, is best remembered (with quiet glee) for dancing into Jerusalem wearing what looks like a nappy. The film never really recovers from that moment, though, including Edward Woodward, Dennis Quilley and Cherie Lunghi.

King Kong
1933 PG 96 ★★★★ ACT/ADV

The original version and now a cult classic. Actually, if you bear its age in mind, it's pretty remarkable. Old Kong may creak a bit but Fay Wray screams up a storm and the mixture of (mild) horror, fantasy and adventure retains the power to move an audience. The odd tear can still be shed when you realise the overgrown gorilla actually *loves* the hysterical Wray. (B&W)

King of Kings
1961 U 163 ★★ DRA

Much credibility is lost once you discover that Jesus (Jeffrey Hunter) has shaved his armpits. Where does it mention that in the Gospels? Pity, really, because otherwise Nicholas Ray's film has a lot going for it, especially in its exploration of the political conflict of the time. Visually spectacular and Orson Welles provides a sonorous narration.

King of the Hill
1993 15 98 ★★★ DRA

Twelve-year-old Jesse Bradford is abandoned by his ailing mother and feckless father (Jeroen Krabbe) in a run-down hotel in St Louis in the 1920s. How this smart, engaging kid learns to fend for himself among the hopeless denizens of the hotel unfolds like a long, rich novel. Director Steven Soderbergh (who also made *sex lies and videotape*) handles the material beautifully.

King Ralph
1991 PG 92 ★ COM

The British Royal Family has been wiped out and the throne descends, by default, to a crass American nightclub entertainer (John Goodman). Not a bad idea but executed without wit or very much comedy and hampered by a script with which neither Goodman nor even Peter O'Toole and John Hurt can be expected to do a lot.

Kismet
1955 U 108 ★★★ MUS

Arabian Nights musical fantasy – adapted from the stage show – with Howard Keel as a Baghdad vagabond whose magic powers are exploited by the wicked vizier. Lively song and dance numbers and Keel and Ann Blyth are, as usual, in fine voice.

Kissin' Cousins
1964 U 87 ★★ MUS

Elvis Presley sings eight songs and plays both a city slicker and his identical (apart from a blond wig) hillbilly cousin. The smoothie tries to persuade the yokel and his family to allow a missile site to be built on their land. Just guess who wins in the end. A pretty soppy tale but if you love Elvis you'll probably find it tolerable.

Kiss Me Kate
1953 U 105 ★★★★ MUS

Howard Keel and Kathryn Grayson, starring in *The Taming of the Shrew*, discover that offstage they're running into exactly the same trouble as Petruchio and Kate. Spectacular stuff with terrific Cole Porter songs, a fine comic turn by Keenan Wynn and James Whitmore ('Brush Up Your Shakespeare'), Ann Miller's dancing and Keel and Grayson at their best.

Kiss of the Spider Woman
1985 15 115 ★★★ DRA

William Hurt won an Oscar as an effeminate homosexual sharing a cell in a South American prison with a political activist (Raul Julia) whom he helps to stay alive with his camp descriptions of old movies. Hector Babenco's film sensitively explores the relationship between two men who have nothing in common except captivity.

K-9
1989 15 97 ★★ MYS/THR

James Belushi is a hard-working cop on the trail of a drugs baron, whose new partner turns out to be a ferocious Alsatian dog. Inevitably the canine (K-9, geddit?) turns out to be smarter than the human. Belushi and the dog have a

certain appeal but on the whole it's all kind of predictable.

Kramer vs Kramer
1979 PG 100 ★★★★ DRA

A tear-jerking wallow of a movie – with, it must be added, a lot of humour – about a divorcing couple (Dustin Hoffman and Meryl Streep) vying for custody of their young son, Justin Henry. Hugely sentimental but beautifully played and hard to resist. Rewarded with numerous Oscars including one, for Best Supporting Actress, that really established Streep's career.

Kuffs
1992 15 97 ★★ ACT/ADV

The inspiration for this silly thriller for teenagers is the existence in America of private police forces – a subject that cries out for serious examination. It doesn't get it in this dumb story of drop-out Christian Slater taking over his murdered brother's private force in San Francisco. Violence and action replace plot and character development. OK for Slater groupies, though not for their younger siblings.

L

Labyrinth
1986 U 98 ★★★ FAM

An amiable fantasy in which young Jennifer Connelly seeks to rescue her baby stepbrother, who has been snatched by wicked goblin David Bowie. Bizarre creatures, concocted by director Jim Henson, lend comedy and thrills as Connelly pursues her quest through a strange maze. Good start, good end, soggy middle.

Lady and the Tramp
1955 U 73 ★★★★ FAM

A piece of classic Disney animation – the story of a streetwise mongrel who comes to the aid of a pedigree spaniel being given a hard time by a pair of Siamese cats. Canine love ensues, naturally. Not least of the delights on offer are several great songs sung by Peggy Lee.

Ladyhawke
1985 PG 118 ★★★ DRA

A robust fantasy (a bit too long perhaps) wherein a knight, Rutger Hauer, and his lover, Michelle Pfeiffer, are cruelly parted by a curse, which has turned her – by day anyway – into a hawk. The villain of the piece is a jealous bishop, spurned by Pfeiffer. Matthew Broderick is the servant who helps Hauer overturn the curse.

Lady in White
1988 15 109 ★★★ MYS/THR

Lukas Haas, locked by his classmates in the school cloakroom, sees a mysterious man who seems to have lost something, and the ghost of a girl his own age. Turning amateur detective, Haas seeks to find out how, or if, the two apparitions are connected. A superior supernatural thriller with lots of suspense, mystery and tension.

Lady Jane
1985 PG 136 ★★★ DRA

In her first film, eighteen-year-old Helena Bonham Carter plays the ill-fated Lady Jane Gray who, after the reign of Henry VIII, became Queen of England for nine days. Plenty of political intrigue and a fine cast of classically trained actors. Trevor Nunn, in his debut as director, makes the film look good but never quite gets the timing right.

Ladykillers, The
1955 U 87 ★★★★ COM

One of the darker Ealing comedies – still very funny, though. A gang of dastardly thieves is thwarted by an innocent old lady. Alec Guinness, sporting sinister fangs, leads the gang; Peter Sellers and a brooding Herbert Lom are two of his sidekicks. Best of all is Katie Johnson as the genteel landlady who messes up their plans.

Lassie
1995 U 79 ★★ FAM

There have been more Lassies than prime ministers (well, almost) and they've been more popular, too. This latest adventure is pretty run-of-the-mill fare starring Helen Slater, about a young streetwise kid finding his way in his new rural home. With the aid of the dog, of course. That collie must be older than God by now.

Lassie Come Home
1943 U 85 ★★★ FAM

The first and possibly the best of the long, long, long-running series, made to seem longer since it's so often repeated. Elizabeth Taylor, Roddy McDowall, Nigel Bruce and Elsa Lanchester are among the humans, though the star of the show is the collie dog, who will have you reaching for the Kleenex as it tries to find its way home to the family it adores.

Last Action Hero
1993 15 125 ★★ ACT/ADV

Arnold Schwarzenegger's first megaflop, a hugely expensive high-concept movie based on only one idea – a magical cinema ticket transfers young Austin O'Brien from his seat in the stalls and into the picture itself but also enables screen hero Arnie and screen villain Charles Dance to escape into the real world. Woody Allen used the same notion much more effectively in *The Purple Rose of Cairo*.

Last Emperor, The
1987 15 156 ★★★ DRA

Bernardo Bertolucci's leisurely story of China's last imperial ruler, who was an emperor at the age of three but ended his days as a municipal gardener. A remarkable story with fine performances by John Lone as the emperor and

Peter O'Toole as his English tutor. A film of stunning visual impact; vivid and colourful but over-earnest and overlong.

Last Great Warrior, The
1994 PG 98 ★★★ ACT/ADV

An atmospheric legend about a seventeenth-century American Indian warrior kidnapped and taken to England where the people and customs are as strange to him as he is to them. The story follows his desperate and dangerous attempt to make it back home to his people. It's unmistakable Disney, i.e., there's a predictable amount of sentiment, action and adventure, but there's also the quality associated with the studio and the richness of character helped by the performances of Adam Beach, Michael Gambon and Mandy Patinkin.

Last of the Mohicans, The
1992 15 107 ★★★★ ACT/ADV

Tense, action-packed drama, based on James Fenimore Cooper's novel, with a splendid hero and a truly terrible villain. Daniel Day-Lewis, as Hawkeye, is the hero who rescues a British colonel's daughters, Madeleine Stowe and Jodhi May, during the North American Indian wars of 1757. Wes Studi is the vengeful Indian chief who wants the women dead. Very violent in places.

LA Story
1991 15 91 ★★★ COM

Steve Martin's affectionate, amusing look at the eccentricities of Los Angeles and its inhabitants. He plays a TV weatherman smitten by English journalist Victoria Tennant. As ever, the path of true love is far from smooth. An uneven tale with some lovely set pieces and Martin himself in very good form.

Late Show, The
1977 15 89 ★★★★ MYS/THR

A delightful comedy-thriller which works both as a detective story and as a homage to the entire genre. Art Carney is the old, beat-up private eye whose attempt to find Lily Tomlin's cat leads them both into a murder investigation. The world-weary Carney and the hyperactive Tomlin make a smashing team.

Laura
1944 U 83 ★★★★ MYS/THR

One of the most satisfying of *film noir* thrillers. Dana Andrews plays the cop who falls in love with a photograph of supposed murder victim Gene Tierney. Ah, but is she really dead? A beautifully told story with a cracking performance by Clifton Webb as a bitchy newspaper columnist. (B&W)

Laurel and Hardy

There are in existence some sixty – yes, count them, sixty – videos featuring Laurel and Hardy. Most of them consist of compilations of the pair's short films and since in our opinion *(well, mine anyway – BN)* Laurel and Hardy are the peerless comedy team you are recommended to try almost any of them. Not only are the couple enormously funny but they created, effortlessly, the kind of pathos that Chaplin worked so hard – and often so irritatingly – to achieve. Stan's simple-minded innocence and Ollie's vast, pompous attempts at dignity are as touching as they are hilarious. It's not our brief in this book to review shorts, though L&H were at their best in their one- and two-reelers *(my opinion again – BN)*. But several of their longer films are also available on video and we list some of them, in alphabetical order, here rather than elsewhere because the video sleeve usually mentions the stars before the movie's title, the format being *Laurel and Hardy* – followed by the name of the film.

Bonnie Scotland (1935 U 77 ★★★ FAM)
What happens is that the boys go to Scotland to claim an inheritance that has been left to Stanley but, as ever, they're out of luck and penniless and so enlist in a Scottish regiment. L&H's trouble was that nobody quite recognised their genius when they were alive, so here – as in all their films – they were deprived of the production values and careful scripting that would certainly be lavished upon them today. Consequently, the film looks rather shabby, though the two principals are as funny as ever when given the opportunity. (B&W)
Bullfighters, The (1945 U 61 ★★ FAM)
Most of Laurel and Hardy's features suffered from being gag- rather than plot-driven and this – their last together – is really no exception. They play private eyes who follow a female suspect down to Mexico. Essentially,

that's just to establish them in the place because the subsequent fun stems from the fact that Stan is the *doppelganger* of a celebrated local bullfighter. In truth, short as it is, it might have worked better even shorter but the boys, inevitably, have their inspired moments, though there's not a lot of talent to back them up. (B&W)

Flying Deuces, The (1939 U 61 ★★★ FAM) A question of unrequited love here – Ollie's unrequited love. What to do? Suicide seems a bit drastic, so he and Stan join the French Foreign Legion with predictably disastrous results. Come on – can you really imagine these two as battle-hardened fighting men? Once again fun stems not so much from the plot as from the L&H set pieces. (B&W)

Nothing but Trouble (1944 U 66 ★★★ FAM) In this one, our heroes are employed as, respectively, chef and butler to a rich couple (Henry O'Neill and Mary Boland). Their well-connected employers are about to entertain a boy king whose wicked uncle is secretly planning to have him bumped off. Pretty thin plot, really, but once again the L&H antics save the day – not just for the story but also for the viewer. (B&W)

Sons of the Desert (1934 U 62 ★★★★ FAM) The henpecked duo – they are nearly always at their best when henpecked – dream up a fantastical excuse to escape from their wives and attend the annual convention of the Sons of the Desert, a sort of fraternity group. The women, of course, see through this deception – women are always smarter than L&H – and the boys come home to a very tricky situation. Much better plotted and written than most of their features, with Stan and Ollie at their best. Unfortunately, this seems to have been issued only in a 'colourised' format, though the film was made in black and white. In our opinion, hanging's too good for whoever invented 'colourization'.

Way Out West (1937 U 63 ★★★★ FAM) This might well be L&H's best feature film. Why they've gone out West is to deliver the deeds to a goldmine to their rightful owner – the daughter of their late partner. But, naturally, on the way they run into all manner of chancers and criminals, chief among them James Finlayson. The action is fast and funny, L&H are on cracking form and – a particular delight – they actually sing their familiar trademark song, 'The Trail of the Lonesome Pine'.

Lavender Hill Mob, The
1951 U 77 ★★★★★ COM

Ealing comedy at its best with Alec Guinness as the meek little bank clerk who plans to steal a truck full of bullion and turn it into Eiffel Tower paperweights. Sid James, Stanley Holloway and Alfie Bass are his unlikely accomplices. Never were there crooks like these and you do so want them to get away with it. (B&W)

Lawnmower Man, The
1992 15 105 ★ MYS/THR

One of the first films to investigate virtual reality, but not very well. Jeff Fahey and Pierce Brosnan star in a dumb story about a dim-witted gardener who, thanks to a scientist's experiment, grows too smart for his own, or anyone else's, good. A virtual-reality sex scene was regarded as pretty steamy at the time. Some may think it still is. They might find the occasional violent scenes off-putting, too.

Lawrence of Arabia
1962 PG 217 ★★★★★ ACT/ADV

David Lean's multi-Oscar-winning account of the life of T E Lawrence. Magnificent to look at and it brought instant stardom to Peter O'Toole. Likewise to Omar Sharif as the Arabian leader, Sherif Ali. The word masterpiece is not too strong for what is an epic movie in every sense.

League of Their Own, A
1992 PG 123 ★★★★ COM

In the 1940s, with America at war, a women's baseball league was established. This is the fictionalised, very funny story of one of the teams and of sisterly rivalry between star player Geena Davis and Lori Petty. Tom Hanks is the team's drunken manager and Madonna is better than usual in a supporting role.

Leap of Faith
1992 PG 104 ★★ COM

Steve Martin as a bogus evangelist who brings his quasi-religious circus to a small town to con money by working 'miracles'. Liam Neeson is the suspicious sheriff who tries to head Martin off but falls for his assistant, Debra Winger. An oddity this, generally serious but with some fine manic moments and the odd, genuine miracle.

Left Handed Gun, The
1958 PG 98 ★★ WES

Being another look at Billy the Kid, America's most notorious and mythologized gunfighter. Paul Newman plays Billy, thus lending the film the reputation of being the first method Western. Possibly too much psychology and too little action but Newman is fine and so is John Dehner as Billy's nemesis, Pat Garrett. (B&W)

Legal Eagles
1986 PG 111 ★★★ MYS/THR

High-flying DA Robert Redford is assigned to prosecute ditsy Daryl Hannah for art fraud and murder. But when Hannah's attorney, Debra Winger, persuades him that her client is not guilty they team up to find the real culprit. The story doesn't hang together too well but the acting is very engaging.

Leon, the Pig Farmer
1992 15 100 ★★★ COM

A young Jew, Mark Frankel, scion of an Orthodox family, discovers that because of artificial insemination he is really the son of a Yorkshire pig farmer, Brian Glover. His original family is appalled, his new family becomes more Jewish than the Jews to make him feel at home. A neat, amusing, nicely played satire on stereotypes and intolerance.

Lethal Weapon 3
1992 15 113 ★★★ ACT/ADV

The only one of the series with less than an 18 certificate. Mel Gibson and Danny Glover play the maverick cops, Joe Pesci is their criminal associate as various lowlife elements try to ensure that Glover won't reach retirement unscathed. Lively and engaging and loads of action. It may be a 15 but it's still pretty violent, though. Contains swearing.

Let Him Have It
1991 15 110 ★★★ DRA

An impassioned, very well-made account of the 1952 murder trial that led to the shameful execution of the simple-minded Derek Bentley for his passive part in the killing of a policeman. Christopher Eccleston and Paul Reynolds play Bentley and Christopher Craig, who actually pulled the trigger but was too young to hang.

Let's Make Love
1960 U 113 ★★★ MUS

Any film that has Marilyn Monroe singing 'My Heart Belongs to Daddy' has got to be worth seeing. Never mind that the rest of it is a run-of-the-mill backstage story about a millionaire and a showgirl: it has Monroe and Yves Montand and Cole Porter's music and that's good enough. (Incidentally, this was Hollywood's attempt to make an international star of Britain's Frankie Vaughan. It didn't work.)

Letter to Brezhnev
1985 15 91 ★★★ COM

Sparky, charming, pre-*Glasnost* comedy in which two Liverpudlian girls, Alexandra Pigg and Margi Clarke, meet and fall for a couple of Russian sailors. Pigg is so smitten that she wants to follow her lad back to Russia and seeks Brezhnev's permission to do so. Contains salty Liverpudlian language.

Letter to Three Wives, A
1949 U 99 ★★★★ DRA

Three wives in upstate New York receive a letter from the local *femme fatale* announcing that she has run off with one of their husbands. But which husband? Delicious suspense, fine performances and a clever script build up to a surprise ending. The fine cast includes Linda Darnell, Jeanne Crain, Ann Sothern and Kirk Douglas. (B&W)

Licence to Kill
1989 15 127 ★★ ACT/ADV

Timothy Dalton's second excursion as James Bond. Not bad but by now much of the original zest has gone from the series. Robert Davi, as a vicious drug baron, makes a good heavy and Carey Lowell is much more liberated and lively than the usual Bond crumpet.

Life and Death of Colonel Blimp, The
1943 U 156 ★★★★ DRA

Roger Livesey gives the performance of his career as a British soldier whose adventures we follow through three wars and three women. One of Powell and Pressburger's most popular and enjoyable tales, liberally sprinkled with laughter, tears and drama. Anton Walbrook and Deborah Kerr lend great support.

Life Is Sweet
1990 15 99 ★★★★ COM

Mike Leigh's funniest, most delightful fly-on-the-wall study of suburbia. Alison Steadman and Jim Broadbent are marvellous as the struggling but resourceful parents; Jane Horrocks is even more so as their bulimic daughter. (The film comes as a double bill with Leigh's short film, *Short and Curlies*.)

Life Stinks
1991 PG 91 ★ COM

But not quite as much as this film does. Mel Brooks, who can be as funny as anyone, directs and stars in this sad botch of a plot about a millionaire who is lured into a bet that he could live on his wits – even if he were broke. The jokes are, too often, crude and obvious and sometimes even patronising.

Like Father Like Son
1987 15 95 ★★ COM

This is what is known as a 'high concept' movie – in other words it's based on a single idea and little else. The idea here concerns identity switching and for some reason there were, at this time, several films around that had latched on to the same notion. In this one Dudley Moore plays a doctor who, after imbibing a magic potion, changes places with his teenage son, Kirk Cameron. The results are fairly predictable and though Moore is, as usual, pretty good value, the possibilities are never realised and the exploration of character is at best skin-deep.

Lion in Winter, The
1968 15 129 ★★★★ DRA

Gloriously rousing account of how Henry II (Peter O'Toole) and his estranged wife, Eleanor of Aquitaine (Katharine Hepburn) meet at Chinon to decide which of their sons will succeed to the throne. The result is a dynamic encounter between two witty, opinionated people. The script is literate, funny and dramatic. O'Toole and the Oscar-winning Hepburn are superb.

Lion King, The
1994 U 90 ★★★ FAM

Disney pulls out all the stops with this, their first venture at an original story, in which a young lion cub is duped into deserting his pride by an evil uncle (voiced by Jeremy Irons). The animation lacks some of the detail of earlier classics, tending to look rather too computerized, but the songs are great. Tim Rice and Elton John collaborated on same and were rewarded for their efforts with an Oscar.

Little Big Man
1970 15 133 ★★★★ WES

Various Western myths and legends – especially the Battle of the Little Bighorn – are explained and exposed by Dustin Hoffman, a 121-year-old adopted Indian, looks back over his long, remarkable life. Hoffman has met everyone from Custer to Wild Bill Hickok and remembers them all – vividly. Lots of action and comedy in an absorbing, unconventional epic.

Little Buddha
1993 PG 118 ★★ DRA

Bernardo Bertolucci's Buddhism for beginners. Two parallel stories here – one, in flashback, tells how 2 500 years ago Prince Siddhartha (Keanu Reeves) became the Buddha; the other, set in modern times, explores whether or not a young American boy might be a reincarnation of a famous lama. The casting is odd and both stories, though interesting, are flatly told.

Little Caesar
1930 PG 75 ★★★★ MYS/THR

'Mother of mercy, is this the end of Rico?' Yes, it was, but it was also the beginning of stardom for Edward G Robinson as a 1920s gangster, modelled on Al Capone. Somewhat dated now but a classic of its era and still much more watchable than most modern thrillers. (B&W)

Little Dorrit
1987 U 168/177 ★★★★ FAM

Nobody's Fault is the first part of Christine Edzard's astonishingly good adaptation of the Dickens novel. Derek Jacobi is the protagonist who first meets Little Dorrit (Sarah Pickering) in the Marshalsea, the debtor's prison where her father, Alec Guinness, has lived for twenty-five years. In this and Part II, *Little Dorrit's Story,* we follow the relationship that springs up between the three of them through fortunes lost and found, triumph and disaster, in a magnificent social drama that is not without its resonance today. The look, the feel and the performances by a huge, talented cast are all quite superb.

Little Lord Fauntleroy
1936 U 98 ★★★ FAM

Freddie Bartholomew plays the little American boy who finds he's a future lord of England. This kid's almost too good to be true, charming even the most unpleasant with his sunny nature, but it's an endearing tale and nicely played. (B&W)

Little Lord Fauntleroy
1994 U 158 ★★★★ FAM

An excellent BBC adaptation of the Frances Hodgson Burnett novel with George Baker, David Healy and Betsy Brantley. The story is unchanged from any other version and, after all, why should it change? A young American boy – so angelic as to make Little Orphan Annie seem positively diabolical – discovers that in succession to his late father he is now heir to an English peerage and a fortune. All goes well as he bonds with his grumpy old granddad (George Baker) until another claimant to the family fortune comes pushingly forward. Opulently made, splendidly acted and full of mirth and tears with a gloriously happy ending.

Little Man Tate
1991 PG 96 ★★★ DRA

Jodie Foster's impressive debut as a director. She also stars as the single, working-class mother of

an seven-year-old prodigy. The film explores the question of what is right for the boy – life with mother or, as child psychologist Dianne Wiest believes, the company of other gifted children? Heartwarming, emotional and not too sentimental.

Little Mermaid, The
1989 U 79 ★★ FAM

Hans Christian Andersen's fairytale, animated and updated by Disney. The basic plot is as it always was – the young mermaid falling in love with and following a human prince. But now she does it to the accompaniment of ballads and calypsos. Not the best of Disney but the young will enjoy it a lot.

Little Monsters
1989 PG 97 ★★ COM

Every child just knows that something creepy lurks under the bed but in Brian's case it happens to be true. Fortunately, though, his monster – Maurice – is a friendly soul, who leads the lad into all manner of adventures. Gentle, amiable stuff for the young.

Little Shop of Horrors
1986 PG 91 ★★★ MUS

When Mushnik's down-market florist shop becomes home to an exotic plant called Audrey II business picks up – until Audrey II starts throwing her weight around. That's the basis for a mélange of horror, music and comedy featuring Steve Martin, Bill Murray, Rick Moranis and many others. On the whole very good fun.

Little Women
1933 U 111 ★★★★ FAM

Louisa M Alcott's story of family life and, specifically, of four sisters growing up around the time of the American Civil War has been made four times now. George Cukor's version, starring Katharine Hepburn and Joan Bennett, was the first and maybe still the best. Lovely, lush enjoyable stuff. (B&W)

Little Women
1995 U 114 ★★★★ FAM

Susan Sarandon as Marmie, Winona Ryder as Jo and Christian Bale as Laurie are spot on in this glossy, heart-warming version of the American classic. Gabriel Byrne looks a little uncomfortable as the German professor with whom Jo strikes up a friendship, but otherwise there's little to fault.

Live and Let Die
1973 PG 116 ★★★ ACT/ADV

Roger Moore's first time out as James Bond. Different from Connery, of course, but he has his own charm. Plenty of palm-tingling chases, with romance provided by Jane Seymour and outright villainy by Yaphet Kotto. Paul McCartney wrote the title song.

Living Daylights, The
1987 PG 125 ★★ ACT/ADV

By contrast, Timothy Dalton's debut as 007 was not so successful. In this tale of drugs, arms dealers and the KGB, Dalton, a very good actor, is handsome enough but, crucially, he can't handle the comic one-liners, so much of the fun vanishes. Also – in the age of AIDS – he only has one girlfriend, Maryam d'Abo. One way and another old 007 comes close to being staid and respectable!

Local Hero
1983 PG 107 ★★★★ COM

Bill Forsyth's lovely story of an American tycoon, Burt Lancaster, who tries to buy a Scottish seaside village to build an oil refinery and runs into stubborn opposition from the locals. A little gem of a film, beautifully played by Peter Riegert, Denis Lawson and indeed the whole cast.

Logan's Run
1976 PG 114 ★★★ SCI/FAN

In a futuristic society where everyone must die at thirty, Michael York is a security guard who has to hunt down those fugitives who reckon thirty, isn't enough. He has a change of heart, though, when he falls for Jenny Agutter. A pretty slender plot but good action sequences and excellent special effects.

Lonely Passion of Judith Hearne, The
1987 15 110 ★★★ DRA

A quite searing story, held together by a marvellous performance from Maggie Smith,

about a lonely, tippling, repressed Irish spinster who believes she has found love at last with a visiting American, Bob Hoskins. But, alas, love and marriage are not what the fast-talking Hoskins has in mind.

Long and the Short and the Tall, The
1960 PG 101 ★★★ ACT/ADV

Directed by Leslie Norman (father/grandfather of the authors). A tough, vivid adaptation of Willis Hall's play about the conflict among a small group of British troops trapped in the jungle behind Japanese lines in the Second World War. Richard Todd, Laurence Harvey and Richard Harris lead a typically strong British cast in an intriguing yarn. (B&W)

Long Day Closes, The
1992 PG 83 ★★★ DRA

The second of Terence Davies's autobiographical films about growing up in working-class Liverpool (*Distant Voices, Still Lives* was the first). Bud, now aged eleven, recalls happy family life and the problems posed by a new school. Measured, fairly uneventful, it either sucks you into its mood or it doesn't.

Longest Day, The
1962 PG 170 ★★★ ACT/ADV

Just about every star who was free, from Richard Burton to John Wayne, took part in this epic reconstruction of the D-Day landings. Splendid action sequences and special effects and enjoyable cameos from the likes of Henry Fonda and Robert Ryan. (B&W)

Longtime Companion
1990 15 95 ★★ DRA

A serious and yet at times touchingly funny drama that explores the effect of AIDS on a gay community in New York. Initially, they're a happy, carefree group but then the modern plague strikes… Fine performance from the Oscar-nominated Bruce Davison.

Look Who's Talking
1989 15 92 ★★★ COM

The clever and amusing gimmick here is having the thoughts of Kirstie Alley's baby voiced by Bruce Willis. Alley is a single mother, George

Segal the shiftless father of her child and John Travolta the New York cabby who becomes Alley's baby-sitter and much more. A charming and funny idea, nicely executed. Sex, sexual innuendo and language account for the 15 certificate for this and the two sequels.

Look Who's Talking Now!
1993 12 91 ★★ COM

This time it's the household pets (voiced by Danny DeVito and Diane Keaton) to whose canine thoughts we are privy as the shadow of adultery raises its head in the Alley-Travolta household on the third outing. Better than the second film (see below), not as good as the first. The original joke is pretty well exhausted by now.

Look Who's Talking Too
1990 15 77 ★ COM

Once again the law of diminishing returns comes in with this sequel in which Alley and Travolta are married and baby Mikey acquires a sister (raucously voiced by Roseanne Barr). The wit, the charm and the fun of the original are nowhere in evidence.

Lorenzo's Oil
1992 15 130 ★★★ DRA

Susan Sarandon's marvellous performance dominates this story – based on fact – of a couple's determination to find a cure for their son's apparently incurable disease. The film claims they succeeded; later developments seem, sadly, to prove them wrong. Nick Nolte, as the father, sounds more like a Mafia godfather than an Italian banker.

Lost Horizon
1937 U 111 ★★★★ MYS/THR

Frank Capra's lovely, heartwarming adaptation of James Hilton's novel, in which Ronald Colman survives an air crash in Tibet and discovers paradise, or rather Shangri-La – a land of peace, love and immortality where time stands still. (B&W)

Love and Death
1975 PG 81 ★★★★ COM

Woody Allen's affectionate, funny satire of Tolstoy and company, in which he plays a condemned man looking back over his life – and his lust for his cousin, Diane Keaton – during the Napoleonic Wars. Allen, bespectacled and neurotic as ever and looking marvellously out of place, is frequently hilarious.

Love at First Bite
1979 15 91 ★★★ COM

George Hamilton makes an agreeably suave and handsome latterday Dracula – a very twentieth-century count – who, among other things, robs blood banks in this often very funny send-up of vampire movies. Susan Saint James is his more-than-willing victim.

Love Bug, The
1969 U 103 ★★★ FAM

Being the first adventure of Herbie, the Volkswagen Beetle with an independent outlook and a marked taste for mischief. Plenty of comedy, slapstick and chaos. Dean Jones and David Tomlinson lend the car fine support. (Three sequels followed in descending order of merit, *Herbie Rides Again* being the best of them.)

Love Field
1992 15 101 ★★★ DRA

Michelle Pfeiffer won an Oscar nomination for her role as a white Southern woman who finds love with a black man, Dennis Haysbert, around the time of the JFK assassination. This is a very good, thoughtful little film, extremely well played, but it was never granted a cinema release in Britain. It should have been.

Love Happy: see Marx Brothers

Love Is a Many Splendored Thing
1955 U 102 ★★★ DRA

A splendid Oscar-winning weepie in which William Holden, as an American journalist, falls in love with a Eurasian doctor, Jennifer Jones, in Hong Kong. (Jennifer Jones? Well, in those days Hollywood didn't allow the romantic pairing of real Eurasians with white actors.) The romance, of course, is ill-fated – as, in those race-conscious times, it had to be.

Love Story
1970 PG 96 ★★ DRA

'Love means never having to say you're sorry'.
Yuk! Incredibly successful sentimental weepie
about how Ryan O'Neal falls in love with
beautiful but terminally ill Ali McGraw in a
New England university town. Millions have
mocked it in public – but only after secretly
shedding buckets of tears.

Lullaby of Broadway
1951 U 88 ★★★ MUS

Tear-jerking musical in which Doris Day
becomes a Broadway star, unaware that her
mother, once a famous actress, has become a
drunk and practically hit skid row. Familiar
backstage stuff, really, but with songs by Cole
Porter and George Gershwin. Day was good in
this kind of thing.

Lust for Life
1956 PG 117 ★★★ DRA

Kirk Douglas simmers and rages effectively in
the turbulent tale of Van Gogh's private and
professional life – neither of them particularly
happy, of course. Very well done, though, and
Anthony Quinn – before he started playing every
role as though it were Zorba the Greek – is
surprisingly good as Van Gogh's friend, Gauguin.

Mac and Me
1988 U 95 ★ FAM

When a cuddly, though not very pretty, alien gets stranded on Earth he ill-advisedly makes his way to suburban LA. The black hole of Calcutta would be more welcoming. Overly cute and far too sentimental, it's a would-be *ET* though it never comes close in quality or style. A largely unknown cast still remains unknown.

Macbeth
1971 15 134 ★★ DRA

Roman Polanski's gory but undeniably gripping adaptation of 'the Scottish play' stars Jon Finch and Francesca Annis as the aggressors with ex-*Professional* Martin Shaw acting his socks off in support. Family viewers beware: there is a good deal of violence here, plus a shot of Annis in the nude.

Madame Bovary
1991 PG 137 ★★ FOR

Considering the sexiness of Flaubert's classic, Claude Chabrol has come up with a rather dull version. Isabelle Huppert plays Emma, the eponymous heroine, who sets out to find love and social status. But this is nineteenth-century France and her methods are unacceptable. (Subtitled)

Madame Sousatzka
1988 15 116 ★★★ DRA

Shirley MacLaine is wonderful as an eccentric Russian piano teacher who becomes obsessed with teaching the beauties of music and the meaning of life to a fifteen-year-old Indian boy. The performance given by MacLaine is inspired, being both amusing and heart-wrenching. Peggy Ashcroft features in the supporting cast.

Made in America
1993 15 106 ★★ COM

A mix-up at the sperm bank means that when Whoopi Goldberg asks for a bright Afro-American to be the surrogate father of her daughter they give her the, er, deposit of a white, second-hand car salesman, Ted Danson, and she's more than a little upset. This is a frenetic, only occasionally funny comedy of errors which is most interesting for sparking

the brief, off-screen relationship between Danson and Goldberg. The film itself opts wimpishly for the politically correct denouement.

Mad Max Beyond Thunderdome
1985 15 102 ★★★ ACT/ADV

The only *Mad Max* movie with a 15 certificate, its main appeal is Mel Gibson – re-creating the futuristic Aussie warrior exiled to the desert. A convoluted post-holocaust plot involves stunts and chases galore and – actually another intriguing point of interest – Tina Turner as the rather splendid ruler of the violent city of Bartertown. (The two previous films, *Mad Max* and *Mad Max 2*, are 18 certificates and not as entertaining or as action-led as this, the last in the series.)

Madonna: Innocence Lost
1995 12 87 ★★ DRA

Based upon the unauthorized biography of Ms Ciccone, this rather intriguing biopic tells of Madonna's early years and her ambition, bordering on the obsessive, to reach the top. Terumi Matthews plays the diva, and with a fair amount of make-up and a carefully positioned mole, quite convincingly too.

Magic
1978 15 113 ★★★ HOR

This is not for the youngsters in the house since it's an eerie story which is, at times, quite terrifying. Anthony Hopkins plays a ventriloquist who is driven mad by his dummy, which begins to dominate his personality. The script is by William Goldman, the creepy direction by Richard Attenborough.

Magic Box, The
1951 U 103 ★★★ DRA

This is a fascinating biopic of William Friese-Greene, the comparatively unsung Briton who was one of the inventors of the movies. Virtually everyone who is anyone in the British film industry crops up, including Robert Donat as Friese-Greene. Laurence Olivier, Michael Redgrave, Richard Attenborough, Glynis Johns, Margaret Rutherford and Peter Ustinov are among the guest stars. John Boulting directs most ably.

Magnificent Seven, The
1960 PG 123 ★★★★★ WES

One of the all-time great Westerns this, which is surprising considering it's based on a Japanese film by Kurosawa – *Seven Samurai*. Seven hired guns collect to protect a Mexican village from marauding bandits. If you haven't seen it before, correct that error at once. Yul Brynner, Steve McQueen and Charles Bronson head the goodies; Eli Wallach leads the bad guys.

Maid, The
1991 PG 86 ★ COM

A silly, straight-to-video farce about a businessman, Martin Sheen, who for reasons that never ring true becomes maid to wealthy Jacqueline Bisset in order to woo her. Lightweight is the kindest way to describe it and the two leads must have been paid well, since it's difficult to see what else, other than a big cheque, could have enticed them to be in it.

Major League
1989 15 102 ★★ COM

To say the Cleveland Indians baseball team is hopeless is an understatement, so when the nasty female owner (Margaret Whitton) plots to sell the club's franchise, it would seem a *fait accompli*. But then she didn't reckon on the players – Tom Berenger, Charlie Sheen, Wesley Snipes and company – who decide to thwart her. It's good fun, light-hearted and enjoyable enough for all the family, not just the sports fans.

Major League II
1994 15 100 ★★★ COM

One of the rare occasions when the sequel is better than the original. Whitton sells the Indians to clapped-out player Corbin Bernsen but they carry on losing. Wesley Snipes has left the team but most of the original cast are back, giving better performances than previously and the comedy is enhanced by Randy Quaid's superb cameo as an increasingly disillusioned fan.

Malcolm X
1992 15 195 ★★★ DRA

Yes, the film is long – too long – but it's a passionate, comprehensive study of the black civil-rights leader who embraced Islam and waited until the end of his life to renounce violence, by which time it was a little late. The movie's frequent *longueurs* are due not to the performances (Denzel Washington is nothing short of excellent in the title role) but to director Spike Lee, who gives the impression of being angry and self-indulgent.

Maltese Falcon, The
1941 PG 99 ★★★★★ MYS/THR

John Huston directed this brilliant *film noir* thriller featuring Dashiell Hammett's private eye, Sam Spade, with a touch that has rarely – if ever – been bettered. Humphrey Bogart (as Spade) is superb, as are Sydney Greenstreet, Peter Lorre and Mary Astor in support. Brilliant stuff considering it marks Huston's directorial debut. Watch out for the cameo by his dad, Walter. (B&W)

Mambo Kings, The
1992 15 100 ★★ DRA

Anyone who stays up for *Come Dancing* will probably have a field day here, as the main point of this film is for hips and groins to sway in time to music. Heart-throbs Armand Assante and Antonio Banderas are lusty Cubans who arrive in New York bringing with them a new form of music and dance called Mambo. The dancing's OK but the over-earnest script and the characterization should have been better.

Man Called Horse, A
1970 15 109 ★★★ WES

A fascinating psychological study of Sioux Indians and their culture – long before Kevin Costner came along with his dancing wolf. It's also one of the best things Richard Harris has done. He gives an outstanding performance as an English aristocrat kidnapped by the Indians, who undergoes torturous ordeals to prove his manhood. (There were a couple of sequels but they amounted to little.)

Manchurian Candidate, The
1962 15 121 ★★★★ MYS/THR

One of the best of all political thrillers, it hinges on brainwashing by the Communists during the Korean War. Laurence Harvey and Frank Sinatra are both pretty well at their best as the returned hero and the soldier detailed to investigate him respectively. Great twists and turns in the plot. Angela Lansbury won an Oscar as Harvey's mother.

Mandy
1952 PG 89 ★★★★ DRA

A heart-warming drama about a deaf-and-dumb girl (Mandy Miller) and the anguish of her mother in deciding whether to send her to a special school where she can be taught to speak. Lovely performances by Miller, Phyllis Calvert and Jack Hawkins and fascinating sequences at the special school. (B&W)

Man for All Seasons, A
1966 U 116 ★★★★ DRA

This marvellous account of Sir Thomas More's fateful refusal to betray his church for his King, Henry VIII, was the deserved winner of six Oscars including one for writer Robert Bolt. All the performances are top notch, though Paul Scofield (also an Oscar winner) in the lead role is outstanding. Wendy Hiller, Robert Shaw, Orson Welles and John Hurt, among others, bring all their skills to the cast.

Man from Laramie, The
1955 U 98 ★★★★ WES

James Stewart is terrific as a mean and moody fellow obsessed with getting revenge on the men who sold rifles to the Indians and killed his brother. The plot may sound familiar because it's a tale oft told by Hollywood, but few others of the genre could match the charm or suspense of this version.

Manhattan
1979 15 92 ★★★★ COM

Woody Allen's New York slice of life, shot superbly in black and white, is basically a comedy, but a very biting one. He plays a comedy writer, heavily influenced by the lives and loves of his friends, who has an affair with a young girl (Mariel Hemingway). By no means a follow up to *Annie Hall*, though the mood is similar. Diane Keaton and Meryl Streep lend elegant support in what is, to a large extent, Allen's love letter to Manhattan. (B&W)

Manhattan Murder Mystery
1993 PG 103 ★★★ MYS/THR

The most user-friendly of Woody Allen's recent movies. He and Diane Keaton star as a couple who think their next-door neighbour has killed his wife and set about trying to prove it. Anjelica Huston and Alan Alda co-star. As far as plots go, this is one of Allen's best. It's light on navel-contemplation and neurosis, heavy on atmosphere, suspense and fast verbal humour and pays an affectionate tribute to films of *The Thin Man* genre.

Man in the Moon, The
1991 PG 95 ★★★ DRA

A gentle, rather inconsequential tale which, at risk of sounding sexist, will appeal more to women since it's about two young girls and their experiences of both love and tragedy while growing up in southern USA. Despite nice performances from the young female cast and Sam Waterston, the real star of the movie is its locale. The recreated Louisiana *circa* 1957 is breathtaking.

Man in the White Suit, The
1951 U 81 ★★★ COM

The trouble with this delightful Ealing comedy is that it's almost too believable to be funny. Alec Guinness turns in a marvellous performance as a scientist who invents everlasting material and makes a lot of enemies in big business because of it. Solid English cast in support, including Joan Greenwood (she of the lovely voice), Cecil Parker (he of the lovely voice) and Michael Gough who, come to think of it, hasn't got a bad voice either. (B&W)

Mannequin
1987 PG 86 ★★ COM

An ancient Egyptian spirit takes possession of a shop window dummy. Andrew McCarthy watches it come to life in the shape of Kim Cattrall and proceeds to fall in love with her. This hardly compares with the screwball comedies of the forties but it's an inoffensive tale that features a young Estelle Getty and an even younger James Spader. It did well enough at the cinema to warrant a sequel, *Mannequin on the Move*. That, however, was a mistake.

Manon des Sources
1986 PG 114 ★★★★ FOR

This follow up to *Jean de Florette* is an equally, if not more impressive film. The young shepherdess (Emmanuelle Béart), learning the truth of her father's death, seeks revenge on Daniel Auteuil and Yves Montand, the men who caused it. It's not necessary to have seen the earlier film, though it helps. Gérard Depardieu may be absent but it's still a great cast and the Provençal scenery is magnificent. (Subtitled)

Man Who Knew Too Much, The
1956 PG 115 ★★ MYS/THR

Alfred Hitchcock made two versions of this thriller about a young boy (a girl in the original) who is kidnapped in order to keep his parents quiet – they being unintentionally involved in an international assassination plot. Trouble is, this is the lesser and later version. It stars Doris Day – who sings 'Que Sera Sera' very nicely – and James Stewart but it's not as thrilling as the 1934 version (which is not available on video).

Man Who Would Be King, The
1975 PG 123 ★★★ ACT/ADV

A rare opportunity to see two of Britain's biggest stars – Sean Connery and Michael Caine – in the same picture. In John Huston's fine adaptation of the Kipling story they play two expatriates in nineteenth-century India who concoct a plan to rob a remote people of their treasures. But the best laid plans of mice and men… Great performances by both stars.

Man without a Face, The
1993 15 110 ★★★ DRA

It could have been titled 'The Man with Two Faces' since Mel Gibson not only stars but directs – and more than competently at that. In fact he plays a man with half a face, horrendously scarred both physically and emotionally by a car crash. His hermit-like existence is changed for ever when a disturbed local lad, Nick Stahl, asks him for help and lands him in considerable trouble. Emotionally charged, but not overly sentimental.

Man with the Golden Gun, The
1974 PG 119 ★★★ ACT/ADV

Or, alternatively, it could be titled 'The Man with the Golden Hair' since this was Roger Moore's second outing as Bond. The film is very nearly stolen from him by Britt Ekland's delightful performance as one of his girls and by Christopher Lee as Scaramanga, the larger-than-life villain. All the usual gimmicks in abundance, plus the obligatory quota of stunts, jokes and derring-do.

Man with Two Brains, The
1983 15 86 ★★★★★ COM

Steve Martin is nothing short of brilliant as an innocent brain surgeon seduced by cunning gold-digger Kathleen Turner. But once her evil intentions are made known, Martin falls in love with a disembodied brain and embarks upon an affair – of sorts – while he tries to find a body for it. Delightful story, script and performances. If you haven't seen it, rectify that oversight at once.

Map of the Human Heart
1993 15 105 ★ DRA

Certain critics went wild over this rather dull wartime drama – were we watching the same film? Jason Scott Lee and Anne Parillaud play a pair of orphans who, having first met in the Arctic, find their paths tend to cross quite regularly, despite moving to Canada and London. Most notable moment is their sexual encounter on a deflated hot air balloon. It takes all sorts but… Probably best watched only by the older members of the family – if then.

Married to the Mob
1988 15 99 ★★★ ACT/ADV

An underrated comedy-thriller with Michelle Pfeiffer playing a gangster's widow who wishes to dissociate herself from the Mob and their overbearing families. Excellent casting sees Matthew Modine as the policeman who helps her. This slipped out with little fanfare, which is a shame since the performances by, and chemistry between, Modine and Pfeiffer warrant attention.

Marx Brothers

Most of the brothers' classics are available on video. In alphabetical order they include:

Animal Crackers (1930 U 93 ★★★ COM) Their second film and an adaptation of their Broadway show. At a very posh party the brothers somehow get involved in a plot to steal a valuable painting. (B&W)

Big Store, The (1941 U 80 ★★ COM) Not one of their best. Groucho is a detective looking into a department store which is the subject of a takeover bid. (B&W)

Day at the Races, A (1937 U 105 ★★★ COM) Enjoyable Marx Brothers caper with Groucho as a horse doctor and Harpo a jockey. The wonderful Margaret Dumont (the best of all straight-women in the movies) is, as usual, Groucho's stooge. Allan Jones and Maureen O'Sullivan are the juvenile leads. The madcap antics of the brothers are the main purpose and appeal of the film so the plot only gets in the way from time to time. (B&W)

Duck Soup (1933 U 66 ★★★★★ COM) The brothers thought *A Night at the Opera* was their best film but in our view this is better still. Groucho becomes prime minister of Freedonia and declares war on neighbouring Sylvania, whose inept agents are Chico and Harpo. Glorious lunacy throughout. Incidentally, this was Zeppo Marx's last film. (B&W)

Go West (1940 U 77 ★★ COM) Despite a glorious sequence on a train the old West is simply not the right environment for the determinedly urban brothers. (B&W)

Love Happy (1949 U 81 ★ COM) Their last film and not really one to cherish. The plot involves hard-up actors, crooks and priceless stolen diamonds. Groucho appears too briefly as a detective and Marilyn Monroe even more briefly as a dumb blonde. (B&W)

Monkey Business (1931 U 74 ★★★ COM) Wherein the brothers stow away on a ship and become involved with gangsters. Lovely stuff when they impersonate Maurice Chevalier to get through immigration. (B&W)

Night at the Opera, A (1935 U 85 ★★★★ COM) Zeppo had retired by now so it's just Groucho, Chico and Harpo doing their best to ruin grand opera for ever more. Some of their best-loved gags appear here, including Groucho riding to his room on a trunk, Harpo flying on the ropes like Tarzan and a riotous backstage finale. (B&W)

Room Service (1938 U 78 ★★ COM) One of the less funny efforts from the Marx Brothers, here playing destitute producers desperately trying to keep their play going and a roof over their heads. Sight gags and one-liners still abound but some go a little wide of the mark. Lucille Ball joins them, as does Ann Miller. (B&W)

Mary Poppins
1964 U 135 ★★ MUS

There are some charming songs in this Hollywood musical about the magical British nanny. Where it goes wrong is firstly by casting Julie Andrews, who is far too nice to be the acerbic Ms P, and secondly by choosing Dick Van Dyke as a cockney. His accent has gone down in East End folklore as the worst of all time. For all its faults, it's a colourful family favourite which kids never seem to tire of.

Mary Shelley's Frankenstein
1994 15 123 ★★★ HOR

Kenneth Branagh's Frankenstein really, since he directed and plays the unbalanced doctor. But it's faithful to Shelley's original story, perhaps too faithful, as thrills are in short supply. An enormously ambitious production which is often too stagey. The story is handled well enough by Branagh, Helena Bonham Carter, Tom Hulce and, to an extent, Robert De Niro, who is touching and sympathetic but not scary enough as the Creature.

MASH
1970 15 111 ★★★★★ DRA

Most people are more familiar with the television series which, though excellent, is not a patch on Robert Altman's brilliant, anarchic, poignant movie version. The story is set during the Korean war in a US military medical unit. Donald Sutherland and Elliott Gould play the irreverent doctors with Robert Duvall, Tom Skerritt and Sally Kellerman making up the rest of the medical team.

Mask
1985 15 115 ★★★★ DRA

If members of your family tend to weep a lot don't let them watch this, or else buy a king-size box of tissues. It's the heart-breaking tale of a young lad and his mother striving for a normal life, despite the boy's disfiguring disease. Outstanding performances by both Eric Stoltz as the son and Cher as the mother, and made all the more moving by being based on fact. Peter Bogdanovich's direction neatly avoids the story's cliché pitfalls.

Mask, The
1994 PG 101 ★★★ COM

Jim Carrey's second starring venture after the enormous success of *Ace Ventura: Pet Detective*. Clever effects and Carrey's rubbery face and manic body language carry the comedy through a lightweight script about a mild-mannered nerd transformed into a hero when he puts on a green mask. Very funny and visually breathtaking.

Matinee
1993 PG 94 ★★ COM

John Goodman gives an appealing performance as the maker of grubby horror films during the time of the Cuban missile crisis. The best part is the movie-within-the-movie – Goodman's appalling, so-bad-it's-funny horror flick about monster ants. But the basic story – people worrying about the possibility of nuclear war – is unconvincing and *Matinee* doesn't work either as comedy or drama.

Maverick
1994 PG 127 ★★★★ WES

Though James Garner played the title role on TV, Mel Gibson does just as charming a job in this big-screen version. Good casting, too, of Jodie Foster as a feisty, poker-playing con woman in whom Gibson meets his match. Garner is, thankfully, not ignored either. He co-stars as a marshal who, like everyone else in the film, is not quite what he seems. The action culminates in the biggest poker game in the West where double-crosses turn into triple-crosses and worse.

Medicine Man
1992 PG 100 ★★ DRA

The problem with this film is that in its attempt to be ecologically correct it forgets to be entertaining and although the leads, Sean

Connery (as a doctor claiming to have found the cure for cancer in a rain forest) and Lorraine Bracco (as an American scientist sent by her boss to check his claim) are both believable and attractive in their roles, the pace of the film drags like a punctured windsock.

Mediterraneo
1991 15 86 ★★ FOR

Quite why this won the Best Foreign Language Film Oscar is not clear. Certainly it's a charming tale, based as it is on the escapades of some Italian soldiers who seem to be in heaven when abandoned on a lovely, peaceful Greek island during the Second World War. But there's little more to it than that. It's sort of bittersweet and is at least based on a true story. (Subtitled)

Meeting Venus
1990 15 115 ★★ DRA

European co-productions rarely come off and this is no exception, though it's better than most. In its study of the difficulties of getting international concert stars to co-operate it's really a satire on the European Community itself. Glenn Close adds American appeal as the diva; Niels Arestrup is the conductor. Worthy and plodding are adjectives that spring to mind, which is a shame considering that the producer and director were David Puttnam and Istvan Szabo respectively. Wagner's *Tannhäuser* music isn't bad, though.

Meet Me in St Louis
1944 U 108 ★★★ MUS

Have the tissues ready, for this is the musical in which Judy Garland sings *Have Yourself a Merry Little Christmas*. If that doesn't get you crying, nothing will. Margaret O'Brien, who plays Garland's younger sister, won a special Oscar for Best Child Actress. The plot revolves around the fates and fortunes of one particular family during the St Louis World Fair of 1903.

Meet the Applegates
1991 15 86 ★ COM

Insects in human guise plot to end the world in this weak but inoffensive fable. Considering it was directed by Michael Lehman, who made the cult movie *Heathers*, it's a disappointment.

Still, there are some nice ideas, many of them quite amusing in places. Ed Begley Jr stars; Stockard Channing is pretty funny, too.

Memoirs of an Invisible Man
1992 PG 95 ★★ COM

Once you've appreciated the way they get around showing what an invisible man is doing, there's little else to appeal in this disappointing remake by John Carpenter. Chevy Chase plays the scientist made invisible in a bungled experiment who becomes inadvertently mixed up in a web of intrigue and potential CIA exploitation. Daryl Hannah provides the love interest.

Memphis Belle
1990 PG 103 ★★★ WAR

Any teenage (or older, or younger come to that) girls in the family will be swooning over this cast of male talent. The likes of Eric Stoltz, Harry Connick Jr, Matthew Modine, Billy Zane, Sean Astin and D B Sweeney make up the crew of the bomber whose twenty-fifth and final mission of the Second World War is told here in spectacular fashion. The film was inspired by William Wyler's 1944 documentary about the plane and its crew. Wyler's daughter, Catherine, co-produced the feature film alongside David Puttnam.

Men Don't Leave
1990 15 110 ★★ DRA

A bit of a tear-jerker this, as Jessica Lange is left widowed and penniless with two young sons to bring up on her own. A sort of touching, very occasionally amusing soap opera, nicely played particularly by Lange but also by a young Chris O'Donnell, Joan Cusack and Kathy Bates. A remake of a French film, La Vie Continue.

Mephisto
1981 15 144 ★★★★ FOR

Klaus Maria Brandauer proves here that he's one of the best and most powerful screen actors in the world. He plays a German actor – particularly noted for his portrayal of Mephistopheles – who is seduced by and delivers himself body and soul to the Nazis. At the centre of what is a sharp examination of corruption, ambition and self-preservation lies Brandauer's positively virtuoso performance. This is great film acting of the kind he was never encouraged, or perhaps allowed to deliver in, for instance, Out of Africa. (Subtitled)

Mermaids
1990 15 105 ★★★★ COM

The music's terrific, the romance charming, the drama effective and the comedy strong – plus there are stirring performances from Cher (who plays a single mother frightened of commitment), Winona Ryder and Christina Ricci (as her daughters) and Bob Hoskins (as the love interest). Ryder is particularly effective as a teenager who has grown tired of her family's shiftless, rootless way of life. Just the ticket for a rainy Saturday afternoon.

Metropolitan
1990 15 94 ★★★ COM

This directorial debut by Whit Stillman is sharp, observant, funny and yet poignant in its portrayal of the way of life of New York yuppies. It's set during the Christmas holidays and Edward Clements is the lonely young man drawn into a small clique of upper-class friends. None of the actors' names are familiar, though they deserved – and found – more work on the strength of this.

Micki + Maude
1984 PG 113 ★★ COM

Dudley Moore is always charming and he needs to be in this immoral tale about a bigamist who decides to settle down with just one of his wives only to discover that both are pregnant. His farcical attempt to do the right thing leads to a fraught double life. At times the attempt to be funny is, like Moore's activities, over-frantic. Amy Irving and Ann Reinking play the two wives.

Midnight Clear, A
1992 15 104 ★★★ WAR

Another one for the females of the family since this Second World War adventure features a line-up of hot male talent: Peter Berg, Kevin Dillon, Ethan Hawke and Arye Gross. A bunch of American troops fraternize briefly with their German counterparts on Christmas Day 1944 before both sides discover how unforgiving war is.

Midnight Sting
1992 15 94 ★★★ COM

More of a comedy-thriller, actually. Ex-convict James Woods sets up an elaborate scam to sting the wealthy ruler of a small town, Bruce Dern. The sting is complicated so pay attention but it revolves around a fight and boxer Louis Gossett Jr. Woods is on cracking form and Dern is suitably creepy as the bad guy who deserves all he has coming.

Midsummer Night's Sex Comedy, A
1982 15 84 ★★★ COM

This marks the first appearance of Mia Farrow in a Woody Allen film as one half of one of the three couples (played by Farrow and Jose Ferrer, Tony Roberts and Julie Hagerty, and Mary Steenburgen with Allen) acting out their fantasies on a weekend holiday in the country *circa* 1900. Visually one of Allen's best, but not as funny as most. One for the grown-ups, really.

Miracle on 34th Street
1947 U 92 ★★★ FAM

For the festive season, this has to be a must. There's enchantment in every snowflake as a department-store Santa Claus (Edmund Gwenn) has to go on trial to prove he really is Father Christmas. Maureen O'Hara and John Payne play the younger adults and Natalie Wood is most appealing as the unbelieving child.

Miracle on 34th Street
1994 PG 100 ★★★★ COM

In this remake Richard Attenborough plays Santa Claus, a part he was obviously born for. His performance is delightful in a story that closely follows the original. Elizabeth Perkins and Dylan McDermott do well as the inconsequential adults. A rare example of a remake improving on the original – though both are worth seeing.

Misérables, Les
1978 PG 138 ★★★ DRA

Victor Hugo's novel of poverty, persecution, pity and redemption in eighteenth-century France filmed here for the fifth time. (The stage musical version came much later.) Richard Jordan is Valjean, sentenced to ten years as a galley slave for stealing bread; Anthony Perkins

and a distinguished cast that includes John Gielgud, Ian Holm, Cyril Cusack and Flora Robson breathe vibrant life into the story.

Misfits, The
1961 PG 120 ★★ DRA

A somewhat downbeat parable from the pen of Arthur Miller, made all the more poignant since it was to be the last film for both its stars, Clark Gable and Marilyn Monroe. Monroe plays a divorcee hanging round a rodeo where she encounters the hard-bitten Gable. Their pairing on screen was as mismatched as their relationship off, if rumours of their arguments are to be believed. (B&W)

Miss Firecracker
1989 PG 90 ★★ DRA

An offbeat comedy about a lonely girl (Holly Hunter) in small-town Mississippi who believes that if she can win the local beauty contest, as her cousin did before her, then love will follow. Tim Robbins provides the local love interest; Mary Steenburgen is the older cousin.

Missing
1982 15 116 ★★★★ DRA

A peerless performance by Jack Lemmon in this true-life drama about a fraught father searching for his son who disappeared in South America. The mystery deepens with revelations of corruption. A smart political thriller which keeps the palms sweaty throughout. The screenplay by director Costa-Gavras and Donald Stewart earned an Oscar.

Mission, The
1986 PG 120 ★★ DRA

Great to look at but this jungle-based story about an eighteenth-century mission of Jesuits in South America is overlong and leisurely. Conflict arises between the missionaries who want to save the Indians and those who want to enslave them. Roland Joffe directs; Robert De Niro and Jeremy Irons star.

Missionary, The
1982 15 82 ★★★ COM

A naughty tale in which ex-missionary Michael Palin, now a rector in Victorian London, finds an intimate way to save 'ladies of the streets'. It's not strong on belly laughs but may raise the odd titter and the supporting cast (Maggie Smith, Denholm Elliott, Trevor Howard, Michael Hordern and Phoebe Nicholls) are always worth watching. Titillating rather than explicit.

Mississippi Masala
1991 15 114 ★★ DRA

Denzel Washington gives a fine performance as a black American conducting a romance with an expatriate Ugandan Asian, Sarita Choudhury, despite the objections of their respective communities. Interesting to see a film about racism that doesn't feature white people. Although melodrama tends to creep in, it makes a change from the usual films about bigotry.

Moderns, The
1988 15 121 ★★ DRA

The arty set in 1926 Paris form the basis of this pretty but convoluted film. The central story has Keith Carradine, as an art forger, rekindling a romance with a former, now married, lover. Linda Fiorentino (who went on to star in *The Last Seduction*), Genevieve Bujold and Geraldine Chaplin are also involved in a milieu that includes painters, writers and art-loving businessmen.

Molly Maguires, The
1970 PG 119 ★★ DRA

Trouble looms among the Pennsylvanian mine workers of the last century when their secret society, led by Sean Connery, is infiltrated by informer Richard Harris. The atmosphere, background and social conditions are effectively created but the story is too downbeat to provide much in the way of family entertainment.

Mommie Dearest
1981 15 124 ★★ DRA

You'll think twice before moaning about your mother when you see what a terrible parent film star Joan Crawford allegedly was to her adopted daughter. Faye Dunaway plays the woman whose eyebrows could have housed a family of beetles and rather overdoes it, but you'll never be able to watch Crawford's films again after knowing how nasty she could be.

Mo' Money
1992 15 86 ★★ COM

Violent comedy-drama in which Damon Wayans plays an amorous young man who takes a job with a credit company to be near the girl of his dreams (Stacey Dash) but soon finds himself mixed up in a fraud. Nice performance by Wayans – who also wrote and produced – with his kid brother Marlon sharing the billing as co-star. Contains violent scenes.

Money Pit, The
1986 15 88 ★★ COM

A mild comedy which benefits from the presence of Shelley Long and Tom Hanks as the young, naive couple who buy a ramshackle house and plan to do it up. However, Murphy's Law intervenes and everything that can go wrong does go wrong. Directed by Richard Benjamin and made by Steven Spielberg's production company, but the comedy doesn't live up to its pedigree.

Monkey Business: see Marx Brothers

Mon Oncle
1958 U 104 ★★★★ FOR

Jacques Tati's first film in colour and a very funny but thoughtful diatribe against the tyranny of machines in modern life. The protagonist is a small boy with parents who are into everything technological and a sympathetic uncle (Tati) who isn't. (Subtitled)

Monsieur Hire
1989 15 82 ★★★ FOR

The basic story comes from a Georges Simenon thriller and involves a peeping tom falling in love with the object of his perversion. Direction by Patrice Leconte is all the more effective for keeping everything tight and short. One for the older members of the household. (Subtitled)

Monsieur Hulot's Holiday
1953 U 83 ★★★★ FOR

Jacques Tati revealing himself as the funniest Frenchmen of all time with a marvellous, if at times farcical, performance as the hapless, good-natured bachelor enjoying a spell at the seaside despite the chaos around him – much of which he causes. (B&W; subtitled)

Month in the Country, A
1987 PG 92 ★★★ DRA

Thoughtful, provocative drama which gently exposes the horror of war. Colin Firth and Kenneth Branagh star as a couple of soldiers back from the First World War and trying to forget it all in a quiet North Country village. But the traumas continue to haunt them. Beautifully acted and shot, with Natasha Richardson and Patrick Malahide providing able support.

Monty Python and the Holy Grail
1975 15 88 ★★★★ COM

Next to *Monty Python's Life of Brian* this is the best of the comic crew's feature films. This time the lads embark on a medieval crusade, mercilessly ripping into the legend of King Arthur. All the usual crowd – Terry Gilliam and Terry Jones (who also co-direct), Graham Chapman, Eric Idle, John Cleese and Michael Palin. Some inspired moments. Some naughty ones, too.

Monty Python's Life of Brian
1979 15 90 ★★★★ COM

Unquestionably the best and most cinematic of the Monty Python movies, the one in which Brian, son of the Virgin Mandy, is mistaken for the Messiah. Lots of people (who hadn't seen it) said it was blasphemous. Nonsense. What it is is a devilishly sly satire of organised religion and extremely funny.

Moonraker
1979 PG 126 ★★ ACT/ADV

Roger Moore as 007 in a James Bond adventure that increasingly resembles a cartoon with gadgets. Michael Lonsdale makes a good, weighty heavy but this is the least satisfying of all Moore's appearances as the man who likes his martinis shaken, not stirred.

Moonstruck
1987 PG 98 ★★★★ COM

A full moon shines over New York's Little Italy and numerous romances alter course – not least Cher's. In the absence of her fiancé (Danny Aiello) she finds herself drawn to his estranged younger brother (Nicolas Cage). There's a magic to this film, which was rewarded by three Oscars. It's joyous and life-enhancing with every performance a gem.

Morning After, The
1986 15 102 ★★ MYS/THR

An alcoholic (Jane Fonda) awakes to find a dead man in her bed. Since she can't remember how he got there she turns to others (specifically Jeff Bridges) for help. It's pretty routine and uninvolving stuff, unworthy of the cast and of Sidney Lumet, who directs without putting his back into it. There was an earlier film with the same title with Dick Van Dyke as an alcoholic. Don't confuse the two, they're very different.

Mother's Boys
1993 15 91 ★★★ HOR

Jamie Lee Curtis is the mother from hell who, having walked out on her husband, Peter Gallagher, and three very young sons, returns three years later to reclaim her family. Tense, chilling and disturbing and well done apart from the over-the-top Hollywood ending.

Mr Baseball
1992 15 104 ★★ COM

Tom Selleck, a top baseball player now past his sell-by date, is transferred to a Japanese team where he learns a thing or two, as do they. In part, a funny examination of the differences between East and West culture. A touch too stereotypical, though, to offer much that's new. Selleck is fun, but then he usually is.

Mr Blandings Builds His Dream House
1948 U 90 ★★★★ COM

Cary Grant is the homemaker of the title who finds that a dream house in the country doesn't necessarily make for an easy life. Well, building the house is not nearly as simple as he had thought. Myrna Loy as Mrs Blandings is excellent, as is Melvyn Douglas, the family friend who arouses Grant's suspicions. A little comic gem. (B&W)

Mr Deeds Goes to Town
1936 U 110 ★★★★ COM

No one handled comedy with a social conscience quite like Frank Capra. All the familiar Capra hallmarks are present in this smashing tale of a philanthropist (Gary Cooper at his best) who, on inheriting twenty million dollars, chooses to give it away and is subsequently thought to be mad. Jean Arthur is delightful as the hard-nosed reporter on the story. (B&W)

Mr Mom
1983 PG 87 ★★ COM

When Michael Keaton gets fired, his wife, Teri Garr, goes out to work while he stays home and minds the kids. Inevitably he finds it's not the cushy number he once believed it to be. A nice, if unoriginal idea, which works quite well thanks mainly to the cast, including Christopher Lloyd.

Mr Nanny
1992 PG 80 ★★ COM

Wrestler Hulk Hogan is hired as nanny to protect the spoilt kids of threatened scientist Austin Pendleton. Pretty brutal in parts, amusing in others, particularly when Hogan dresses in a pink tutu to please the little girl. Younger audiences will derive the most pleasure, since unsophisticated is the word for it.

Mrs Doubtfire
1993 PG 120 ★★★ COM

Suddenly unemployed actor Robin Williams, kicked out by wife Sally Field, disguises himself as a nanny to gain access to his children. Pretty funny in parts, horrendously sentimental elsewhere but it was one of the most popular comedies of all time. Much of the humour is provided by Pierce Brosnan's cameo as Field's new boyfriend.

Mrs Miniver
1942 U 128 ★★★★ DRA

Greer Garson gives the performance of a lifetime heading her English family drastically shaken by the advent of war. A great movie (winning seven Oscars, including Garson as Best Actress) which succeeded in rallying US support for the war. (B&W)

Mr Smith Goes to Washington
1939 U 124 ★★★★ DRA

Frank Capra again, this time with the help of James Stewart as an idealistic schoolteacher who, on election to the US Senate, is horrified to discover just how corrupt it is. Jean Arthur and Claude Rains add to the movie's caustic, witty appeal. The idea became a short-lived TV series and there was a remake – thankfully relegated to the movie graveyard – entitled *Billy Jack Goes to Washington*. (B&W)

Mrs Parker and the Vicious Circle
1994 15 124 ★★★ DRA

Dorothy Parker was the jewel in the Algonquin set's crown, but she of the snappy one-liners and rapier wit was an unhappy, unfulfilled woman, a fact that is stressed here. Jennifer Jason Leigh gives a marvellous performance, though almost too much so since she sounds so like Mrs Parker that her diction is difficult to follow and half the dialogue is hard to understand. The story tells of her life, her loves – mostly unrequited – and her career from the early Jazz Age days to Hollywood (as a scriptwriter) and lonely old age. Beautifully atmospheric, but you do have to listen closely.

Mrs Soffel
1984 PG 107 ★★★ DRA

An unusual love story in which Diane Keaton, as the wife of a prison warden, becomes deeply involved with two prisoners on death row – Matthew Modine and, especially, Mel Gibson. She starts by reading them scripture and ends by planning their escape from death.

Mr Wonderful
1993 15 98 ★★★ COM

Matt Dillon tries to persuade ex-wife Annabella Sciorra to remarry and relieve him of crippling alimony bills. So he sets out to find her a new husband but with, for him, surprising results. Director Anthony Minghella (who made *Truly, Madly, Deeply*) does a first-class job and though we know perfectly well who will end up with whom, it's quite plausible that the characters don't.

Much Ado about Nothing
1993 PG 106 ★★★★ COM

Kenneth Branagh's glorious, lusty, totally accessible version of Shakespeare's comedy. He also does a grand job as Benedick, the confirmed bachelor duped into falling for confirmed spinster Beatrice – nicely played by Mrs Branagh, Emma Thompson. An all-star cast includes Denzel Washington, Keanu Reeves, Michael Keaton and Richard Briers. An ideal introduction to Shakespeare for anyone.

Muppet Christmas Carol, The
1992 U 85 ★★★ FAM

Michael Caine stars as the miserly Scrooge using and abusing his poor employee Bob Cratchit (Kermit the Frog). In a role she was born to, Miss Piggy plays Mrs Cratchit, determined that her family should get better treatment from Scrooge this Christmas. A sweet musical tale which should appeal to Muppet fans and non-Muppet fans like.

Murder by Death
1976 PG 91 ★★ COM

More interesting for its cast than its plot. Truman Capote plays the host at a murder party to which he has invited the world's greatest detectives. Peter Sellers, Maggie Smith, Peter Falk, Alec Guinness and David Niven are among those involved. Writer Neil Simon sends up such literary dicks as Charlie Chan and Miss Marple. A nice enough idea that amounts to no more than a silly spoof.

Murder on the Orient Express
1974 PG 122 ★★★ MYS/THR

Albert Finney as Hercule Poirot solving the murder – of an American tycoon – aboard the famous train. A super supporting cast all do their bit: Lauren Bacall, Ingrid Bergman, Jacqueline Bisset, Sean Connery, John Gielgud, Vanessa Redgrave, Richard Widmark… the list goes on and on. Sidney Lumet directs it all at a good pace.

Murder, She Said
1961 PG 84 ★★★ MYS/THR

Based on Agatha Christie's *4.50 from Paddington* and starring Margaret Rutherford as Miss Marple. The usual satisfying Christie puzzle. It's the gloriously eccentric Rutherford, though, who carries the film and provides the appeal and charm. Other films featuring Rutherford as Miss Marple are *Murder at the Gallop*, *Murder Most Foul* and *Murder Ahoy*. They're all undemanding but agreeable and all have U certificates.

Music Box
1989 15 120 ★★★★ DRA

Jessica Lange gives a powerful performance as a lawyer defending her own father (Armin Mueller-Stahl) against a charge of war crimes. As she uncovers the evidence, so she learns that she never really knew her father. Cleverly scripted and beautifully directed by Costa-Gavras. For most of the film you're as much in the dark as Lange is about her father's possible involvement in the atrocities.

Music Man, The
1962 U 151 ★★★ MUS

Robert Preston plays a con-artist salesman who arrives in a small town where he proceeds to form a brass band. Best known of the songs is '76 Trombones' but there are also great renditions of 'Till There Was You' and 'Trouble'. A rousing, enjoyable movie.

Music of Chance, The
1993 15 94 ★★★ DRA

A strange, frightening tale that has the feel of a Roald Dahl story about it. It recounts the chilling experiences of two itinerant men who owe a pair of strange millionaires a lot of money and are forced to pay them back by building a wall in their grounds. The performances by James Spader and Mandy Patinkin are top-notch.

Mutiny on the Bounty
1962 15 177 ★★ ACT/ADV

This version with Trevor Howard and Marlon Brando reprising the 1935 Laughton and Gable roles (not available on video) is a great disappointment. Brando is simply miscast and self-indulgent, though Howard gives his usual fine performance. The film looks good but it's more violent than the earlier picture and far too long. (The most convincing and perhaps most accurate version of the story is *The Bounty* –

also a 15 – with Anthony Hopkins and Mel Gibson.)

My Beautiful Laundrette
1985 15 93 ★★★ DRA

An unusual drama about racism and intolerance generally. Daniel Day-Lewis stars as the white lover of a Pakistani (Gordon Warnecke) who helps Warnecke take over and run a launderette in South London. Pakistani playwright Hanif Kureishi wrote the script; Stephen Frears directed. It was originally intended as a television movie but was made so well as to warrant a cinema release.

My Blue Heaven
1990 PG 91 ★★★ COM

Steve Martin as a gormless but eccentric mobster who is relocated to suburban LA in the witness-protection programme. Helping him fit into his new life is straight-laced FBI agent Rick Moranis. Not really Martin at his best. (Another video – with a U certificate – called *My Blue Heaven* is a 1950 movie which stars Betty Grable and Dan Dailey as a couple of radio stars who adopt a child. It's a little sticky-sweet but a pleasing film for the family.)

My Cousin Vinny
1992 15 114 ★★★ COM

Two lads who steal a tin of tuna in Alabama are incorrectly charged with murder and call in dodgy cousin Joe Pesci, a barely qualified Brooklyn lawyer, to defend them. But since all he does is antagonise the judge (Fred Gwynne – very good) they might be better off defending themselves. Marisa Tomei shines as Pesci's feisty girlfriend. Funny at the start and finish, drags a lot in the middle.

My Darling Clementine
1946 U 93 ★★★★★ WES

John Ford, the master of the Western, is on absolutely top form in this lyrical, thrilling version of the story of Wyatt Earp, Doc Holliday, the Clanton gang and, of course, the gunfight at the OK Corral. Henry Fonda plays Earp and Victor Mature is surprisingly good as the alcoholic, consumptive Doc Holliday. A must for all Western fans. (B&W)

My Fair Lady
1964 U 163 ★★★★ MUS

A lovely score distinguishes this musical version of Shaw's play, including 'I Could Have Danced All Night'. Rex Harrison is spot on as the professor trying to turn a flower girl (Audrey Hepburn) into a lady. Hepburn's cockney accent is nearly on a par with Dick Van Dyke's in *Mary Poppins*, but who cares, she looks wonderful.

My Favourite Year
1982 PG 88 ★★★★ COM

Peter O'Toole bears a marked resemblance to Errol Flynn in his wonderfully comic performance as an alcoholic actor who can't get the roles any more and is obliged to take part in a live TV show. Mark Linn-Baker has the onerous task of trying to get the drunk to turn up sober and on time for the programme. A delightful relationship develops between the two vastly different men. Good direction by Richard Benjamin.

My Girl
1991 PG 98 ★ DRA

Anna Chlumsky comes of age when she experiences death and her first kiss (with Macaulay Culkin, no less) during the course of one summer. Her father (Dan Aykroyd) also finds love in the shapely form of Jamie Lee Curtis. A rites of passage tale that benefits from the adult performers, and could have been better if only they had a little more to do.

My Girl 2
1994 PG 95 ★ DRA

Chlumsky's back, older and wiser this time, not only wondering about boys, but about her late mother. So she heads off to LA to find out more. Jamie Lee Curtis and Aykroyd return but in parts that are even smaller than before. No Culkin this time, though.

My Left Foot
1989 15 99 ★★★★ DRA

Daniel Day-Lewis and Brenda Fricker won Oscars for their performances as, respectively, cerebral palsy victim Christy Brown, who so painfully taught himself to write, and his determined mother. Jim Sheridan's lively film exudes anger, hope and the indomitability of the human spirit. It's never downbeat, always uplifting. Ray McAnally provides great support as Christy's father.

My Life as a Dog
1985 PG 97 ★★★★ FOR

Many people whose opinions are worth listening to think this was the best film of the 1980s. It's based on a largely autobiographical novel about a twelve-year-old Swedish boy sent to live with his uncle and aunt in the country, *circa* 1950. He's a mischievous lad and his adventures switch between the comic and the poignant. It's most suited to the older family members who should find it a delight. (Subtitled)

My Stepmother is an Alien
1988 15 103 ★★ COM

A novel idea, quite nicely explored by director Richard Benjamin. A widowed scientist, Dan Aykroyd, meets the woman of his dreams, marries her and looks forward to a life of domestic bliss. Trouble is his new wife, Kim Basinger, is an alien intent on saving her planet. At times fairly amusing but the main attraction is the two leads, who work surprisingly well together.

Mystery of Edwin Drood, The
1993 15 97 ★ DRA

If Charles Dickens had managed to finish his novel, he'd have done it a lot better than this movie did. Talk about artistic licence – a nineteenth-century story ends up with a very twentieth-century denouement. Robert Powell manages to shine as the jealous fiancé and there are some familiar faces in the cast. (An earlier and better version in 1935 starred Claude Rains and Douglas Montgomery.)

Mystic Pizza
1988 15 104 ★★★ DRA

An enchanting tale of three young women (Julia Roberts, Annabeth Gish and Lili Taylor) who work in a pizza joint in Connecticut and seek romance and a better life. The performances are the movie's appeal. It was Roberts's first film and remains one of her best. A well-written, character-led drama that never got the recognition it deserved. (Don't let the male members of the household dismiss it as 'a women's movie'.)

Nadine
1987 PG 80 ★★ DRA

Soufflé-light comedy-thriller set in 1950s small-town America where the local hairdresser (Kim Basinger) witnesses the murder of a photographer while she's trying to steal back some nudey shots he has of her. Jeff Bridges plays the loser husband she's about to divorce. Good natured, with nice interaction between Basinger and Bridges.

Naked Gun, The: From the Files of Police Squad!
1988 15 81 ★★★★ COM

From the people who brought you *Airplane!* and the TV series *Police Squad* and done in the same knockabout style. Leslie Nielsen stars as blundering cop Lt Drebin who, somehow, manages to get the job done. Few of the gags miss the mark and some will have you crying with laughter. Priscilla Presley is a revelation as a comedienne. Also features O J Simpson, who later became prominent for far less hilarious reasons.

Naked Gun 2½, The: The Smell of Fear
1991 15 82 ★★★ COM

Lt Drebin returns to tackle the threat of toxic waste. Priscilla Presley's back to help him, as are George Kennedy and O J. Again, it's very funny but probably the weakest of the series. Some of the jokes look a little stale but there are still enough good ones to make it well worth watching.

Naked Gun 33⅓: The Final Insult
1994 12 79 ★★★★ COM

It's a toss up between this and the original as to which film is funnier. Drebin's having trouble coping with retirement so when a dastardly crime challenges all the guys at the police station, he picks up his badge and returns to the force. This time the makers are back on top form with fresh gags and a wonderful finale at the Oscars.

Narrow Margin
1990 15 93 ★★ MYS/THR

Despite the presence of Gene Hackman as an assistant DA assigned to accompany murder witness Anne Archer to trial, the film tends to pall. Chemistry is lacking between the two leads and, rather than adding to the suspense, the claustrophobic location – a train – merely confines. (An earlier, more gripping version exists from 1952, available on *The Video Collection*.)

Nasty Girl, The
1990 PG 93 ★★★★ FOR

A German film about a young woman (Lena Stolze) who delves into her Bavarian hometown's record during the war and becomes obsessed with uncovering its involvement with the Nazis. Biting drama and a lot of ironic humour. (Subtitled)

National Lampoon's Animal House
1978 15 106 ★★★ COM

Director John Landis kicks off the first of the *National Lampoon* series, which still remains the best. In this intermittently hilarious spoof of American college life most of the better gags spring from below the belt – either lavatorial or sexual – and involve irreverent student John Belushi. Donald Sutherland, Tim Matheson and Tom Hulce share the acting credits.

National Lampoon's Christmas Vacation
1989 PG 93 ★★ COM

Poor old Chevy Chase is having financial troubles over the festive period but despite it all enters the spirit of the occasion and, along with Beverly D'Angelo (back for a third time as Mrs Griswald), entertains their extended family at home. The Christmas tree burning down is one of the calmer moments. Chase is ably supported by Randy Quaid, Diane Ladd, John Randolph and a very young Juliette Lewis.

National Lampoon's European Vacation
1985 15 90 ★ COM

As a follow up to *Vacation* (see below) this is very disappointing. The jokes are weaker for being familiar and the situations are more farcical than ever. The absence of Randy Quaid is compensated for to some extent by the presence of Robbie Coltrane, Mel Smith and Eric Idle as a polite British cyclist.

National Lampoon's Loaded Weapon 1
1993 PG 79 ★ COM

Despite the involvement of those who produced the *Airplane!* and *Naked Gun* series this is an all-too-often unfunny spoof of action movies like *Lethal Weapon*. Emilio Estevez and Samuel L Jackson don't have the comic touch for farce that, say, Leslie Nielsen has, though there are moments which will make you roar.

National Lampoon's Vacation
1983 15 94 ★★ COM

In which the hapless Griswald family – Chevy Chase, his unfortunate wife Beverly D'Angelo and children – heads off across the USA in search of a holiday. What ensues is a reasonably amusing catalogue of fiascos. Randy Quaid and John Candy are just a couple of the horrors the family encounters en route.

National Velvet
1944 U 118 ★★★ FAM

Most notorious for being the film that broke the back of Elizabeth Taylor – both metaphorically and literally – but most loved for being a sentimental tale about a young girl who, against all the odds and helped only by a stable lad (Mickey Rooney), gets to ride in the Grand National. A charming tale of courage and determination with fine support performances. Anne Revere won a Best Supporting Actress Oscar for her role as Taylor's mother.

Natural, The
1984 PG 118 ★★★ DRA

Robert Redford shines as a baseball player whose talent is so great as to be other-worldly. Robert Duvall, Kim Basinger and Glenn Close join the cast but it's still way too long. Sensitive direction from Barry Levinson tends toward sentimentality but the score, photography and performances are spot on.

Navy SEALS
1990 15 109 ★ ACT/ADV

A silly, suspenseless thriller about a couple of crack commandos from the US Navy (Charlie Sheen and Michael Biehn) who, SAS-like, go into the areas other units cannot reach. Macho posturing and ludicrous daredevil escapes make up most of the action. (For those interested in such things, SEALS is an acronym of Sea, Air and Land Services – those boys go everywhere.)

Necessary Roughness
1991 15 103 ★ DRA

Scott Bakula (he of TV's *Quantum Leap*) plays a quarterback returning to college to save its football team. There he finds some of the teachers aren't the strict unapproachables he once thought them. You'd be forgiven for missing the comedy since it certainly isn't marked by laughs. As predictable as it is formulaic, with the thirty-four-year-old Bakula looking very uncomfortable as a college kid, particularly in those tight sports trousers.

Network
1976 15 117 ★★★ DRA

This biting satire of the television world features just about everyone you've ever heard of. Sidney Lumet directs the likes of Peter Finch (who won a posthumous Oscar), Faye Dunaway, William Holden, Ned Beatty, Robert Duvall and Ken Kercheval – remember him as the boozy Cliff Barnes in TV's *Dallas*?

NeverEnding Story, The
1984 U 90 ★★★ FAM

A lovely idea, enhanced by breathtaking special effects, about young Bastian (Barret Oliver) who enters the mystical world of his adventure book. But there's no such thing as a free lunch. Once there it falls to him to save the world, too. Directed by Wolfgang Petersen, it was a German/British venture which suffered in the following sequels by Hollywood's increasing involvement. America may have improved the effects but it destroyed the magic.

NeverEnding Story II, The: The Next Chapter
1990 U 86 ★★ FAM

Despite the improved special effects, this is a disappointing sequel since the story's lost its way as badly as our hero, Bastian. He's having a hard time: his mum's died and his dad is preoccupied, so he seeks refuge in the pages of his storybook.

NeverEnding Story 3, The
1994 U 85 ★ FAM

'Interminable story' is more accurate as a title since all the magic of the first film has vanished and what is left is a crass, thin tale of cheesy characters carried over from the previous movies. Special effects are clever but it lacks excitement and one hopes it heralds the last of the series.

Never Say Never Again
1983 PG 128 ★★★ ACT/ADV

Sean Connery returns for his final outing as Bond (after a twelve-year break), accompanied by the usual clever gadgetry, Kim Basinger, Klaus Maria Brandauer, Max von Sydow and Edward Fox. It's a slick remake of *Thunderball* but tends to go on too long.

News Boys, The
1992 PG 117 ★★ MUS

At the turn of the century, the USA experienced a newspaper-boy strike. This musical and ineffectual account fails to convey any drama. The talented Christian Bale leads the rebellious lads and Robert Duvall plays Joseph Pulitzer, the robber baron who puts the boys out of work. Not at all a bad score, though.

New York, New York
1977 PG 156 ★★★ MUS

Martin Scorsese bites off more than he can chew with this elaborate tale of a couple (Robert De Niro and Liza Minnelli) set against the background of the Big Band era. It's well worth watching since individual features are impressive – the score and the design particularly. But as a whole it doesn't quite gel. Based loosely on the drama *The Man I Love*.

New York Stories
1989 15 125 ★★★ DRA

A diverse trilogy of short films from Woody Allen, Martin Scorsese and Francis Coppola. Not only does the subject matter vary greatly, but so does the form. Allen's *Oedipus Wrecks* is the best – a ghostly Jewish mother gives her son a roasting for his choice of girlfriend (Mia Farrow). Scorsese's *Life Lessons*, an intense

drama of the art world with Nick Nolte and Rosanna Arquette, isn't bad, but Coppola's *Life without Zoe* is, being a sentimental, poorly portrayed tale of a lonely rich girl.

Next of Kin
1989 15 103 ★★ ACT/ADV

Patrick Swayze is convincing as a backwoodsman, less so as a cop. The ol' country boy is down from the hills in Chicago, on the trail of a mobster. Luckily he's got his brother, Liam Neeson, to help. The formula's too rigid to provide much in the way of novelty, though the casting is interesting and the action, at times very violent, is well staged.

Niagara
1953 PG 85 ★★ DRA

Most notable point about this thriller, which falls flat in the suspense department, is that it's the first starring vehicle for Marilyn Monroe, who oozes sex appeal playing the promiscuous wife planning to do away with her husband (Joseph Cotten) at the falls.

Nicholas and Alexandra
1971 PG 165 ★★★ DRA

Lavish historical drama depicting the events leading to the Russian revolution. Michael Jayston stars as Tsar Nicholas, who strives to keep self and family together. It's a somewhat overblown epic, although the cast impresses. Janet Suzman is excellent as the Tsarina, as is Tom Baker as Rasputin, and there are cameos from the likes of Laurence Olivier and Michael Redgrave.

Night and the City
1992 15 104 ★★ MYS/THR

Disappointment's the overriding factor here as a period thriller pairing Robert De Niro and Jessica Lange should be better than this. De Niro plays a 1950s ambulance-chasing lawyer who wants to make the big time and aims to do so via boxing promotion with the aid of his married girlfriend's money. Unlikeable characters and a lack of atmosphere is the overall impression.

Night at the Opera: see Marx Brothers

Night of the Hunter, The
1955 PG 91 ★★★★ MYS/THR

With 'love' and 'hate' tattooed on his knuckles Robert Mitchum plays a bible-basher preying on some runaway children whose mother he has murdered. It's a suspenseful examination of good and evil, with fine work all round, though most notably by the director – Charles Laughton – who, despite showing such an aptitude for it, never directed again. (There was another version made in 1991 with Richard Chamberlain. The remake has a different ending.)

Night on Earth
1991 15 124 ★★★ DRA

Five stories, all of which take place in or around a taxi cab. LA, New York, Paris, Rome and Helsinki provide the backdrops for the vaguely amusing, always poignant tales written by Jim Jarmusch. Winona Ryder, Rosie Perez, Beatrice Dalle, Gena Rowlands and Armin Mueller-Stahl are just some of the people cruising the cities searching for something missing from their lives. (Partly subtitled)

Night to Remember, A
1942 PG 88 ★★★ MYS/THR

Brian Aherne plays a novelist who finds himself embroiled in a mystery similar to one he might have written when he discovers a body in his New York flat. A neat little thriller is enlivened by humour and the light touch of Loretta Young as Aherne's wife. Not to be confused with the following film.

Night to Remember, A
1958 PG 118 ★★★ DRA

A straightforward – and all the better for that – account of the sinking of the *Titanic* on its maiden voyage in 1912. The main problem with it is that there are just too many characters so that leading players Kenneth More and Honor Blackman have little chance to shine. But the build up to the collision with the iceberg ('I know I ordered ice but this is ridiculous') is well done.

1941
1979 PG 113 ★★ DRA

This is one of Spielberg's few flops. He bit off more than he could chew with this extravaganza about a Japanese submarine arriving in LA, 1941, just after the news of Pearl Harbor. Dan Aykroyd, Ned Beatty and John Belushi star and it's spectacular to look at but the comedy is far too frenetic and desperate and the story is unconvincing.

Nine to Five
1980 15 105 ★★★ COM

A boardroom farce in which secretaries Jane Fonda, Lily Tomlin and Dolly Parton plan revenge on their chauvinistic boss, Dabney Coleman. Laughs owe more to the women's performances than the script, though it had enough moments to spark a successful TV series and launch the acting career of Ms Parton.

Ninotchka
1939 U 105 ★★★★★ COM

When a tough, no-nonsense Russian envoy (Greta Garbo) is dispatched to Paris, it's not long before the Communist in her is lost to the lure of the city and the appeal of fun-loving socialite Melvyn Douglas. This is a joyous romantic comedy. While Garbo and Douglas do a splendid job with the romance, the fun is provided by the three KGB spies sent to keep an eye on their colleague who themselves succumb to the capitalist lifestyle. The original publicity billing announced: 'Garbo Laughs!'

No Escape
1994 15 118 ★★★ ACT/ADV

Ray Liotta stars as a grade 'A' prisoner sometime in the future who is sent to a new type of jail – an island from which there's no escape and on which there are no wardens, only violent prisoners. Interesting ideas are never fully explored, though it's good to see Liotta given the lead role, a task for which he proves more than able.

Noises Off
1992 15 99 ★★ COM

Director Peter Bogdanovich has turned Michael Frayn's very funny play into a vaguely amusing farce about a bunch of touring thespians bumbling their way toward their New York debut. It worked far better on the stage but the cast, including Michael Caine, Denholm Elliott, Christopher Reeve and Marilu Henner, has a certain appeal.

Norma Rae
1979 PG 110 ★★★ DRA

An Oscar-winning performance by Sally Field in the title role of this tear-jerker about a Southern mill worker who organises a union to push for better working conditions. Beau Bridges plays her husband. Great performances all round, though a little heavy going at times.

North
1994 PG 83 ★★★ COM

Formulaic Hollywood family fare in which a young boy (Elijah Wood) searches the length and breadth of the world for the perfect parents. Silly story but a good vehicle for a number of cameos (from Kathy Bates and Alan Arkin, for instance) and offbeat performances – not least that of Bruce Willis as the Easter Bunny.

North by Northwest
1959 PG 131 ★★★★ ACT/ADV

One of Hitchcock's best adventure films, in which Cary Grant plays an advertising executive who finds himself in very hot water when he's mistaken for a spy. James Mason is impeccably smooth as the baddie. The camerawork makes the most of the locations, not least the memorable finale at Mount Rushmore.

North West Frontier
1959 U 125 ★★★★ ACT/ADV

British film-making at its best. Action-packed, humorous and nicely written story set in war-torn India around 1905. British officer Kenneth More is assigned to take a train across the country to save a young prince. Also aboard are the prince's governess, Lauren Bacall, plus Herbert Lom and Wilfrid Hyde White. Upper lips were never stiffer and there are some palm-sweating moments as the train encounters no end of trouble en route. (Americans know this movie as *Flame Over India*.)

Notorious
1946 U 97 ★★★ MYS/THR

Hitchcock thriller with a nice dash of romance between Cary Grant and Ingrid Bergman mixed up in a Nazi plot. Needless to say Claude Rains makes a terrific baddie though the deep characterization means no-one's entirely black or white. The suspense is maintained right to the very end and, of course, romance blossoms nicely. (B&W)

Not without My Daughter
1990 15 111 ★★ DRA

A true story about a woman (played by Sally Field) whose beloved child was snatched by her father and taken from her home in America to live in Iran. Despite all appeals, the mother got no co-operation from the authorities. So, she went it alone and decided to escape with her daughter. Alfred Molina as the father is excellent; Field tends to cry a lot.

No Way Out
1987 15 109 ★★★ MYS/THR

Kevin Costner stars as a young naval officer who finds himself the prime suspect in a murder case but is convinced the defence secretary (Gene Hackman) is the guilty party. Sean Young provides the link between the two men. Keep your wits about you with this one, the mystery's complex. (To an extent this is a remake of the 1947 thriller *The Big Clock* but the new version adds a strange but interesting twist at the very end.)

Nowhere to Run
1993 15 91 ★ ACT/ADV

This just about passes muster for a rainy Saturday afternoon when there's nothing on the TV. Outlaw Jean-Claude Van Damme pitches up at the farm of single mother Rosanna Arquette, who's in the throes of fighting off nasty Joss Ackland, who wants her farm for development. Oh, how sorry Ackland will be for tangling with the Muscles from Brussels. The script is cornier than the farm fields and the plot as predictable as Van Damme's expressions.

Now, Voyager
1942 PG 113 ★★★★ DRA

Bette Davis gives so good a performance that she earned herself a fifth successive Oscar nomination. This is the melodrama in which she falls in love with the married Paul Henreid and utters the immortal line, 'Let's not ask for the moon when we have the stars'. They just don't make weepies like this any more. Indeed, they rarely made weepies like this at any time.

Nukie
1992 U 95 ★ FAM

An interracial, intergalactic fantasy about a couple of aliens who land on Earth in Africa. This is an attempt to cash in on the success of such movies as *ET*. But it needs to be an awful lot better to stand much chance. The characters simply aren't rounded enough – and we don't mean portly.

Nuns on the Run
1990 15 88 ★★★ COM

A broad but often hilarious film about a couple of smalltime crooks (Robbie Coltrane and Eric Idle) who unwittingly get involved with the big boys and hide out in a convent, posing as nuns. Undemanding but fun and quite exciting. The surprise find of the film was Camille Coduri as Idle's love interest; the bigger surprise is that she's not been in anything since.

Nun's Story, The
1959 PG 145 ★★★★ DRA

A moving, reflective story with Audrey Hepburn as a nun working deep in the heart of the Belgian Congo who finds conditions there make her doubt her faith. Peter Finch, as the attractive local doctor, doesn't make her vows any easier to keep. Edith Evans and Dame Peggy Ashcroft play fellow nuns. Fred Zinnemann directed – very well, too.

Nurse on Wheels
1963 U 82 ★★★★ COM

A perfectly charming British comedy in which district nurse Juliet Mills, complete with bicycle and elderly mother, takes up residence in a small village community. Love and romance crop up in the shape of a local farmer. Comedy stalwarts such as Joan Sims and Jim Dale help things along. At times, very funny indeed.

Nuts in May
1976 PG 81 ★★★★ COM

Mike Leigh's hilarious and forward-looking comedy about an environmentally correct couple – all open sandals and falafels – who hit the country on a camping holiday. With acute observation, Leigh exposes the absurdities of 'enthusiasts' whether they be environmentalists, vegetarians or campers. Alison Steadman is unrecognisable as the mousey Candice-Marie dominated by her ill-matched husband Keith – a superb performance by Roger Sloman.

Octopussy
1983 PG 125 ★★★ ACT/ADV

Roger Moore picks up his licence to kill in his sixth outing as James Bond and – unlucky for some – thirteenth adventure for the secret agent (fourteen if you count *Casino Royale* – but who does?). Among his adversaries are a sexy smuggler, Maud Adams, and Louis Jourdan, who simply wants to rule the world. Again the gadgets are the real stars, though Moore is at his most charming and the locations – India, Berlin and the Middle East – are pleasing. Nice cameo from then tennis ace Vijay Amritraj.

Odd Couple, The
1968 PG 101 ★★★★ COM

Sharply written and acutely observed comedy from the pen of Neil Simon about two men, one very tidy, the other a slob, sharing a flat in the aftermath of divorce. Jack Lemmon (the tidy one) and Walter Matthau are on splendid form. A long-running TV series followed, though it lacked the winning partnership of Matthau and Lemmon.

Odessa File, The
1974 PG 123 ★★ DRA

Jon Voight leads Frederick Forsyth's thriller about a German reporter on the trail of Nazi war criminals who had hitherto escaped retribution. An average plot is adequately performed by a cast that includes Maria Schell, Maximilian Schell and Derek Jacobi. The music is by Andrew Lloyd Webber.

Officer and a Gentleman, An
1982 15 119 ★★★ DRA

Richard Gere is the naval cadet who eventually earns the description of the title, thanks in part to the love of a good woman, factory girl Debra Winger. This was the film that spawned the song 'Up Where We Belong' and garnered Louis Gossett Jr the Oscar for Best Supporting Actor for his portrayal of the harsh sergeant who licks Gere into shape. All the performances are pretty good. This is perhaps one for the romantics among you.

Of Mice and Men
1992 PG 106 ★★★ DRA

John Steinbeck's touching, ultimately tragic 1930s tale of two itinerant workers, one able

and competent (Gary Sinise), the other simple and too strong for his own good (John Malkovich), is beautifully played and shot. Contains some sex and much that is emotionally quite harrowing. (There was also a 1981 TV movie starring Robert Blake and Randy Quaid, which was competent but not so good as the later film. The 1939 version in black and white with Burgess Meredith and Lon Chaney Jr is probably the best of the three but is not available on video.)

Oh, Mr Porter!
1937 U 80 ★★★★ FAM

Will Hay, much underrated nowadays, was one of the finest of British film comedians and here he turns in a hilarious performance as the officious stationmaster running an isolated wayside halt on the Irish border. Along with Graham Moffatt, his incompetent and sarcastic assistant, and the near-senile Moore Marriott, he encounters supposed ghosts that turn out to be gun-runners. There is plenty here to amuse all the family.

Oklahoma!
1955 U 134 ★★★★ MUS

The winning musical combination of Rodgers and Hammerstein strikes gold again with such cracking numbers as 'Oh, What a Beautiful Morning' and 'I'm Just a Girl Who Can't Say No'. Shirley Jones belts out the numbers as the country girl romanced by cowboy Gordon MacRae. But with an amorous and dangerous ranch hand, Rod Steiger, lurking in the woodshed there's a darker twist to the plot than in most musicals. A must for fans of musicals.

Old Gringo
1989 15 115 ★★ DRA

Pancho Villa's 1913 Mexican revolution provides the setting for an intriguing *ménage-à-trois* between a spinster (Jane Fonda), a journalist (Gregory Peck) and a dashing Mexican general (Jimmy Smits). Individually they're fine but somehow the three don't spark the chemistry needed to make the relationships believable. Like Sandown racecourse on a March morning – a little heavy going at times.

Old Yeller
1957 U 81 ★★ FAM

Prepare to weep. Disney pulls out all the emotional stops in this endearing tale about a young lad (Tommy Kirk) and his faithful stray dog struggling against the hardships of farm life in nineteenth-century Texas. The younger children will love it.

Oliver!
1968 U 140 ★★★★ MUS

Mark Lester is most appealing as the eponymous orphan who asks for more and gets more than he bargained for. Ron Moody's Fagin takes the acting honours in Carol Reed's (and Lionel Bart's) Oscar-winning musical. The characters, the score and the choreography are all impressive and Dickens's genius as a storyteller means there's enough excitement between the songs to keep everyone happy.

Oliver Twist
1948 U 111 ★★★★ FAM

David Lean's version is devoid of songs but offers Alec Guinness – brilliant as Fagin – in a faithful adaptation of Dickens's saga. Also noteworthy: an early appearance by Anthony Newley as the Artful Dodger and an appealing piece of acting by John Howard Davies in the title role. (B&W)

Oliver Twist
1982 PG 98 ★★ DRA

This later version with George C Scott, Michael Hordern and the Tims Curry and West is worth watching since it's smartly adapted by James Goldman, but it doesn't measure up to Lean's film. Scott is particularly good as Fagin but the very young may find it a little frightening, hence the PG certificate.

Olivier Olivier
1992 15 104 ★★★ FOR

A young French boy disappears from his country home. His mother is distraught but nothing she does can find him. Years later he returns, to be warmly welcomed back by her but looked on suspiciously by his sister. Is he indeed, as he claims, the real Olivier? An intriguing, atmospheric tale. Warning: there are a couple of scenes suggestive of incest. (Subtitled)

Once Upon a Forest
1993 U 68 ★★ FAM

A politically correct animated tale with songs provided by Michael Crawford. A tanker has crashed, releasing its toxic contents into the air, thereby killing most of the forest. It's left to three little adventurers – a mouse, a mole and a hedgehog – to fetch the necessary herbs to cure the survivors. The animation's good, the story worthy and the ensemble generally pleasing.

One-Eyed Jacks
1961 PG 135 ★★★ WES

A psychological Western in which an outlaw (Marlon Brando) seeks revenge on his one-time friend, now a sheriff (Karl Malden). The novel on which it's loosely based told the story of Pat Garrett and Billy the Kid but the names and the outcome were changed for the film. Moody and atmospheric with magnificent seascapes – it's set in the Monterey Peninsula – and good direction by Brando, who stepped in behind the camera at the last minute.

One Million Years BC
1966 PG 96 ★★★ ACT/ADV

Three stars might be a touch generous but Ray Harryhausen's prehistoric special effects are ingenious and there's always the sight of Raquel Welch in her natty, off-the-shoulder designer bearskin. In the time of the title Rock man John Richardson falls for Shell woman Welch but has to overcome tribal opposition, dinosaurs and earthquakes before winning her. The dialogue consists of grunts and there are some enjoyable, unintended laughs.

One of Our Aircraft Is Missing
1942 U 97 ★★★ WAR

A Powell and Pressburger thriller about the crew of a British bomber forced to bale out on their way back over Holland. The enemy may not only be the Germans. Intriguing and tense, admirably played by the likes of Eric Portman, Hugh Williams and Bernard Miles. Hitchcock-esque cameo by Michael Powell as an air-traffic controller.

One of Our Dinosaurs is Missing
1975 U 90 ★★★ FAM

Disney does England – again with fog and cockneys as shorthand for London and every foreigner a baddie. But it's entertaining all the same. A spy hides a secret formula in a dinosaur bone and farce ensues as good guys and bad guys scramble to recover it first. A splendid cast – Peter Ustinov, Helen Hayes, Joan Sims, Roy Kinnear and Joss Ackland – makes up for the faults.

One, Two, Three
1961 U 110 ★★★ COM

James Cagney, an American executive for Coca-Cola trying to sell the drink to the Russians, is given the even trickier task of preventing his boss discovering that his daughter has made the most unsuitable marriage – to a Communist. A Billy Wilder comedy that verges on the farcical, though it's worth watching since it marks Cagney's last starring role.

On Golden Pond
1981 PG 104 ★★★ DRA

Although essentially a drama about a father/daughter reconciliation one summer, there's a great deal of humour in this heartwarming tale, made all the more poignant for starring real-life estranged father and daughter Henry and Jane Fonda. As the father and daughter make up on screen, so did the Fondas off screen. And not a moment too soon, for it was to be Henry's last film. He and Katharine Hepburn both won Oscars.

On Her Majesty's Secret Service
1969 PG 127 ★★ ACT/ADV

This is the James Bond movie they hoped to forget. George Lazenby plays 007 with as much vivacity as a totem pole. Rumour has it that he and leading lady Diana Rigg hit it off so badly that she would eat bulbs of garlic the evening before a love scene. Pity, because the plot is stronger than most and there's some cracking action. Indeed, some Bond fans reckon this is the best of the lot, but they're in the minority.

Only the Lonely
1991 15 100 ★ COM

A sad little tale about a policeman (John Candy) living with and dominated by his mother (Maureen O'Hara). Things get even sadder when he falls for undertaker's daughter Ally Sheedy and mum strives to scupper the romance. Well played but the direction, by Christopher Columbus, fails to exploit the humour and only develops the poignant side. James Belushi, Anthony Quinn and Macaulay Culkin join the cast.

On the Town
1949 U 93 ★★★ MUS

All-singing, all-dancing, all-starry musical about three sailors (Gene Kelly, Frank Sinatra and Jules Munshin) on leave for a day in New York. It's an action-packed day with the lads intent on making the most of their twenty-four hours. A brilliant score includes 'New York, New York' plus a ballet by Leonard Bernstein and Kelly's choreography.

On the Waterfront
1954 PG 103 ★★★★ DRA

Unrelenting drama about the New York harbour union striking against its oppressive boss (Lee J Cobb). Marlon Brando is superb as the ex-boxer trying to do what's right. Rod Steiger, Karl Malden and Eva Marie Saint provide terrific support. No surprise really that it won eight Oscars, among them one for director Elia Kazan, one for Brando and one for Saint.

Ordinary People
1980 15 119 ★★★ DRA

This poignant tale about a family which falls apart when their teenage son commits suicide is almost too painful to watch. For those with a sensitive disposition and a tendency to weep easily – steer clear. Donald Sutherland and Mary Tyler Moore play the parents, while Robert Redford stays behind the camera to direct. And a very good job he does too, winning the Oscar for his efforts.

Orlando
1992 PG 89 ★★★ DRA

Director Sally Potter's excellent adaptation of a Virginia Woolf story about an Elizabethan man/woman who lived for 400 years. Tilda Swinton does a smashing job portraying the androgynous heroine and is ably supported by Billy Zane and Quentin Crisp.

Oscar
1991 PG 105 ★★ COM

Sylvester Stallone's first attempt at period comedy – with varying results. The story, about a 1930s Mafia boss whose daughter is planning an unsuitable marriage, is too much of a drawing-room farce. But the characters are likeable and Stallone does well enough at the comedy in such distinguished company as Don Ameche, Marisa Tomei and even Linda Gray – a name from the past, better known as 'S'wellen' from TV's *Dallas*.

Other People's Money
1991 15 96 ★★ COM

A gentle comedy about a financial asset-stripper, Danny DeVito, who finds a good deal of opposition to his bid to buy Gregory Peck's family business. Wall Street ruthlessness meets old-fashioned values. Norman Jewison directs; Penelope Ann Miller, Piper Laurie and Dean Jones co-star.

Outcast of the Islands
1951 PG 96 ★★ DRA

Carol Reed directed this adaptation of Joseph Conrad's novel with Trevor Howard in fine form as the eponymous outcast, a man who is driven to crime and deceit partly through external circumstances, partly because of his own shiftless character. An honourable attempt to translate an excellent book to the screen. The Malaysian background makes a pretty setting and there's a strong supporting cast – Ralph Richardson, Wendy Hiller, Robert Morley and Kerima as the native girl with whom Howard becomes obsessed. (B&W)

Outlaw, The
1943 U 111 ★★ WES

It was for this raunchy Western that Jane Russell had that pointy bra specially made. By present standards it's quite tame but in its day this was considered to be very sexy. The story brings Billy the Kid together with Doc Holliday (Walter Huston), though the kid finds time to huddle in the hay with Russell. Suitable for all members since there's nothing here that would shock or offend modern audiences.

Out of Africa
1985 PG 154 ★★★ DRA

The beautiful game parks of Africa provide the backdrop to this touching tale (based on the life of Karen Blixen) of a love affair between a married society woman (Meryl Streep) and a white hunter (a somewhat miscast and curiously small-looking Robert Redford). Klaus Maria Brandauer is terrific in support. Sydney Pollack directs but the real star of the movie is the landscape.

Outrageous Fortune
1987 15 95 ★★★ COM

A comedy of errors which owes most of the laughs to its female stars, Bette Midler and Shelley Long, since the script is weak and the plot poor. An ill-matched pair of women join forces to find the man with whom, it transpires, they were both having an affair. Peter Coyote is the rat who has supposedly perished in a mysterious explosion.

Overboard
1987 PG 107 ★★ COM

A quite entertaining tale of redemption. Wealthy, selfish Goldie Hawn loses her memory when she falls off her yacht. Widowed Kurt Russell saves her and, persuading the amnesiac that she is his wife, uses her as a housekeeper and nanny for his unruly kids. Distasteful? Well, yes, it is a bit. Otherwise it's a light romantic comedy of the type Hawn can do with her eyes shut.

Pacific Heights
1990 15 98 ★★★ MYS/THR

A happy couple (Melanie Griffith and Matthew Modine), renovating their dream home, make a BIG mistake by taking in psychotic lodger Michael Keaton. Not only do their lives become a nightmare, they're also endangered. Creepy, thanks to a great performance by Keaton, and one to be watched with the lights on and, preferably, in company.

Package, The
1989 15 103 ★★ ACT/ADV

A Cold War thriller which will leave you cold since it's pretty run-of-the-mill stuff. Gene Hackman plays a soldier who discovers he's being used as the fall guy in an American/Russian conspiracy. Excitement's kept to a minimum and the action's unsurprising. Despite the cast, among them Tommy Lee Jones, Joanna Cassidy and John Heard, there's not much to recommend it.

Paint Your Wagon
1969 PG 153 ★★★ MUS

A musical Western with Lee Marvin and Clint Eastwood singing. Whatever next? Actually they do it rather well, though their tongues would seem firmly ensconced in their cheeks throughout the film. The macho crooners buy the same wife (Jean Seberg) at an auction, and a whole lot of trouble to boot. Marvin's rendition of 'Wand'rin' Star' remains a classic.

Pajama Game, The
1957 U 96 ★★★ MUS

Doris Day rouses fellow factory workers to demand better conditions in between songs. Politics takes a back seat to music and romance but the capital-versus-labour plot is meatier than in most musicals. Day is as robust as ever and the tunes are catchy.

Pale Rider
1985 15 111 ★★ WES

Directed by and starring Clint Eastwood, there's strong atmosphere to this Western but an awful lot of pretension. Again he plays the enigmatic stranger, riding into a dirty town to clean it up, but along the way it becomes a self-indulgent piece which aspires to be something more mythical than just a shoot-'em-up. It isn't. Clint's first venture back in the saddle since *The Outlaw Josey Wales*, and not a patch on it.

Pal Joey
1957 PG 105 ★★★ MUS

A Rodgers and Hart musical with songs better than the story. Frank Sinatra is the nightclub-owning object of both Kim Novak's and Rita Hayworth's attentions. 'The Lady is a Tramp' and 'My Funny Valentine' are both featured here. Sinatra is so thoroughly charming you can quite see why both women fight over him.

Paper, The
1994 15 108 ★★★ DRA

Supposedly a witty drama based on a day in the life of a New York tabloid (*The Sun*) this sharp, fast-moving film by Ron Howard centres more on the twenty-four hours of its assistant editor (Michael Keaton), a man so obsessed with getting a possible exclusive he's in danger of forgetting an important dinner date with his heavily pregnant wife (Marisa Tomei). The most memorable aspects are the peripheral performances by Robert Duvall, Glenn Close and Randy Quaid. Exciting, amusing stuff.

Paper Chase, The
1973 PG 107 ★★ DRA

A gentle look at young love and rebellion with Timothy Bottoms as a Harvard graduate who falls for his nasty teacher's daughter, Lindsay Wagner (TV's *The Bionic Woman*). Nicely written and pretty to watch. Should keep the early teenagers happy, at least.

Parallax View, The
1974 15 97 ★★★ MYS/THR

Alan J Pakula keeps things nice and tight in a neat thriller starring Warren Beatty as a journalist delving into the murder of an American senator. The story, based on a conspiracy theory, was apparently inspired by the assassination of JFK. Beatty does an able job, but the film never really fulfils its promise as the characters remain rather one-dimensional. *All The President's Men* or *JFK* are better examples of the genre.

Parenthood
1989 15 118 ★★★ COM

This observant comedy about an extended family is often too real to be funny, though it has some hilarious moments. Steve Martin and Mary Steenburgen are having trouble with their brood, while Dianne Wiest experiences the nightmare of a rebellious teenage daughter. Rick Moranis wants a three-year-old genius for a daughter and black sheep Tom Hulce turns up with an illegitimate child. Add to that all the adults working through their problems with their father, Jason Robards, and there's enough material for two films.

Paris, Texas
1984 15 140 ★★ DRA

A disturbing film, well directed by Wim Wenders, which has developed a cult following. Harry Dean Stanton turns up years later to recover the child he had abandoned as a babe and with him sets off to find the wife (Nastassja Kinski) whom he had been deserted by, only to discover that she is leading a seedy existence as a peep-show model. Hugely atmospheric but, unless you belong to the cult, an unlikeable tale.

Passage to India, A
1984 PG 157 ★★★ DRA

Accomplished direction by David Lean brings E M Forster's novel to life. So sumptuous you can almost smell 1920s India where a young, confident Brit (Judy Davis) has her eyes opened by the differences between the Indian culture and her own. Peggy Ashcroft won Best Supporting Actress for her part as Davis's chaperone and mother-in-law to be. Alec Guinness is badly miscast but on the whole it's an absorbing film.

Passenger 57
1992 15 80 ★★ ACT/ADV

Gripping adventure in the sky, on the ground and up in the air again. Wesley Snipes plays the heroic airline cop accompanying arch villain Bruce Payne to trial. With security that would make Group 4 blush, Payne slips away and leads his pursuers a merry dance. Payne is fine as the psychotic prisoner and it's nice to see Snipes given the leading role. But despite the action it's a preposterous yarn.

Passion Fish
1992 15 130 ★★ DRA

The beautiful Deep South setting of this gentle drama makes it a visual feast. Newly paralysed Mary McDonnell finds her confinement impossible to deal with until home help Alfre Woodard, who has problems of her own, stops her feeling so sorry for herself. The ensuing friendship between the two women provides the backbone of the story. Strong language and some sex account for the certificate.

Passport to Pimlico
1949 U 80 ★★★★★ COM

Ealing comedy at its best and lightest. Residents of a London borough, led by Stanley Holloway, find a cache of treasure in a bomb crater and also unearth an ancient charter declaring the area an independent kingdom. The characters and situations are charming and the script won T E B Clarke an Oscar nomination. A must for every member of the family from babe to granny.

Pat and Mike
1952 U 90 ★★★★★ COM

A joyous Spencer Tracy/Katharine Hepburn vehicle. He's a boxing promoter who, spotting her sporting ability, decides to represent her. The only problem is she goes to pieces every time her fiancé is around. Aldo Ray plays Tracy's petulant boxer client, none too pleased to be sharing his coach with a woman. Delightful stuff, with the partnership rarely better. (B&W)

Patriot Games
1992 15 112 ★★ ACT/ADV

The second of Tom Clancy's thrillers featuring CIA agent Jack Ryan. This time Alec Baldwin (who played him in *The Hunt for Red October*) is replaced by Harrison Ford. Ryan, in London with wife (Anne Archer) and daughter, foils an IRA plot to blow up high-ranking James Fox, then becomes the target of the terrorists' wrath which follows him back to the USA. Sean Bean is good as an IRA fanatic but it's a pretty daft tale.

Patton: Lust for Glory
1970 PG 162 ★★★ WAR

George C Scott won one of the film's seven Oscars for his superb portrayal of the gung-ho

American general. Following the man's extraordinary Second World War career, it's a well-rounded insight into how his mind worked. Francis Ford Coppola co-wrote, Franklin J Schaffner directed and a great job was done by all. As a history lesson, the kids could do worse.

Peggy Sue Got Married
1986 15 98 ★★ COM

'Could have done better' would be the school report on this time-travel comedy about an unhappy, thirtysomething woman (Kathleen Turner) who gets to go back to her high school days and have a second bash at life. Director Francis Coppola lets his nephew, Nicolas Cage, get away with a hammy performance as her husband and cute though Turner is, she doesn't pass muster as a sweet sixteen-year-old. The 1960s setting is nice though.

Pelican Brief, The
1993 12 135 ★★ MYS/THR

This confirms it – Julia Roberts is just a pretty face. Whatever acting ability she showed in *Pretty Woman* is not visible in her flat performance as a law student whose life is threatened when she uncovers dirty dealings involving the highest members of the government. Denzel Washington is better as the journalist who helps her but even he seems to be freewheeling. The story, by John Grisham, is intriguing enough, if only the characters weren't so wooden.

Pelle the Conqueror
1988 15 150 ★★★ FOR

The length and dour content of this Danish epic makes it unsuitable for the youngsters, though that doesn't detract from its plus points – after all, it won Best Foreign Film Oscar that year. Max von Sydow is remarkable as an impoverished Swedish farmer who, accompanied by his nine-year-old son, struggles to find a better life in Denmark. The pace is slow, the mood too ponderous at times, but it packs a punch. (Subtitled)

Perfect World, A
1993 15 132 ★★★ ACT/ADV

Touching story about an escaped convict (Kevin Costner) who takes a young boy hostage but soon forms a strong bond with him. Clint Eastwood (also wearing his director's hat for this one) plays the Texas Ranger trying to track them down. Hankies at the ready, though, since you just know this isn't going to end up happy ever after.

Peter Pan
1953 U 76 ★ FAM

Walt Disney took J M Barrie's children's classic and turned Peter into a shrew-faced cartoon, Wendy became a witless wonder and Captain Hook merely a tetchy physically disadvantaged seadog. But, if your children prefer cartoons to books, they'll probably glean enjoyment from it.

Peter's Friends
1992 15 97 ★★★ COM

This engaging comedy by Kenneth Branagh didn't do as well as it deserved since it suffered from comparisons to *The Big Chill*. True, both centre on the long-awaited reunion of old college friends, but the similarities end there. Branagh stars as one of the house guests of Stephen Fry (in the title role) who has something to tell his old mates. The cast includes Emma Thompson, Hugh Laurie and Rita Rudner (co-writer). Sometimes sad and frequently amusing.

Pete's Dragon
1977 U 106 ★★ FAM

A young orphan runs away from his greedy foster parents accompanied by a friendly dragon which none but he can see. Despite being a Disney venture, the human characters are real – only the dragon is drawn – and the mix doesn't work as well as it did in *Mary Poppins*. But the story's cute and the cast – Mickey Rooney, Jim Dale and Shelley Winters – are enthusiastic.

Philadelphia
1993 12 120 ★★★ DRA

The first mainstream movie about AIDS, despite being predictably sentimental, manages to generate humour and optimism thanks to the inspired casting of Tom Hanks, who won an Oscar as the dying homosexual. Antonio Banderas plays his lover, Olympia Dukakis is his mother. As well as examining the onset of the condition, it deals with some of the prejudices that gays encounter. Tears are guaranteed.

Philadelphia Experiment, The
1984 PG 101 ★★★ SCI/FAN

All sorts of mayhem ensues when a couple of US sailors (Michael Paré and Bobby Di Cicco) are plucked out of the Second World War and dumped in 1984 when a naval experiment goes wrong. A neat science-fiction movie with romance, adventure and more than a little suspense. The sequel, imaginatively titled *Philadelphia Experiment 2*, sees the time travel work the other way and is not nearly as good.

Piano, The
1993 15 120 ★★★ DRA

The interesting (but frankly overrated) story of an inexplicably mute nineteenth-century Scottish widow (Holly Hunter) arriving in New Zealand with her daughter for an arranged marriage with a man (Sam Neill) she's never met. There she finds comfort, initially from her beloved piano and then from sexual encounters with a neighbour (Harvey Keitel). Oscars for director Jane Campion's script, Hunter and young Anna Paquin as Best Supporting Actress, but it's a film to admire rather than like. There's a gruesome scene you may want to avoid.

Picnic at Hanging Rock
1975 PG 111 ★★★ MYS/THR

All the more effective for being inspired by a true incident, this is an evocative and haunting account of three Australian schoolgirls and a teacher who, in 1900, disappeared without trace during a school outing to Hanging Rock. The brooding, mystical atmosphere owes much to Peter Weir's direction.

Pied Piper, The
1971 PG 86 ★★ DRA

A word of warning: this movie may be unsuitable for the very young since parts, like the child-catcher in *Chitty Chitty Bang Bang,* are surprisingly frightening. Donovan plays the strolling minstrel who is employed to rid Hamelin of the rat infestation and takes away the children when the town refuses to pay

him. Donald Pleasence, Michael Hordern, John Hurt and Diana Dors also feature. If young children do choose to watch it, stay with them.

Pink Floyd: The Wall
1982 15 91 ★★ MUS

Fans of the Floyd will love this colourful visualization of their bestselling album. Bob Geldof plays the rock star who's growing madder by the minute. Alan Parker directs with flamboyance and the animation for 'Another Brick in the Wall' (by cartoonist Gerald Scarfe) is eye-catching. Contains swearing, sex and violence.

Pink Panther, The
1964 PG 110 ★★★ COM

Blake Edwards does a competent job directing David Niven as the dashing cat-burglar who always manages to stay one step ahead of the incomparable and incompetent Inspector Clouseau. Peter Sellers shows his comic brilliance as the bungling French cop in the first of a series which often – though not always – maintained a pretty high comic standard. Great theme tune, too, of course.

Pink Panther Strikes Again, The
1976 PG 98 ★★★ COM

Sellers returns for the fifth of the Panther films as the hapless Clouseau. Herbert Lom is hilarious as his boss, driven deeper and deeper into insanity by his subordinate's monumental blunders. Leonard Rossiter, Colin Blakely and Lesley-Anne Down provide support. The jokes are beginning to look a little stretched, though the running gag of Clouseau fighting his manservant, Burt Kwouk, every time he comes home is still very funny.

Pinocchio
1940 U 84 ★★★★ FAM

Walt Disney does a superb job combining brilliant animation, smashing songs and a whole host of colourful characters to tell the touching tale of a puppet that comes to life and whose nose grows longer every time he tells a lie. (Small children, take note!) Again, there are sections which may be frightening to the very young if they're left to watch alone.

Pirates
1986 PG 106 ★ ACT/ADV

Generally regarded as a disaster, this was an expensive attempt by director Roman Polanski to make a period comedy about a British pirate (Walter Matthau) who, taken captive on a Spanish galleon, stirs the crew to mutiny. Originally, it was planned for 1976 with Jack Nicholson in the starring role but ten years later the casting changed and the budget had soared to a reported thirty million dollars, eight million alone being spent on the galleon.

Pirates of Penzance, The
1983 U 107 ★★★ MUS

A delightful version of Gilbert and Sullivan's best-loved operetta with Kevin Kline superb as the dashing young pirate in search of a wife – he just oozes sex appeal. Angela Lansbury is nicely cast as a fellow pirate and the numbers are beautifully choreographed and belted out with a gusto the D'Oyly Carte company never matched.

Places in the Heart
1984 PG 111 ★★ DRA

Too heavy going for the young, though Sally Field won the Oscar for her role as a 1930s widow struggling during the Depression to keep her family and Texas farm intact. A lot of breast beating and a rather distancing natural approach to the production make it somewhat hard work, even for the more mature audience. (It was when accepting this Oscar that Field made her 'You like me, you really like me!' speech.)

Planes, Trains and Automobiles
1987 15 89 ★★ COM

Not as funny as you'd think considering it's a John Hughes movie pairing Steve Martin with John Candy. If the roles were reversed it might have worked better. Martin plays a stressed-out businessman striving to get home for Thanksgiving despite severe weather and air, road and rail problems. Adding to his misery is Candy, an unfailingly cheerful salesman, who does little to help.

Planet of the Apes
1968 PG 107 ★★ SCI/FAN

Taken on surface level, this is a rollicking good sci-fi adventure. On a deeper level, it's a social allegory. Charlton Heston is the second Adam, an astronaut whose abortive space mission leaves him and crew twenty centuries away from Earth, on a planet where apes have taken over. It sparked a highly successful TV series and numerous sequels.

Platoon
1986 15 115 ★★★ WAR

One of the better Vietnam films that were as popular in the eighties as Filofaxes. Director Oliver Stone, who served in 'Nam himself, shows considerable insight in his harrowing portrayal of infantry life and troop atrocities. Tom Berenger, Charlie Sheen and Willem Dafoe give their best performances yet. Stone and the film collected four Oscars.

Playboys, The
1992 PG 104 ★★ DRA

Overly long and rather uneventful tale of an unmarried mother (Robin Wright) who finds life in her 1950s Irish village disrupted by the arrival of a travelling troupe of actors. Aidan Quinn, as the attractive stranger accompanying the players, and Albert Finney, the rather brutish, local policeman, both vie for her favours.

Player, The
1992 15 119 ★★★★ COM

Robert Altman's blistering, hilarious satire on Hollywood. Tim Robbins plays a studio script commissioner who accidentally kills the scriptwriter who, he believes, has been sending him hate mail. Does retribution follow? Not a bit of it. Robbins goes on to glory in a funny, amoral story packed with in-jokes and sixty famous faces – from Cher to Julia Roberts – in walk-on parts.

Play It Again, Sam
1972 15 82 ★★★ COM

An ingenious Woody Allen vehicle in which the self-deprecating comic plays a writer deserted by his wife (Susan Anspach) after she can take no more of his fascination with Humphrey Bogart – the ghost of whom takes to dropping by. Brilliant editing interweaves bits of old Bogie films into this one. Allen's old faithful Diane Keaton plays the love interest.

Playtime
1967 U 115 ★★★ FOR

Monsieur Hulot (as always played by writer-director Jacques Tati) has a number of comic adventures in an airport, restaurant and office block on his way to a meeting. Everything, from American tourists to inanimate objects, conspires to thwart and frustrate him. From start to finish, it's a delight. (Subtitled)

Plaza Suite
1971 PG 109 ★★★ COM

Walter Matthau features in all three Neil Simon playlets which take place in the bridal suite of New York's Plaza Hotel. The first sketch sees Maureen Stapleton as the nervy wife of the unfaithful Matthau. The second sees our hero as a film producer romancing old flame Barbara Harris and, in the third, Matthau is the father of the bride who locks herself in the bathroom. Each one a winner.

Please Sir
1971 PG 97 ★★★ COM

Delightful – and only dated by some of the fashions – version of the hit TV series which featured the fifth formers of Fenn Street comprehensive school. John Alderton plays the innocent teacher accompanying the pupils on a nature ramble. Wonderful hoity-toityness from Joan Sanderson as the stuffy schoolmistress. Your children will have seen it all before in the classroom, no doubt.

Plenty
1985 15 119 ★★ DRA

Meryl Streep turns in yet another good performance as a neurotic young woman involved with the French Resistance during the Second World War and falling for commando Sam Neill. The film then follows her – and Britain's – postwar fortunes, none of which gives much cause for cheer. David Hare's script is thoughtful and serious but the action is slow to build and never quite gets there. Charles Dance, Tracy Ullman, John Gielgud and Sting are among the distinguished cast.

Police Academy
1984 15 92 ★★★ COM

The first and best of a series of six films – please, let there not be any more – which, despite being broad, crude, sexist and pretty well mindless, have proved unaccountably popular with the younger set. Well, not so unaccountable perhaps if what the younger set really likes is broad, crude, sexist, etc. This initial outing, featuring Steve Guttenberg, Kim Cattrall and a host of more-or-less unknowns, concerns the farcical adventures and misadventures of a bunch of pretty inept recruits at the police academy of the title. It's quite funny in parts – funnier than its successors, anyway – and does have the virtue of poking gentle fun at authority.

Police Academy 2: Their First Assignment
1985 15 84 ★★ COM

Guttenberg again, plus such survivors of the first film as Bubba Smith and Michael Winslow, as the hapless crime-fighters tackle a gang of paint-spraying yobs. For devious reasons of his own, Art Metrano, as an ambitious police lieutenant, wants the rookies to fail. More farcical, less amusing than the first.

Police Academy 3: Back in Training
1986 PG 80 ★★ COM

As you can see, the films were turned out so fast they might as well have been on a conveyor belt. Here, Guttenberg, Smith and company have gone back for more training – and boy, do they need it. But now they find their beloved academy is in danger of closing and must find a way to save it.

Police Academy 4: Citizens on Patrol
1987 PG 83 ★★ COM

Same old stuff, really, only this time the recruits – Guttenberg, Smith and Winslow among them – have to train civilians, an outfit called Citizens on Patrol, in spotting and fighting crime. The format is beginning to look distinctly weary, hence perhaps the PG certificate – an attempt to rope in an even younger audience.

Police Academy 5: Assignment Miami Beach
1988 PG 86 ★★ COM

By now Guttenberg had had enough – and who could blame him? – and is no longer among those present as the dimmest bunch of cops since the Keystone lot go to Miami for a police convention. The plot involves crooks, switched baggage and a backstage power struggle in the academy itself.

Police Academy 6: City under Siege
1989 PG 80 ★★ COM

Bubba Smith finally gets the leading role as the city is terrorized (well, sort of) by a gang of criminals using fairly ingenious methods. The result is the kind of stuff that plays adequately in off-peak hours on TV, for by now the police academy milch cow really has dried up. No doubt the series made a lot of money but it didn't make any reputations. It did little for Steve Guttenberg and even less for Michael Winslow, whose vocal virtuosity was one of the best things in each of the films but who hasn't been heard of since. Still, let's look on the bright side – there hasn't been a *Police Academy* movie since 1989, so may be we really have heard the last of them.

Pollyanna
1960 U 129 ★★ FAM

A film for all ages but beware – while adults may sigh tenderly at the goody-goodyness of the little heroine, their offspring may take a robustly antagonistic view. Hayley Mills is the orphaned twelve-year-old who comes to stay with her rich, cantankerous aunt (Jane Wyman) and soon wins everyone round to being nice to each other. There's a lot of charm, some of it tearful, but don't expect your own children to behave like Hayley.

Poltergeist
1982 15 110 ★★★ HOR

Some moments in Steven Spielberg's movie of the paranormal are downright frightening, making it all the more enjoyable for the older family members. As the daughter of pleasant, middle-class Craig T Nelson and JoBeth Williams, Heather O'Rourke seems to set the furniture flying round the room and has a tendency to disappear into walls. Well acted and entertaining, though a deeper examination of poltergeists would have been welcome. Two sequels followed and progressively worsened.

Pope Must Die, The
1991 15 95 ★★ COM

Unfathomable why this hit-and-miss comedy of errors from the *Comic Strip* team should have such a restrictive certificate. Apart from a few swear words and bad jokes there's really little to offend here. Robbie Coltrane plays a country priest elected, by computer error, to the Papacy and making a lot of enemies when he unearths deep corruption within the Vatican. Pretty daffy, but funny enough.

Pope of Greenwich Village, The
1984 15 116 ★★ COM

Underrated, slice-of-life tale about a couple of friends in New York – restaurant manager-cum-hustler Mickey Rourke and his waiter cousin Eric Roberts – who, on losing their jobs, become involved in a crazy robbery and discover they've stolen from the Mafia. It's acutely observed, and all the funnier for it, with both men showing a hitherto hidden talent for comedy.

Popeye
1980 U 92 ★★ FAM

Robert Altman's live action film doesn't quite work, mostly because he tries to add depth and poignancy to the cartoon character who, after a can or two of spinach, develops muscles to rival Arnie Schwarzenegger's. Robin Williams plays the sailor man and looks the part but somehow he's not funny enough. Shelley Duvall is better as Olive Oyl – a part she was born for – but neither can do much with the overloaded plot.

Poseidon Adventure, The
1972 PG 112 ★★★ ACT/ADV

One of those disaster movies top-heavy with big names. On board the sinking liner are Gene Hackman, Ernest Borgnine, Roddy McDowall and many other familiar faces. It's pretty run-of-the-mill, who-will-survive stuff, though the special effects were good enough to earn an Oscar.

Posse
1993 15 106 ★★ WES

This is the first black Western and it's not very good thanks to a cliché-ridden plot that can be predicted from a hundred paces. Mario Van

Peebles (doubling up as director) forms a renegade bunch of soldiers who head for his home town in search of vengeance. On their trail is a posse headed by their colonel, Billy Zane. You can probably guess the rest already.

Postcards from the Edge
1991 15 97 ★★★ DRA

Much funnier than you'd think, this story, which some claim is loosely based on the relationship between actress Carrie Fisher (who wrote the original book) and her mother, Debbie Reynolds. Meryl Streep plays the Fisher role, a drug-addicted actress who, despite entering her middle years, is still overpowered and overshadowed by her famous mum. Shirley MacLaine is brilliant as the bitingly sharp, self-obsessed stage mother.

Power of One, The
1992 15 122 ★★ DRA

Rites of passage stuff featuring a young cast but dealing with a serious, grown-up subject. Young Stephen Dorff is an orphan sent to boarding school in Zimbabwe, *circa* 1930. There he's bullied by Afrikaners and offered friendship only by a black prisoner (Morgan Freeman), who coaches him to become a champion boxer and heralds him as a peace-bringer. Dorff then travels round South Africa denouncing racism as he goes.

Prancer
1989 U 98 ★★ FAM

A sweet tale of a desperately unhappy and lonely little girl who believes she has found Santa's missing reindeer. A largely unknown cast (apart from Sam Elliott and Cloris Leachman) meant that this film slipped out unnoticed, but it's full of Christmas spirit and the promise of magic for the young heroine.

Presidio, The
1988 15 94 ★★ MYS/THR

This average thriller is as predictable as rain in Wimbledon fortnight. The chief of military police at a San Francisco army base (Sean Connery) clashes with a local cop (Mark Harmon) over the investigation into the murder of one of Connery's men. They also clash over the fact that Harmon falls in love with

Connery's daughter (Meg Ryan). The action sequences are pretty good though.

Pretty Woman
1990 15 114 ★★★★ COM

Gather the clan (well, the older ones anyway), open the chocolates and settle down for a delightful two hours, as Julia Roberts becomes a modern-day Cinderella. She's an LA hooker hired by billionaire Richard Gere to spend the week with him. Love, of course, intervenes enchantingly. It's not just Gere and Roberts who delight either; Laura San Giacomo and Hector Elizondo provide smashing support. Some sex and ripe language.

Pride and Prejudice
1940 U 113 ★★★ DRA

Though nothing comes close to the book, this is the best attempt of any to bring Jane Austen's wonderful tale of romance to the screen. Greer Garson and Laurence Olivier play Elizabeth and Darcy, ideally suited to one another but unable to see it because of their respective prejudices. The ending's been Hollywoodized but on the whole it's a relatively faithful adaptation. (B&W)

Priest
1995 15 103 ★★★ DRA

The pressures of life as a Catholic priest – and, particularly, the problems of celibacy – are the subjects under examination here. The priest in question is Linus Roache, whose homosexuality is as much a problem for him as the Liverpool ghetto to which he's been sent. The resident father (Tom Wilkinson) sets no very good example, co-habiting as he does with his housekeeper (Cathy Tyson). The drama arises mainly from the revelation of Roache's sexual preferences and from a case of incest which he learns about in the Confessional. It's a hard, even bleak story and the central character is not as sympathetic as he might be. But Wilkinson is fine and the writing – by Jimmy (*Cracker*) McGovern – is sharp, witty and often warm.

Prime of Miss Jean Brodie, The
1969 15 111 ★★★ COM

The book could have been written with Maggie Smith in mind, so good is she as the risqué schoolmistress guiding her pupils carefully through the obstacles of girlhood. Set in Edinburgh during the 1930s, it has as much resonance today as when first written and the humour is abundant.

Prince and the Pauper, The
1937 U 113 ★★★ DRA

Mark Twain's emotional story about an unhappy young prince who swaps clothes with a pauper who resembles him. Out in the big world the young prince finds his kingdom in a sorry state. Errol Flynn plays the young royal's champion; Claude Rains is his dastardly adversary. (B&W)

Prince and the Pauper, The
1977 PG 115 ★★★ DRA

Mark Lester plays both prince and beggar; Oliver Reed, Raquel Welch, George C Scott, Rex Harrison and Ernest Borgnine amply fill the adult roles in a very respectable remake.

Prince of Tides, The
1991 15 126 ★★ DRA

An ideal film to do the ironing to, this one-woman effort by director/star Barbra Streisand. She inadvertently becomes the psychiatrist to middle-aged Nick Nolte who has lost his job and self-respect and is in danger of losing his wife. As she drags up his horrific past, Streisand falls in love with him. Powerful performances but the story is too pat and manipulative.

Princess and the Goblin, The
1993 U 78 ★★ FAM

An average, animated tale of a princess kidnapped by goblins. Listen hard for the voices of Rik Mayall, Joss Ackland, Roy Kinnear, Claire Bloom and Molly Sugden.

Princess Bride, The
1987 PG 94 ★★★★ COM

Settle down and wallow in this charming, very funny fairy tale adventure wherein a young farmhand (Cary Elwes) – seeking to rescue his long-lost love (Robin Wright) when she's kidnapped by the evil prince (Chris Sarandon) – must do battle with all manner of nasty folk, including a giant and a Spanish swordsman. Wallace Shawn leads the band of ruffians Wright encounters. An enchanting tale.

Prisoner of Zenda, The
1952 U 97 ★★★ ACT/ADV

The best version, but hardest to come by, is the one with Ronald Colman made in 1937, but the plot's so romantic and adventurous that either version should keep the family enthralled for an hour or two. This stars Stewart Granger as the Englishman who so closely resembles the king that his services are called upon to impersonate him for a while. Deborah Kerr is the king's betrothed with whom Granger falls in love.

Private Benjamin
1980 15 105 ★★★ COM

Goldie Hawn is at her cutest as a spoiled, pampered young woman who, widowed on her wedding day, drowns her sorrows by joining the army. It's not long before she's rudely awakened to the fact that polished nails and a soldier's life don't mix. Very funny in parts.

Private Function, A
1985 15 92 ★★★ COM

The presence of a pig in a food-rationed, postwar Northern town causes all manner of dirty dealings and double crossings and a nightmare time for timid chiropodist Michael Palin, who has to look after the animal against the wishes of his houseproud wife, Maggie Smith. A witty, funny script by Alan Bennett and hilarious performances by Palin and Smith in particular.

Private Life of Henry VIII, The
1933 U 90 ★★★ DRA

A spectacular production makes the ideal framework for Charles Laughton's extravagant, Oscar-winning performance in the title role. A good few liberties are taken with the historical facts but never mind – the gusto and humour of the performances and production are hugely enjoyable. Strong support from Merle Oberon, Robert Donat and Elsa Lanchester (Mrs Laughton). Alexander Korda directed. (B&W)

Private Life of Sherlock Holmes, The
1970 PG 125 ★★★ COM

Despite never knowing whether it's a comedy or a spy thriller, Billy Wilder's inventive tale is an interesting and novel examination of the fictional detective and his amazingly successful career. Robert Stephens dons the deerstalker; Colin Blakely, as Watson, holds the stethoscope.

Private Lives of Elizabeth and Essex, The
1939 U 102 ★★★ ACT/ADV

A sumptuous historical drama with Bette Davis formidable as the queen and Errol Flynn at his most dashing as her loyal, but ultimately over-ambitious subject. Somewhat economical with the truth as far as history is concerned but the drama is gripping and Davis is at her best.

Private's Progress
1956 U 96 ★★★ COM

A very pleasing army farce that could as well be called 'Carry On Soldier'. Ian Carmichael is the naive, rather delicate recruit ill-suited to the macho life and totally exploited by his crooked uncle to help him loot stolen German treasures. A bit dated now but Terry-Thomas, Richard Attenborough and Dennis Price add lustre to the cast. Written, directed and produced by the Boulting brothers.

Prizzi's Honor
1985 15 124 ★★★ MYS/THR

As much a black comedy as anything else when Mafia hit man Jack Nicholson marries hit woman Kathleen Turner. Jealous Anjelica Huston poses a threat to what seems an idyllic partnership. So do the machinations of the Mob. Great performances all round. John Huston (Anjelica's dad) directed and his daughter won the Oscar for Best Supporting Actress.

Problem Child
1990 PG 77 ★ COM

For 'Problem Child' read 'Disturbed Little Boy'. Michael Oliver is the orphan adopted by unsuspecting and childless John Ritter and Amy Yasbeck. What passes for mischief in this unpleasant little film looks more like the behaviour of a child in urgent need of psychiatric care. The whole thing leaves a nasty taste in the mouth and we include it here only so that you will know to avoid it, along with its sequels. There is little to laugh at, much to pity and even more to deplore.

Producers, The
1968 PG 84 ★★★★ COM

This is probably writer-director Mel Brooks's most completely satisfying film. Down-at-heel impresario Zero Mostel lures gullible accountant Gene Wilder into a get-rich-quick scheme whereby theatrical 'angels' are conned into investing in a sure-fire flop. The show in question, a musical called *Springtime for Hitler*, is in such horrendous bad taste that it certainly should be a flop, but... This is one of those rare films in which everything works to perfection.

Programme, The
1994 15 109 ★★ DRA

A cliché-ridden, action-strewn tale about football hopefuls finding their way through college. The emphasis is on the fact that, despite the differences between them, all are united by one thing: American football. The way it's treated here, such a notion tends to stick in the throat but at least the story has James Caan – as college coach – to recommend it and for the sentimental among you, there's the odd love story or two thrown in as well.

Proof
1991 15 86 ★★ DRA

A strange, affecting Australian movie about a blind photographer. 'A what?' we hear you cry. But, oddly enough, it works rather well. Blind, distrustful Hugo Weaving learns to operate a camera and uses the snapshots he takes to ensure that his friends and colleagues are honest with him. It all takes a bit of swallowing but you're pretty well convinced by the end.

Prospero's Books
1991 15 120 ★★ DRA

For visual content Peter Greenaway's version of *The Tempest* earns nine out of ten. For entertainment value, it scores rather less. John Gielgud plays Prospero, narrates the story and voices all the parts while the screen is bombarded by a myriad of stunning images.

The tale is all there but somehow it's in pieces. The film stretches the boundaries of the cinema, perhaps, but it also stretches the patience. Contains nudity.

Psycho
1960 15 109 ★★★★ HOR

Even in this more tolerant age this is not at all one for the younger members of the family. Alfred Hitchcock's classic horror story (set in Bates Motel where the guests go in but rarely come out) still has plenty of power to shock. Janet Leigh, you will recall, takes the fatal shower and Anthony Perkins takes the knife as Norman Bates. Don't watch it too late, or alone, or you'll have nightmares. (B&W)

Public Enemy, The
1931 PG 80 ★★★ MYS/THR

Few remember the plot of this early gangster movie, but everyone remembers the hilarious scene where James Cagney squashes a grapefruit into Mae Clark's face. Not a very nice thing to do, but then he's the hoodlum, the 1920s bootlegger whose rise and fall is being recounted. It was Cagney's sixth film and the one that made him a star. Worth watching for the grapefruit scene alone. (B&W)

Public Eye, The
1992 15 94 ★★ MYS/THR

Atmospheric attempt at a modern *film noir*, with Joe Pesci as a 1940s, ambulance-chasing tabloid photographer (longing to take quality pictures of something other than corpses) who gets involved with the Mafia after promising to help widowed nightclub owner, Barbara Hershey. To his horror, Pesci finds himself piggy in the middle between two warring gangs.

Pumping Iron
1977 PG 82 ★★ DRA

The only reason anyone but a body-builder would want to watch this is to see how Arnold Schwarzenegger looked before he became Mr Box Office. No, that's not quite fair. The film follows Arnie's (and Lou Ferrigno's) elaborate preparations for the Mr Universe contest and

the behind-the-scenes atmosphere is quite absorbing as preparations hot up and the veins in Arnie's bull neck stand out like worm casts.

Pump Up the Volume
1990 15 98 ★★ COM

An early starring vehicle for Christian Slater, who plays a teenage renegade inciting his high school mates to rebellion via his night-time pirate radio show. The plot's pretty silly but Slater, given a fairly wide-ranging acting opportunity – he's shy by day, dynamite by night – is magnetic. Teenagers will love it.

Punchline
1988 15 117 ★★ COM

An oddly downbeat tale about a housewife (Sally Field) who wishes to become a stand-up comic. Tom Hanks plays the (fairly) established comedian who teaches her. The trouble is, there's more to be laughed at than with. On the whole, it's pretty sad. Any budding Jo Brands will be discouraged.

Pure Hell of St Trinian's, The
1960 U 90 ★★ COM

The pupils from hell are standing trial for burning down their school. By various means they are acquitted and offered a new St Trinian's by a suspicious fellow claiming to be a professor (Cecil Parker). All the favourites are back (except Alastair Sim), including George Cole as Flash Harry, running a matrimonial service for the sixth form, and Joyce Grenfell as an amorous policewoman. (B&W)

Purple Rose of Cairo, The
1985 PG 78 ★★★★ COM

A delightful fairy tale directed by but not featuring Woody Allen. Mia Farrow plays a downtrodden waitress who, in the gloomy days of the 1930s Depression, finds her fantasy comes to life at the local cinema when her movie idol, Jeff Daniels, steps from the screen into the auditorium and her life. A similar idea was used less well – and certainly with far less charm, wit and humour – in *Last Action Hero*.

Queen of Hearts
1989 PG 107 ★★ COM

Quirky dramatic comedy in which an Italian family find that in running a café in London they've bitten off more than they can chew. There's a strong sense of family life and the atmosphere is so authentic you can almost smell the coffee, but despite a promising, amusing start, it falls into melodrama all too soon and never quite recovers.

Quick Change
1990 15 85 ★★★ COM

A sometimes sparkling comedy about three bank robbers (Geena Davis, Randy Quaid and their leader, Bill Murray) who pull off an ingenious heist, planned to precision, only to find their escape plans are disastrous. They simply can't get out of town. Murray and Quaid are a winning combination while Davis more than holds her own in such company.

Quiet Man, The
1952 U 124 ★★★ DRA

If you can overlook Hollywood's twee depiction of 'Oireland' – all thatched cottages and smiling, genial peasants – then there's much pleasure in this romantic, humorous tale of an ex-boxer (John Wayne) who arrives in the Emerald Isle to find his roots and discovers feisty redheaded beauty Maureen O'Hara into the bargain. John Ford directs but can't resist a bit of macho action with a fight sequence that lasts so long as to be ludicrous.

Quigley Down Under
1990 15 115 ★★ WES

An Australian Western which might have qualified for a PG if it weren't for a violent scene of a beating. That apart, it's a standard story with a fair bit of action, about an evil rancher (Alan Rickman) and his honest hired hand (Tom Selleck). Selleck is most appealing as the American troubleshooter bemused by turn-of-the-century Australia, but it's Rickman, as usual, who steals the show.

Quince Tree Sun, The
1993 U 132 ★★★ FOR

To say this is like watching paint dry is a perfectly accurate description because that's what the viewer does. An artist, Antonio Lopez, tries to paint a quince tree in his garden before the fruit drops and rots. And that's just about all that happens. But Victor Erice's film depicts the preparations and the actual painting with such loving detail that you find yourself lulled and almost hypnotized into a mood of peaceful contemplation. (Subtitled)

Quo Vadis
1951 PG 162 ★★★ DRA

A Roman epic that should keep the more mature family members occupied for nigh on three hours but may test the patience of the younger ones. The story is of a love affair between a Roman centurion and a Christian girl during the reign of the Emperor Nero. Fights, chariot races, Christians thrown to the lions – all ancient Roman life is here. Robert Taylor and Deborah Kerr are the lovers; Peter Ustinov overshadows everyone else as the demented Nero.

Radio Days
1987 PG 85 ★★★★ COM

One of Woody Allen's best, this nostalgic, affectionate look at a Jewish boyhood in Queens, New York, *circa* 1940. Allen narrates the story of a young lad and his family with snippets from the radio shows of the day. Mia Farrow, Julie Kavner, Josh Mostel, Dianne Wiest and Michael Tucker are among the familiar Allen regulars.

Raiders of the Lost Ark
1981 PG 110 ★★★★ ACT/ADV

The brainchild of Hollywood's two most successful movie-makers, producer George Lucas and director Steven Spielberg, could hardly fail – and it doesn't. A gripping, ripping adventure yarn with an attractive hero, a smart script and a generous serving of romance offers all anyone could want from an action movie. Harrison Ford cracks the whip as archaeologist and adventurer Indiana Jones, trying to recover the Ark of the Covenant before the Nazis get it.

Railway Children, The
1971 U 104 ★★★★★ FAM

Delightful story of three children who come to live by a railway when their parents fall on hard times. Adventures and friendships abound and a truly classic family film is the result. Jenny Agutter is marvellous as the eldest girl and Bernard Cribbins gives a lovely performance as the stationmaster. Lionel Jeffries directs. Gather the extended family around you for this one.

Raining Stones
1993 15 87 ★★★★ DRA

Ken Loach's harsh but funny study of working-class Northern life is also a bitter, spirited attack on the legacy of Thatcher's Britain. It's sharply written and acutely observed and you'll find yourself laughing even while you weep for the victims of the recession of the early nineties. Unemployment, religion, friendship and loan sharks are all explored minutely. Excellent performances from a little-known cast make it all the more effective.

Rain Man
1988 15 127 ★★★ DRA

Although Dustin Hoffman won the Oscar for his fine portrayal of an autistic savant, it is Tom Cruise who gives the better performance. He has the harder, less showy role of Hoffman's selfish brother, who undergoes a gradual change in his personality as the fraternal relationship develops while the pair drive across America. The script and Barry Levinson's direction were also recognized by the Academy.

Raising Arizona
1987 15 90 ★★ COM

Make sure you've got your tea, biscuits and family all ready in front of the telly before you press the 'play' button since the pre-credit sequence is easily the funniest part of the Coen brothers's movie. Although the film has been much admired, the rest never quite lives up to that early promise. Nicolas Cage and Holly Hunter are a childless couple who steal one of a set of quintuplets. Things get out of hand when the child's father is prepared to resort to violence to get his baby back.

Raising Cain
1992 15 88 ★ MYS/THR

An untidy, disappointing thriller with John Lithgow (he of the face like a Cabbage Patch doll) as a psychological disaster. On the one hand, he's a loving father and husband (Lolita Davidovich plays his wife); on the other, a dangerous psychotic who steals children for his father to experiment on. Director Brian DePalma never hits the right note between comedy and violence but Lithgow, going easily through the paces, is always good to watch. Contains a lot of violence.

Rambling Rose
1991 15 107 ★★ DRA

A genteel, conservative family in 1930s Georgia find their lives totally disrupted when promiscuous Laura Dern comes to work for them. Robert Duvall takes a more modest part than usual, as the reserved head of the household. Diane Ladd (Dern's mother in real life) is more prominent as the matriarch. For the first time ever, a mother and daughter were nominated for an Oscar for the same movie. Now that's what we call a family film – apart from the sexier scenes, of course.

Ran
1985 15 153 ★★★★ FOR

Essentially this is *King Lear*, relocated to feudal Japan and reinterpreted by Oriental maestro Akira Kurosawa. When an ageing warlord hands over his kingdom to his eldest son rivalry, jealousy and war break out. 'Ran' means chaos and that's precisely what happens. Magnificent battle scenes, complex personal relationships and a striking portrayal of evil from Meiko Harada as the wife of the eldest son. Quite simply, this is a great film. (Subtitled)

Reach For the Sky
1956 U 130 ★★★ WAR

Kenneth More gives a rousing portrayal of Second World War flying ace Douglas Bader. If the story were not true you'd never believe the gripping screen biography of this amazingly courageous man who overcame a double leg amputation to get back into the cockpit and fight for his country. Lewis Gilbert directs with unfussy skill. (B&W)

Real McCoy, The
1993 15 100 ★★ MYS/THR

Raffles would have sneered at this uninvolving thriller about a cat burglar (Kim Basinger) who longs to give up the day job but is forced back to commit one last theft by the evil Terence Stamp. Hardly an original thought seems to have gone into the entire movie and Val Kilmer is wasted in a thin part as the love interest. Stamp overacts but Basinger at least brings energy to her role.

Rear Window
1954 PG 107 ★★★★ MYS/THR

Hitchcock's stylish romantic thriller is based on a Cornell Woolrich story about a photographer (James Stewart) who, confined by a broken leg to a wheelchair, sits looking out of his window all day. Boredom is replaced by danger when he thinks he witnesses a murder across the way and ropes in his girlfriend (Grace Kelly) to help him investigate. It's a dynamic pairing which increases the sense of the sultry summer.

Rebecca
1940 U PG 130 ★★★★ MYS/THR

Alfred Hitchcock does a smashing job bringing Daphne du Maurier's romantic thriller to the screen. The performances are super, especially Joan Fontaine as the mousy second wife of brooding widower Laurence Olivier, striving to live up to the first wife's image. Judith Anderson scores as the creepy Mrs Danvers. (B&W)

Rebecca's Daughters
1992 15 93 ★★ COM

One point of interest in this romp that's not as funny as it thinks it is, is that the original script was by Dylan Thomas. It's based on a true incident in the mid-nineteenth century when the rebellious Welsh dressed as women to fight the English imposition of tollgates. Paul Rhys is their leader, Rebecca; Peter O'Toole, bearing a marked resemblance to the Virgin Queen, is an oppressive English landowner.

Rebel without a Cause
1955 PG 106 ★★★ DRA

Keep your teenage children away from this one, for despite looking pretty dated, it still speaks to the generation of pubescents who see their parents as the enemy and a barrier to self-expression. It was the second of three films (the others being *East of Eden* and *Giant*) that made James Dean the teenage idol that he is to this day. Natalie Wood, Sal Mineo and Dennis Hopper all do justice to their supporting roles.

Red Badge of Courage, The
1951 U 66 ★★★ WAR

John Huston's full version of Stephen Crane's book has rarely been seen, since a lukewarm reception led to it being hacked down to sixty-six minutes. But even as it stands this story of a young soldier stricken with guilt for being cowardly during the American Civil War is quite riveting. It's certainly the best film Audie Murphy ever made. (There is a longer, 1974 made-for-TV version with Richard Thomas – a.k.a John Boy Walton – in the leading role but it doesn't compare to Huston's film, no matter how much the latter was butchered.) (B&W)

Red River
1948 U 121 ★★★★ WES

Howard Hawks's epic Western centres on the conflict during a cattle-drive along the Chisholm Trail between the tyrannical leader

(John Wayne) and the young, ruggedly independent Montgomery Clift. Actually, it's a sort of *Mutiny on the Bounty* with cows. (When John Ford saw this film he said of John Wayne: 'I never knew the sonuvabitch could act'.) The original film ran for 133 minutes, so this could be a somewhat butchered version with Walter Brennan's narration acting as an edit. *Caveat emptor.* Incidentally, the TV movie remake with a PG certificate and James Arness starring is not good. (B&W)

Red Rock West
1993 15 94 ★★ MYS/THR

Keep your wits about you for this amusing thriller of mistaken identity. Nicolas Cage stars as an itinerant Texan who lands a bar job in a one-horse Wyoming town. But his employer, J T Walsh, believes him to be the hit man he's hired to kill his wife, Lara Flynn Boyle. Things take an unexpected turn when Cage informs her of her husband's intentions and everyone starts double-crossing everyone else. Funny in places with a nice performance from Dennis Hopper.

Reds
1981 15 187 ★★★ DRA

Laudable, though far too long, account of an American journalist's involvement in the Russian Revolution. Warren Beatty does a fine job not only in the lead role but as director – so fine he was awarded an Oscar for his directorial debut. Diane Keaton provides the romantic interest. Old favourites Gene Hackman and Jack Nicholson co-star.

Red Shoes, The
1948 U 128 ★★★★★ DRA

The winning combination of Michael Powell and Emeric Pressburger again delivers the goods with this marvellous, tragic fairy tale about a young ballerina (Moira Shearer) and the two men she's torn between – her jealous husband, Marius Goring, and her domineering impresario, Anton Walbrook. This is a truly classic film; any dancers in the family *must* watch it.

Red Sorghum
1987 15 88 ★★★ FOR

Zhang Yimou's poignant historical saga about the life of a young Chinese woman, Gong Li,

from her marriage in the 1920s up to and including the Japanese invasion some ten years later. Funny and tragic by turns and at times visually stunning. (Sorghum, incidentally, is a ubiquitous and indispensable Chinese crop.) (Subtitled)

Regarding Henry
1991 15 103 ★★ DRA

If all mental injury was as cute as it's portrayed here, then community care might actually work. Harrison Ford plays a ruthless lawyer whom nobody much likes until he's accidentally shot and the resulting brain damage makes him a far more loveable chap. An unconvincing performance by Ford but then he's not given any believable material to work with. Annette Bening plays his wife.

Regle du Jeu, La
1939 PG 102 ★★★★★ FOR

A weekend outing to the country for servants and masters alike results in a variety of richly complex situations, including love, romance and accidental death. It's a marvellously plotted film anyway but what makes this Jean Renoir's masterpiece is that, on another level, it's a wise and mocking satire of the social system in prewar France. It's usually included in every critic's list of the all-time ten best. (B&W; subtitled)

Remains of the Day, The
1993 U 129 ★★★★ DRA

Beautiful and evocative adaptation by Merchant and Ivory of Kazuo Ishiguro's quintessentially English period drama. It's a story of wasted lives and missed opportunities and of a gullible Englishman's exploitation by the Nazis. But it is also full of warmth and quiet humour and contains outstanding performances, both by Anthony Hopkins as the butler reflecting on his life and finding it full of regrets and Emma Thompson as the feisty, independent housekeeper.

Repossessed
1990 15 85 ★ COM

The biggest and best joke of this spoof on *The Exorcist* is that Linda Blair – the demonically possessed little girl of the original film – is possessed all over again as a projectile-vomiting housewife. Other than that most of the jokes go wide of the mark, despite Leslie Nielsen giving his all as the devil-destroying exorcist.

Rescuers, The
1977 U 74 ★★★ FAM

An inoffensive, animated adventure from Disney about the exploits of a pair of troubleshooting mice who are called in to find a kidnapped girl. Thrilling adventures and some nice songs are helped along by first-class animation, featuring characters like Orville the albatross and Evinrude the dragonfly. Bob Newhart and Eva Gabor provide the voices of the romantic rodents.

Rescuers Down Under, The
1990 U 95 ★★★ FAM

The mighty mice are back to do battle with evil but the fresh angle is that they must go to Australia, where a young lad is up to his ears in trouble. This time the voices of George C Scott and John Candy join those of Newhart and Gabor. As sequels go, this one is perfectly acceptable.

Return of Martin Guerre, The
1982 15 105 ★★★ FOR

This was remade quite well in 1993 as *Sommersby*, with Richard Gere and Jodie Foster. But the original is still a shade better. Gérard Depardieu plays a soldier who returns to his sixteenth-century French village a much improved character. Even his wife can't believe the change in his personality and so begins a trial to decide whether Depardieu is, in fact, the man he claims to be or an imposter. All the more interesting for being based on fact. (Subtitled)

Return of Swamp Thing
1989 15 84 ★★ SCI/FAN

Cute B-movie about a comic-book superhero who fell into a toxic swamp a weedy nerd and emerged as the vegetable equivalent of Arnold Schwarzenegger. Heather Locklear is the appealing heroine; Louis Jourdan her evil uncle determined to do her wrong.

Return of the Jedi
1983 U 126 ★★★★ SCI/FAN

Final, delightful part of the *Star Wars* trilogy, which sees Luke Skywalker and friends banding against the threat of an evil Deathstar. Harrison Ford, Carrie Fisher, Alec Guinness and the disembodied voice of James Earl Jones (as Darth Vader) are all on top form and the special effects are better than ever. It helps if you've seen the earlier films but you can still enjoy this one anyway.

Return of the Pink Panther, The
1975 PG 108 ★★ COM

Peter Sellers returns as Clouseau ten years after *A Shot in the Dark*. By now Christopher Plummer has replaced David Niven as the cat burglar but the plot still revolves around a stolen diamond. Plenty of knockabout jokes and Herbert Lom is a definite plus as the much put-upon Inspector Dreyfus.

Return of the Musketeers , The
1989 PG 98 ★★★ ACT/ADV

In this, the third of the *Musketeer* films made by director Richard Lester, we catch up with our heroes twenty years later. Their old enemy, Milady, is dead by now, of course, but her son crops up as the villain of the piece. The musketeers come to the aid of the French queen as she tries to stop the execution of King Charles I. Michael York, Oliver Reed and Frank Finlay lead the cast. (This was the film on which Roy Kinnear was killed when he was thrown from a horse.)

Reuben, Reuben
1982 15 96 ★★ COM

An offbeat comedy set in New England where an alcoholic poet (Tom Conti) takes advantage of mature, married women until a beautiful young girl comes along – Kelly McGillis, in her first film. Loosely based on Dylan Thomas's American tour and nicely played and wittily written, but it never quite gels.

Reversal of Fortune
1990 15 107 ★★★ DRA

A cold account of the notorious von Bulow affair in which the social-climbing husband, Claus (Jeremy Irons) was accused – mainly by his stepchildren – of attempting to murder his wealthy wife, their mother (Glenn Close) by means of an insulin overdose. Even now, nobody really knows what happened. Flawless performances by Close and Irons (who won an Oscar) but it is Ron Silver, as the lawyer Alan Dershowitz, who adds the colour and warmth and thereby runs away with the movie.

Richard III
1955 U 150 ★★★ DRA

A very theatrical production, directed by and starring Laurence Olivier, who is no less than magnificent as Shakespeare's hunchback king. Reprising his stage triumph, Olivier gave what was for several decades regarded as the definitive portrayal. John Gielgud, Ralph Richardson, Claire Bloom and Cedric Hardwicke lend lustre to the supporting cast.

Rich in Love
1993 PG 100 ★★ DRA

Fans of *Driving Miss Daisy* will be delighted by this gentle family drama made by the same director, Bruce Beresford. Beautifully shot and set in the Deep South, USA, where a young girl (Kathryn Erbe) tries to maintain her family's status quo when her mother (Jill Clayburgh) walks out. Albert Finney is charming as the bemused husband, still unsure why his wife left. Suzy Amis plays the elder daughter returning with a husband (Kyle MacLachlan) in tow and Ethan Hawke provides further love interest.

Riff-Raff
1991 15 95 ★★★ COM

Like *Raining Stones* this is a biting satire of Thatcherite Britain by Ken Loach – and, let's face it, who does it better? Most of the action revolves around a building site and the various labourers employed there. Actually, the social comment is more muted in what is, in effect, Loach's first out-and-out comedy. (Don't confuse this with two other, much earlier films with the same title. One's a comedy with Jean Harlow and Spencer Tracy; the other is an action drama with Pat O'Brien.)

Ring of Bright Water
1969 U 102 ★★★ FAM

Nominally, the stars are Bill Travers and Virginia McKenna, but it's Mij the otter who

scampers off with the movie. It's an adaptation of Gavin Maxwell's autobiographical book in which he tells how he attempted to keep a young otter in his London flat – not an easy thing to do – before deciding to give up flat and job and take off with Mij to a seaside cottage in Scotland. A charming tale which benefits mightily from the fact that it's both true and unsentimental.

Rio Bravo
1959 PG 136 ★★★ WES

A delightful Western by Howard Hawks in which John Wayne plays a sheriff assigned to guard a killer whose brothers swear to spring him from jail. An odd assortment of deputies, including a drunken Dean Martin and Walter Brennan, are Wayne's only allies. Well, there's Angie Dickinson, too, but she's not around for the shooting. Familiar, but all the same smashing stuff.

Rio Grande
1950 U 102 ★★★ WES

Following on from *Fort Apache* and *She Wore a Yellow Ribbon*, this is the last in director John Ford's cavalry trilogy. John Wayne stars as the hard-bitten leader of a frontline troop who finds his job is made difficult when his son is among the new recruits. A much more personal view of the Wild West than usual.

River, The
1984 15 119 ★★ DRA

One of a batch of rural dramas that were made around this time. A farming family lives under the constant threat that the river running through their land will flood. It does. Mel Gibson and Sissy Spacek turn in impressive performances, though the script doesn't really flesh out their characters. Scott Glenn is pretty good, too, as the local heavy. A sombre but thoughtful tale. (Jean Renoir made an Indian film also entitled *The River* in 1951. It has a U certificate but is hard to get hold of on video, if not impossible. Look out for it on TV, though. It's a moving story, adapted from Rumer Godden's novel, about English children growing up in Bengal.)

River Runs Through It, A
1992 PG 118 ★★ DRA

Although this film, revolving around
fly-fishing, is beautiful to look it, you soon
realise angling is not a spectator sport. The
story's pretty uninvolving, too, as a couple of
sons (Brad Pitt and Craig Sheffer) reassess their
relationship with each other and their father
(Tom Skerritt). Nicely acted, with director
Robert Redford narrating, but ultimately, and
despite tragic incidents, less moving than it
might have been.

River Wild, The
1994 12 106 ★★★★ ACT/ADV

Cracking adventure story which the females of
the household in particular will love right up to
the final scene. Meryl Streep plays the all-action
heroine taking her son and husband on a
dangerous trip down the Colorado River rapids.
But the terror of the white water is nothing in
comparison to the threat posed when she picks
up a couple of stranded young men. We soon
learn that they have just committed robbery
and murder, and that the river is their only
getaway route. Can Streep foil the psychos and
save her family? Streep is magnificent, as is
Kevin Bacon as the more deadly of the killers,
while David Strathairn handles the role of the
feeble husband nicely. Gripping stuff.

Road to Morocco
1942 U 78 ★★★ COM

Dorothy Lamour as an Arabian princess wooed,
as ever, by Bob Hope and Bing Crosby (see
Road to Singapore, below). It's all rather wild
and disjointed but is also very funny. (B&W)

Road to Singapore
1940 U 81 ★★★ COM

The first of the very successful series featuring
Bob Hope and Bing Crosby, with Dorothy
Lamour as the object of both men's desire.
Some of the comedy has dated now but Hope
and Crosby play off each other most
engagingly. This one – in which they travel to a
South Sea island, fall for Lamour and find
themselves short of cash – set the tone for the
rest of the series. Crosby is invariably the sharp,
laidback smart one while Hope is the fall guy.
Whatever the setting, they usually turn up as
penniless and inept adventurers. (B&W)

Road to Utopia
1945 PG 86 ★★ COM

Centres on a gold rush in the Klondike and
ownership of a gold mine. Actually, it belongs
to Lamour, who turns up later looking for the
bad guys who stole it from her family in the
first place. (B&W)

Road to Zanzibar
1941 PG 87 ★★ COM

Again involves a gold mine but only briefly.
After Crosby and Hope have bought and sold it
the story takes another direction with the male
leads, plus Lamour and Una Merkel, going on
safari. The series was extremely popular in its
time, largely because Hope and Crosby were
then at the peak of their movie fame. Besides,
the combination of Hope's wisecracks and one-
liners and Crosby's crooning is a guaranteed
crowd-pleaser. Lamour, too, though given more
or less a supporting role, shows a nice comic
touch. (B&W)

Roaring Twenties, The
1939 PG 102 ★★★ ACT/ADV

One of the classic gangster movies with the
classic gangster figures – James Cagney and
Humphrey Bogart – as a couple of soldiers who
take opposing but intertwining career paths
after the First World War. A touch dated,
perhaps, but there's bootlegging, gang rivalry
and a sharp eye for the period shown by
director Raoul Walsh. Cagney is the star;
Bogart hadn't quite made it to the top then.
(B&W)

Robin and Marian
1976 PG 102 ★★★ DRA

Attention to detail here is so authentic you can
almost smell the forest. Sean Connery plays the
older Robin, returning to Sherwood after the
Crusades and hoping to take up where he left
off with Marian (Audrey Hepburn). Again he
finds his plans hampered by his arch enemy, the
Sheriff of Nottingham (Robert Shaw). Less a
swashbuckler than a grown-up love story.

Robin Hood
1990 PG 100 ★ ACT/ADV

Run-of-the-mill Robin (Patrick Bergin) and his
mealy-mouthed men is the overall impression

given by this dreary account of Hood's adventures in and around Sherwood. Uma Thurman adds a little spark as Maid Marian but the film tries to be both serious and comic and signally fails to be either.

Robin Hood: Men in Tights
1993 PG 100 ★ COM

Spoofs of movies that weren't particularly good in the first place can't possibly work. Mel Brooks's send-up of Kevin Costner's epic (see below) is simply desperately unfunny. The title's the most amusing joke in it.

Robin Hood: Prince of Thieves
1991 PG 137 ★★ ACT/ADV

No-one has equalled the Errol Flynn version but at least Kevin Costner didn't attempt to. He tackled the legend from a different angle and did it reasonably well. This is one of the most popular videos ever. Of course, it owes a great deal to Alan Rickman, who goes gloriously over the top as the cackling Sheriff of Nottingham. Could have done without the Bryan Adams dirge, 'Everything I Do, I Do it For You', though.

Rock-a-Doodle
1990 U 71 ★★ FAM

Animated film with a great deal of humour and some rather bland songs. An Elvis-like rooster's ego is badly dented when the sun rises before he crows. Humiliated, he leaves the farmyard and heads for appreciation in the city. Fame and fortune befall the rooster but the animals left at the farm face a terrible future unless they can coax him back. Kids will love it.

Rocketeer
1991 PG 104 ★★ ACT/ADV

This is a great one for the near-teens, much underrated when released in the cinema. It's based on a 1930s-set comic-strip character, played here by Bill Campbell, who, on discovering a unique flying machine, becomes embroiled in espionage, world-domination plots and the like. A cute little love story is thrown in for romantics.

Rocking Horse Winner, The
1949 PG 88 ★★★ DRA

An evocative tale (based on a D H Lawrence story) about the knock-on effects of a young boy's talent for picking the names of race track winners as he rides on his rocking horse. Would that work with Lottery numbers, we wonder? John Mills stars and produced. (B&W)

Rocky
1976 PG 114 ★★★ ACT/ADV

A small-time boxer (Sylvester Stallone) gets the opportunity to make the big time when he's given a shot at the title. The then-unknown Stallone packed a mighty punch with this. Having written the script himself, he held out against making the movie until it was agreed that he could star. Smart guy and obviously not just a pretty face. He does a convincing job and the movie won Best Film Oscar that year.

Rocky II
1979 PG 114 ★★ ACT/ADV

The message, as usual, is find a winning formula and flog it to death, though this first sequel is entertaining enough. Rocky marries his long-suffering girlfriend (Talia Shire) and steps into the ring for another shot at the title. The formula is already beginning to look all too familiar.

Rocky III
1982 PG 95 ★★ ACT/ADV

Now Rocky's wife wants him to quit, leading contender Mr T wants him to fight. So Rocky does fight and loses his title. Golly, can he get it back? What do you think?

Rocky IV
1985 PG 88 ★ ACT/ADV

It's getting pretty silly now as matters become all too personal for our Rocky. His great friend and rival (Carl Weathers) is killed, so the Rock takes on Soviet hero Dolph Lundgren for revenge, the world title and peace.

Rocky V
1990 PG 99 ★ ACT/ADV

You'd be forgiven for not noticing that Rocky has incurred some brain damage over the course of his career (so have the people who keep making this stuff, come to that). He's also down on his uppers (as is the series) and working as a trainer. One interesting point is that Sage Stallone (Sly's son) plays Rocky's son. (Sage? Does he have a sister called Onion?). This is quite the worst of the five and, one can only hope, the last.

Rocky Horror Picture Show, The
1975 15 99 ★★★ COM

It may have had them rocking in the aisles in the theatre but it doesn't translate to the cinema with the same appeal. Barry Bostwick and Susan Sarandon play the young innocents who inadvertently pitch up at a house full of the weirdest, campest, most tuneful people on Earth including Tim Curry as Frank N Furter. Meat Loaf puts in an appearance among the supporting cast. A little too raunchy for the youngsters.

Roger & Me
1989 15 87 ★★★ DRA

A documentary, pretty hard to get hold of, but worth a look by the older members of the household. Michael Moore (of *Michael Moore's TV Nation* fame) investigates the boss of General Motors, Roger Smith, who was responsible for the redundancy of an entire Michigan town when he moved his company out. Sometimes funny and frequently sad, it's surprisingly entertaining.

Rollerball
1975 15 118 ★★ ACT/ADV

Since there is no crime in the future, sport provides the only outlet for violence and James Caan's the star of the most violent sport of all – rollerball (a kind of hockey-cum-basketball on rollerskates and motor bikes). It evolves into a plot about the individual versus the Establishment and involves some very vicious action.

Romancing the Stone
1984 PG 101 ★★★★ ACT/ADV

A wonderful fantasy adventure in which a romantic novelist (Kathleen Turner) finds herself living one of her books for real as she searches for her kidnapped sister in South

America. Michael Douglas is the intrepid adventurer who helps her – but with an ulterior motive. Danny DeVito joins the pair as a comic crook. Lots of action, some sex and violence and fruity language. Followed by a sequel, *The Jewel of the Nile*.

Roman Holiday
1953 U 113 ★★★ DRA

An utterly romantic fairy tale about a beautiful, bored princess (Audrey Hepburn, who won the Oscar for Best Actress) who slips away one night to enjoy the delights that Rome has to offer. While on the loose she meets a journalist (Gregory Peck), who falls in love with her, ignorant of her identity. Smashing acting from Peck and Hepburn, who have enough electricity between them to light up the Vatican.

Room Service: see Marx Brothers

Room with a View, A
1985 PG 112 ★★★★ DRA

Merchant/Ivory pull out all the stops in a breathtaking adaptation of E M Forster's novel. Helena Bonham Carter plays the young woman romanced by Italy and Julian Sands while on a visit to Florence with her aunt (Maggie Smith). The supporting performances are humorous gems. Denholm Elliott, Daniel Day-Lewis, Simon Callow and Judi Dench provide them. Beautiful photography enhances the experience.

Rosalie Goes Shopping
1989 15 90 ★★ DRA

A quirky, wry satire on the dangers of credit cards. Marianne Sagebrecht is a bored housewife with countless children and a compulsion for shopping. With mounting debts she continues to spend, spend, spend. More a comment on consumerism than a mainstream movie.

Rosencrantz and Guildenstern Are Dead
1990 PG 113 ★★ COM

Tom Stoppard's play, despite his best efforts to turn it into a movie, still works best on the stage. It's a touch too wordy for the screen though Tim Roth and Gary Oldman give their all as the courtiers charged with ensuring that Hamlet doesn't return from England. The sparkling wit is there but a more experienced director than Stoppard himself would probably have given it some much-needed punch. Richard Dreyfuss appears as the Player King.

'Round Midnight
1986 15 126 ★★★ MUS

Writer/director Bertrand Tavernier's affectionate tribute to the great black American jazz musicians who settled in Paris in the 1950s. Dexter Gordon, a dab hand at the jazz but comparatively new to the acting lark, plays the lead in a story inspired by the lives of Bud Powell and Lester Young. Herbie Hancock's score is one of the film's best features. (Subtitled in parts)

Roxanne
1987 PG 102 ★★★ COM

Steve Martin's funny, touching, modern version of *Cyrano de Bergerac*. He's the local fire chief, friend to all but lover of none due to his unusually large nose. When the beautiful Roxanne (Daryl Hannah) comes to town, Martin woos her, ostensibly on behalf of a hunky fellow fireman. Beautifully balanced performances from Hannah and Martin and a pleasingly romantic ending.

Ruby
1992 15 106 ★★ MYS/THR

Not the jewel, but Jack, the man who shot the man (Lee Harvey Oswald) who shot JFK. Danny Aiello turns in a very tidy performance in a film that's never quite sure if it's compounding the conspiracy theory or just telling a fictional tale. The docu-drama approach of British director John Mackenzie is interesting but doesn't quite come off.

Rudyard Kipling's The Jungle Book
1995 PG 108 ★★ ACT/ADV

This film owes little more to Kipling's original story than the Walt Disney version and is only half as good. Jason Scott Lee plays Mowgli, the lad who goes into the jungle as a toddler and

emerges a muscle-bound hunk with the wolves, a panther and a bear for family. Once he becomes involved with the neighbourhood army, all manner of troubles ensue. Lena Headey provides the love interest; Cary Elwes the action and villainy and John Cleese the humour. Disappointing overall.

Running on Empty
1988 15 111 ★★★ DRA

On the run for an act of terrorism they committed as hippies in the sixties, Christine Lahti and Judd Hirsch are unable to provide the stable home life their son, River Phoenix, needs when he's offered a music scholarship. An impressive drama about priorities, love and sacrifice by director Sidney Lumet, which owes an enormous amount to Phoenix, who's quite brilliant.

Russia House, The
1990 15 118 ★★ MYS/THR

Unless you have a particular penchant for spy thrillers, this post-Cold War John Le Carré story is past its sell-by date. Sean Connery plays a London publisher who receives an intriguing manuscript from Russia. The result is a web of intrigue that lands him between the British and Russian intelligence services. Still, he does get to romance a beautiful Muscovite (Michelle Pfeiffer). The cast is more attractive than the tale.

Ryan's Daughter
1970 15 186 ★★★ DRA

David Lean's emotional saga about an Irishwoman (Sara Miles) who – despite being married to the local schoolteacher (Robert Mitchum) – shocks the close-knit coastal community when she embarks on an affair with a British soldier. Trevor Howard turns in a lovely performance as the priest but it was John Mills, as the village idiot, who won the Oscar. The film, much vilified on its cinema release, wears surprisingly well. (The adverse criticism it received so depressed David Lean that he didn't make another film until *A Passage to India* fourteen years later.)

Saint of Fort Washington, The
1994 15 99 ★★★ DRA

Heart-rending drama about homelessness.
Matt Dillon plays a young schizophrenic
released into 'community care', i.e. chucked
out onto the streets, who is taken in hand by
hardened street dweller Danny Glover. Tears
before bedtime stuff, so watch it armed with
tissues.

Salaam Bombay!
1988 15 109 ★★★ FOR

A young country boy's experiences on the
rough streets of Bombay form the basis of
this fascinating Indian drama, which is
remarkable for the strength of its
characterizations. Many of the prostitutes and
urchins are the real McCoy and in telling
what happens to them the film does not pull
its punches. (Subtitled)

Same Time, Next Year
1978 15 113 ★★★ DRA

Charming, bittersweet story about a couple
(Ellen Burstyn and Alan Alda) who meet on
holiday every year when, for an all-too-brief
time, they conduct an adulterous affair. Very
obviously originating from a stage play since
Alda and Burstyn are the only people in it, but
so sufficient are they, you don't miss a
supporting cast.

Sandlot Kids, The
1993 PG 97 ★★ COM

A gentle, uneventful story about a young boy's
first summer in a new town. Thanks to the
local lads' love of baseball he immediately finds
friends and adventure – albeit undramatic
adventure. Engaging enough, though.

Santa Claus
1985 U 103 ★ FAM

As Santa's little helper, a part he fits rather
well, Dudley Moore is very cute but
unfortunately the feeble storyline and the
script let him down. There's a sort of plot
about a disgruntled elf selling Santa's secrets to
a toy manufacturer but it's not up to much. As
a festive fantasy for the children, though, it
serves its purpose and should keep them
amused for a while.

Sarafina!
1992 15 112 ★★ MUS

A rousing, colourful musical set in South Africa.
Unfortunately, the political content – an
uprising by the Soweto schoolchildren, many of
whom were massacred – is too heavy for such a
light framework. Nice songs and choreography
though, and Whoopi Goldberg as a teacher and
Leleti Khumalo as the young heroine are both
good to watch. The violence of the massacre and
torture scenes account for the 15 certificate.

Saturday Night and Sunday Morning
1960 PG 86 ★★★ DRA

Dramas about angry young men tend to look
pretty dated now, but in its day this was a
powerful tale about an anti-hero (Albert
Finney) who has an affair with a fellow factory
worker's wife. Karel Reisz directs Finney in his
first, hugely impressive starring role. The use of
black-and-white photography and the drab,
rugged Midlands locations add to the
grippingly realistic atmosphere. (B&W)

Scarlet Pimpernel, The
1934 U 94 ★★★★ DRA

Leslie Howard plays Baroness Orczy's Regency
fop who doubles as the daring rescuer of
endangered French aristocrats. Splendid he is,
too, in both parts. Merle Oberon is the
Pimpernel's unsuspecting wife; Raymond Massey
the revolutionary Chauvelin, Howard's arch
enemy. First-rate rousing adventure. (B&W)

Scenes from a Mall
1991 15 83 ★★ COM

For once Woody Allen stars in a film he's
neither written nor directed, so don't expect the
usual angst and trauma. What you have here is
a comedy in which numerous marital
revelations and schisms appear when Bette
Midler and Allen go shopping to celebrate their
wedding anniversary. Midler's smashing as a
female foil to Allen. Paul Mazursky directs,
though he fails to exploit a lot of the comic
opportunities the situation offers.

Scent of a Woman
1992 15 150 ★★★ DRA

Well-performed but implausible drama about a
young preppy (Chris O'Donnell) hired for the

holiday weekend to keep an eye on a blind Vietnam veteran (Al Pacino) while his family has a break. Pacino takes the boy on a no-holds-barred weekend in New York, which he plans to be his last. Oscar-winner Pacino's occasionally flamboyant performance contrasts with young O'Donnell's quieter approach and the sentiment tends to stick in the throat by the end. Eminently watchable, though.

Schindler's List
1993 15 187 ★★★★★ DRA

A powerhouse production by Steven Spielberg which recounts the story of Oskar Schindler, an Austrian businessman who, during the Second World War, saved hundreds of Jews from the gas chamber. Magnificent performances from Ralph Fiennes and Ben Kingsley, not to mention Liam Neeson in the title role, meant that finally Spielberg got the Oscar that was so long owing to him. (B&W)

Scott of the Antarctic
1948 U 105 ★★★ ACT/ADV

Since you know this trip is going to end in tears, be prepared. It's evocatively told and you're as closely involved with Scott (John Mills) and his team as if you were actually there with them on the frozen wastes. James Robertson Justice, Kenneth More and Christopher Lee support.

Scout, The
1994 12 98 ★★★ COM

Despite missing a cinema release this is a neat little comedy which should appeal to all tastes. Albert Brooks is grand as the unsuccessful scout for the New York Yankee baseball team, despatched by his irate boss to talent-spot in the outer reaches of Mexico. Among the enchilladas and on a pitch on which you wouldn't graze cattle, he spots the brilliant all-rounder Brendan Fraser. Only trouble is, Fraser has some psychological difficulties which may be insurmountable. Nice performances, aided by a sharp script ensure some, if not very many laughs.

Scrooge
1951 U 86 ★★★ FAM

Alastair Sim's quite frightening Scrooge is ably backed up by Jack Warner, Michael Hordern,

George Cole and others in a delightful feel-good adaptation of Dickens's tale. The film was made in black and white but has been released on video in a 'colourized' version. If you possibly can, watch it in black and white.

Scrooge
1970 U 108 ★★★ MUS

A musical version, with lyrics by Leslie Bricusse. Scrooge is played by Albert Finney and the various Christmas ghosts are portrayed by Alec Guinness, Edith Evans and Kenneth More. Quite a cast, one way or another. The music and songs are pleasant but, as always, it's the story that really pleases.

Scrooged
1988 PG 97 ★★ COM

Lethal Weapon director Richard Donner takes the helm here with a modern-day, comic version of Dickens's *A Christmas Carol*. A TV executive (Bill Murray) is devoid of the festive spirit until he's taken in hand by three ghosts. Murray's always good value and there's a number of starry cameos to look out for.

Sea Hawk, The
1940 U 122 ★★★ ACT/ADV

Errol Flynn is on his finest swashing and buckling form as the English sea captain graciously permitted by Flora Robson's formidable Queen Elizabeth to plunder the Spanish fleet. There's plenty of rousing action but do listen carefully to the dialogue, for the film also served as anti-Nazi propaganda in the early part of the Second World War. (B&W)

Searchers, The
1956 U 114 ★★★★★ WES

One of the best Westerns ever made, impeccably directed by the maestro John Ford. John Wayne stars as an Indian-hating pioneer searching for his niece (Natalie Wood) who has been abducted by the Comanches. He believes she has been ruined and would be better off dead. His young companion, Jeffrey Hunter, wants to bring her back alive. A richly intelligent character study, superbly directed and beautifully played. Not to be missed.

Secret Garden, The
1993 U 97 ★★★★ FAM

Beautifully staged adaptation of Frances Hodgson Burnett's children's classic. A little orphan girl is sent to stay with her remote uncle (John Lynch) and his hard-nosed housekeeper (Maggie Smith). Locked doors and mysterious noises hide all manner of secrets and adventures. Despite a woeful waste of Lynch in a minute part, it's a delight – and not just for the children. (There are earlier versions also well worth watching: a TV movie – the lesser of the three – and a 1949, vaguely creepy version with Margaret O'Brien and Elsa Lanchester, which also has a U certificate.)

Secret Honor
1984 15 86 ★★★★ DRA

A most remarkable film – a one-man show (directed by Robert Altman) in which Philip Baker Hall plays a ranting Richard Nixon who, on the verge of suicide, delivers what purport to be his reminiscences. The revelations are so jaw-droppingly horrendous, and indeed criminal, that you wonder Nixon did not sue.

Secret Life of Walter Mitty, The
1947 U 106 ★★★ COM

Charming vehicle for Danny Kaye to do what he does best – impersonate. As the naive, timid fantasist of the title he enlivens his drab existence by daydreaming himself into heroic and dangerous situations, only to find himself deeply involved in one. Virginia Mayo provides some normality as the love interest but it's the loveable Kaye who makes this film, travesty though it is of Thurber's short story, such a gem.

Secret of My Success, The
1987 PG 105 ★★ COM

Michael J Fox offers the main appeal of this thin tale about a country boy who lands a job in the big city and encounters naughtiness for the first time. Corruption lurks in the office, outside the office and, specifically, in the bedroom. Fox is energetic, as is Helen Slater as the object of his affections.

See No Evil, Hear No Evil
1989 15 97 ★★ COM

A daft comedy designed as a vehicle for Richard Pryor and Gene Wilder. It's a good pairing but could have worked so much better if the material had been up to scratch. They play a blind man (Pryor) and a deaf man (Wilder) who are mistaken for murderers and can only prove their innocence by catching the real culprits. Lame jokes, too many of them aimed at the afflicted – though funnily enough, it was one of the first videos to be released with subtitles. Wonder if deaf people will laugh much?

Seven Brides for Seven Brothers
1954 U 98 ★★★★ MUS

Joyous story about seven brothers on a remote farm, headed by Howard Keel, who decide it's time they got themselves some wives. Jane Powell is the first of the young women kidnapped to make a comfortable home for Keel and the boys. Magnificent songs – 'Bless Your Beautiful Hide' and 'When You're in Love' among them – are accompanied by some of the best dancing and choreography you could hope to see. Despite its unapologetic sexism, it's a must for all the family.

Seven Samurai
1954 PG 190 ★★★★★ FOR

This story of sixteenth-century Japanese villagers who, exploited by bandits, enlist the aid of seven wandering warriors, may sound familiar. That's because it was this superb film, by Akira Kurosawa, which was remade by John Sturges as the Western, *The Magnificent Seven*. Both pictures are hugely recommended but Kurosawa's is the undoubted classic. (B&W; subtitled)

Seventh Seal, The
1957 PG 92 ★★★★★ FOR

This magical, classic Swedish gem from Ingmar Bergman remains one of the most intelligent movies ever made. A fourteenth-century Knight (Max von Sydow), on his way back from the crusades, ponders the meaning of life as he plays a game of chess with Death. A quite brilliant film, one of the jewels in Bergman's crown. (B&W; subtitled)

7th Voyage of Sinbad, The
1958 U 84 ★★★ FAM

The great Ray Harryhausen's effects enhance this rollicking fantasy adventure in which Sinbad's love has been reduced to the size of a pea by an evil magician, setting Sinbad off in search of a restorative. Adventures galore as Sinbad (Kerwin Mathews) and company run into the cyclops and skeletal swordsmen. Great fun for all the clan.

Seven Year Itch, The
1955 PG 100 ★★★★ COM

The Marilyn Monroe comedy famed for the scene in which her skirt is blown above her shoulders by a New York subway vent. (No, it's OK – her knickers are very chaste and unrevealing.) Apart from that she plays a dumb blonde who moves into the flat above Tom Ewell. Ewell's wife is away and he's reached that 'certain' age… But again it's all right – director Billy Wilder handles the story with wit and decorum.

Shadow, The
1994 12 103 ★★ SCI/FAN

Alec Baldwin lurks in corners as the comic-book superhero who was dealing with the dastardlies long before Superman was a twinkle in his daddy's eye. The Shadow has the ability to cloud men's minds, which while a useful talent to possess isn't a very exciting one to watch, at least not in this somewhat banal story. Like all superheroes, the Shadow rounds up the bad guys and, incidentally, saves the world from domination by a descendant of Genghis Khan.

Shadowlands
1993 U 126 ★★★★ DRA

Richard Attenborough's superb account of the gentle love affair between the *Narnia* creator, C S Lewis (a quite outstanding performance by Anthony Hopkins) and a brash American divorcee (Debra Winger, who is every bit as good as Sir Anthony). Subtle evocation of the differences between the ivory tower-based writer and the worldly woman. Hankies at the ready. (There's also a very fine made-for-TV version from 1985 starring Joss Ackland and Claire Bloom.)

Shadows and Fog
1992 15 82 ★★ COM

You need to be a committed fan of Woody Allen to list this as one of your faves. Shot in black and white, it's a pastiche of 1920s/30s German Expressionist movies in which a strangler lurks in the city smog. The cast list reads like an Oscar roll-call with cameos from Madonna, John Malkovich, Jodie Foster, Donald Pleasence, Wallace Shawn and Lily Tomlin. Hollywood's finest may be present, shame the humour isn't. (B&W)

Shag
1988 15 95 ★★ COM

The title (referring to a dance, incidentally) should raise a titter even if the film doesn't. Phoebe Cates, Bridget Fonda, Annabeth Gish and Page Hannah (Daryl's sister) play the four friends who take off for Myrtle Beach for a last weekend of fun before Cates gets married. Set in 1963, it's a cute tale, enhanced by a likeable cast.

Shane
1953 PG 113 ★★★★★ WES

One of the all-time classic Westerns, often imitated but never bettered. Alan Ladd plays the enigmatic stranger who has to buckle on his gunbelt to protect the homesteaders threatened by Jack Palance and his gang of killers. Perfect combination of action, drama and strong, brooding emotion. Ladd was never better, neither was Palance and there's great support from Jean Arthur and Van Heflin.

Shanghai Surprise
1986 15 93 ★ ACT/ADV

Teenagers may be attracted to this because it stars Madonna but they'll almost certainly be disappointed. It's a wheezy old vehicle for her or anyone. It's a comedy-thriller in which she and her then husband, Sean Penn, hunt for stolen opium in 1930s China. Villains, of course, are after it too. The result is neither exciting nor amusing.

Shattered
1991 15 94 ★★ MYS/THR

'Shocked' is more like it – that such a good cast could have agreed to such a poor film. Tom

Berenger stars as Greta Scacchi's wealthy husband who, following a car crash, wakes up with amnesia and a personality change. Bob Hoskins is the detective he hires to answer the questions he has about his wife and her friends Corbin Bernsen and Joanne Whalley-Kilmer. By the time the mystery comes to light you're long past caring.

Shawshank Redemption, The
1994 15 143 ★★★★ DRA

Magnificently powerful story about a mild accountant (Tim Robbins) sentenced to life imprisonment for the murder of his wife, despite protesting his innocence. The film revolves around jail life and the various ways the inmates handle it. Robbins gives the performance of a lifetime and should at least have been nominated for an Oscar alongside co-star Morgan Freeman, who plays the prison's Mr Fix-It – the man who can get you anything from a chisel to a poster of Rita Hayworth. Despite some truly brutal scenes this missed an 18 certificate. Brilliant as it is, we personally would feel uncomfortable letting a 15-year-old child watch certain scenes.

She
1965 U 101 ★★ ACT/ADV

Fine ironing movie, or the sort of movie you welcome when your brain needs a rest. Ursula Andress plays the beautiful young queen who has found the secret of eternal youth. Christopher Lee and Peter Cushing co-star, but it is Andress as the sexy narcissus who steals the show. Be careful, though, with the very little ones – despite the U certificate, it's a little raunchy in parts.

She-Devil
1989 15 95 ★★ DRA

If you can get hold of the BBC television version, do so. It's far superior to this Hollywood adaptation of Fay Weldon's novel about a plain housewife getting revenge on her cheating husband. All the magic and subtlety of the book and TV series is lost with poor casting and cheap humour. Roseanne Barr plays the fat wife and mother, Meryl Streep is the slim, wealthy mistress and Ed Begley Jr the hapless male in the middle.

She Wore a Yellow Ribbon
1949 U 98 ★★★★ WES

The second of John Ford's US cavalry trilogy (*Fort Apache* and *Rio Grande* being the others) in which John Wayne stars as the grizzled veteran officer who has reached retiring age but is reluctant to go since the Apaches are on the warpath again. Wayne is at his best and Ford at his most elegiac in a story that encompasses far more than exciting frontier action.

Shining Through
1992 15 127 ★★ WAR

Sit back and enjoy this film. It's one of those rare treats – a movie so bad that you'll love it. Most of the laughs – all of them unintentional – are to be had from the terrible performance, not to mention voice, of Melanie Griffith, totally unbelievable as a spy in Germany during the Second World War. Poor old Michael Douglas is almost equally ludicrous as the intelligence officer who appointed her. If only all bad films were as funny as this.

Shirley Valentine
1989 15 104 ★★★★ COM

One for the women, this, as a bored Liverpudlian housewife (Pauline Collins) leaves the drudgery of her monotonous life and unromantic husband (Bernard Hill) and heads off on holiday to a Greek island where she finds her heart's desire in the shape of Tom Conti. A delightful comedy from Willy Russell. Mind you, though, while Shirley telling her story to a wall may have worked on stage, it jars a little on screen.

Shooting Party, The
1984 15 93 ★★★★ DRA

Observant and moving tale based around a weekend shooting party in 1913. James Mason is brilliant in his last role as the host to a bunch of aristocratic guests come for the ritual slaughter of the birds. What develops is a study of class and social attitudes and an ironic commentary on the impending war. A graceful, poignant film enhanced by the presence of John Gielgud, Edward Fox, Dorothy Tutin and Gordon Jackson.

Shootist, The
1976 PG 95 ★★★ WES

A most moving performance by John Wayne, who was soon to die of cancer, as an old gunfighter, dying of cancer, who seeks a peaceful, dignified death. Fate, however, intervenes. In Don Siegel's elegiac Western, Lauren Bacall plays Wayne's landlady and, as the town doctor, James Stewart has some memorable toupee-to-toupee confrontations with the Duke.

Short Circuit
1986 PG 94 ★★★ SCI/FAN

A cutesy robot (fondly known as Number Five) surprises its creator, Steve Guttenberg, when it comes to life. Number Five escapes from the military establishment where it was made, falls into the hands of animal-loving Ally Sheedy and begins to proclaim peace and love, rather than war. A nice, gently amusing piece of romantic science-fantasy.

Short Circuit 2
1988 PG 106 ★★ SCI/FAN

Number Five – now called Johnny Five – is back but most of the original cast aren't. Perhaps they knew when they'd had enough of a good thing. The new story is less cute and more streetwise and this time the robot falls into bad company. Teenagers may still see something amusing but older generations may want to give this one a miss.

Shout
1991 PG 85 ★★★ DRA

According to this quiet but appealing story, rock 'n' roll developed in a reform school somewhere in Texas, sometime in the fifties. Not just any old reform school, but one at which the teachers included understanding music man John Travolta. James Walters is the inmate with a talent for rock tunes and an eye for the warden's daughter, Heather Graham.

Show Boat
1951 U 103 ★★★★ MUS

One of the all-time great musicals with some splendid numbers by Jerome Kern. So good, indeed, that both this and the 1936 version (with Paul Robeson crooning 'Ol' Man River')

are enthusiastically recommended. The story is a big, fat melodrama involving gamblers, show people, racial bigotry, love, romance and tragedy, all centring on a Mississippi show boat. Those dramatically and tunefully involved include Howard Keel, Kathryn Grayson and Ava Gardner. (The earlier version is not on video but is sometimes shown on TV.)

Sibling Rivalry
1990 15 84 ★★ COM

Good idea, shame about the show. For a Carl Reiner comedy this is woefully unfunny. Kirstie Alley in the lead role provides something to recommend it but the script certainly doesn't. A browbeaten housewife (Alley), awaiting the arrival of her husband's long-lost brother, is swept off her feet in the greengrocer's by a stranger with whom she has torrid sex. His dying on her is bad enough; the fact that he's the missing brother-in-law is a lot worse...

Silas Marner
1985 PG 90 ★★★ DRA

Effective and relatively faithful adaptation of George Eliot's classic novel about a miser. Ben Kingsley plays Silas Marner, who finds his life takes on new importance when a young orphan adopts him. This was a BBC production and very few people make this kind of costume drama better than Auntie.

Silkwood
1983 15 125 ★★★ DRA

Dynamic performances by both Meryl Streep, as Karen Silkwood, and Cher, as her best friend, in a disturbing film based on fact. Silkwood worked at a nuclear processing plant where she inadvertently discovered that safety precautions were frighteningly poor. The film itself is an alarming commentary on the power of big business over the life and death of the individual.

Silverado
1985 PG 127 ★★★ WES

Lawrence Kasdan's brave attempt at a Western, which, though well made, doesn't quite hang together. Four very different men join forces against corruption in a remote town. Plenty of comedy, thrills and shoot-outs but in a cast that includes Scott Glenn, the Kevins Kline and Costner, John Cleese and Jeff Goldblum there are too many who look as if they would sooner phone for a lawyer than reach for a gun.

Sinbad the Sailor
1947 U 112 ★★★ FAM

In this one Sinbad is played by the dashing Douglas Fairbanks Jr. Here he's off in search of lost treasure and loads of exciting adventures in which mythical monsters abound. Maureen O'Hara is the object of his affections. Rousing stuff for all the family.

Singin' in the Rain
1952 U 98 ★★★★★ MUS

Sometimes regarded as the best of all musicals and certainly it's hard to think of anything better. Gene Kelly as co-director, choreographer and star provides the most beautiful footwork, of course, and is admirably abetted by Donald O'Connor and Debbie Reynolds in an affectionate spoof of the movies at the dawn of the sound age. Great songs, of course, and a lovely, funny performance by Jean Hagen.

Singles
1992 15 95 ★★★ DRA

An intelligent comedy-drama set in a condo full of twentysomethings, all of whom are ready to settle down whether they know it or not. The cast – Bridget Fonda, Campbell Scott, Matt Dillon, Kyra Sedgwick among them – makes an ill-assorted but likeable bunch of young hopefuls. One for the romantics; cynics should steer clear. (Only a '12' in the cinema but upped for video since it contains some choice language.)

Sirens
1994 15 90 ★★★ DRA

A spectacularly visual film set in the Bohemian household of an Australian artist (Sam Neill) where beautiful people swan around in various states of undress – most notably the supermodel, Elle Macpherson, who put on a couple of stone for the role and looks stunning. Hugh Grant, as an uptight clergyman, and Tara Fitzgerald, as his wife, react in markedly contrasting ways when they're forced to stay with the artist. Contains nudity.

Sister Act
1992 PG 90 ★★★ COM

An implausible comedy – though it has its moments – about a raunchy cabaret artist (Whoopi Goldberg) who, after witnessing a Mob killing, takes refuge in a convent. In spite of the personality clash between her and Mother Superior Maggie Smith, she begins to enjoy it and shapes the choir into a flock of swinging penguins. The numbers are a delight.

Sister Act 2: Back in the Habit
1993 PG 103 ★ COM

Whoopi and most of the cast are back, thank goodness, but the quality isn't. It's a weak sequel, much the same as before only not so good. This time Goldberg is urged into taking up the habit again to save an inner-city school from closure. An expensive habit to put Ms Goldberg back in – she cost Disney a reported seven million dollars.

Six Wives of Henry VIII, The
1972 U 541 ★★★★ DRA

Fascinating, comprehensive saga (told in six parts – each video is ninety minutes) of the King with more wives than Rod Stewart. Keith Michell makes an excellent Henry, turning from an ambitious lad into a tyrannical monarch, while the wives – Annette Crosbie, Barbara Leigh-Hunt, Dorothy Tutin, Anne Stallybrass, Rosalie Crutchley and Elvi Hale – are perfect to a woman. Great entertainment and a history lesson to boot.

Sleeper
1973 PG 83 ★★★★★ COM

Woody Allen at his very best as a man who is deep-frozen in 1973 only to awaken 200 years later in a world where they've found that alcohol, sugar, salt and smoking are good for you. Mind you, it's also a police state in which enemies of the government are forced to watch endless TV reruns, than which nothing could be crueller. Allen joins Diane Keaton and the rebels. Unmissable for Allen fans.

Sleeping Beauty
1959 U 75 ★★★★ FAM

Brushed up and dusted down, Sleeping Beauty looks lovelier than ever now she's been re-released on a sparkling new print. Charming animated fairy tale from Disney with music adapted from the Tchaikovsky ballet and a host of memorable characters. Reportedly, it took seven years to make and cost over six million dollars – it's made that back a few times though.

Sleeping with the Enemy
1991 15 93 ★★ MYS/THR

Sleeping's probably the best thing to do while watching this, since it's an ill-conceived thriller with unbelievable characters. Julia Roberts is pretty uninspiring as an unhappy wife who leaves her brutal husband, Patrick Bergin, and pretends to be dead. By the time he catches up with her, seeking revenge, she has taken up with Kevin Anderson, who must be the most wimpish hero in the cinema. Pretty violent and even more so if you pick up the video version with the 18 certificate.

Sleepless in Seattle
1993 PG 101 ★★★★ COM

One of those films which leave you feeling all's right with the world. The romantics amongst you will have a ball. Meg Ryan is about to make a disastrous marriage until she hears lonely widower Tom Hanks talking on the radio and falls in love. The setting is Christmas-time, the finale's on top of the Empire State Building and the humour and the sentiment flow thick, if not always fast, throughout. Charming.

Slipper and the Rose, The
1976 U 136 ★★★ FAM

A pretty musical version of Cinderella with Gemma Craven as the girl who keeps losing her footwear and Richard Chamberlain the dashing royal who finds it. Annette Crosbie is delightful as the fairy godmother and almost every reliable British supporting actor appears in it. One for everybody to enjoy.

Snapper, The
1993 15 81 ★★★★ COM

Although this story by Roddy Doyle – who wrote *The Commitments* – was originally made for TV, it was so well received that they released it later in the cinema. It's the affectionate,

funny heart-warming account (directed by Stephen Frears) of the reactions of a Dublin family when the young, unmarried daughter falls pregnant. Tina Kellegher and Colm Meaney are delightful as daughter and father.

Sneakers
1992 15 120 ★★★ ACT/ADV

Just as you're beginning to think they don't make good caper movies any more, they do: this one. Robert Redford leads a band of fiendishly clever computer experts (Dan Aykroyd, Sidney Poitier, David Strathairn and River Phoenix) who are forced into pitting their wits against both the FBI and technical wizard and arch baddie, Ben Kingsley. Expertly plotted with gadgetry to rival any Bond movie, it's a cracking adventure with something for everybody. And you don't need to know a thing about computers to understand what's going on.

Sniper
1992 15 95 ★★ ACT/ADV

A silly excuse for lots of testosterone as hunky chaps Tom Berenger and Billy Zane play sparring US snipers sent in to the jungle to dispatch some drug barons. With their constant bickering, it's surprising the baddies don't hear them a mile off, but selective deafness seems to rule the day. Selective viewing would be advisable, too.

Snowman, The
1982 U 26 ★★★★ FAM

Raymond Briggs's magical tale about a snowman who comes to life is beautifully depicted in this short, but rich animated film. Makes a splendid Christmas present for anybody.

Snow White and the Seven Dwarfs
1937 U 80 ★★★★ FAM

Disney's first and, some would argue, best feature-length animated film. Nearly sixty years later it still stands comparison with his – and other studios' – later work. There is a freshness and vivacity about it that doesn't seem to fade with time and some of the songs ('Some Day My Prince Will Come', for instance, and 'Whistle While You Work') have bcome standards. Here's a question for you: what are the names of the dwarfs? We know, but we're not telling. Do yourself a favour – watch the film and find out.

Soapdish
1991 15 92 ★★★ COM

Not a bad comedy, with an impressive cast. Sally Field plays the aging doyenne of a daytime soap opera who fears she may be written out of the plot. Scriptwriter Whoopi Goldberg comes up with an ingenious twist for her character but it involves her ex-husband, Kevin Kline, and leads to an off-set story more outlandish than the soap itself. Nicely paced, which is just as well since most of the comedy borders on farce. Robert Downey Jr and Carrie Fisher are among the cast.

Soft Top Hard Shoulder
1993 15 91 ★★★ COM

Peter Capaldi stars in this gentle comedy (which he also wrote) about an unemployed graduate, hopelessly accident-prone, who decides to drive from his London home to Glasgow for his father's sixtieth birthday. Picking up a kooky hitchhiker en route (Elaine Collins) proves a bad idea. Nice images and pleasing gags line the route.

So I Married an Axe Murderer
1993 15 90 ★★★ COM

A nightclub poet (Mike Myers) loves the women but just can't commit to them until, that is, he's whisked off his feet by the woman of his dreams (Nancy Travis). But after they're married he begins to suspect she may be the local axe murderer. Some of the comedy goes wide of the mark but Myers is very appealing and there are nice cameos from Alan Arkin and Charles Grodin. Don't be put off by the title, there's no blood or mayhem here.

Some Like It Hot
1959 U 117 ★★★★★ COM

If any member of your family has not yet seen this Billy Wilder classic, rectify that oversight at once. Musicians Jack Lemmon and Tony Curtis hide out from the Mob – in drag – in an all-women band after witnessing the Saint Valentine's day massacre. Hilarious complications ensue when Curtis woos the lead singer, Marilyn Monroe, and Lemmon is pursued by a wealthy, randy old man (Joe E Brown), leading to the unforgettable line, 'Nobody's perfect'. (B&W)

Someone to Watch Over Me
1987 15 102 ★★★★ MYS/THR

Steaming thrills, romance and adventure as a beautiful heiress (Mimi Rogers) needs police protection until she can testify at a killer's trial. Tom Berenger's the married cop who, in the course of playing bodyguard, falls in love with her. Intelligent and well written, with enough chemistry between Rogers and Berenger to light up the National Grid. Some violence and sex account for the certificate.

Sommersby
1992 15 109 ★★★ DRA

A period drama about a soldier (Richard Gere) returning from a lengthy absence fighting the American Civil War to the wife (Jodie Foster), child and farming community he left behind. Trouble is, he's a changed man – for the better. The question then arises: is he the *real* Sommersby? The truth only emerges at a murder trial. Well made, though the original French version, *The Return of Martin Guerre*, is better.

Son of the Pink Panther
1994 PG 85 ★ COM

Blake Edwards's attempt to revive the famous inspector by having Clouseau's son (Roberto Benigni) take over really doesn't work. The original series depended on Peter Sellers and only Peter Sellers: few have his comic genius.

Sophie's Choice
1982 15 144 ★★★ DRA

Only those with a heart of stone could fail to be moved by the harrowing story and the magnificent portrayal, by Meryl Streep, of a Nazi concentration-camp survivor striving to find happiness in New York. Kevin Kline plays her hot-blooded lover. Sophie's choice, when finally we learn what it was, is desperately moving. A standard box of hankies may not be enough – family size should do it.

Sound Barrier, The
1952 U 111 ★★★ ACT/ADV

Not David Lean's best, but even his lesser films are head and shoulders above most. Ralph Richardson is an aircraft designer who will risk everything to be the first to break the sound barrier. Ann Todd is his long-suffering daughter; Nigel Patrick and John Justin play the test pilots dicing with death. The cinematography is marvellous. (B&W)

Sound of Music, The
1965 U 165 ★★★★ MUS

Bringing the hills to life with Rodgers and Hammerstein's fantastic score is Julie Andrews as the lapsed novice who became nanny to seven children and saved them from the Nazis. The story (of the von Trapp family) is, of course, based on fact. Joyous songs and splendid choreography mark this uplifting and unashamedly sentimental tale. Five Oscars show just how good a movie it is.

South Pacific
1958 U 143 ★★★★ MUS

The Second World War is the era, an exotic South Sea island the setting for a string of vignettes enlivened by Rodgers and Hammerstein's superb music. This is the show where you'll find those all-time favourites, 'Nothing Like a Dame', 'Some Enchanted Evening' and 'Happy Talk'. Rossano Brazzi is the French planter, Mitzi Gaynor the American nurse who falls for him and tries to wash him right out of her hair.

Spartacus
1960 PG 186 ★★★ ACT/ADV

An intelligent and spectacular epic about society's attitude towards violence. A Roman slave, Spartacus (Kirk Douglas), rebels against his masters and almost overcomes the might of the empire. Well, maybe the real uprising wasn't quite like this but Stanley Kubrick directs with flair and the casting – Laurence Olivier and Charles Laughton, Tony Curtis and Peter Ustinov – is splendid. (There are two versions: a shorter one and this slightly longer, spruced-up one, which reintroduces a homo-erotic scene between Olivier and Curtis that was excluded from earlier prints.)

Speed
1994 15 111 ★★★★ ACT/ADV

Gob-smacking action and terrific special effects are the real stars of this adventure, though Keanu Reeves is more than capable as the Los Angeles cop up against explosives expert Dennis Hopper over land, under land and in the air. First Reeves must rescue the occupants of a lift, then he's on a bus primed to explode if its speed drops below fifty and then it gets a little silly on an underground train. But for the most part this is a two-hour chase you won't tire of.

Spellbound
1945 PG 107 ★★★ MYS/THR

Alfred Hitchcock's psychologically based thriller sees Ingrid Bergman as the shrink and Gregory Peck as the occupant of her couch who must be cured of amnesia if he's to clear his name of murder. Well played by the cast, though Hitchcock might have been better advised to remove the out-of-place Salador Dali-designed dream sequence. (B&W)

Splash
1984 PG 105 ★★★★ COM

Another delight for all generations (except the very young). This romantic comedy concerns a mermaid (Daryl Hannah) who lands up in modern-day New York where she's housed and helped by Tom Hanks who thinks she's merely a foreigner. It's not long, of course, before he falls in love with her; she's already in love with him. John Candy is a joy in a supporting role but it's Hannah and Hanks who provide the magic.

Splitting Heirs
1992 15 83 ★★ COM

A half-hearted attempt at comedy co-written by ex-Python Eric Idle. In a weak story of mistaken identities, Idle plays an English lad swapped at birth and then cheated out of his inheritance by Rick Moranis. Killing Moranis is the solution and frantic farce the outcome as Barbara Hershey and Catherine Zeta Jones, John Cleese and Eric Sykes also become involved.

Spymaker: the Secret Life of Ian Fleming
1990 15 95 ★ ACT/ADV

Best thing about this fictional biography of the creator of James Bond is that it stars Jason Connery, Sean's son. Connery junior does a fair enough job with what he's given but the material's weak. Fleming did serve in naval intelligence but the film tries to suggest that he actually was Bond and shared his creation's adventures, which seems, to say the least, doubtful.

Spy Who Loved Me, The
1977 PG 120 ★★★★ ACT/ADV

A great soundtrack accompanies one of the very best Bond movies. Roger Moore's 007 forms an alliance with Russian agent Barbara Bach to stop Curt Jurgens fulfilling his plans for world domination. Hectic brawls ensue against the iron-mouthed Jaws (Richard Kiel). Able direction by Lewis Gilbert; Marvin Hamlisch's song, 'Nobody Does It Better' (performed by Carly Simon) was Oscar-nominated.

Stagecoach
1939 U 91 ★★★★★ WES

Possibly the greatest Western of them all (*Emma's opinion, not mine. I like this a lot but I still vote for 'The Searchers' – BN*). The pedigree is impeccable: John Ford directed, John Wayne starred – as the Ringo Kid – Red Indians looming on the horizon were never more menacing and there's very pleasing romance in the shapely form of Claire Trevor. The story was loosely inspired by de Maupassant's *Boule de Suif* and the film was the first to make Hollywood realise that Westerns did not need to be merely B-pictures. (B&W)

Stakeout
1987 15 112 ★★★ MYS/THR

Two cops (Richard Dreyfuss and Emilio Estevez) are staking out the home of Madeleine Stowe, the girlfriend of escaped killer Aidan Quinn. Trouble is, Dreyfuss takes a fancy to Stowe and jeopardises the whole scheme by his reckless pursuit of her. A highly amusing tale with an exciting climax and all the characters, bar Quinn, thoroughly likeable. A poor sequel, *Another Stakeout*, followed in 1993.

Stalag 17
1953 PG 115 ★★★★ WAR

A brilliant depiction by Billy Wilder of life in a concentration camp during the Second World War. William Holden, at his most charismatic, plays the gloomy American sergeant suspected by his colleagues of being a Nazi spy. Otto Preminger is equally impressive as the nasty Nazi commandant. The combination of humour and high drama gives it widespread appeal.

Stand and Deliver
1987 PG 99 ★★ DRA

There's not much action here, but a lot of thought as a tough Hispanic headmaster shakes up his inner-city school and, against all odds, makes his underprivileged pupils proud of themselves. Lou Diamond Phillips – playing one of the more rebellious students – is the most familiar face but Edward James Olmos, as the teacher, takes the acting honours. All the better for being based on fact.

Stand by Me
1986 15 85 ★★★ DRA

Strong on nostalgia but rather slow on pace is the overall impression of Rob Reiner's rites of passage story about childhood and friendship in 1950s America. Four young friends – River Phoenix and Corey Feldman among them – set off to find a missing boy. Kiefer Sutherland's a big bully of a kid and Richard Dreyfuss is the only adult encountered. It's a warm affecting story by, surprisingly, horror writer Stephen King.

Stanley & Iris
1990 15 100 ★★ DRA

The acting combination should have been a winning one but as it is the heavy story and ponderous script mean that Jane Fonda and Robert De Niro are largely wasted. She plays a poor widow who barely earns enough to feed her children; he's a dyslexic whom she teaches to read. The emphasis on economic hardship detracts from the budding romance. Worthy, yes, but not really worth making.

Stargate
1994 PG 116 ★★★★ SCI/FAN

Star Wars for the 1990s. This is a smashing adventure, as well thought out as it is executed.

James Spader is an archaeologist – not quite of the macho Indiana Jones mould – who, along with a military attachment headed by Kurt Russell, is sent through an ancient Egyptian gate and finds himself in another world whose inhabitants are ruled by a tyrannous alien (Jaye Davidson of *The Crying Game*). The special effects are impressive and the story fresh. Great fun for the family.

Star is Born, A
1937 U 111 ★★★ DRA

William Wellman directed this first version of Hollywood's favourite tear-jerker – the story of the star (Fredric March) whose own career wanes as that of his actress wife (Janet Gaynor) begins to soar. It's very well played and Wellman eschews any temptation to tug too fiercely on the heartstrings. The basic tale has been remade, with variations, twice (see below). Why, though, so much interest in what is essentially old-fashioned melodrama? Could it be that it touches painfully on a deep-rooted masculine fear of being superseded by and subservient to a woman?

Star is Born, A
1954 U 168 ★★★★ DRA

Actually, 'musical drama' is a better description of this George Cukor version in which James Mason plays the star drowning his career in alcohol and Judy Garland is the young singer who, at his urging, successfully strikes out for movie stardom. Of the three films, this is the best, thanks largely to Garland's musical ability and a hugely touching performance by Mason. The film was badly hacked about on first release and was only restored to something like its full length in 1983. This video release is some seven minutes shorter than Cukor's original cut.

Star is Born, A
1976 15 134 ★★ MUS

A big mistake – huge. Here, in a desperate attempt at topicality, the story is taken away from the Hollywood milieu and transplanted to the world of rock music. Now drugs, as well as drink, contribute to the decline and fall of Kris Kristofferson, while the star who is born is played by Barbra Streisand. Neither of the principals is bad but the film simply doesn't

convince. In the two earlier versions you cared deeply about the fate of the protagonists; this time, in the words of Rhett Butler, you don't give a damn.

Starman
1984 PG 110 ★★★ SCI/FAN

There'd be no complaints from the female inhabitants if all Earth-visiting aliens looked like Jeff Bridges. He's a charming extra-terrestrial, stranded in America, who takes on the form of Karen Allen's dead husband and hijacks her into taking him back to his spaceship. The problem is, if he doesn't get there soon, he will die. Lots of car chases and lovely romance, but it's not at all gooey so young boys shouldn't be deterred. John Carpenter directs with aplomb.

Star Trek: The Motion Picture
1979 U 126 ★★ SCI/FAN

Only the most hardened of Trekkie fans could fail to be disappointed with this big-screen version of the fantastic TV series. Boldly going where it had gone many times before the Starship *Enterprise* and all the familiar crew head off into the galaxy to save Earth once more from wicked space invaders. The familiar cast, of course: William Shatner, Leonard Nimoy, DeForest Kelley and all your other favourites. (The full version, running 144 minutes, is also available on video.)

Star Trek II: The Wrath of Khan
1982 15 108 ★ SCI/FAN

Not a good sequel, despite a stronger story line than the first movie. Here, the evil Ricardo Montalban is out for revenge on Captain Kirk. Spock steps in to save him and it looks like curtains for the pointy-eared Vulcan. All the trusty old crew members are on board the *Enterprise* once more. More explicit violence accounts for the restrictive certificate.

Star Trek III: The Search for Spock
1984 PG 101 ★ SCI/FAN

This rather gives away the ending to the previous *Star Trek* but then nobody really watches for the suspense factor. Spock (or anyway Leonard Nimoy) is actually behind the camera as director and doing a pretty good job of it. The trouble is, if we're really being critical, the crew are now all so old they're beginning to look embalmed.

Star Trek IV: The Voyage Home
1986 PG 117 ★★★ SCI/FAN

Now things are hotting up. This is a really good, witty adventure, just as the TV series used to be. The *Enterprise* has found social awareness and is off to save the whale, threatened with extinction by the uncaring inhabitants of twentieth-century Earth. Again Nimoy directs and gives a rollicking good performance as Spock to boot.

Star Trek V: the Final Frontier
1989 PG 102 ★★ SCI/FAN

It's now Captain Kirk (a.k.a. William Shatner) who steps behind the camera but unfortunately he doesn't do as good a job as his Vulcan friend. This is a rather incongruous mission in which Kirk meets God, or anyway someone purporting to be God. Far too much of the metaphysical and not enough action.

Star Trek VI: The Undiscovered Country
1991 PG 109 ★★★★ SCI/FAN

The best of the lot, directed by Nicholas Meyer, who does a far better job here than he did in *Star Trek II*. He sets and maintains a cracking pace as the *Enterprise*, on an intergalactic peace mission, is assigned to conduct the Klingons to Earth for treaty talks, but as any Trekkie knows, you can't trust a Klingon… By now the tried and trusty crew are so aged that the *Enterprise* might as well be an intergalactic zimmerframe.

Star Trek: Generations
1995 PG 115 ★★★ SCI/FAN

A pretty successful attempt to introduce the new, small-screen crew of the starship *Enterprise* to a cinema audience. Kirk, Chekov and Scotty are the only original cast members to show up and they're not around for long. Once they've gone – though Kirk does show up again – the story settles down as an absorbing adventure in which the new *Enterprise* (under captain Patrick Stewart) must save the galaxy from mad scientist Malcolm McDowell. Fans of TV's *Star Trek: the Next Generation* will probably like it best.

Star Wars
1977 U 121 ★★★★ SCI/FAN

The ultimate in sci-fi movies from George Lucas, whose special effects are so realistic that cinema audiences the world over were ducking in their seats as the spaceship first appeared. Mark Hamill's at the helm as the intergalactic pilot encountering such exotic heroes as Harrison Ford, Carrie Fisher, Alec Guinness and the cutest couple of robots, R2-D2 and C-3PO. Their adversaries, of course, are the evil Empire and the dreaded Darth Vader. (This is the widescreen version; the pan and scan one is shorter.)

Stay Tuned
1992 PG 85 ★★ SCI/FAN

Couch potatoes everywhere take note – satellite TV can damage your health. Or at least it nearly does for John Ritter and Pam Dawber, who get sucked into their TV set and find themselves appearing in the programmes. If they can survive twenty-four hours on Hellvision they'll be allowed home; if they can't, they'll be dead. Some good gags but a largely wasted opportunity to send up the medium.

Steel Magnolias
1989 PG 113 ★★★ DRA

Send the men out, this is undoubtedly a women's movie. It revolves around five friends in a close-knit community and the effect on their relationship when the daughter of one of them falls ill. Sally Field plays the mother, Julia Roberts the ailing daughter. Olympia Dukakis, Daryl Hannah, Dolly Parton and Shirley MacLaine who, incidentally, is hilarious as the most eccentric of the bunch, make up the assorted friends. You'll laugh and cry as the girls act their socks off.

Stella
1990 15 104 ★★ DRA

Hankies at the ready – if you're easily moved, that is. Bette Midler (and thank heavens for her feistiness or this movie would have been too outrageously sentimental to bear) is the independent woman, sacrificing everything in her battle to raise her young daughter alone. This is a remake, and an inadequate one at that, of *Stella Dallas* (see below).

Stella Dallas
1937 U 101 ★★★ DRA

Here it's Barbara Stanwyck who plays the struggling mother who marries out of her class and only succeeds in embarrassing her socially upward daughter. This is quite as much a tearjerker as *Stella* but Hollywood made this sort of thing with greater conviction in the 1930s. John Boles co-stars as the well-connected husband finally put off by Stanwyck's vulgarity. (In both films the well-to-do middle classes are the bad guys.) (B&W)

St Elmo's Fire
1985 15 104 ★★★ DRA

Probably more appealing to older teenagers since this is a Brat Pack vehicle, featuring the likes of Rob Lowe, Emilio Estevez, Judd Nelson and Demi Moore. A newly graduated bunch of friends find life after college is not as easy as they'd thought. Drugs, rejection, unwanted pregnancy and virginity are just some of the problems encountered.

Stepping Out
1991 PG 104 ★★ DRA

An unassuming little story about a tap-dance class (led by teacher Liza Minnelli) in an upstate New York town and the various problems of each member. Julie Walters turns in a lovely comic performance as the snobbish English woman whom no-one much likes. Shelley Winters is the piano player with attitude and Bill Irwin is the only man in the group. Everything is worked out in a rousing, upbeat musical happy ending.

Steptoe and Son
1972 PG 93 ★★★ COM

A little too raunchy for the very young since young Steptoe, Harry H Corbett, marries a stripper – much to his father's disgust. What worked so well on TV doesn't quite transfer to the bigger, longer cinema format, but Corbett and Wilfrid Brambell nicely re-create their sad/funny claustrophobic father-son relationship.

Sting, The
1973 PG 123 ★★★★ MYS/THR

Best of the 'con' movies, not only because it pairs Paul Newman with Robert Redford again but also because it's so expertly and deviously plotted. You can't afford to nod off in this one because the story is very complex. Robert Shaw, who plays a most unpleasant racketeer, is the object of the Newman/Redford sting. Everyone should have a thoroughly good time watching it. But, be warned, the sequel (below) is not worth bothering with.

Sting II, The
1983 PG 97 ★ MYS/THR

The cast includes Jackie Gleason, Karl Malden and Oliver Reed – but none of the originals – and the story is about Reed (in the Shaw role) trying to get revenge on Gleason and Mac Davis, who take the parts played much better by Newman and Redford.

Stop! or My Mom Will Shoot
1992 PG 83 ★★ COM

Sylvester Stallone, essaying comedy, is not as awful as you might expect in this silly but not altogether unappealing story of a manly cop whose image is rather ruined by having a domineering, bossy mother – all four foot ten inches of her (Estelle Getty). When Mom comes to stay, she not only tries to sort out sonny boy's love life but solve his cases, too. Getty overacts dreadfully.

Stowaway
1936 U 86 ★★★ FAM

No child actor has ever matched the young Shirley Temple in dimpled cheeks or heart-tugging cuteness. Here she's an orphan – yet again – who gets lost in Asia and smuggles herself aboard an American ship. Alice Faye co-stars. Young kids may despise the little girl for her strong moral tone, parents might well wish some of it would rub off on their own offspring. (B&W)

Straight Talk
1992 PG 87 ★★★ COM

Brilliant casting drags this implausible tale of a small-town girl who makes it big in the city into a thoroughly entertaining and romantic comedy. Dolly Parton's the country girl who accidentally lands a radio show and becomes an overnight success as an agony aunt. James Woods is the journalist assigned to check her background who falls in love with her. In a similar charming vein to the comedies of the thirties and forties.

Strangers on a Train
1951 PG 97 ★★★ MYS/THR

Hitchcock more than does justice to Patricia Highsmith's psychological thriller about two men who meet on a train and plan to swap murders, so that each can establish an airtight alibi. Trouble is, one of them's not so keen… Farley Granger and Robert Walker play the plotters. There's a marvellous, memorable denouement in a fairground. (A similar plot was used in the Danny DeVito comedy *Throw Momma from the Train*.) (B&W)

Strapless
1989 15 95 ★★★ DRA

A salutary tale about marrying in haste and repenting at leisure. David Hare directed his own screenplay in which an American doctor in London (Blair Brown) marries Bruno Ganz, whom she meets on holiday, and then begins to realise how very little she knows about him. As a study of independent womanhood this doesn't quite hit the mark, although Bridget Fonda is good as Brown's freewheeling, free-spirited sister.

Streetcar Named Desire, A
1951 15 117 ★★★★ DRA

Elia Kazan's admittedly stagey but nevertheless powerful and absorbing screen version of Tennessee Williams's play. This account of the passionate relationship between a widowed Southern belle (Vivien Leigh) and her brutish young brother-in-law (Marlon Brando) is domestic drama at fever pitch. Remarkably, Leigh and the main supporting players (Karl Malden and Kim Hunter) won Oscars and Brando didn't – yet it's the surly, brooding, exciting Brando whom everyone who has seen the film remembers most vividly. (B&W)

Streets of Fire
1984 15 94 ★★★ ACT/ADV

This film looks better than it sounds – that's because it's a rock 'n' roll thriller tale about a singer (Diane Lane) who is kidnapped by bikers. Michael Paré is the cool, macho posturer

called in to save her. A pretty run-of-the-mill plot but the music and garishly visual style are unusual elements. Plenty of action, violence and four-letter words, as you might expect from director Walter Hill.

Strictly Ballroom
1992 PG 94 ★★★★ COM

Fans of TV's *Come Dancing* will think it's Christmas with this endearing tale about a plain Australian girl (Tara Morice) who longs to be a ballroom dancer. When hot-hoofer Paul Mercurio is abandoned by his beautiful, accomplished partner for not dancing the official steps, ugly duckling Morice puts herself forward to accompany him in the championships. Not quite the fairy tale it could have been. The drama's a little disturbing but there's much that's romantic and funny.

Suburban Commando
1991 PG 86 ★★★ COM

Few wrestlers have the charm of Hulk Hogan, which is just as well or we'd have a lot of them turning to acting. As it is, one OK muscleman-turned-thespian (not counting Arnie) is bearable. Hulk plays a fighter from another planet who takes a vacation on Earth and gets embroiled in the misadventures of a suburban family which befriends him. Some violence, but generally this is much funnier than you'd expect.

Subway
1985 15 98 ★★★ FOR

Too much style and not enough characterization mars this French thriller by Luc Besson. Its hero, Christophe Lambert, on the run for stealing important documents from Isabelle Adjani's husband, hides out in the Paris Metro system where a weird community resides. Doesn't make a lot of sense but it's bold and dashing and Isabelle Adjani is not the only thing that's stunning to look at. (Subtitled)

Sugarland Express, The
1974 PG 105 ★★★ COM

An underrated comedy, directed by a very young Steven Spielberg, in which Goldie Hawn, William Atherton and a baby are chased across Texas by the police. Hawn had helped

Atherton escape from jail in order to rescue their baby from care. The story is based on fact. The humour, chases and stunts are great and Hawn, still easily young enough to play cute, gives one of her most appealing performances.

Summer Holiday
1963 U 104 ★★★ MUS

All together now, 'We're all going on a...' Cliff Richard, his chic sixties pals and Una Stubbs board a double-decker for a swinging European vacation. A pleasant tale with likeable youths and toe-tapping songs ('Bachelor Boy' among them) which all the family should enjoy. Granny will be particularly enchanted because 'when that nice Cliff – beg his pardon, *Sir* Cliff – Richard sings songs you can understand what he's saying.' The young will probably regard Cliff as decidedly uncool these days.

Summer School
1987 15 93 ★★ COM

A pleasant, teenage flick neatly directed by Carl Reiner and attractively acted by Kirstie Alley and Mark Harman. He's a teacher forced to instruct a bunch of delinquents during school vacation. You won't be clutching your sides with mirth, but it will certainly raise a smile, if not a titter.

Sunset
1988 15 103 ★★ COM

A film-within-a-film (all of it directed by Blake Edwards) which never quite works but deserves points for trying. Bruce Willis plays the Western star Tom Mix, who is obliged by manipulative studio boss Malcolm McDowell to make a film about Wyatt Earp with the real Earp (James Garner) on hand to advise. Things get a little complex thereafter as the story develops into a thriller. Garner is easily the best of the cast.

Sunshine Boys, The
1975 PG 106 ★★★★ COM

Walter Matthau and George Burns are a winning combination as a pair of antagonistic comics who are reluctantly reunited in old age to appear on a TV show and fall to bickering just as they had in their prime. A blisteringly funny script by Neil Simon and Herbert Ross's canny direction help make this a cracker from

start to finish. Both stars are superb and Burns, who had not appeared in a film for thirty-six years, won the Oscar for Best Supporting Actor.

Supergrass, The
1985 15 93 ★★★ COM

The Comic Strip hit the big screen to great effect with this irreverently amusing tale about a geek (Ade Edmondson) who becomes embroiled with a gang of smugglers. All the *Comic Strip* usuals – except Rik Mayall – appear. Co-starring roles are played by Peter Richardson (who also directed and co-wrote), Dawn French and Jennifer Saunders. Alexei Sayle has a few hilarious scenes as a thick policeman.

Superman
1978 PG 137 ★★★ SCI/FAN

Still the best of the comic-book heroes, though visually the *Batman* films have moved into a higher class. Here Christopher Reeve dons the Lycra to set off and save the world from dastardly villain Gene Hackman. Margot Kidder makes her first appearance as Lois Lane, the love of Clark Kent's life. This was the film for which Marlon Brando was paid an astronomical sum for a few seconds on screen. What he does, he does very well, he just doesn't do much of it. Good stuff, though better was yet to come.

Superman II
1980 PG 127 ★★★★ SCI/FAN

An improvement on the first, this sequel (directed by Richard Lester) sees Superman in romantic mood, making love to Lois (Margot Kidder again) while Gene Hackman, Ned Beatty and a number of other cronies plan to destroy him and – yes, you guessed it – rule the world. Terence Stamp is very good as the leader of three villainous Kryptonians who possess the same powers as Superman.

Superman III
1983 PG 120 ★★ SCI/FAN

Margot Kidder bows out (except for a brief appearance as Lois Lane) and the new girl in Superman's life is Annette O'Toole. Not that Superman really notices, since he's being wooed by fiendish villainess Pamela Stephenson, who is working for smooth and dastardly Robert Vaughn. Comedy is the order of the day here, with Richard Pryor sadly wasted as a nervous and exploited computer wizard. Not nearly as good as its predecessors.

Superman IV: the Quest for Peace
1987 PG 89 ★ SCI/FAN

Best to leave it here, though better to have left it there with *Superman III*. Christopher Reeve wrote the story for this one, not that it's terribly good. It's a worthy plot about the nuclear threat and, despite the return of Gene Hackman and also Margot Kidder, there's not a lot of fun to be had. *Superman* movies are simply not the place for earnest messages about peace and the environment. But, especially in view of his dreadful riding accident, it should be said that Reeve – here wearing his knickers outside his tights for the last time – was excellent in the role in all four films, his performance always going a long way towards transcending deficiencies in the scripts and storylines.

Super Mario Bros
1993 PG 100 ★★ ACT/ADV

The film version of the computer game – it seemed a bizarre idea at the time but since then we've had *Street Fighter* as well, so perhaps computer games are to be the new source of Hollywood inspiration, if 'inspiration' is the right word. Surprisingly, this is quite a lot of fun – bright, colourful and imaginative – so don't dismiss it out of hand. Bob Hoskins and John Leguizamo are well cast as the Brooklyn plumbers who dive into a parallel world of dinosaurs and mutants to save Samantha Mathis.

Support Your Local Gunfighter
1971 U 88 ★★★ WES

This is a follow-up to the film below. It's not quite as good but it's still appealing. James Garner returns, this time very much in his *Maverick* persona, as a con man mistaken for the hired gun the town are awaiting. Jack Elam's back in support.

Support Your Local Sheriff
1969 PG 89 ★★★★ WES

A charming Western spoof in which a stranger riding through a lawless town is reluctantly bamboozled into becoming sheriff. (A lovely performance in this role by James Garner). Familiar faces of the old Western movies such as Walter Brennan and Jack Elam appear. Naturally Garner, though protesting that he's basically on his way to Australia, has to stay and clean up the town.

Sure Thing, The
1985 15 90 ★★★ COM

Young lovers will identify strongly with this sweet tale of young love (and lust) in which John Cusack and Daphne Zuniga share a ride across the USA on their way to meet the respective, presumed loves of their lives. But the course of true love.... and all that. After some initial sparring, the couple find themselves increasingly drawn to each other and Cusack becomes less enamoured of 'the sure thing' he's travelling to meet. The comedy's good thanks to the deft handling of director Rob Reiner.

Suspect
1987 15 116 ★★★★ MYS/THR

Brilliant, much-underrated thriller about an attorney handling what would seem to be a hopeless defence case, until a juror provides help, albeit illegally. Cher is outstanding as the lawyer, Dennis Quaid at his most attractive as the jury member-turned-investigator and Liam Neeson is thoroughly convincing as the deaf mute accused of murder. A fair ration of thrills and twists and turns will keep you in suspense right to the end.

Suspicion
1941 PG 95 ★★★ MYS/THR

That man Hitchcock again, this time with Joan Fontaine (in Oscar-winning form) as the nervous new bride of dashing Cary Grant. She suspects he may be trying to kill her and, it must be said, he is really far too attentive for a man with no ulterior motive. Or is he? Good but not one of Hitch's best. (B&W)

Swallows and Amazons
1974 U 89 ★★★★ FAM

All family members, from the oldest to the youngest, with no-one excluded in the middle, should watch this captivating romp about six children, a couple of boats and an exciting game of pirates. Arthur Ransome's magical tale lends itself beautifully to the screen and the performances by all concerned – especially Ronald Fraser as a somewhat disreputable uncle – are delightful.

Sweetie
1989 15 95 ★★★ DRA

Jane Campion, the writer/director who brought you *The Piano,* made her feature debut with this strange, but curiously fascinating film about two very weird sisters Down Under. One is afraid of trees and the other is just plain mad. It's a bizarre tragi-comedy, the failing of which is that it loses sight of the humour and opts for the tragedy. Not to everyone's taste but imaginative, at least.

Swing Kids
1993 15 109 ★★ DRA

Although his name doesn't appear on the credits, the best thing about this rather remote film is Kenneth Branagh as a Nazi. The story concerns a bunch of youngsters who, in Germany in 1939, and in face of the oppression of Hitler and the encroaching war, embrace the freedom of the new jazz culture. Robert Sean Leonard and Christian Bale do a nice job as the swinging lads but it's a film which starts promisingly then cops out and ends absurdly.

Swiss Family Robinson
1960 U 126 ★★ FAM

John Mills and Dorothy McGuire head the family who, shipwrecked on a desert island, have to fend for themselves in an ideal treehouse home and cope with pirates. It's a wholesome affair, jollily adapted by Disney. An earlier version starring Freddie Bartholomew was narrated by Orson Welles.

Switch
1991 15 99 ★★ COM

A mildly diverting comedy in which a male chauvinist pig is murdered and returned to Earth to learn his lesson – in a woman's body. Mind you, he's not done badly since the body in question is Ellen Barkin's. Pity the poor fellow who gets Nora Batty's. Watch out for some ripe language.

Switching Channels
1988 PG 100 ★★ COM

This is a prime example of how *not* to remake an old movie. In what is one of the clearest cases of 'If it ain't broke don't fix it', Burt Reynolds, Kathleen Turner and Christopher Reeve star in a contemporary version of *The Front Page,* only now it's set in a TV station. Here the star reporter (Turner) is engaged to wealthy Reeve, much to the jealousy of her boss and ex-husband Reynolds. Reeve is quite good as a wimp but otherwise the comedy falls flat and you'd be better advised to watch almost any of the other versions.

Sword in the Stone, The
1963 U 76 ★ FAM

We implore you to make your child read the book instead of being introduced to the delights of this story via Walt Disney's rather crass cartoon. The magical story – and it's a magic best captured in words rather than drawings – tells how a young boy became King Arthur after an enchanted childhood in which he was taught by Merlin. The book is by T H White and is part of a longer work entitled *The Once and Future King.*

Table for Five
1983 PG 116 ★★ DRA

Nicely written but terribly sentimental tale about a father (Jon Voight) taking his three children on a cruise in an attempt to spend some 'quality time' with them. Bonding takes a while since he prefers the women to the kids and he has a lousy sense of responsibility. Good acting from all, particularly Voight. Certainly more for the parents than the offspring.

Taking of Pelham One Two Three, The
1974 15 104 ★★★ ACT/ADV

It's not the best of days for transport cop Walter Matthau when a New York subway train is hijacked. Robert Shaw – whoever made a better bad guy? – and Hector Elizondo head the kidnappers, holding the passengers ransom for one million dollars. It's a tense tale with Matthau only given an hour to save the day and with Shaw at his most nasty.

Tale of Two Cities, A
1935 U 121 ★★★★ ACT/ADV

Loyal and spectacular adaptation of Charles Dickens's classic story based around the French revolution. Heads roll off the guillotine like peas from a factory line and the bloodthirsty rabble around it cheer lustily. If that's not enough to whet your appetite, then what about the prospect of Ronald Colman in the lead role and Elizabeth Allan as the heroine? Have the family and the tissues handy and prepare to weep buckets. (B&W)

Tales of Beatrix Potter
1971 U 86 ★★★ FAM

Not the TV series of videos, but the ballet version incorporating some of Potter's best-loved animals. Jeremy Fisher springs around in tights, pirouetting with the best of them, Jemima Puddleduck just manages to escape the fox and Mrs Tiggywinkle's still washing away. The costumes are amazing and the choreography, by none other than Frederick Ashton, is delightful. A joy for all ages.

Talk of the Town, The
1942 U 113 ★★★★★ COM

One of the all-time great romantic comedies, up there beside *It's a Wonderful Life* and *Bringing Up Baby*. The plot's adequate, but it's the casting that works so perfectly. Cary Grant plays the hero, a wrongly convicted jailbird who escapes and hides out in the home of Jean Arthur. The house is empty but only for a night as it's about to be rented by Ronald Colman, a law professor due to be elected to the Supreme Court. The comedy of the situation works perfectly, as do the developing friendships amongst the trio. Do not miss it. (B&W)

Tall Guy, The
1989 15 88 ★★ COM

American actor Jeff Goldblum has been the fall-guy to Rowan Atkinson's egotistical comic for several years in their West End play. Until, that is, he comes under the tender loving care of a nurse, Emma Thompson, with whom he's immediately in love. But, as his relationship with her improves, his partnership with Atkinson takes a nose dive. It's a pleasing romantic comedy which almost hits the mark, but never quite gets there.

Taming of the Shrew, The
1967 U 116 ★★★★ COM

Franco Zeffirelli's version of Shakespeare's comedy is an energetic, colourful one which stars Elizabeth Taylor and Richard Burton. That aside, its appeal is mainly for Bard fans since it's very stagey. Michael Hordern, Cyril Cusack and Victor Spinetti complete an enthusiastic cast.

Taps
1981 PG 121 ★★ DRA

This film has found its way into the movie annals, not for its artistic or entertainment value, but for featuring a very young, inexperienced actor called Tom Cruise. He's one of a number of military cadets who, under the leadership of upright young Timothy Hutton, take over their army school in an attempt to stop it closing. Sean Penn and George C Scott are also in amongst the cast.

Target
1985 15 112 ★★ MYS/THR

Coupling Gene Hackman and Matt Dillon (the latter as the former's son) gives this dour spy thriller a much-needed boost. They're a warring couple who find they must join forces when wife/mother Gayle Hunnicutt – having taken a well-earned break in Paris – is kidnapped. From start to finish it's totally predictable and the pacing tends towards the erratic, but Dillon and Hackman generate a chemistry which makes it watchable.

Teenage Mutant Ninja Turtles
1990 PG 87 ★★ ACT/ADV

Four pizza-loving dudes, who just happen to be giant turtles turned into heroes in green shells after a toxic-waste accident, hang out in sewers, emerging every now and again onto the streets of New York to right wrongs. Here, Leonardo, Donatello, Raphael and Michelangelo high-kick their way round Manhattan to help TV anchor woman April (Judith Hoag). The comedy may make it more universally appealing, but it tends to be one for the young.

Teenage Mutant Ninja Turtles II: The Secret of the Ooze
1991 PG 84 ★★ ACT/ADV

Toxic trouble for the turtles this time as David Warner, inventor of the ooze that made the boys green and their rat friend enormous, tries to destroy the stuff. April's back, in the guise of Paige Turco this time, and the quartet are as cute as ever. There's little difference between the original and sequel.

Teenage Mutant Ninja Turtles III: The Turtles are Back... in Time
1993 PG 92 ★★ ACT/ADV

The four fighting fellows are forced back in time to ancient Japan where their dear friend April (Paige Turco again) has been kidnapped. Samurai politics and rebellions pose more danger than the streets of Harlem ever did. Not quite as good as the first two.

Teen Agent
1991 PG 84 ★★ MYS/THR

During a school outing to Paris, cool pupil Richard Grieco – who really must do something about his French vocabulary if he hopes to pass his exams – is mistaken for a CIA agent. British intelligence (or non-intelligence as would seem more appropriate here) then brief him in the 007 stuff. Despite the silly plot, the presence of Linda Hunt, Roger Rees,

Geraldine James and even Roger Daltrey supplies a certain charm. Not bad for the nippers.

Teen Wolf
1985 PG 88 ★★★ COM

Strange choice of movie for Michael J Fox, though he does a very good job as the high-school shortie who finds his basketball abilities improve considerably when he turns into a werewolf. Don't ask how – it's a long story. The chest, facial – not to mention nasal – hair seem to go down a treat with the chicks too. Innocuous stuff but made palatable by the presence of Fox. He bowed out of the sequel, which isn't worth bothering with.

Ten Commandments, The
1956 U 219 ★★★★ ACT/ADV

No-one has ever parted the Red Sea with the panache of Charlton Heston as Moses. This enormous biblical epic by Cecil B DeMille is worth watching for that alone, but if you want more you'll certainly get it here in what is an overblown, lavish early soap opera. With Yul Brynner (cutting quite a dash as Pharaoh), Edward G Robinson, Anne Baxter, Cedric Hardwicke and Vincent Price, for a cold, rainy weekend's viewing what more could you want?

Tender Mercies
1983 PG 88 ★★★ DRA

Smashing story about an alcoholic Country and Western singer, Robert Duvall, who is down on his luck but hoping to change his fortunes after meeting a young widow (Tess Harper). Bruce Beresford keeps tight control on the subject matter, preventing any sentimentality, while the performances, particularly that of Duvall, who won an Oscar, are quite excellent.

10 Rillington Place
1970 15 106 ★★★ MYS/THR

This smashing British drama is based on the John Christie/Timothy Evans murder case of the 1940s which saw one of the greatest examples of British misjustice. Richard Attenborough as the wife-murdering Christie and John Hurt as his gullible lodger are terrific.

Tequila Sunrise
1988 15 110 ★★ MYS/THR

An attractive cast enlivens an otherwise routine thriller about two childhood chums (Mel Gibson and Kurt Russell) who find they've taken very different paths to reach adulthood but still share the same taste in women (Michelle Pfeiffer).

Terminator 2: Judgment Day
1991 15 130 ★★★★ ACT/ADV

Although the first *Terminator* was an 18 certificate, don't worry. This is just as good, while the special effects are even better. Arnold Schwarzenegger returns – as promised in the original – but this time as a friendly metal monster, ready to do battle with a state-of-the-art cyborg (Robert Patrick) in order to save Linda Hamilton and her boy (Edward Furlong) for the sake of the future. Quite dazzling effects make this scintillating viewing. The film was cut by eighteen seconds to get a 15 certificate on video.

Terms of Endearment
1983 15 126 ★★★ DRA

This is essentially two movies. One – a comedy – is very funny, with Jack Nicholson and Shirley MacLaine a winning combination as sparring neighbours. The other is a different, soppy kettle of fish with Debra Winger – as MacLaine's daughter – dying from cancer. The soapy and the humorous mix as well as oil and water. Perfect for video and the fast-forward button.

Tess
1979 PG 164 ★★ DRA

Roman Polanski's beautiful but unfulfilling adaptation of Thomas Hardy's *Tess of the D'Urbervilles*. The story is about a beautiful young peasant girl sometime last century whose fate and fortune are sealed when she is misused by a wealthy squire's son. A pretty cast, including Nastassja Kinski, Leigh Lawson and Peter Firth, add to the look of the movie, but the power of the emotional drama is lost. Appealing mainly to those who like their romance melodramatic.

Texasville
1990 15 120 ★★ DRA

Peter Bogdanovich's long-awaited sequel to *The Last Picture Show* proved not worth the wait. Despite reuniting the original cast (Jeff Bridges, Cybill Shepherd and Timothy Bottoms), the script lacks bite and the characters' lives in the 1980s aren't nearly as interesting as they were in the 1970s.

That Hamilton Woman
1941 PG 125 ★★★ DRA

Directed by Alexander Korda and starring Laurence Olivier and Vivien Leigh, this film couldn't fail. Leigh is superb as Lady Hamilton who embarks on a passionate – and most scandalous for its day – affair with Admiral Nelson (he of the column in Trafalgar Square fame). A great production, ideal family viewing accompanied by large bags of sweets. (B&W)

That'll Be the Day
1973 15 87 ★★★ MUS

Historical document of the early days of rock 'n' roll with young men busy contemplating their boring young navels and seeing music as the only way to a better life. David Essex fair shines as the star of the piece though Ringo Starr, Keith Moon and Billy Fury aren't half bad. The 1950s setting dates it badly, as does the 'angry young man' subject matter, but it's well made and thoroughly enjoyable nostalgia for all that.

That's Entertainment!
1974 U 122 ★★★★ MUS

For fans of the big production musicals, this is a must. All-singing, all-dancing stars of MGM's best help to celebrate the studio's fiftieth birthday with this medley of great numbers. The section on Judy Garland narrated by her daughter, Liza Minnelli, is particularly special. Fred Astaire, Bing Crosby, Gene Kelly and Donald O'Connor join the festivities.

That's Entertainment, Part II
1976 U 121 ★★★ MUS

Gene Kelly proves he's more than just a hot-hoofer with clever direction of this MGM back-slapping sequel. Hundreds of clips – not all of them musical – are linked by the likes of

Kelly and Fred Astaire. Music and memories in abundance.

That Sinking Feeling
1979 PG 86 ★★★ COM

Prior to making *Gregory's Girl* and *Local Hero*, Bill Forsyth cut his teeth on this, his own screenplay about a mixed bunch of young unemployed Glaswegians who steal a number of steel sinks in the hope of making some money. None of them, however, is really suited to a life of crime. Funny in parts, though its setting – the danker regions of Glasgow – tends to emphasize the poignancy of it all. John Gordon Sinclair is among the young cast.

Thelma and Louise
1991 15 124 ★★★★★ ACT/ADV

Don't miss this. And certainly don't dismiss it as a 'women's movie'. This is the road-movie genre at its best. Good story, witty script, fine acting, brilliant locations and altogether great fun. Ridley Scott directs Geena Davis and Susan Sarandon as a couple of bored, working-class friends who take off for a weekend away only to murder a man and be forced to go on the run. There's more charm than there is tarmac – and there's plenty of that.

They Died with Their Boots On
1941 U 135 ★★★ WES

Errol Flynn as Colonel George Armstrong Custer lends the story of events leading up to the battle of the Little Bighorn great panache – a quality enhanced by Olivia de Havilland as his justifiably anxious little wife. Note: this is Custer as all-American hero, before the revisionists reconstructed his image. (B&W)

They Shoot Horses, Don't They?
1969 15 119 ★★★★ DRA

Sydney Pollack's effective depiction of how fitting the term 'Depression' was during the 1930s in America. The story of competitors vying for money in a marathon dance contest set in a rundown hall is an allegory of society in general and an ironic commentary on the American way of life, in which, as the master of ceremonies Gig Young points out, there can only be one winner. Young, who won the Oscar, was quite brilliant in his seedy,

untrustworthy role, though he was pretty well matched by Jane Fonda as a tough, cynical competitor.

Thief of Bagdad, The
1940 U 102 ★★★★★ FAM

Despite an earlier version in 1924 with Douglas Fairbanks and a later, 1978 Roddy McDowall version, this remains the most lavish adaptation of the *Arabian Nights* fantasy. Sabu plays the thief but Conrad Veidt walks off with the show as the Vizier, though it's a close-run thing between him and the genie. Every member of the family will delight in this.

Things Change
1988 PG 96 ★★★ COM

Gently amusing caper about an innocent shoe-cleaner (Don Ameche), who looks just like the local Mafia boss. Said Godfather is wanted on a murder charge but if the shoe-shine man (watched over by Joe Mantegna) will pretend to be him, then the Mob will grant him his heart's desire. Only problem is that the minder feels sorry for the lackey and allows him a couple of days final fling before going to the law. Very charming and sweet.

Third Man, The
1949 PG 100 ★★★★★ MYS/THR

A lesson in movie-making by director Carol Reed, who re-creates an electric atmosphere in postwar Vienna. Joseph Cotten stars as a naive American newly arrived in the city in search of an old friend, Orson Welles. Only thing is his friend is believed dead and the police are most interested in him. Trevor Howard plays the investigating army major, while Cotten and, of course, Welles are superb. *Film noir* at its best. (B&W)

39 Steps, The
1935 U 91 ★★★★★ MYS/THR

John Buchan could certainly write a blistering adventure tale and Alfred Hitchcock, as he proves here, could certainly direct one, even if he did take several liberties with the original plot. Robert Donat's charming in the lead as the debonair Richard Hannay who's wrongly suspected of murder and is forced to go on the run. Madeleine Carroll is his reluctant accomplice. Not only is it a great story and script, the humour and romance between the stars make it a winner all ways round. One for every member of the clan, old or young. (B&W)

Thirty Nine Steps, The
1978 PG 98 ★★ MYS/THR

Not nearly as good as the Hitchcock film, though the plot still owes more to Hitch than to Buchan. This rather dated version stars Robert Powell and, despite a nail-biting, palm-sweating climax, lacks the excitement and suspense of the earlier picture.

This Boy's Life
1993 15 110 ★★★ DRA

Brit Michael Caton-Jones directs this project, with ineffectual results. The story is the main reason for this film's lack of appeal, as it's a rather dour, rites of passage tale about a young man, nicely played by Leonardo DiCaprio, who has parental problems. It's enhanced slightly by the presence of Robert De Niro as his stepfather and Ellen Barkin as his mummy. Contains violence.

This Is My Life
1992 15 90 ★★ COM

Observant, touching tale about a woman who has always lived for others and now decides to grab life by the horns and do her own thing. Julie Kavner stars as the mother who finds success as a stand-up comedian but risks her relationship with her two young daughters (Samantha Mathis and Gaby Hoffmann) to do so. Nora Ephron directs with an experienced touch though she tends to be a little heavy-handed with the sentimentality and wastes some of the Jewish jokes.

This Is Spinal Tap
1984 15 79 ★★★★ COM

Director Rob Reiner's spoof of rock-band documentaries still remains the best, despite spawning numerous imitations, none of which touch this for humour and satire. The fictional band are British, and the camera follows their disastrous tour of America. Reiner also narrates. If you've got any head-bangers in the family, they may identify with this.

Thomas Crown Affair, The
1968 PG 98 ★★★★ MYS/THR

Norman Jewison's slick direction effortlessly guides Steve McQueen through the tricky central role as a wealthy industrialist who plans a bank robbery for something to do. Faye Dunaway's charming as the insurance detective sent to investigate him. It won an Oscar for the song, 'The Windmills of Your Mind'.

Thoroughly Modern Millie
1967 PG 130 ★★★ COM

Don't be deterred by the fact that this comedy stars Julie Andrews. She shows a hitherto hidden talent for comedy and is perfect as an innocent flapper from the country enjoying life in the big city – until, that is, she discovers a market for white slavery is being conducted from her boarding house. Mary Tyler Moore plays her best mate; Beatrice Lillie their landlady. Delightful stuff with some catchy tunes.

¡Three Amigos!
1986 PG 99 ★★ COM

Silly comedy intended as a starring vehicle for the lead trio – Steve Martin, Chevy Chase and Martin Short – but someone forgot to write any good jokes for them. Three washed-up entertainers take up a *Magnificent Seven*-type offer to help clean up a one-horse town south of the American border. Farce is the order of the day and if you like juvenile slapstick, you'll enjoy this. More sophisticated palates should look elsewhere for laughs.

Three Faces of Eve, The
1957 PG 87 ★★★ DRA

This haunting tale of a woman with three diverse, distinct personalities is all the more disturbing for being based on a true story. Deft performances from Joanne Woodward as, in turn, a sluggish housewife, a harpy and a smart, intelligent female. A little sanitized considering the subject matter is mental illness but most moving nonetheless. (B&W)

3 Men and a Baby
1987 PG 98 ★★★ COM

Lovely idea, well executed by three attractive leads and deftly directed by none other than Mr

Spock - Leonard Nimoy. When three lusty bachelors – architect Tom Selleck, actor Ted Danson and artist Steve Guttenberg – find a baby girl left on their doorstep, the possibility that any one of them could be her father overwhelms the men with varying emotions of paternal love, abhorrence and fear of dirty nappies. The boys are charming struggling to coochy-coo the little bundle and continue with their lives. Delightful.

3 Men and a Little Lady
1990 PG 99 ★ COM

A case of not knowing when to stop. Much of the humour in *3 Men and a Baby* was down to the situation. Once Mary, the baby, has grown up a bit and her mother's back to take care of her, most of the comedy's already been lost. The rest went with a bad script and a contrived tale. Selleck discovers he loves Mary's mum, Nancy Travis, and chases her to England where she's about to marry Christopher Cazenove. Life's too short to bother with this for any but the most devoted fans of the trio.

Three Musketeers, The
1973 U 102 ★★★★ ACT/ADV

Prior to this version there had already been four earlier films of Alexandre Dumas's swashbuckling adventure. But not all are on video nor worth hunting through the archives for. So, by the time this was made, the story had been pulled about, pushed around and moulded nicely into shape for the silver screen. Michael York joins the French queen's most loyal guards – Oliver Reed, Richard Chamberlain and Frank Finlay – with Raquel Welch and Faye Dunaway providing the heaving bosoms. Romping fun.

Three Musketeers, The
1993 PG 106 ★ ACT/ADV

By now, so many versions of the story had been made that it was difficult to find a new angle so Hollywood obviously decided not to bother and pinned the film's hopes on Kiefer Sutherland, Charlie Sheen and Chris O'Donnell. But the boys just don't cut a dash with flowing hair and skirts. The only one with any panache is Oliver Platt and that's because he gets the funny lines.

3 Ninjas
1992 PG 80 ★★★ ACT/ADV

If you want to keep the youngsters quiet for a while, sit them down in front of this modern tale about a trio of children who learn the martial arts at their Oriental granddad's knee. Just as well since they need all the help they can get if they're to help their FBI agent father (Alan McRae). Adults will blanch a little at the contrived plot, but kids should accept it on face value as a piece of fun where the little guys save the day.

3.10 to Yuma
1957 U 87 ★★★ WES

Classic Western story with Glenn Ford as a captured outlaw being held by the inhabitants of a small town until the train comes to take him to jail. Ford is perfect as the charming villain with a heart of gold. (B&W)

Throne of Blood
1957 PG 105 ★★★★★ FOR

If you like your *Macbeth* Japanese and bloody then this splendid Samurai version of That Play shouldn't be missed. Director Akira Kurosawa takes a number of liberties with the original work in transposing it to the Orient but it's a powerful piece of which the Bard would be proud. (B&W; subtitled)

Throw Momma from the Train
1987 15 84 ★★ COM

If the plot of this vaguely amusing comedy seems familiar, it's basically that of Alfred Hitchcock's classic mystery, *Strangers on a Train*. When lecturer Billy Crystal recommends his thickest, most impressionable student, Danny DeVito, to go see Hitchcock's movie, DeVito gets the idea that his teacher wants to swap murders and decides to kill the former's ex-wife in return for Crystal returning the favour with his overbearing mother.

Thumbelina
1994 U 83 ★★★ FAM

Animated story about a little girl knee-high to a grasshopper who searches for love in an oversized, hostile world. Great songs, lots of colour and a perfect video to keep young kids amused for a bit.

Thunderball
1965 PG 125 ★★★ ACT/ADV

Sean Connery's fourth appearance as the secret agent licensed to kill and faced with the threat of world destruction. Armed with clever gadgets, suave sophistication and oodles of sex appeal, not even the most fiendish baddie is a match for James. Adolfo Celi's the evil one with some hungry sharks at his disposal. This was remade many years later as *Never Say Never Again* – again with Sean Connery.

Thunderheart
1992 15 114 ★★ MYS/THR

Interesting, politically correct tale depicting the harsh life the remaining Native Americans face in modern-day USA. Val Kilmer plays a literally red-blooded (since he's half Indian) FBI agent who's sent by boss Sam Shepard to investigate a murder on a Sioux reservation. There he finds his loyalties torn between the white man and his inner self. A lot of atmosphere but ultimately little else.

Tiger Bay
1959 PG 102 ★★★ MYS/THR

A tender story about a small girl (Hayley Mills) who witnesses a murder but is so attached to the killer that she hampers the investigation and takes off with the man. A lot of the charm comes from the performances – particularly the twelve-year-old Mills – and the fact that, like Tatum O'Neal in *Paper Moon*, her daddy (Sir John) was on set to guide her, cast as the detective out to catch them. (B&W)

Time Bandits
1981 PG 111 ★★★★ COM

Some very naughty but very funny gags from ex-Python Terry Gilliam, who directs the likes of John Cleese, Sir Ralph Richardson, Sean Connery, Shelley Duvall, Michael Palin and a bunch of dwarfs. Said diminutive heroes are packed off on a romp through history where they encounter other vertically challenged folk such as Attila the Hun, Napoleon and Hitler, and turn up in places as diverse as Ancient Rome and the *Titanic*. Some scenes must surely have you splitting your sides.

Timescape
1991 15 90 ★★★ SCI/FAN

Adventurous sci-fi tale that is too subtle for its own good and thereby loses much of its impact. Jeff Daniels plays a lonely widower struggling to raise his young daughter in small-town America who finds there's something fishy about his new lodgers. What starts very slowly as a drama develops into a race against time to save the town. Good plot but executed badly.

Tin Men
1987 15 108 ★★★ COM

Delightful pairing of the diminutive Danny DeVito and the not much taller Richard Dreyfuss, who get off on the wrong foot when they crash into one another. Unbeknown to each other, both are ruthless door-to-door salesman who go on to employ their devious ways to get even with the other. Dreyfuss gets hoisted by his own petard when he tries to steal DeVito's wife, Barbara Hershey. Some very funny moments, nicely held together by director Barry Levinson.

Titfield Thunderbolt, The
1953 U 80 ★★★★ COM

Ealing comedy's on top form here as a village decides to fight the Government's decision to close the local railway line. And so Stanley Holloway, George Relph and John Gregson band together to keep the station going. Gentle humour and good characterization help to highlight the English eccentricity.

To Be or Not to Be
1942 U 95 ★★★★★ COM

During the Second World War a theatre company in Warsaw develops its own underground resistance, headed by husband-and-wife team Jack Benny and Carole Lombard. Their sabotage escapades are hilarious, as are their attempts to outwit the Nazis. In this Ernst Lubitsch classic Lombard is superb, Benny hilarious. In the sensitive days of wartime the film was accused of bad taste. But if the taste is bad, it's also glorious. (B&W)

To Be or Not to Be
1983 PG 103 ★ COM

Farce and crude comedy replace the subtlety and wit of the original in this quite unnecesessary remake. But real life husband-and-wife team Mel Brooks and Anne Bancroft are likeable enough reprising the roles made famous by Jack Benny and Carole Lombard. This time the bad taste is all down to Brooks.

To Catch a Thief
1955 PG 102 ★★★ MYS/THR

Slick, almost too oily a caper about a retired Cannes-dwelling cat burglar Cary Grant, determined to trap the robber who is employing his old MO to steal from the wealthy on the Riviera. Bored young heiress Grace Kelly offers her help. It's pretty to look at but very contrived. Director Hitchcock should stick to horror movies. A good one to iron to.

To Have and Have Not
1944 PG 96 ★★★★ ACT/ADV

Lauren Bacall is dynamite in her screen debut as the love interest of Martinique fisherman Humphrey Bogart, who somewhat reluctantly gets embroiled with the Free French movement. The chemistry on-screen between Bogey and Bacall must surely have been helped as they fell in love off-screen while making the movie. Howard Hawks directs an Ernest Hemingway plot. (B&W)

To Kill a Mockingbird
1962 PG 124 ★★★ DRA

The book's better, but this is a faithful, evocative adaptation which captures some of the intensity of small-town, Southern USA life. Gregory Peck gives a spellbinding performance as the father, Atticus. Children should identify with the central characters – a couple of youngsters maturing from tree-climbing tearaways into responsible small adults over the course of a long, hot summer. (B&W)

Tokyo Story
1953 U 130 ★★★★ FOR

When an old couple travel from their Japanese village to the capital city on a visit to their children, they become aware of the rifts that have developed between them and their offspring. The provocative, uneventful tale is expertly depicted by director Yasujiro Ozu. Grandparents should sit down in front of this one, maybe with a glass of sherry or two. (B&W; subtitled)

Tom and Jerry: The Movie
1993 U 80 ★ COM

Fred Quimby was the man who made the best Tom and Jerry cartoons – where was he when this film was made? A talking – and, heavens above, whatever next – even singing cat and mouse is just not on. Unless you're total toon junkies avoid the feature-length movie and stick to the TV shorts.

Tom Brown's Schooldays
1951 U 95 ★★★ FAM

A more accessible version than the 1940 film (not available on video), this takes a more light-hearted approach to the heady childhood days of boarding school. John Howard Davies plays the eponymous hero Tom, Robert Newton is the innovative headmaster and John Forrest is marvellously threatening as the spiteful bully Flashman. (B&W)

Tombstone
1993 15 124 ★★ WES

A star-studded cast enhances this rather slow account of the life and times of Wyatt Earp and his brothers. Kurt Russell, Val Kilmer, Billy Zane, Michael Biehn and Jason Priestley are testosterone-in-chaps, so female interest may be sustained even if male attention may wander.

Tom Jones
1963 PG 117 ★★★★ COM

Henry Fielding's bawdy novel is brought to life thanks to a fine screenplay by John Osborne and a quite superb performance by the young Albert Finney in the title role. Tony Richardson keeps tight control over the cast, which also includes Susannah York, Joan Greenwood and Dame Edith Evans. A must for any budding Lotharios.

Tom Sawyer
1973 U 95 ★★★ FAM

Johnny Whitaker plays the ruffian orphan who attracts adventure like pollen does bees. Celeste

Holm's his aunt who battles in vain to keep him home, and Jeff East his great pal, Huckleberry Finn. Straightforward telling of the book, though you'd be better off reading it because it's much more exciting. Look out for a young Jodie Foster.

Too Hot to Handle
1991 15 112 ★★ COM

Prior to becoming Mr and Mrs, Alec Baldwin and Kim Basinger made this rather dashing romp about a wealthy playboy (Baldwin) who, on his stag night, falls for a cabaret singer (Basinger). If his impending society wedding wasn't enough of a deterrent to dampen their lusty ardour, her position as a gangster's moll doesn't help matters. Despite it all the pair can't help themselves. So dynamic are the duo that it's not surprising to learn they cemented their on-screen relationship off it. Otherwise entitled *The Marrying Man*.

Tootsie
1982 15 111 ★★★★ COM

The movie that made cross-dressing popular. Dustin Hoffman gives a fantastic performance as the out-of-work actor so desperate to get a job he poses as a woman and finds national celebrity on a daytime soap. While his career is helped by wearing a dress, he finds his love life severely hampered. Bill Murray is hilarious in a small part as Hoffman's flatmate, Jessica Lange adorable as Tootsie's colleague, friend and the object of his affections.

Top Gun
1986 15 105 ★★★ ACT/ADV

There's much to ogle at here as pretty young things and death-defying aeroplane stunts do much to pass a very enjoyable couple of hours. Tom Cruise plays the ambitious trainee naval pilot who falls in love with his instructress, Kelly McGillis, mostly to the tune of 'Take My Breath Away'.

Top Hat
1935 U 93 ★★★★ MUS

No-one ever matched the combination of the dancing and singing pairing of Fred Astaire and Ginger Rogers and the music of Irving Berlin. Here the dynamic duo perform such numbers

as 'Isn't It a Lovely Day?', 'Top Hat, White Tie and Tails' and 'Cheek to Cheek'. The combo never worked better. (B&W)

Top Secret!
1984 15 86 ★★ COM

An OK spoof on old spy movies, made by the *Airplane!* team. Val Kilmer shows comic timing as the teen rock idol touring Nazi Germany. The plot wanes early, though the jokes keep going.

Tora! Tora! Tora!
1970 U 137 ★★★ WAR

This lavish adventure about the Japanese attack on Pearl Harbor in the Second World War was the most expensive movie to be made at the time, costing a reported twenty-five million dollars. Most of the money went on special effects while the cast, including Joseph Cotten and Jason Robards, are hard-pressed to keep up with them. It's an intelligent film which examines the event from both sides.

Torch Song Trilogy
1988 15 114 ★★★ DRA

A lonely Jewish drag queen is the touching core of this no-holds-barred depiction of gay life. Originally this was three Tony-award-winning, one-act plays scripted by and starring Harvey Fierstein. All linked together and once again starring Fierstein, the plays pack just as much impact on-screen, being in turn funny and moving. Homophobes should be forced to watch it.

To Sir with Love
1967 PG 101 ★★ DRA

Entertaining, avant-garde story about the problems posed when a black man (Sidney Poitier) comes to teach in a hard, all-white London school. Junking the more conservative attitude to teaching, Sir has to adopt a more dramatic approach to win the class's respect. Judy Geeson, Christian Roberts and Lulu are among the schoolkids.

Toto the Hero
1991 15 87 ★★★★ FOR

Good production values but a slow plot mark this Belgian movie centring on an old man, the eponymous Toto, who sets about getting the revenge he's dreamed of all his life. Children may get nightmares as this is an elderly gent who, since a babe-in-arms, has wanted to kill the child he believed took his rightful place with a wealthy family. (Subtitled)

Tous les Matins du Monde
1992 15 110 ★★★ FOR

You'd be forgiven for thinking Gérard Depardieu is the only actor France has. To ensure that if not he, at least one of his offspring are in every French movie, his son Guillaume has taken to the profession and makes his debut here. Gérard plays a court composer as an old man, Guillaume the character as a boy, in a tale about love, regrets and memories. (Subtitled)

Towering Inferno, The
1974 15 160 ★★★ ACT/ADV

The daddy of disaster movies was enormously successful, not so much for its simple plot about a newly built tower block which bursts into flames, but for the celestial cast trapped on the top floor – Paul Newman, Fred Astaire, William Holden, Robert Wagner and Faye Dunaway – while fireman Steve McQueen battles to save them. Special effects are impressive. Just the thing for older members of the family.

Town Like Alice, A
1956 PG 111 ★★★ ACT/ADV

A splendid movie with great adventure and loads of romance, which is based on the novel by Nevil Shute. Set in Malaya during the Second World War, it recounts the plight of some female POWs who have to trek across the country from one camp to another. Peter Finch is the Australian who helps the women, Virginia McKenna the one with whom he falls in love. Everyone should like this. (B&W)

Toys
1993 PG 116 ★★ COM

Even if you don't like the film – and it certainly has a number of flaws (including a plot that is at best wayward) – this is a visual delight.

Director Barry Levinson makes the most of the movie's setting, a toy factory, and goes to town on creating a bright and colourful playroom look to the production. The story centres on good guy/bad guy fighting for control of the factory. Robin Williams wants to make safe, nice toys; his evil uncle, Michael Gambon, wants to make weapons.

Toy Soldiers
1991 15 108 ★★★ ACT/ADV

Troublesome prep-school boys – so young they should still wear short trousers – prove their worth in khaki when their school is overrun by terrorists. OK, it's not very likely but the sight of the little guys beating the big guys is always a welcome one. Sean Astin leads the boys' brigade, Denholm Elliott the school and Andrew Divoff the baddies.

Trading Places
1983 15 112 ★★★ COM

The first half of this comedy is spot on, very funny and played to perfection by Eddie Murphy and Dan Aykroyd. The second half, however, slips into sentimentality and seems to forget its object is jokes. Murphy's the beggar who swaps place with spoilt, city rich kid, Aykroyd. If you only watch an hour of this, you're in for a treat.

Trapped in Paradise
1994 PG 107 ★ COM

Brothers Nicolas Cage, Dana Carvey and Jon Lovitz are trapped at Christmastime by the kindness of the town they've just robbed. Not that the townsfolk know they're robbers, of course. Seasonal it may be but there's little of the festive spirit about this rather dim comedy. The brothers – even Cage – are not particularly likeable so it becomes increasingly hard to see why everyone should be so nice to them. All three leads, especially the very funny Lovitz, deserve better.

Treasure Island
1934 U 98 ★★ FAM

Rollicking adventure with Jackie Cooper as Jim Hawkins, Wallace Beery a leering Long John Silver. Stirring stuff, faithful to Robert Louis Stevenson's story. (B&W)

Treasure Island
1972 PG 85 ★★ DRA

Orson Welles makes a superb, if rather hammy, Long John Silver, kidnapping Jim Hawkins and dragging him off in search of gold.

Treasure Island
1990 PG 128 ★★ DRA

Don't be put off by Charlton Heston as the peg-legged pirate. He may be more convincing as God, but he's not half bad. The direction, by his son Fraser, keeps the action exciting, the pictures pretty and the characters intriguing. Christian Bale turns in a nice performance as Jim, while Julian Glover, Oliver Reed and Christopher Lee lend considerable weight.

Treasure of the Sierra Madre, The
1948 PG 121 ★★★★ DRA

John Huston's cracking adventure deals with the flaws of human nature which come to light when lots of money is involved. Three gold prospectors – Humphrey Bogart, Walter Huston (John's daddy) and Tim Holt – fight to stake their claims. Both Hustons won Oscars for their respective roles in the production. It was the first time father and son had achieved this for the same film. (B&W)

Trial, The
1993 15 115 ★★ DRA

Only for the most dedicated Kafka fans, this. It's an oblique mystery about a man in Eastern Europe (Kyle MacLachlan) who is unable to find the reason for his arrest. If you like your movies surreal fine, but somehow the structure is wrong and the menace and desperate frustration of the book are lost.

Tron
1982 PG 92 ★ SCI/FAN

The special effects are a wow but that's all that is in this *Innerspace* with computers. Hot-shot Jeff Bridges has his ideas stolen by scheming David Warner, who ingeniously deconstructs him and inserts him into a terminal. There he must use his knowledge of video games to survive in the computer architecture as he is forced to play the Master Control Program to decide his fate.

Troop Beverly Hills
1989 PG 106 ★★ COM

Shelley Long's such a cutey that it's hard to dislike her movies however weak the plot. In this one, she plays a goofy and obscenely wealthy housewife who leads her daughter's Guides group, awarding them badges for shopping, manicures, telling real Gucci from fake etc... She's funny even if the script isn't, and the idea's quite appealing.

Trouble with Harry, The
1955 PG 95 ★★★ MYS/THR

Not the usual type of Hitchcock movie, this. The emphasis is strongly on comedy as, individually, a local community uncovers a dead body and each in turn tries to bury/ignore it. Shirley MacLaine gives a good performance – her first, incidentally – as does John Forsythe, almost unrecognisable without his blue hair in TV's *Dynasty*.

True Grit
1969 PG 128 ★★★ WES

When a feisty young teenager appeals to a slobbish, embittered marshal (John Wayne) to abandon his unconstructive retirement and help her trap her father's killer, so begins a friendship which develops with an intricacy and subtlety good enough to earn Wayne his one and only Oscar. The film's not his best, but it's a good Western nonetheless.

True Identity
1991 15 89 ★★ COM

Lenny Henry's make-up is the main appeal of the film as he plays an actor who, to hide from the Mob, employs a number of shape-changing, colour-swapping disguises. Lenny Henry does justice to the make-up, it's just a shame the script doesn't.

Truly Madly Deeply
1991 PG 102 ★★★★ DRA

Some classic moments make this touching tale of bereavement quite hilarious. Juliet Stevenson plays a woman vainly trying to come to terms with her boyfriend's (Alan Rickman) death. Her grief is alleviated when he returns from the dead to console her, but she becomes increasingly irritated by his selfish behaviour, bringing home ghoulish friends to watch videos being an example. Delightful, with performances rarely equalled.

Turner & Hooch
1989 PG 95 ★★★ MYS/THR

It's difficult to judge which is the cuter, Tom Hanks or the big, slobbering mastiff dog he's lumbered with. Hanks is a houseproud cop, the dog's an unhousetrained orphan and the only witness to a murder and Hanks has to look after him until the case is solved. The plus side for the cop is that local vet Mare Winningham takes an interest, too.

Turtle Diary
1985 PG 92 ★★★ DRA

Should anyone need reminding that before becoming an MP Glenda Jackson was a considerable actress, one of her final roles was here as a frustrated, middle-aged woman who is obsessed with the plight of some giant turtles kept in the zoo. Ben Kingsley, equally as repressed, shares her concern and together they plan to free them. Nice script by Harold Pinter, who makes a Hitchcockian appearance in a bookshop.

12 Angry Men
1957 U 92 ★★★★★ DRA

Few films have ever equalled the power of this courtroom drama in which Henry Fonda plays the spokesman of a jury who is undecided about the guilt of a young murder suspect. The brilliance of the script – one man trying to persuade eleven – is matched only by that of the performances and direction (Sidney Lumet's first and possibly best). Jury service will never seem the same after this. (B&W)

Twelve O'Clock High
1949 U 127 ★★★★ WAR

Smashing Second World War adventure focusing on a squadron of American pilots based in Blighty and the problems they and, more importantly, their commanding officers (particularly Gregory Peck) experience under the pressure. Peck is quite superb, as is Dean Jagger (no relation to Mick) who won an Oscar. (B&W)

20,000 Leagues under the Sea
1954 U 122 ★★ SCI/FAN

An impressive cast and slick Disney production values do justice to Jules Vern's nautical adventure. James Mason plays a crazed Captain Nemo who snatches a scientist (Paul Lukas) and sailor (Kirk Douglas) to man his state-of-the-art submarine. Action-packed stuff which should keep the clan quiet for a couple of hours.

Twice Round the Daffodils
1962 PG 85 ★★★ COM

Delightful British comedy set in a nursing home for TB patients. Romance and drama abound as the likes of Donald Sinden, Kenneth Williams, Donald Houston and Lance Percival cough and joke their way to health with the aid of such appealing nurses as Nanette Newman and Juliet Mills. When the patients are well enough to walk around the flower bed twice they're well enough to go home. A real charmer. (B&W)

Twins
1988 PG 102 ★★ COM

A one-joke film which relies on the fact that Danny DeVito and Arnold Schwarzenegger as twins should keep you laughing all the way through. An unreasonable assumption, amusing as the sight of little and large is. It's not that funny and nor is the plot. Predictable yarn about an unlikely couple reunited after a lifetime of separation to discover who their parents were.

Two Jakes, The
1990 15 132 ★★ MYS/THR

Don't give up the day job, Jack. Mr Nicholson directs himself in this dreary sequel to the smashing *Chinatown*. He reprises his earlier role as Jake Gittes, private eye, investigating adultery and fraud. The story's woefully over-plotted and the result is a confusing mishmash which wastes its cast – Harvey Keitel, Madeleine Stowe, Meg Tilly, Eli Wallach and Frederic Forrest. A little on the raunchy side and a fair bit of violence.

2001: A Space Odyssey
1968 U 133 ★★★★★ SCI/FAN

If at all possible, introduce your family to this innovative sci-fi via the large screen. Stanley Kubrick's marvellous direction of Arthur C Clarke's space fantasy is sadly diminished on the small screen though still splendid if you don't have the choice. Avoid the sequel – *2010* – it makes turkeys look like Oscar material.

Ugly American, The
1962 PG 115 ★★★ DRA

Marlon Brando, not that he could ever be ugly, plays the title role of a US ambassador sent to a Communist country in Asia where the political situation demands a great deal of tact, something he lacks.

Uncle Buck
1989 15 95 ★ COM

If it weren't for the presence of John Candy as the eponymous hero, this feeble effort from John Hughes would be high in the minus-rating league. The daft plot centres on a family who have no alternative but to leave their spoilt brats with the relative from hell. The teenage daughter, experiencing a hormone explosion, can't bear him and the two lock horns. The comedy's weak, the jokes rarely work and the children are unattractive. One other notable point is that a very young Macaulay Culkin appears. Only for those too young to have developed a sophisticated sense of humour.

Undercover Blues
1993 15 86 ★ MYS/THR

Again, a movie where the stars outshine the story, but even Dennis Quaid and Kathleen Turner are hard pushed to keep momentum going in this crime caper. They play a couple of karate-kicking spies who marry and have a cute baby. But their hoped-for retirement vanishes out of the window when they're promptly involved in espionage. Both are appealing, it's just a shame the script isn't. Too tedious for an ironing movie. One for when you're completely whacked.

Under Fire
1983 15 123 ★★★★ DRA

An exceptional political drama, which was something of a flop at the American box office largely because it showed the US of A in rather a dim light. The story takes place during the Nicaraguan uprising of 1979 and revolves around the adventures of two experienced American newspapermen, reporter Gene Hackman and photographer Nick Nolte. What the film condemns most strongly is the behaviour of the American media, as exemplified by the methods of Hackman and Nolte when they set out to find and interview a shadowy rebel leader. Also involved in a situation that becomes increasingly fraught is a radio journalist, Joanna Cassidy, who veers romantically between the two men. Roger Spottiswoode's film powerfully conveys the fear, sweat and tension of the civil unrest in a trouble-torn country.

Under Siege
1992 15 98 ★★ ACT/ADV

Utter nonsense, but enjoyable nonetheless as a naval chef (Steven Seagal, would you believe) has to save the day after his ship is hijacked by the evil, psychotic Tommy Lee Jones. Luckily, for the bap-watchers, Jones arrives on board with stripper Erika Eleniak so there's a bit of romance and titillation as well as an abundance of action. Implausible that one man can defeat so many, but then you don't watch this sort of film for a reminder of reality. Youngsters should be warned there's a lot of killing and ample cleavage.

Unforgiven
1992 15 125 ★★★★★ WES

Superb, intelligent Western directed by and starring the maestro, Clint Eastwood. Again he plays the enigmatic hired gun who, lured out of retirement, leaves his family to do one last job. Gathering help en route from old friend Morgan Freeman, he heads in to town to take revenge for a prostitute whose face has been slashed. Terrific performances from the men, including Richard Harris as gunfighter English Bob and Gene Hackman as the sheriff every town should be without. Very violent, so mind who watches it but – if you're over 15 – make sure you do.

Untamed Heart
1993 15 97 ★★★ DRA

Oodles of tissues needed for this one as a quiet washer-upper, Christian Slater, falls in love with waitress Marisa Tomei. She's an incurable romantic who eventually falls in love with him, too, only to learn that her Prince Charming has a fatal heart defect. Hearts are large all round here and despite the sentiment, there's a lot of humour, too, mainly from Rosie Perez – she of the marvellously grating voice – who gives quite a comic turn.

Untouchables, The
1987 15 115 ★★★★ MYS/THR

At last, a film about the Mafia that doesn't glorify the institution and is on the side of the good guys – including FBI agent Eliot Ness, the man who eventually brought to justice Al Capone. A supreme piece of direction by Brian DePalma with inspired casting. Kevin Costner is Ness, Andy Garcia his sidekick and Sean Connery the policeman who helps them. Robert De Niro has a much smaller role as Capone.

Up Pompeii
1971 15 86 ★★★ COM

Inimitable Frankie Howerd comedy which defies you to 'titter ye not'. This is the film version of the highly successful, raunchy TV series in which Howerd played the Roman slave who first made his appearance in the stage play *A Funny Thing Happened on the Way to the Forum*. Michael Hordern, Patrick Cargill and Lance Percival are among the talented cast. Wonderfully smutty.

Used People
1992 15 111 ★★ COM

Quirky comedy-cum-drama about a Jewish widow, Shirley MacLaine, who, despite her persistent rejection of his advances, is courted by a charming Italian gent, Marcello Mastroianni, a man who's admired her from afar for a very long time. Despite her daughters's opposition to the match, MacLaine eventually succumbs to his charms. Delightful roles for the two leads, who handle them with a perfect balance of sentimentality and humour.

U2: Rattle and Hum
1988 15 95 ★★★ MUS

The boys from Dublin are followed on their world tour in a much-better-than-average rock documentary. The backstage banter's interspersed nicely with concert footage so that even those who don't like the lads' music should find it entertaining. Amusing scene where Bono and the boys visit Graceland. (B&W and colour)

Vanishing, The
1988 15 102 ★★★★ FOR

George Sluizer made two versions of this chilling suspense thriller. This is his first venture (in French), with the hero being a Dutchman (Gene Bervoets) whose girlfriend is inexplicably kidnapped while they're holidaying in France. The tale follows his obsession with finding out what happened to her, however long it takes. A brilliant ending makes this the more frightening version. (Subtitled)

Vanishing, The
1993 15 105 ★★ MYS/THR

Although this is the same plot, it's been given the Hollywood make-over and as the more sanitized version, it's the less thrilling. That's not to say you won't be gripping tightly to the arm of your chair, but you might be able to dispose of the cushion for this one. Kiefer Sutherland's the man whose vacation's cut short by the disappearance of his girl; Jeff Bridges the nutter who snatches her. Not for the faint or weak-hearted.

Verdict, The
1982 15 128 ★★★★ DRA

There are two movies with this title but they're very different, though both are worth watching. The 1946 *Verdict* is a crime thriller with Sydney Greenstreet; this *Verdict* is a courtroom drama, equally as thrilling in its way, with has-been lawyer Paul Newman being given a last crack at a case of medical negligence. This is a superb work, intelligent, smartly written and performed to perfection.

Vertigo
1958 PG 122 ★★ MYS/THR

Alfred Hitchcock's rather mediocre thriller in which James Stewart's the man with no head for heights who, since he's a retired copper, is hired by an old friend to watch his wife, Kim Novak. The story's enhanced by the evocative atmosphere only Hitch could create.

Vice Versa
1988 PG 94 ★★ COM

There seemed to be a plethora of role-reversal movies all released around the same time. The best of them was *Big* with Tom Hanks, but this wasn't bad either, though it's a weak story. Judge Reinhold is a workaholic father who gets to know what life's like for his young son, Fred (*The Wonder Years*) Savage.

View to a Kill, A
1985 PG 126 ★★ ACT/ADV

This poor Bond movie marks the beginning of the end of 007's mass popularity. Despite Roger Moore still being licensed to kill, some of the charm has been omitted, and though Christopher Walken makes an imposing baddie there's not enough villainy to challenge James. Moore bowed out gracefully after this one and who can blame him?

Vikings, The
1958 PG 111 ★★★ ACT/ADV

Smashing production about marauding Norwegians swashing and buckling all over Europe. Kirk Douglas and Tony Curtis are the charismatic leads. Great attention to detail gives it the authentic touch.

Vincent & Theo
1990 15 134 ★★★ DRA

Brotherly love is the basis of this atmospheric Robert Altman film about Vincent Van Gogh (Tim Roth) and his brother Theo (Paul Rhys). This is a cut above the usual Hollywood biographies, painting, if you'll excuse the pun, a much fuller picture than you'd expect.

Virgin Queen, The
1955 U 87 ★★★ DRA

Ideal casting marks this historical depiction of the life and times of Elizabeth I. Bette Davis again dons a wig and crown to reprise her royal role, this time opposite Richard Todd who plays Sir Walter Raleigh. Not as romantic as *The Private Lives of Elizabeth and Essex*, but then Todd lacks the panache of Errol Flynn. Bette's brilliant, though.

Visiteurs, Les
1993 15 102 ★★ FOR

French farce which confirms that different countries have different senses of humour which don't translate that well. Jean Reno plays a medieval knight who, along with his grubby valet, are transported into the present day. Some of the situations, though lavatorial, are very funny, but comedy's a little thin on the ground. (Subtitled)

Vital Signs
1990 15 99 ★★ DRA

To hail this comedy-drama as an American *Doctor in the House* is to pay it a compliment it never quite earns, though the subject matter's similar: students trying to make the grade while distractions such as sex and stuff keep interfering. Good cast including Adrian Pasdar, Diane Lane, Laura San Giacomo and Jimmy Smits.

Viva Zapata!
1952 PG 109 ★★★★ ACT/ADV

Marlon Brando may not be many people's idea of a Mexican brigand but he will be after watching this. As the notorious revolutionary who rose from nothing to the top job, he is superb. Oscar-winning support provided by Anthony Quinn. Good adventure yarn, just right for a lazy evening in. (B&W)

V I Warshawski
1991 15 85 ★★ MYS/THR

In Sara Paretsky's thrillers, V I Warshawski is a woman with – excuse the expression – balls. Here, all the feistiness Kathleen Turner usually brings to a role is missing and so as the heroine detective she's rather too mild. That's not the actress's fault, the script is so bland. Turner gives some high kicks and takes a number of punches, but she's not fast-talking enough and so the story falls flat. Shame – as Warshawski in the BBC Radio 4 series Turner was just right.

Wall Street
1987 15 120 ★★★ DRA

If one film were to sum up the 1980s, this would be it. A movie about greed, both corporate and personal, in which yuppies abound, mobile phones and Filofaxes are worn like watches and people 'do' breakfast. Oliver Stone's direction shows remarkable perception of the stockbroking world – one of which he's obviously not fond – and Michael Douglas and Charlie Sheen play the high-flying bankers to perfection.

War and Peace
1956 U 200 ★★★ ACT/ADV

If director King Vidor had managed to shorten this adaptation of Tolstoy's masterpiece he'd have made a much better film. As it stands, it's enjoyable and lavish but sprawling and slow. Money certainly wasn't stinted on either the Russian battle scenes or the cast, since the likes of Audrey Hepburn, John Mills and Henry Fonda don't come cheap.

WarGames
1983 PG 108 ★★★ COM

The computer literate in the family will love this and even those who still think a mouse is just a furry animal will glean a lot of fun out of this crime-caper comedy in which computer hacker Matthew Broderick accesses his way into the White House's defence computer program. Lovely stuff from the very young, rosy-cheeked Broderick.

War of the Buttons, The
1994 PG 90 ★★★ DRA

This bittersweet tale of a couple of warring children's gangs in Ireland never seems to know where it's going. Not satisfied with the engaging portrayal of the two sides' intriguing *modus operandi*, it tries to be something more when it gets sidetracked by the sub-plot involving the miserable home life of one side's leader. Considering that David Puttnam produced and Colin Welland wrote the script, it should have been better.

War of the Roses, The
1989 15 111 ★★★★ COM

Anyone who's ever had a relationship go wrong will adore this side-splitting black comedy about a divorce. Initially, the marriage of Mrs and Mr Rose (Kathleen Turner and Michael Douglas) is perfect but, ever so slowly (and this is the genius of the movie – its subtlety), cracks begin to appear until they are separated and fighting what amounts to the Third World War over their beloved house. Danny DeVito directs with a talent for the comic which is complemented perfectly by his two stars.

War of the Worlds, The
1953 PG 82 ★★ SCI/FAN

So convincing is H G Wells's story about an alien invasion, that when Orson Welles read it on American airwaves, people actually believed that Martians had landed. This screen version, narrated by Cedric Hardwicke and starring Gene Barry and Ann Robinson, is also fairly absorbing, thanks in no small measure to the Oscar-winning special effects.

Water Babies, The
1978 U 81 ★★★ FAM

A brilliant combination of live action and cartoon enabled director Lionel Jeffries to bring Charles Kingsley's magical novel to the screen. The story, for those who haven't read the book, is about a little chimney sweep who escapes from the misery of Victorian life to one of fantasy and adventure under the sea. James Mason, Billie Whitelaw and Bernard Cribbins are among the human cast.

Waterdance, The
1992 15 102 ★★★ DRA

Heart-warming tale set in and around a rehabilitation centre ward where three men (Eric Stoltz, William Forsythe and Wesley Snipes) confront the changes that paraplegia will bring to their lives. Despite the subject matter, the tone is remarkably upbeat and amusing.

Waterland
1992 15 91 ★ DRA

Based on an English novel set in the fen country but here set awkwardly in America. Jeremy Irons plays a rather dour schoolteacher who goes off into a reverie during class and tells his life story to his students. Irons's real-life wife Sinead Cusack plays his screen wife, their meeting forming the basis of his stories.

Watership Down
1978 U 88 ★★★ DRA

A splendid, animated version of Richard Adams's rabbit novel. Despite the subjects being bunnie-wunnies, basic human values of love, courage and survival are in abundance. Hankies at the ready though for the more touching moments and for Art Garfunkel's song 'Bright Eyes'. Some of the scarier moments may be a little too much for the nippers.

Wayne's World
1992 PG 90 ★★ COM

This is *Bill and Ted* with attitude. Similar in speech and mindless good nature, Mike Myers and Dana Carvey aren't quite as appealing as Reeves and Winter but there are some comic moments that are gems (such as their head-banging singalong to Queen's 'Bohemian Rhapsody') as the two lads, hosts of a TV show broadcast from their home, cruise town hoping to find babes. Nice casting of Rob Lowe as the villain.

Wayne's World 2
1993 PG 91 ★★★ COM

A superb sequel, much funnier and better plotted than the first, with Myers and Carvey again. This time, Wayne restages Woodstock (as Waynestock) with a number of jibes at popular movies and the help of Jim Morrison, while Garth makes out with Kim Basinger. Meanwhile Tia Carrere, Wayne's girlfriend, is being seduced by the evil Christopher Walken. Great fun.

Wedding Banquet, The
1993 15 103 ★★★ FOR

Oriental comedies don't come much better than this, though it's mixed with some pretty dramatic scenes. The story centres around a young gay Taiwanese man living in America with his lover, who gets married in order to please his parents and help his bride get a Green Card. The wedding, which takes on enormous proportions, goes badly wrong. (Subtitled in parts)

Welcome Home, Roxy Carmichael
1991 15 92 ★★★ DRA

Quirky story about a lonely teenager (Winona Ryder) coming to terms with encroaching womanhood and her parentage. The imminent homecoming of a Hollywood star leads Ryder to believe that she is in fact her long-lost mother. Jeff Daniels turns in a performance only matched in subtlety and grace by Ryder herself. Teenagers will identify, no doubt.

We're No Angels
1989 15 102 ★ COM

We're not a good combination either – Robert De Niro and Sean Penn in a comedy is not the best piece of casting the cinema industry's ever seen. They look awkward in a violent piece which is desperate rather than funny. Freshly escaped from jail, the boys try to pass themselves off as men of the cloth. Humphrey Bogart and Aldo Ray did it rather better in 1955.

West Side Story
1961 PG 145 ★★★ MUS

Modernized and melodized, Shakespeare's tragic romance *Romeo and Juliet* is set in 1950s New York with Richard Beymer and Natalie Wood as the lovers from opposing gangs. Fights take the form of splendid dance choreography and the score, by Leonard Bernstein, is fantastic. It won ten Oscars.

Westworld
1973 15 85 ★★★ SCI/FAN

Intelligent and imaginative horror set in a futuristic American Butlins camp, where the yellow coats are robots – Yul Brynner among them. But, due to a short-circuit, the robots malfunction, turn into psychotic killers and the *Hi-De-Hi* atmosphere takes on nightmare proportions. Where's that Peggy when you need her? Contains a good deal of violence.

What About Bob?
1991 PG 95 ★★★ COM

When a neurotic patient (Bill Murray) becomes fixated with his psychiatrist (Richard Dreyfuss), the emphasis of their relationship slowly changes. The mad one whose allergies even had allergies calms down, while the doctor turns into a nervous wreck. Great casting and a lovely performance by Murray make the situations very funny. Kids will love it and so will Grandma.

What's Eating Gilbert Grape
1993 12 112 ★★★ DRA

Johnny Depp stars as the title character, a caring young man who lives with his obese mum (Darlene Cates – discovered while taking part in a 'fat' discussion on an American talk show), his mentally challenged younger brother and two sisters. As their house is collapsing under the mother's weight, so is Gilbert's life. Bittersweet and quirky with support from Juliette Lewis, Mary Steenburgen and Crispin Glover.

What's Up, Doc?
1972 U 90 ★★★★ COM

Brilliant comedy directed by Peter Bogdanovich based around confusion in a hotel over four identical bags: one with rocks in; one with sparkling rocks in – jewels; one containing underwear and another, top-secret spy papers. Barbra Streisand never had a part so good and Ryan O'Neal was never as attractive. Great chases, script and characterization. Don't miss it.

When a Man Loves a Woman
1994 15 120 ★★ DRA

An incongruous story and misguided casting mar the basic tale about alcoholism. Meg Ryan – who's dreadful, bouncing off the walls like a weeble – is the drunk mother and wife. Andy Garcia – who is the best thing in it – plays the saint-like husband whose pleasantness would seem to have driven her to the bottle. Not one for after the pub, that's for sure.

When Harry Met Sally...
1989 15 91 ★★★★ COM

Prepare to explain to the more naive viewers just what Meg Ryan is doing in THE restaurant scene. That's hilarious, but then the whole film is a delight to watch as Ryan and Billy Crystal try to steer a platonic friendship through the course of their lives. Charm and comedy in abundance.

When the Whales Came
1989 U 96 ★★★ DRA

Hankies at the ready – whole boxes for the animal-lovers in the household. This is the touching story of a lonely, deaf old man (Paul Scofield) who lives a hermit's existence on a remote island. His life is soon changed when he's befriended by two young children and together they try to save a beached whale. The story moves along a little too slowly for the very young to keep attending, but nice support from Helen Mirren and David Threlfall helps sustain interest.

When Worlds Collide
1951 U 79 ★★ SCI/FAN

Scientists are busy preparing for the end of the world, which, according to this somewhat predictable tale, is nigh. Still, they manage to find time to bicker and love as they do so and the sight of New York slipping into the Hudson is impressive. Special effects are the best bits and duly won awards.

Where Angels Fear to Tread
1991 PG 108 ★★★ DRA

Possibly the hardest of E M Forster's novels to adapt and director Charles Sturridge concentrated more on the look of the movie version rather than the effect, so some of the dramatic impact is lost. Based in England and Italy, the story tells of a young widow who, while holidaying in Tuscany, marries a local peasant to her British in-laws' disgust. Helena Bonham Carter, Rupert Graves and Helen Mirren star.

Where No Vultures Fly
1951 U 103 ★★ ACT/ADV

Or *Ivory Hunter* as it was originally titled. In a semi-documentary style, not always convincing, this dramatic tale recounts the establishment of the Mount Kilimanjaro Game Preserve Park, Kenya. Anthony Steel, Dinah Sheridan and Meredith Edwards head the cast.

Whisky Galore!
1949 PG 80 ★★★★★ COM

One of the all-time greats, designed to make you feel better for having watched it. This is a delightful, often hilarious tale about a remote Scottish fishing village which hides a consignment of whisky washed up from a shipwreck. Basil Radford, Joan Greenwood, James Robertson Justice et. al. are all present and most correct in one of Ealing's best comedies. Incidentally, Americans knew it as *Tight Little Island*. (B&W)

Whistle Down the Wind
1961 PG 95 ★★★ DRA

When three children discover a fugitive (Alan Bates) hiding in their barn, they believe him to be Jesus Christ and treat him accordingly. The story, a poignant, often moving one, is based on the novel by Mary Hayley Bell whose daughter, Hayley Mills, stars in the film. (B&W)

White Christmas
1954 U 115 ★★★ MUS

Singalong-a-Bing-and-Danny, as Messrs Crosby and Kaye get festive while entertaining residents at a winter resort. Irving Berlin's score is delightful, as are the boys, but the story is basically that of *Holiday Inn* – at least it's familiar.

White Fang
1991 PG 104 ★★ ACT/ADV

Teenie heart-throb Ethan Hawke stars as a young orphan prospecting for gold in the hostile Klondike where he's befriended by an orphan wolf cub, Seymour Cassel and Klaus Maria Brandauer. It's nicely filmed and adequately presented, though its appeal lies with the younger generations on the whole.

White Fang 2: Myth of the White Wolf
1994 U 102 ★★ ACT/ADV

Scott Bairstow takes the role vacated after the first film by Ethan Hawke (who appears in a cameo at the beginning) as the sidekick to the half-wolf. Gold prospecting is again the pivot around which the action rotates. It has its moments.

White Hunter, Black Heart
1990 PG 107 ★★ DRA

The basic plot to this occasionally dragging drama was inspired by the problems caused by the director John Huston while he was making *The African Queen*. As rumour has it, he was more concerned with shooting elephants than film and this obsession nearly jeopardised the entire production. Clint Eastwood takes the lead role (acting and directing) with the help of Jeff Fahey and George Dzundza. Its ponderous feel will bore the young.

White Men Can't Jump
1992 15 111 ★★★ COM

Hilarious, sharp-shooting comedy about a couple of competitive basketball players who get into all sorts of trouble hustling around the New York courts. Woody Harrelson's the guy supposedly unable to jump, Wesley Snipes his partner and competitor. In certain European countries it was unfortunately retitled *White Men Can't Get It Up*. Older kids will love it, so will the grown-ups, though the language may be a little fresh.

White Nights
1985 15 131 ★★ MYS/THR

Dynamic combination of ballet dancer Mikhail Baryshnikov and American hoofer Gregory Hines enhances what is otherwise a plodding thriller. The Russian attempts to defect from the USSR, while the American, a tap dancer, is employed to prevent him. Good support from Isabella Rossellini, John Glover, Helen Mirren and Geraldine Page.

White Sands
1992 15 97 ★ MYS/THR

Don't miss the opening credits or else you'll have missed out on the best bit of this plodding thriller. Willem Dafoe gives a tortuous performance as a deputy sheriff who gets embroiled in FBI intrigue after discovering a dead body. The plot's so confusing it's hard to keep up with, though the small part by Mickey Rourke enlivens it for a while.

Who Framed Roger Rabbit
1988 PG 99 ★★★★ COM

Fantastic family fun thanks to a lively story about a Toon Town murder and an Oscar-winning mix of live action and cartoons. Bob Hoskins and Christopher Lloyd provide the human roles, though the voices of Kathleen Turner (as the sexy Jessica Rabbit), Charles Fleischer and Amy Irving feature.

Whose Life Is It Anyway?
1981 15 113 ★★ DRA

Poignant and thought-provoking tale about a wisecracking artist (Richard Dreyfuss), almost paralysed after a road accident, who argues for his right not to live but to die. The conflict is between his wishes and the medical profession's duty to preserve life wherever possible. Powerful performance by Dreyfuss, whose acting is confined to eyes alone. John Cassavetes and Christine Lahti lend support.

Who's Harry Crumb?
1989 PG 87 ★ COM

Although funny in parts, there's too much slapstick and slapdash humour for this comedy to work. John Candy's appealing, though, as the useless private eye hired to find a kidnapped girl.

Who's That Girl
1987 PG 88 ★ COM

Unfortunately it's Madonna, who needn't have stuck to the day job if she'd kept on accepting scripts the calibre of *Desperately Seeking Susan*. But here the advice must be run not walk back to the recording studio. The film's a daft caper with Griffin Dunne accompanying jailbird Madonna out of town.

Wild One, The
1954 PG 76 ★★★ ACT/ADV

Grease those leathers, polish the Harley and settle down in front of this, the best, if not the very first, of the biker films. Marlon Brando's the angry, misunderstood leader of the pack whose very presence terrorizes a small American town. (B&W)

Willow
1988 PG 120 ★★★ SCI/FAN

Delightful fairy-tale adventure from the pen of *Star Wars* creator George Lucas, made all the more romantic since it brought together Val Kilmer and Joanne Whalley (as she was then, Whalley-Kilmer as she is now). A dwarf (Warwick Davis), helped by the gallant Kilmer, protects an abandoned baby destined to rule the kingdom currently presided over by an evil Queen (Jean Marsh). Lovely effects and amusing script.

Willy Wonka & the Chocolate Factory
1971 U 95 ★★★ FAM

Roald Dahl's anti-greed tale is imaginatively brought to life by some delightful sets and a fittingly eccentric performance from Gene Wilder as Mr Wonka. The songs are OK, too, but it's not for the very young as some of the scenes are surprisingly scary.

Wilt
1989 15 89 ★★ COM

Alison Steadman is hilarious as the catalyst in this otherwise silly comedy about a teacher (Griff Rhys Jones) who dreams of murdering his domineering wife (Steadman). When she disappears, the police detective (Mel Smith) immediately suspects him. Not for the very young, since the humour tends to be a little risqué (and, occasionally, unfunny).

Winchester '73
1950 U 92 ★★★★ WES

One of the most intelligent Westerns ever made, with James Stewart on splendid form as, through a series of adventures, he tracks down his beloved stolen gun. Shelley Winters and Rock Hudson are among the familiar faces, along with an as-yet unknown Anthony Curtis. (B&W)

Wings of the Apache
1990 15 83 ★ ACT/ADV

Nicolas Cage and Sean Young do with helicopters what Tom Cruise and Kelly McGillis did with aeroplanes in *Top Gun*, only Cruise and co did it better. This is a silly story acted with little conviction, only worth watching for the flying sequences.

Winslow Boy, The
1948 U 113 ★★★★ DRA

Brilliant viewing for a rainy Saturday afternoon. Gather the family and the chocolates and sit back for two pleasurable hours as the plot unfolds. Cedric Hardwicke's young son is expelled for stealing and the family, with the help of lawyer Robert Donat, fight to clear the boy's name. Charming stuff with a great deal of humour and a bit of romance thrown in. (B&W)

Wish You Were Here
1987 15 88 ★★★ COM

Emily Lloyd burst onto the scene with her stunning performance as a young girl flowering into womanhood despite the dreariness of postwar Britain. Writer/director David Leland based the character on Cynthia Payne, about whom he was to write more later with *Personal Services*.

Witches, The
1990 PG 88 ★★★ COM

Nicolas Roeg's sharp adaptation of a Roald Dahl story where a young lad and his granny (Mai Zetterling) while on holiday, get mixed up with a witches' convention at their hotel. Anjelica Huston's superb as the head witch and Rowan Atkinson hilarious as the hotel manager. Humour's heavily mixed with horror so stay with the littler ones while watching it.

With Honours
1994 PG 96 ★ COM

Bypassing the cinema, this went straight to video, a far more suitable place for it since it's the kind of movie during which you can get on with other things and still not miss too much. Joe Pesci plays a down-and-out who has in his possession the treasured thesis of Harvard student Brendan Fraser. For the return of said essay, Fraser must provide Pesci with accommodation. The comedy is crude, not in the lewd sense but lacking in sophistication, though Fraser and Pesci give it their best.

Withnail and I
1987 15 103 ★★ COM

Two 'resting' actors, Richard E Grant and Paul McGann, decide to leave the drudgery of city life and head for the country, only to discover the horrors it holds are even worse. Period comedy set in the late sixties which never gets past the obvious and stereotypical. Good performances by the boys, though. Contains swearing and drug-taking.

Without a Clue
1988 PG 102 ★★ MYS/THR

For a movie about Sherlock Holmes, starring Michael Caine as he of the deerstalker headgear and Ben Kingsley the good Doctor Watson, you'd expect a great deal more than this offers. The idea is a send-up of Sir Arthur Conan Doyle's hero. Caine is a drunken actor employed by the brilliant writer, Dr Watson, to impersonate his fictional creation, Mr Holmes. Nice enough, though the laughs are in short supply.

Witness
1985 15 107 ★★★★ MYS/THR

Dynamic thriller whose intricate story is matched by the characterization and the performances to a man (and woman) are sublime. The appealing young Lukas Haas plays the only witness to a murder. Harrison Ford is the policeman who enters Haas's Amish community to protect himself, the boy and his mother, Kelly McGillis, from the desperate killers. Delicious little details and a palm-sweating climax.

Witness for the Prosecution
1957 U 111 ★★★ MYS/THR

Whatever you do, make sure you don't pick up the 1982 remake. Billy Wilder does a superb job adapting Agatha Christie's whodunit into a witty vehicle for Charles Laughton, who, hilarious as the grouchy lawyer, shows his versatility. Tyrone Power is the husband accused of murder; Marlene Dietrich his wife. (B&W)

Wizard of Oz, The
1939 U 98 ★★★★★ FAM

If your children – or you, or granny for that matter – haven't seen this supreme musical then rush to the video store immediately. Beautiful songs, wonderful imagery and characters as familiar as old friends make this a must for everyone to enjoy. Guaranteed there won't be a dry eye in the house after Judy Garland's rendition of 'Somewhere over the Rainbow'. (Colour and B&W)

Wolf
1994 15 125 ★★★★ HOR

Publisher Jack Nicholson finds his life takes a nosedive after being bitten by a beast in Vermont – not a nice place to be bitten. His wife, Kate Nelligan, does the dirty on him and he loses his job to his own protégé, James Spader. The only comfort is to be found in his new, albeit hirsute, lease of life and the arms of boss's daughter, Michelle Pfeiffer. Scintillating, despite the sight of Nicholson baying at the moon in Central Park.

Wolves of Willoughby Chase, The
1989 PG 89 ★★ DRA

A corny tale saved by hammy performances from Stephanie Beacham and Mel Smith as the evil guardians of two young heiresses, whose fortune they plan to steal. A childish tale, though not for the very young since some moments may frighten them.

Woman in Black, The
1989 15 99 ★★★ HOR

Not for the faint-hearted this, a bloodcurdling ghost story by Susan Hill. Set earlier this century, a lawyer goes to a remote house to unravel the late occupant's affairs and finds he's not the only one there. Despite being made for TV, the production values are as good as any cinema movie and the story better than most. Definitely not for the children.

Woman of the Year
1942 U 114 ★★★★ COM

This sparkling comedy marks the first pairing of Spencer Tracy and Katharine Hepburn – she of the title. Hepburn's a political expert, Tracy the sports writer she falls in love with, though their respective careers threaten to come between them. Brilliantly played and very witty. There was a remake to which the hopeless task of reprising the central roles went to Renee Taylor and Joseph Bologna. (B&W)

Women on the Verge of a Nervous Breakdown
1988 15 85 ★★★★ FOR

Spain's answer to Steven Spielberg, Pedro Almodovar, directs this exuberant farce about some nutty women, mainly a soap-opera actress (Carmen Maura) who, when pregnant, is abandoned by her boyfriend (Antonio Banderas). There's energy, verve and oodles of charm here. (Subtitled)

Wooden Horse, The
1950 U 98 ★★★ WAR

Solid Second World War movie that has 'British best' stamped all over it. Leo Genn, Bryan Forbes and David Tomlinson are just some of the brave POWs who plan an escape from their camp by tunnelling out under the gymnasium's pommel horse. Rousing patriotic stuff; just

what you need for an indulgent afternoon. (B&W)

Woodstock
1970 15 177 ★★ MUS

Fans of the sixties music scene are well served by this documentary, which is all about the experience that was Woodstock: lots of cheesecloth, beads and flares, not to mention love and peace, as the likes of The Who, Jimi Hendrix, Joe Cocker and Sly and the Family Stone hammer away on stage. Contains nudity.

Working Girl
1988 15 109 ★★★ COM

Delightful story about a secretary (Melanie Griffith) who, after her boyfriend (Alec Baldwin) does the dirty on her, decides to concentrate on her career and passes herself off as her ruthless boss (Sigourney Weaver). Harrison Ford's charming as the businessman she dupes as well as falls in love with.

World Apart, A
1988 PG 108 ★★★ DRA

The young Jodhi May gives a heartbreaking performance as the neglected daughter of a political activist mother (Barbara Hershey) in South Africa. This was a time when apartheid was still the official policy and Hershey is regarded as an enemy by the authorities, and indeed imprisoned, because of her support for the African National Congress. The film was directed – very well, too – by the cinematographer Chris Menges and adapted from her own autobiographical book by Shawn Slovo. May, therefore, plays Slovo herself and Hershey her mother, Ruth First. There are some harrowing scenes of Hershey's ill-treatment at the hands of the police. The political situation is handled splendidly but the heart of the film is the touching relationship between mother and daughter, both roles played so well that Hershey and May shared the Best Actress award at Cannes.

Wuthering Heights
1939 U 100 ★★★ DRA

Though only telling half Emily Brontë's classic novel, William Wyler's movie tells it well. Laurence Olivier is a masterful Heathcliff and

Merle Oberon touching as Cathy (despite the rumour that she had spots and was photographed through gauze). Photography won an Oscar. (B&W)

Wyatt Earp
1994 12 183 ★★★★ WES

A thorough examination of the man and his methods. Kevin Costner plays the reluctant lawman (Michael Madsen turned down the John Travolta role in *Pulp Fiction* to play Virgil Earp) but the scene-stealer is Dennis Quaid as the TB-riddled Doc Holliday (he lost nearly four stone to look the part; so much, in fact, that he's totally convincing as a man dying of consumption). Solid, but Costner could have given a bit more dynamism to his character.

Yankee Doodle Dandy
1942 U 121 ★★★ MUS

Although an all-singing, all-dancing Jimmy Cagney doesn't immediately appeal, the man's a useful hot-hoofer and does a smashing Oscar-winning job portraying George M Cohan, a song and dance star of the First World War. Includes such numbers as 'Give My Regards to Broadway'. (B&W)

Yanks
1979 15 133 ★★★ DRA

Richard Gere burst into women's hearts the world over after his subtle portrayal of an American GI, posted to the north of England during the Second World War, where he falls in love with a local girl (Lisa Eichhorn). Worth getting in a big box of chocolates to consume along with the nostalgia and romance offered here. Lovely gooey stuff.

Year My Voice Broke, The
1987 15 100 ★★★ DRA

Yes, all right, this is essentially another rites of passage story but it's an unusually good one. It's set in a small Australian town in 1962 where young Noah Taylor is smitten in adolescence by Leone Carmen, a girl he has virtually grown up with. She, however, is maturing faster than he, being equally smitten with the local bad boy, Ben Mendelsohn, with whom she doesn't practise safe sex. Mixed in with Taylor's attempts to win Carmen's affections are some vaguely supernatural goings on and a mystery concerning a past scandal in the town. The performances are spot on and writer/director John Duigan handles the characters, the situations and the period with commendable ease.

Year of Living Dangerously, The
1983 PG 110 ★★★ DRA

Intelligent political drama set in Indonesia where Mel Gibson's a journalist whose investigative work lands him in deep trouble. Linda Hunt won an Oscar for her transvestite performance as a male photographer helping Gibson. Sigourney Weaver provides the love interest.

Young at Heart
1954 U 112 ★★ MUS

Doris Day seems an unlikely object of Frank Sinatra's affections but she is here in what is a musical version of *Four Daughters*. The songs are smashing, including 'Someone to Watch Over Me', 'Just One of Those Things' and 'One for My Baby'.

Young Frankenstein
1974 15 106 ★★★ COM

Funny, farcical parody of Hollywood horror movies by Mel Brooks. Gene Wilder is the mad scientist; Madeline Kahn his fiancée who becomes the monster's wife. (B&W)

Young Guns II
1990 15 99 ★★ WES

Young Guns was better but doesn't make it here since it's an 18 and is pretty violent. Mind you, this has its fair share of shoot-outs, but it's not as gory. Emilio Estevez again as Billy the Kid, brother Charlie Sheen's gone, but newcomer Christian Slater makes up for his absence. The casting is a teenage girl's dream.

Young Lions, The
1958 PG 160 ★★★★ ACT/ADV

Marlon Brando's not only a blond but a German in this Second World War adventure which examines the fighting from the perspective of two American soldiers (Dean Martin and Montgomery Clift) and a Nazi officer. Good performances and an intelligent story make it riveting viewing. (B&W)

Young Winston
1972 PG 120 ★★★ DRA

Simon Ward does a good job portraying Mr W Churchill during his early life, from the terrible schooldays through his outstanding days as a soldier to his entry to Parliament. If it weren't all true, you'd never believe one man could achieve so much. The support cast are some of the cinema's best, including Robert Shaw, Anne Bancroft, Jack Hawkins, Ian Holm, Anthony Hopkins and John Mills.

You Only Live Twice
1967 PG 112 ★★★ ACT/ADV

Jaw-dropping gadgetry, Japanese locations, Sean Connery as the suave gent who's licensed to kill and Donald Pleasence as arch-villain Blofeld make this one of the best Bond movies.

Zardoz
1974 15 101 ★ SCI/FAN

Nice scenery, shame about the story since this sci-fi adventure by director John Boorman has great effects but little substance. Sean Connery plays a savage in a future world, 2293, run by eternally young intellectuals. Charlotte Rampling does her best but in the end it's pretty hollow.

Zelig
1983 PG 76 ★★★ COM

Avant-garde special effects lend this spoof documentary much of its appeal. Woody Allen writes, directs and stars as Zelig, a sort of human chameleon, who appears to have no personality of his own but always fits perfectly into whichever background he is in. So, with the aid of those special effects, we follow his life story as he crops up in the company of such as Chaplin, Eugene O'Neill, Franklin D Roosevelt, the Pope and, most hilariously, Adolf Hitler. Zelig is discovered, blinking nervously behind his glasses and clad in Gestapo uniform, sitting just behind the Führer at a Nazi rally. It's not actually as funny as it should be but the intercutting of new footage and newsreel works quite as well here as it does in *Forrest Gump*.

Zorba the Greek
1964 PG 136 ★★★ DRA

A lavish story greatly enhanced by its setting, the Greek island of Crete, where a young intellectual Brit (Alan Bates) falls under the spell of the locale and the local character (Anthony Quinn). Since it tends toward the lusty at times, the very young should be steered clear, but it's fine for the more mature family members. (B&W)

Zulu
1964 PG 132 ★★★★ WAR

Tremendous account of the battle at Rorke's Drift, where a small band of Welsh soldiers held off a large Zulu army, winning eleven V.C.s. No expense was spared: as well as superb battle sequences there's narration by Richard Burton and a celestial cast including Jack Hawkins, Michael Caine, Stanley Baker and Nigel Green. Good history lesson, too.

Barry & Emma Norman's
Top Twenties

Choosing our favourite twenty films for each certificate has not been easy. In fact, we've had to resort to a spot of cheating at times by including trilogies. With the likes of *Dumbo*, *Sleeping Beauty*, etc, we included all of those in what we call 'The Disney Classics Collection'. Another problem was the '12' certificate, since it's only very recently been introduced and there aren't, as yet, many 12s on video. As the only one we fancy is *Forrest Gump*, we have chosen to ignore that category entirely (along with the Uc's, which are mainly for the tinies) – but do watch *Forrest Gump*!

In the meantime, here are our top twenty U, PG and 15 films – *not* in any order of preference within each classification.

U Certificate
The Adventures of Robin Hood
All About Eve
Bringing Up Baby
Casablanca
Citizen Kane
The Disney Classics Collection
E.T. The Extra-Terrestrial
Gone with the Wind
High Noon
I Know Where I'm Going
It Happened One Night
Kind Hearts and Coronets
Ninotchka
The Railway Children
The Searchers
Singin' in the Rain
Some Like it Hot
Stagecoach
The Talk of the Town
The Wizard of Oz

PG Certificate
Back to the Future trilogy
The Big Sleep
Butch Cassidy and the Sundance Kid
Edward Scissorhands

Field of Dreams
The Grapes of Wrath
The Great Escape
Great Expectations
Jaws
Lawrence of Arabia
The Magnificent Seven
The Maltese Falcon
La Regle du Jeu
Romancing the Stone
Seven Samuri
The Seventh Seal
Shane
Sleeper
The Third Man
Whisky Galore!

15 Certificate

Blade Runner: The Director's Cut
The Commitments
Cool Hand Luke
Desperately Seeking Susan
Fearless
A Fish Called Wanda
In the Name of the Father
Life is Sweet
The Man with Two Brains
MASH
Monty Python's Life of Brian
My Left Foot
Schindler's List
Speed
Someone to Watch over Me
Thelma and Louise
Tootsie
Unforgiven
The Untouchables
Witness

Index by film category

Action/Adventure

Comedy

U

Drama

U

Family

Uc

U

Foreign

U

PG

Horror

Musicals

U

PG

15

Mystery/Thriller

U

PG

Science fiction/Fantasy

U

PG

Westerns